Common Worlds and Single Lives

EXPLORATIONS IN ANTHROPOLOGY
A University College London Series

Series Editors: Barbara Bender, John Gledhill and Bruce Kapferer

Daniel Miller, *Modernity – An Ethnographic Approach: Dualism and Mass Consumption in Trinidad*

Robert Pool, *Dialogue and the Interpretation of Illness: Conversations in a Cameroon Village*

Cécile Barraud, Daniel de Coppet, André Iteanu and Raymond Jamous (eds), *Of Relations and the Dead: Four Societies Viewed from the Angle of their Exchanges*

Christopher Tilley, *A Phenomenology of Landscape: Places, Paths and Monuments*

Victoria Goddard, Josep R. Llobera and Cris Shore (eds), *The Anthropology of Europe: Identity and Boundaries in Conflict*

Pat Caplan, *Understanding Disputes: The Politics of Argument*

Alisdair Rogers and Steven Vertovec (eds), *The Urban Context: Ethnicity, Social Networks and Situational Analysis*

Saskia Kersenboom, *Word, Sound, Image: The Life of the Tamil Text*

Daniel de Coppet and André Iteanu (eds), *Cosmos and Society in Oceania*

Roy Ellen and Katsuyoshi Fukui, *Redefining Nature: Ecology, Culture and Domestication*

William Washabaugh, *Flamenco: Passion, Politics and Popular Culture*

Bernard Juillerat, *Children of the Blood: Society, Reproduction and Imaginary Representations in New Guinea*

Karsten Paerregaard, *Linking Separate Worlds: Urban Migrants and Rural Lives in Peru*

Daniel Miller, *Capitalism: An Ethnographic Approach*

Nicole Rodriguez Toulis, *Believing Identity: Pentecostalism and the Mediation of Jamaican Ethnicity and Gender in England*

Jerome R. Mintz, *Carnival Song and Society: Gossip, Sexuality and Creativity in Andalusia*

Neil Jarman, *Material Conflicts, Parades and Visual Displays in Northern Ireland*

Gary Armstrong and Richard Giulianotti, *Entering the Field: New Perspectives on World Football*

Deborah Reed-Danahay, *Auto / Ethnography: Rewriting the Self and the Social*

Marianne Elisabeth Lien, *Marketing and Modernity*

R. D. Grillo and R. L. Stirrat (eds), *Discourses of Development: Anthropological Perspectives*

Simon Sinclair, *Making Doctors: An Institutional Apprenticeship*

Gary Armstrong, *Football Hooligans: Knowing the Score*

Barbara Bender, *Stonehenge: Making Space*

L.R. Goldman, *Child's Play: Myth, Mimesis and Make-Believe*

Common Worlds and Single Lives: Constituting Knowledge in Pacific Societies

Edited by
Verena Keck

Oxford • New York

First published in 1998 by
Berg
Editorial offices:
150 Cowley Road, Oxford, OX4 1JJ, UK
70 Washington Square South, New York, NY 10012, USA

Published with the aid of the Swiss Academy of Humanities and
Social Sciences.

Berg is the imprint of Oxford International Publishers Ltd.

Library of Congress Cataloging-in-Publication Data

A catalogue record for this book is available from the Library of
Congress.

British Library Cataloguing-in-Publication Data

A catalogue record for this book is available from the British
Library.

ISBN   1 85973 164 3 (Cloth)
       1 85973 169 4 (Paper)

Typeset by JS Typesetting, Wellingborough, Northants.
Printed in the United Kingdom by WBC Book Manufacturers,
Bridgend, Mid Glamorgan.

Contents

Introduction

Verena Keck

In 1988 I visited the Nankina Valley, a remote area in the Finisterre Range in the Madang Province of Papua New Guinea (PNG). I was doing fieldwork among the neighbouring Yupno and I was curious about Nankina culture. When I arrived there, a young man who was full of resentment said in answer to my questions:

> We have always been here. Then came the missionaries and threw everything out. They prohibited all the traditional things. And we gave them up. Now you come and ask us about the traditions of our ancestors and we don't know anything anymore. We are totally confused. Is it our fault?

I assume that many anthropologists have had this experience. But I also assume that many anthropologists upon reading these innocuous introductory lines might have an uneasy feeling – something isn't quite right here. So I did fieldwork (Keck 1992, 1993, 1994) among the 'Yupno' (in actual fact, the 'Yupno' do not have a name for themselves). After a while, I became curious about the 'Nankina' who live in the neighbouring Nankina Valley. I knew, however, that 'Nankina' just like 'Yupno' was only the name of the respective river, that many 'Nankina' had immigrated into the Yupno Valley by crossing the mountains and that some of them also lived in the towns of Madang and Lae. Nevertheless, for the time being I equated 'Nankina' with the valley of the same name. I then had numerous talks with 'Nankina' informants but only with middle-aged men as they were the only ones to speak Tok Pisin. Yet they readily supplied me with information on kinship structure, settlement patterns, growing things in their gardens, life cycles – but still I suspected their single lives to be more varied and more complex; that the young people, the elderly and the women looked upon many things differently from their opinion leaders. In the end, it set me thinking how the young man quoted

1

above talked about 'traditional things' that the Lutheran catechists had 'prohibited' and that could be disposed of like a commodity while, as it seemed to me, in his everyday life he behaved in a most 'traditional' way.

I suppose that in the beginning we all felt something was not right with the description because, at the close of the twentieth century, the traditional concepts of 'culture', 'individual' and 'knowledge' are simply lost to us and we have at least to question and, depending on the case, to 'invent' them anew.

Deterritorialized Cultures

The idea of culture appears today in an amazingly wide variety of contexts and has experienced a veritable boom since the 1970s, spawning a whole string of new compound words formed with 'multi-', 'pluri-', 'inter-', 'trans-' and 'culturalism', as well as many different ethno-fashions. The traditional concept of culture is passing through a period of widespread and indiscriminate use in different social spheres. It starts 'behaving in a "global" way – ubiquitous, encompassing, all-explanatory' (M. Strathern 1995: 155). Any people, sect, company, band or maker of brands may draw on 'culture' but, above all wherever people differentiate between people, culture is evidence for diversity. In the course of the 'shrinking' of the world due to globalization (Harvey 1989) and of the increasing movement of people towards 'common worlds', the concept was appropriated by 'others' and anthropologists lost control over one of their most basic terms (Comaroff and Comaroff 1992). The paradoxical result is that anthropological writings are increasingly being consulted by people wishing to construct cultural identities of a totalizing sort – which the anthropologists now find highly problematic. This has to be explained.

Few concepts have been as pervasively effective in anthropology as the often quoted passage from E.B. Tylor's *Primitive Culture* of 1871, which describes culture and civilization as, in the widest sense, a *complete whole* that includes knowledge, religious beliefs, art, morals, laws and customs; in other words, all the skills and characteristics human beings acquire as members of a society. However, these ideas of homogeneity, coherence and continuity have to be called into question. Wicker (1997) lists two main kinds of disapproval. Critics of the first kind view the classical definition of culture as a continuation of older concepts of race deriving from Herder's notion of the *Volksgeist*. Culture, like race, is perceived as defying definition. This emphasis on the collective 'we' implies the incommensurability of the different cultural forms and renders this view attractive for the political and cultural New Right as well. Critics of the second kind are the ethnicity researchers investigating the ethnic borders themselves and the mechanisms used to preserve them. Ethnic lines of separation were found to constitute and preserve themselves through processes of ascription – to self and others. It was not possible, however, to trace the origins of these processes of ethnicity to the different cultural representations of the groups involved (Barth 1969; Glazer and Moynihan 1975).

In the course of the history of anthropology obviously there have also been other attempts to more precisely define the object of research but it seems that the starting point has always been three kinds of emphasis that were believed to fit together and also appear together (Hannerz 1996: 8). One is that culture is learned, acquired in everyday social life, as it were; the software needed for programming the biologically given hardware – which, thanks to the cognitive sciences, is becoming increasingly better known. The second emphasis is that culture is something that comes in various packages, distinctive to different human collectivities, and that, as a rule, these collectivities belong to territories. Finally, culture should somehow be integrated, fitting in neatly – something equally 'distributed' among all its members.

The three above-mentioned emphases in the traditional understanding of culture appear to be contested in varying degrees. The idea that culture is learned still seems to be valid, although it refers to a life-long process that is not only limited to childhood, but the two other notions are generally put in question by anthropologists as well.

In view of the increasing integration of societies into networks of global interdependence, as people move with their meanings, and meanings find ways of travelling via mass media even when people stay in one place, anthropological conceptualizations, as in the second of the three emphases mentioned above, postulating *a natural connection of cultures, societies and nations with fixed geographical and territorial spaces*, seem increasingly inappropriate. Territories cannot really contain cultures any more.

In anthropology, space has long served as a seemingly value-free idiom for defining clear and permanent divisions among cultures, an idiom assigning to each culture an original place – a cultural habitat based on the assumption that spatial separation correlates with cultural difference. This reciprocal indexation of topology and culture, of territory and nation, has become questionable. Whether criticism of the isomorphic construction of space and culture is directed at the 'incarceration' of cultures in fixed places (Appadurai 1988), or at the metaphor of the 'localness' of cultures (Clifford 1988), or whether the latent functionalist search for cultural stability and sedentary equilibrium is deconstructed (Malkki 1995), a call is being issued from all sides for a more dynamic, process-oriented theoretical interpretation of culture, identity and space.

Pacific societies are no exception. The Pacific region has had a long history of migration and foreign cultural influence, spreading originally along ancient trade routes and culminating in a process of colonization (Fox, Bellwood and Tryon 1995), but in the post-colonial era the rate of cultural exchange has increased tremendously and taken new forms and directions (cf. for example Otto 1993; van Meijl and van der Grijp 1993).

In the contemporary historical context, *migration* on a regional (as in the case of the Nankina), national and transnational level is one of the most important aspects of mobility in the region (see the contributions by Adams, Stanek and Weiss and Hoëm in this volume). Transnational migration and the resettlement of rural populations in urban areas have been construed rather negatively, by an anthropology focussed on territorial 'anchoring', as an 'uprooting' of people involving a loss of tradition, culture and identity. These movements have raised questions as to the relevance of conceptual boundaries that have been erected between 'town' and 'country', between 'centre' and 'periphery', or between 'us' and 'others'. Processes of urbanization and of international-ization can open up new horizons for the study of space, identities and inter-ethnic relations (Friedman 1994; Wassmann 1998a). According to Epeli Hau'ofa (1994), for example, transnational migration movements contribute to the expansion of 'local' cultures; suggesting that the so-called 'small nations' of the Pacific region may be becoming larger even as they become part of the 'global village' in a presumably shrinking world. One might also ask to which national or cultural 'territory' enclaves of Pacific islanders living 'overseas' more truly belong – to the state and culture of their present domicile or to those of their origin?

Focusing on *displacement* can raise our awareness of the cultural processes of constructing spaces/localities and identities. The image of the place and the country of origin, as cultivated in the imaginations of people living in the diaspora, is conveyed through their memories and perhaps motivated by nostalgia. International networks formed through emigration are being used to gain positions of power within the structure of the nation state at home (Marcus 1993). The diverse processes of displacement also have tangible consequences for the people who have remained at their places of origin. Thus success stories of affluent migrants may lead to a conviction of living in the 'wrong place', especially among the younger generation of those remaining 'at home'. Even regions with only moderate demographic changes through migration and regular commuting may show the effects of a displacement caused by the exertion of global influences. International tourism plays an important role in the economies and cultural construction of Pacific nations from Indonesia to Polynesia. Colonial and post-colonial influences, for example the different waves of Christian-ization, have contributed to, and continue to lend support to, a phenomenon where new centres of mythical origin and pathways of migration are being thought up and lived in, which are often hotly disputed within the respective society and may lead to the formation of local factions.

The place-focused concept of culture as rooted in the native soil of the people was a popular image (Handler 1985; Kahn 1989; Gupta and Ferguson 1992) but there are no separate worlds any more – just common worlds which overlap and are available to various degrees. We are definitely confronted with a 'shifting anthropological object' (Olwig and Hastrup 1997) and a global space consisting of 'deterritorialized ethnoscapes' (Appadurai 1991).

Local Agency

The shifting relationship between culture and territory is not the only relevant topic. The assumption, as in emphasis three, *that the carrier of 'a culture' is 'a people'* – that strongly sociocentric, collectivist understanding of culture – is also being challenged. The idea of culture as the expression of a complex whole, manifesting itself in fixed social structures, in stereotyped patterns of thought, actions and beliefs, was clearly influenced by the pattern-, configuration-, theme-, ethos-, eidos- and super-organic models of early American cultural anthropology. In these there was no need at all for an active subject. However, there has recently been a resurgence of interest in the acting subject, in individual agency, in context-oriented appropriation of knowledge and significations within the framework of guided participation (Rogoff and Lave 1984; Lave 1988; Rogoff 1990). For homogeneously distributed 'culture' within collectivities becomes problematic once we notice how their 'members' have highly varying experiences, how their biographies differ – especially, but not only, after they have visited other places in other countries or are reacting differently to the global offers of the mass media. Single lives in common worlds differ. In this way, the concept of complex culture should yield to the concept of a flowing cultural complexity (Barth 1993; Wicker 1997).

At the same time, however, this local context is not autonomous but rather a kind of arena in which a variety of influences come together and are acted out, in a unique combination under those special conditions. Globalization may have a levelling influence, but the local contexts differ, just as the actors differ as well. Thus, on the local level, old, formerly more separate currents of meaning and knowledge are blended together, and new, creolized, idiosyncratic 'cultures' also come into existence. If we start out from the acting individual, culture is no longer a reality *sui generis* but a principle of semiotic practice. Culture as a set of specific dispositions, acquired by individuals in the process of living, permits the intersubjective formation of signification and meaningful action. The point of departure is those nodal points in the networks of interrelations where there is mutual construction of identities through cultural encounters (Hastrup and Olweg 1997). Wicker (1997: 41) vehemently declares: 'Culture has no *facultas* of its own – no independent *proprietas*. Culture is a modal *accidens* equipped only with *dispositio* and *habitus*, and thus has no proper force of its own – it neither resists nor adapts and assimilates. There is no cultural being.'

At best – following the *praxiology* of Bourdieu (1977, 1989) – culture is expressed in and through those durable dispositions that form the habits of people. In this sense, Wicker continues, it is not *the* Turkish culture that determines the integration process of Turks in, say, Switzerland but, on the one hand, the migrants' social field of origin (rural, urban, social class, degree of literacy) that generates and naturalizes durable dispositions in the form of action strategies and world views, and on the other hand the social fields in the country of admission. However, since dispositions are inert – *hysteresis* is Bourdieu's term – the dynamics of adaptation are thus reduced; change is slow. It is not cultural persistence, therefore, but the staying power of habits. Thus the existence of social and political collectivities – which are found all the same – cannot be explained through culture but only through the social and political practice of local actors.

Personal experiences of the invasion of new ideas and objects or of displacement, understood as a liminal phase (Westen 1985), may vary but generally tend to vacillate between the exciting prospect of discovering new potentials within an unfamiliar form of life and a sense of 'uprootedness' and loss. Regardless of the actor's condition, as a 'victim' of anomy, discrimination, on a downward spiral into social 'pathology', or as a trickster between locations and cultural worlds who realizes the opportunities in the 'second sight' (Chandler 1996) he or she has gained from the experience of hybridity, it seems that the experience of new cultural worlds or of dislocation places a special emphasis on actors (Sørensen 1997) as it simultaneously ruptures the structure of both the home and the new 'culture' at the moment of their collision in an everyday world of *praxis*.

One way of unravelling the complexities of this historical process, given that it evolves through a dynamic and practical encounter between agents, events and, in this case, multiple structures, is the use of *theories of praxis*, especially if they are combined with *processual ethnography*. Well-known representatives of the *praxis* approach are Pierre Bourdieu and Marshall Sahlins (see also Giddens 1984 and Ortner 1984). Individual agency, structure and event are the crucial dimensions. Such an analysis would focus on how actors continuously respond to new situations. Sally Falk Moore (1975, 1987, see also Sahlins 1991), drawing on the rich tradition in processual ethnography of the Manchester school, has argued that, in each new situation, active 'processes of regularization', attempts to fix or hold the situation within a frame (often erroneously represented as continuous in a static sense), occur in conjunction with necessary 'processes of situational adjustment'. Thus, social reality can be seen as fluid and 'indeterminate'. Change and continuity may be dealt with simultaneously instead of being considered in opposition to each other. Moore acknowledges a partial impact of cultural models (see below) in the social process, but, in contrast to Bourdieu's homogeneous concept of *habitus*, she accounts more adequately for heterogeneity in culture and practice. She strategically seeks to detect how part structures are built and torn down in sequences of local, small-scale events that can be located in a long-term historical process. The methodological focus on these so-called 'diagnostic events' helps to situate *praxis* theory firmly within processual analysis. The next step is to find out how people, in the words of Sahlins, 'creatively reconsider their conceptual schemes'. In particular the biographies of cultural brokers and the way they operate in various domains could be central (see the contributions by A. Strathern, Josephides, Stanek and Weiss and Venbrux in this volume).

Knowledge and Knowing

A fundamental question, however, remains unanswered. What is the relationship between the single individual experience of social action and that which, in whatever form, is collectively in existence already? Bourdieu's concept of *habitus* is an attempt to understand the unity of social practices via the production of clearly differentiated sets of dispositions to action and interpretations of the world in different sectors of a population. Zygmund Bauman (1992) proposes connecting the actor not to a system but to a flexible sense of habitat, to 'habitats of meaning'. Habitats may expand and contract. There is definitely a danger of viewing the individual actor too individualistically, simply disregarding the publicness and collectiveness that are also more-or-less part of a cultural entity and thereby going from one extreme to the other. This would be wrong for, as individuals, the actors are acting within contexts, in 'settings of activity' (Lave 1988: 116) that are valid for all or for most individuals. In the same way, the experiences of individual 'just plain folks' ('jpfs') (Rogoff and Lave 1984) are, as it were, put at the disposition of the other 'jpfs', without these having individually to have the same experience. A large part of knowledge appears to be transferred or acquired in this way.

Abstract knowledge, a 'pool of information' to varying degrees actively internalized by the individual, and those individually acquired 'private' experiences, the 'routines of everyday living' (Lave 1988: 14) that also result in active knowledge, appear to exist side by side. To put it more precisely: there is a pool of common-sense knowledge, of special knowledge, which for the most part is linguistically encoded, and there are innumerable partial versions of this knowledge and additional alternative knowledge in the individuals who in their everyday lives perceive, think, interact and apply specific capabilities and skills. This more individual knowledge appears to be encoded less in language and more in the form of actions or images. It is the kind of knowledge a housewife needs when she goes shopping (Murtaugh 1985), a milkman when distributing the dairy products to his customers following a specific pattern (Scribner 1984), a Yakan in the Philippines when he wants to enter a house correctly (Frake 1954). 'Everyday knowledge' is not the static knowledge of a *sujet épistémique* (Dasen 1992), but applied knowledge in action (situated practice, knowledge as practice, knowledge as performance). It is not only the way this kind of knowledge is organized that is of interest but the way it actually functions: thus knowledge that is directly connected to actions or is expressed by them, is also given a specific structure, in addition causes further actions, determines their aims and guides them (see the contributions by Telban and Grau). Linguistic abstractions alone, whatever we can elicit verbally, are not sufficient for grasping this kind of knowledge. 'Everyday knowledge' is less a conceptual kind of knowledge than a procedural knowledge connected to specific contexts. It is knowledge that is not only an understanding system but at the same time and in particular an acting system as well. Since it is learned by observation or by doing, it remains mostly implicit – just try asking a football player how he dribbles round his opponent and you will hardly get an articulate answer.

To take an example from Schank and Abelson (1977): I am in New York and somebody asks me the way to Coney Island; I tell him to take the 'N'-train to the end of the line. This instruction only makes sense 'if this improperly specified algorithm can be filled out with a great deal of knowledge about how to walk, pay for subways, get in the train and so on' (Schank and Abelson 1977:

20). 'Script' is the name for this tacit knowledge that enables us to understand even incomplete instructions and hints, as it refers to a structure that describes appropriate sequences of events in a particular context because it handles stylized everyday situations. 'Riding the subway', 'playing tennis', 'going to a birthday party', 'making coffee in the morning' are such standardized situations. The strongly simplified version of a 'restaurant visit script' (from the point of view of the customer) might, in the USA, run somewhat like this: (scene: entering) entering the restaurant, waiting to be attended to, looking for a free table, going to the table (together with the waiter/waitress), sitting down; (scene: ordering): calling the waiter/waitress to the table, waiter/waitress comes to the table, asking for the menu etc. This is an everyday script that has not been written down anywhere, which is implicit and culturally defined. Yet in a Swiss restaurant the script would differ slightly: there you go directly to the table and sit down and in most cases you pay the waiter/waitress and not the cashier. Giddens (1984: 4) writes: 'The vast bulk of the "stocks of knowledge" . . . incorporated in encounters is not directly accessible to the consciousness of the actors. Most such knowledge is practical in character, it is inherent in the capability to "go on" within the routines of social life' (cf. Connerton 1989).

The traditional anchoring of cultures to specific territories has been questioned, the Durkheimian concept of culture as collective representation has been queried, so we also need to call into question our traditional *conception of knowledge*. After what has already been mentioned, it would seem to be advantageous to distinguish between knowledge (i.e. understanding that is definite and lineated, *what* is known, as an abstract pool of information) and knowing (i.e. understanding that is more fluid and flexible in character, *how* something is known, knowledge in practice), between a more declarative and a more procedural knowledge. We may reorient our analysis and reverse the process – starting with knowing and seeing how knowledge is constituted from it (Borofsky 1994) – as we already did with the traditional concept of culture when we started out from the individual agency. People share certain knowledge/knowing because they have learned how to interact with one another. What people share culturally is the experience of getting along with one another, of participating in meaningful activities together, experiencing common everyday lives (Holland and Quinn 1987; Lave 1988; Rogoff 1990; Lave 1993).

These actions are based on accepted social practices or *habitus* – Goodenough's (1957) definition of culture as what people have to know in order to be able to act in a culturally acceptable way in their respective social environment appears still to be surprisingly relevant. Nevertheless, considerable knowledge diversity and differences in its distribution exist in many cultural groups. How do we make sense of this? We probably still focus too exclusively on the declarative, verbalized knowledge (thereby following the tradition of our discipline) and we overlook the hidden, implicit, common knowing. In addition, the 'emphasis on habituated experiences as unconsciously embedded in the body fits well with Bourdieu's . . . concept of "habitus"' (Borofsky 1994: 341). Much of what we might term 'the cultural' is stored in scripts, schemas, in 'simplified worlds', and it is primarily accessed through performance.

Let us look at Wassmann's research (1995) for an ethnographic example of the distribution of knowledge/knowing. He analyzed the distribution of knowledge/knowing among the Yupno in four different areas (calling to mind that the Yupno are the neighbours of the Nankina). In the case of the 'counting system', it is, surprisingly, the individual variations (same/different) that catch the eye ('surprisingly' because a counting system is, at least for us, really a normative thing). The variations both between individuals and for the same informants over time are so great that it is not possible to speak of an actual collective model. As counting is usually done in public, however, this does not play an important role.

On the other hand, the 'hot/cool/cold' system is known to all the Yupno; it is a true shared model, but is at their disposal (more/less) in varying degrees: only those who actually work with it, rather than those who only know of it, use it spontaneously – i.e. the sorcerers.

In classifying 'foodstuffs', three different models are simultaneously available, depending on the context, one of which is probably only significant in interaction with an anthropologist (a perfect taxonomy), and two further non-taxonomic models that are important in everyday life, i.e. when discussing foodstuffs during gardening and when cooking the food.

There also appear to be different models (mental images) in the conception of one's own settlement area as space (investigated with the help of drawings on the ground, hence without verbal interaction): one's own 'world' is conceived differently by those with an 'outside world' experience, i.e. those who have left their valley to go to the coast, than by those who don't have this experience. At the same time, personal conceptions (as in the case of numbers), daily usage (as in the case of 'hot/cool/cold' classification) or the context (as with foodstuffs) do not play a role: the course of one's own life seems decisive.

All this knowledge is fragmented between the young and the old, between women and men, between those with and those without experience of displacement; in addition, cultural rules also play a role. Thus it is culturally inappropriate that women count in public and men refuse to publicly comment on food, which is 'women's domain': *'on sait faire mais on ne fait pas'* (Chamoux 1981: 71).

In attempting to analyze the ways in which 'culture' shapes individual decision-making or, in other words, to operationalize Bourdieu's concept of *habitus*, a possible approach seems to be to investigate in which form knowledge/knowing is *mentally at the disposal* of the actor. Here we do not mean concrete, complete, practical 'external' knowledge, the facts or acts, but the 'inner' representation of this knowledge in the mind. These representations cannot consist of a mere picture of the world or even of a set of concepts that refer to or stand in a one-to-one relationship with elements of the external world. On the contrary, they are abstractions or 'cultural models' (script, schema, frame), gained by reducing stereotyped situations or events to their typical and common characteristics. Quinn and Holland (1987: 32) write 'cultural models are composed of prototypical event sequence set in simplified worlds', conceived as 'presupposed, taken-for-granted models of the world that are widely shared (although not necessarily to the exclusion of other alternative models) by members of a society' (Quinn and Holland 1987: 4; see Rosch and Lloyd 1978; Keesing 1987; D'Andrade and Strauss 1992). In addition, these models are probabilistic and partial, they are actual frames: with their help, a person is able to also confront atypical or unexpected situations or information; these models allow room for creativity by making it possible to come to conclusions regarding new situations. They are organized in such a way that it is possible to link this organization to what is known about the way human beings think (Bloch 1991; see Wassmann 1994; Wassmann and Dasen, in press). It seems that these models of knowledge/knowing appear in two different basic forms, in the form of the proposition schemata and in that of the image schemata, to use Lakoff's terminology of 1987. In the first case, we have a linguistic or procedural model that shows the proto- typical of a simplified world and the causative interconnection of prototypical events (through a process of pars-pro-toto or through metonymy). The restaurant script mentioned above is an example. In the second case, however, the representation consists of schematized, visual images. These images are able to make comprehensible physical manifestations or logical relationships which cannot be conceptualized and to make them 'conceivable' (by using an analogy or a metaphor). 'Rage' can be imagined as a hot liquid in a container, 'evaporation' as ascending molecules jumping out of the water like popcorn; the above-mentioned mental maps of the Yupno of their own settlement area are a further example.

Appropriating Knowledge

Let us change our perspective. There is a long history of changing Western representations of other societies. A striking feature of these representations is that they are often agentive. By this is meant that they depict a state of affairs requiring action or intervention, as 'the peoples of much of the world have been portrayed as savage, decadent or merely pagan and unen- lightened' (Hobart 1993: 2). Thus they require law and order, effective government or Christianity and civilization. This idea of necessary development has often been linked to, or equated with, modernization; this is the transformation of traditional into modern societies, characterized by advanced technology, material prosperity and political stability. The way to this transformation is by means of *scientific knowledge*. Significantly, such knowledge requires the homogenization and quantification of what is potentially qualitatively different: thus kinds of food become cash crop and human activities become labour (Hobart 1993: 6). Common to this modernization theory and the competing dependency theory (according to which structures of dependence are set up by the world capitalist system which penetrates local societies) is the absence of local agents. Traditional societies are thought to need guidance; agency is attributed to foreign planners or to imported Western legal structures (Benda-Beckmann 1993). Scientific knowledge is conceived as true propositions about the world and seeks information, which can be applied to any spatial and social situation and is therefore not context-bound. It is a 'world-ordering knowledge' (Hobart 1993: 1) and thereby plays an almost hegemonic role. From this point of view, not only are indigenous knowledges ignored or dismissed, but the nature of the so-called 'problem of underdevelopment' and its solution are defined by reference to this world-ordering knowledge. Local knowledge is no more than an obstacle to rational progress. Parallel to this, Western (and native) experts believe themselves to be rational and to 'know' something whereas the local population is irrational and only 'believes' (Long and Long 1992; Antweiler 1995). Experts' knowledge and local knowledge/knowing are seen as a dichotomy with only the former being treated as a valuable resource for which one also has to pay – although at the moment an increasing interest in local knowledge can be noted, for example, about medicinal plants on the part of the pharmaceuticals industry. It is not by chance that a discussion arose on the associated intellectual property rights (Brush 1993; see contribution by M. Strathern in this book).

Yet the term 'local knowledge' is far from ideal since the kind of knowledge hereby understood is frequently not at all limited to specific locations, it is often regionally distributed or the term is used for the knowledge of nomads. 'Local' is rather to be understood as the contrast to 'globally valid'. The term 'indigenous knowledge' is just as much of a problem as, depending on the continent and the political objective, 'indigenous' means very different things and, in addition, also contains the danger of idealization – the transfiguration of the people 'close to nature' into ecological saints. Both terms, 'local knowledge' and 'indigenous knowledge', denote a kind of human knowledge that is culturally situated and is not at all to be equated with 'non-Western' knowledge (Schröder 1995). As we already know, everyday knowledge in Western societies does not differ in principle from that of non-Western groups (Rogoff and Lave 1984; Flick 1995). This exaggerated dichotomization and standardization only reflects the myth of Western scientific thinking, with its claim to being global, to which non-Western thinking is compared – as if elsewhere people do not reflect, as if only in the West people think scientifically (cf. Sperber 1985).

Pacific islanders have been fiercely confronted with 'external' or 'foreign' knowledge/knowing, through missionaries, development experts, urban administrators, the mass media or when they themselves have visited urban centres or worked on plantations. If, formerly, knowledge was something the older people handed down to the younger ones as the tradition of their society, 'globalization' is aimed directly at the sector of the younger and mostly male population – which has resulted in a loss of status for the old people and also, above all, for the women (see the contributions by Firth, Toren, Obrist van Eeuwijk and Moral). For a long time development theorists believed that traditional and modern knowledge were incompatible, and that the feasibility of modernization was based on the possibility of replacing the first by the second. Of course, anthropologists held a different view – although they also separated local knowledge/knowing from the lived context just by recording it in writing, making it definite in the sense that it was no longer negotiable, theorizing it into folk models (see Warren, Slikkerveer and Brokensha 1995 for an example). Ironically, local communities whose members feel themselves to be 'beleaguered by the inexorable encroachment of "mainstream" culture, may well feel that they *are* involved in the confrontation of such a dichotomy: that extraneous knowledge does indeed threaten their own knowledge. It depicts itself as 'expert' and is thereby felt to impugn local knowledge as ignorance' (Cohen 1993: 32). Such 'expert' knowledge comes from outside, mostly in the form of declarative knowledge (about technologies, agriculture, Christian morals, politics etc.) or in the mass media as the model of a lifestyle; in both cases it is obvious that it is linked with power. Therefore it is even more difficult to resist. Localities thus either capitulate, discard or even repugn their 'traditional' knowledge, they may make a syncretic accommodation, or they may subtly subvert the extraneous (see the contributions by Paini, Jeudy-Ballini and Lemonnier). These may be unconscious, subtle changes, but often the local actors discuss quite deliberately the 'route' they want to take – if we only think of the discussions about *kastom* and *bisnis* in Melanesia. In their local arena, they may thus manage to deal with the new global knowledge in a highly superior manner and to use it for their own, often traditionally shaped aims (see the contributions by Stanek and Weiss, A. Strathern and Venbrux). The division between 'global' and 'local' becomes meaningless. M. Strathern questions this common distinction by describing the first contact between white people and Highlanders in PNG at the beginning of this century.

> [The Highlanders] ... did not realise they ... were actors in a universal historical defeat, part of colonial expansion or entering the world market for gold. Rather, they saw versions of familiar beings, first in spirit and then in human form. This interpretation was totalising ... Highlander's knowledge practices led them to demonstrate a potential for relationship which the strangers did not know they were presenting ... Yet one could cast the Highlanders' strategy as global (totalising the strangers as versions of themselves) and the Australians as local (dreadfully conscious of the place they had come from and the place they were in now) (M. Strathern 1995: 164).

The Organization of the Book

The aim of this collection[1] is to provide an analysis of the nature of knowledge transmission in post-colonial Pacific societies. This is being attempted with the help of ethnographic studies demonstrating the social and political implications of Pacific islanders' knowledge/knowing in five major domains: embodiment, life history, local Christianity, global relations, and new forms of knowledge. Two 'book end' essays by Firth and M. Strathern address the intricacies of investigating the nature of 'knowledge' and 'creativity'.

The contributions reflect a post-colonial world where everything is on the move and where traditional concepts like 'culture' (as a collectivity tied to specific territories), 'individual' (as a carrier of a culture) or 'knowledge' (as static declarative specialist knowledge) are called into question. The contributors Adams, Stanek and Weiss and Hoëm write about the *experience of an outside world*; the *local agencies as cultural brokers* between two worlds are the topic of A. Strathern, Josephides, Stanek and Weiss and Venbrux – whereby the changing status of women in particular is the central theme (Toren, Obrist van Eeuwijk, Moral); Telban and Grau deal with *knowing* 'in' and 'through' the body, the contributors Paini and Jeudi-Ballini write about the reciprocal appropriation of Christian knowledge; the appropriation of *new forms of knowledge* is the focus of Lemonnier, Stanek and Weiss, Venbrux and Hoëm.

The present contributions have been grouped under the following headings for the purpose of this volume and in order to form a plausible sequence; a summary of the articles in their order in this volume follows below.

Prologue

In his introductory contribution, *Sir Raymond Firth* relates the nature of knowledge to some Oceanic problems. The subject of knowledge has a long philosophical history in which the meaning of the concept has been elaborately scrutinized. It is clear that assertions of or about knowledge often conceal approximations and uncertainties. Oceanic languages seem to have concepts of knowledge, though their relation to perception and to belief varies greatly. Questions of knowledge in relation to personal identity are raised by the categorization of Polynesian pronouns and by variations in the use of personal names. As regards the problem of quality of knowledge, Firth maintains that descriptions of Oceanic phenomena by historians, geographers and anthropologists are evidential, not part of a self-constructed world.

Embodied Personhood

Borut Telban begins his chapter with the statement that the Ambonwari, the Karawari speaking people from the East Sepik Province of PNG, like many others do not have a term for any kind of physical body removed from the totality of human existence. People refer to the 'body' in its active, behavioural state as *kay* (way, habit, manner; ritual; being) which refers to embodied processes, both collective and individual, mythical and historical. The concept of *habitus*, known from the work by Mauss and elaborated by Bourdieu, is thus evoked. The other – for Melanesianists more familiar – reference to body is *arm* (skin). Thus it may be said that 'body' has meaning for Ambonwari people only through the external appearance of skin and the way it is observed in action. By using examples from daily practices, habitual life, healing ceremonies and ritual, Telban endeavours to make a significant connection between body and being which is central for Ambonwari understanding of their identity.

Andrée Grau takes as a starting point the notions of 'bodily intelligence' proposed by Howard Gardner and 'body memory' proposed by Paul Connerton as being important factors in the way individuals acquire knowledge about themselves and their societies. These ideas are developed by looking at material from the Tiwi of Melville and Bathurst islands, Northern Australia, where she carried out fieldwork between 1980–4. Grau concentrates on a group of dances which, following Goodale, she labels the 'kinship dances' because each dance shows a specific kinship relationship between the dancer and the person for whom the dance is being performed. Although kinship is present throughout Tiwi society, providing a framework for social action, it is only in dance that it is articulated in such a clear 'theoretical' way. She argues that dance plays a important role for kinship in three different ways: First, it teaches the system to the youngsters by 'putting it in their bodies'; secondly, it allows people to remember not only contemporary but also past kinship relationships between individuals; and thirdly through dance, kinship theories are elaborated through the use of bodily intelligence.

The contribution by *Christina Toren* concerns nineteenth-century Fijian conversion to Christianity and concomitant transformations in ideas of the person. The chapter examines archival data concerning death, birth and sacrifice to show how *mana* (literally 'effectiveness') resided in what one could be seen to consume and how it informed relations between kin. With Christian conversion one finds the elaboration of ideas of mutual compassion so that *mana* becomes a residual, though still implicitly crucial, category. The analysis suggests that while conversion effected certain profound transformations in Fijian ideas and practice, it ultimately resulted in a distinctively Fijian Christianity, as well as a distinctively Fijian concept of personhood.

Changing Life Histories

Andrew Strathern notes that 'life-history' is a genre that anthropologists have suggested to the people with whom they work, and the conditions of their 'production' have varied. Two such histories, or 'self-accounts', already published, illustrate this point and show clear differences in the personalities and orientations of their authors. Ongka's self-account, published in 1979, reveals a self-confident and eloquent narrator and rhetorician, versed in custom, history, aesthetic expression, and viewpoints on recent change. Both the account and the introduction to it written by the author as editor/translator, reflect the time of early transition from colonial rule to independence in PNG in the mid-1970s. The later account, by Ru, published in 1993 but originally composed prior to 1987, displays a quieter approach to life and a different moral stance towards exchange, as an element constitutive of kinship relations, as well as an element of individual and intergroup politics. Ru is a man some twenty years younger than Ongka, but these differences cannot be attributed – subjectively perceived by the author – to 'social change' *tout court*. Ru's attitudes do not represent any shift in the overall ethos of the exchange system (*moka*) from inter-group to inter-personal contexts, as both men have been equally involved in life-long processes whereby these contexts are intertwined. From the perspective of practice theory, however, Ru's orientations reflect his efforts over the years to build and rebuild networks of relationships from fragile material bases whereas Ongka's orientations reflect the centrality of his position in group affairs and the politico-emotional continuity of these since his childhood as the son of a leader or 'big man'. The author further explores these dimensions of comparison and contrast and also looks outside of the two texts at contextual issues of change that have impinged on the lives of Ru and Ongka and their contemporaries and the possible impact on concepts of the person and overall ontologies.

Lisette Josephides' portraits of some Kewa people from PNG bring together different kinds of material: solicited self-accounts ('autobiographies') and her observations of the eliciting strategies in people's daily interactions, their fights, disputes, responses to others, jokes, gossip and 'eliciting talk'. She analyzes them not as metadiscourses on culture but as active attempts to construct the self – especially in cross-sex relations – and its (changing) surroundings, including the moral sphere. What emerges is people's own discourse rather than perceptions elicited in ethnographic interviews. In the long and excessive accounts that break up and fragment – and thus subvert – any 'master narrative' the ethnographer or individual Kewa may wish to tell about 'Kewa culture', we glimpse the contours of a particular theory of action emerging from action as performed and recounted by the people rather than a generalized theory of action distilled from 'typical' ethnographic examples. As these accounts also implicate the ethnographer, she traces the process of anthropological knowledge as empathy developing in the encounter.

Local Recasting of Christianity

According to *Anna Paini*, Catholics and Protestants of a Christianized village on the west coast of the island of Lifu (Loyalty Island, New Caledonia) do not perceive their present-day practices and commentaries in terms of displacement of indigenous knowledge by Christian principles. Rather, they stress the mutual accommodation or coexistence of indigenous and Christian elements. (Yet she does feel uncomfortable in speaking either of syncretism or of compartmentalization of domains.) Although cast in an idiom that does not speak of the abuse of colonial power that emerges from other narratives, nevertheless Protestants' and Catholics' present-day accounts of how they embraced one Christian Church or the other differ. The Catholic perception that Church standards were set outside the village's domain, though narrated as something belonging to the past, is not found in Protestant narratives where the perspective taken is aimed at reducing the foreignness of the imported religion.

The data presented by *Monique Jeudy-Ballini* are mainly based on her fieldwork research among the Sulka people of East New Britain, PNG. It concerns the local appropriation of imported religions. First, she points out that such a process of appropriation is not unilateral. Thus, she shows that while Christian beliefs have been reinterpreted by the Sulka, a symmetric process of reinterpreting Sulka beliefs was at work among the first Catholic missionaries – who, to put it briefly, considered the Sulka as Christians unaware of their own Christianity. She insists on the experimental dimension that underlies the process of reinterpretation and that, for instance, leads individuals to test the imported knowledge in a quite pragmatic way, through provocative and defiant acts directed against the ancestral spirits. Dealing with the case of the Seventh Day Adventists' movement, Jeudy-Ballini examines the relationship between imported religions – once locally appropriated – to show what role their on-going interaction plays in the Sulka's construction of their own cultural identity.

Experiencing Outside Worlds

In his contribution, *Ronald Adams* describes the labour recruitment of the Tannese people of Efate, Vanuatu, in the second half of the nineteenth century. Before the contact with traders, the end of the known world for the Tannese was just to the north of Efate; but for the great majority of the Tannese, most of their own island was beyond the realm of immediate experience and only a few men were permitted to venture beyond their particular *niko* ('canoe') or territory, and even then only along traditionally sanctioned pathways leading to precise destinations. This political control of space left little room for innovation and closely regulated the range of relationships available to local groups. After 1842, with regular European contact, and with the establishment of European plantations throughout the Pacific and in Queensland from the 1860s on, things changed and the range of travel available to the coastal inhabitants of southern Vanuatu increased. An unprecedented number of Tannese men – and increasingly women as well – would undertake journeys of exploration abroad, to places as far afield as Australia, Fiji, New Caledonia, Samoa, Hawaii and the Carolines. Adams analyzes how the Tannese experienced this outside world in the light of Tannese culture, how they returned from these journeys abroad with new identities transcending traditional descent lines and with new ident-ifications, and he addresses the difficulty of conceptualizing experiences which would appear to have been simultaneously revolutionary and traditional.

Many anthropological studies, writes *Brigit Obrist van Eeuwijk,* describe the dilemma faced by PNG men: whether they should follow the traditional ways of gaining power and prestige, i.e. the men's cult and the exchange system, or the new ways, i.e. business and politics. It is often overlooked that PNG women face a similar dilemma. Obrist van Eeuwijk's research among the Kwanga in the East Sepik Province has shown that, according to the local tradition, the practical aspects of human procreation, i.e. contraception, menstruation, childbirth and childcare, formed the core of the female realm. With the integration into the colonial and later the national administration, new institutions of the missions and the state have progressively intruded into these formerly female domains. The author analyzes responses of Kwanga women to these intrusions.

Beatriz Moral's contribution focuses on an Micronesian society. In a traditional context, Chuukese women's status was defined by their role as guardians of the transcendental unity and harmony of the lineage and the rules derived from the incest taboo. Women's status was a mixture of power and silence, respect and male superiority. These circumstances were the foundation for the new elements introduced into the Chuukese culture. The result of this new situation – where some of the traditional elements have been forgotten and some maintained but, in most cases, with their meaning changed – is a deterioration in women's status. The legitimization of male power, a decrease in opportunities for women to interfere in decision-making processes, and an increase in the control over women have been some of the results of this situation. The elements responsible for this new situation are, basically: Christianization, North-Americanization and the introduction of Western ways of government and administration.

Appropriating New Forms of Knowledge

Pierre Lemonnier notes that since the late 1960s, as feud and tribal warfare has declined among the Ankave-Anga in PNG, aggression by invisible cannibal flying spirits has increased. Although police parties visit this remote area only once every two or three years, and patrol officers even less, the reference to the state is constant. This is the basis for the informal courts where most political power is presently located. At the same time, thanks to knowledge imported from a nearby group, a new specialist, the *bos sanguma*, is now able to 'see' and denounce publicly the human hosts or patrons of the invisible cannibal spirits held responsible for many illnesses. This gives them political power of a kind unheard of among the Anga. Lemonnier analyzes these new local procedures – courts and divination – with the aim of showing invisible powers and rendering them tangible.

Milan Stanek and *Florence Weiss* address the adaptation strategies of the first and second generations of Sepik migrants to the town of Rabaul. The original colonial labour regulations were abolished in the 1960s and the 'natives' were allowed to migrate and to seek jobs freely. Successively, the urban work force of single men was replaced by a more proportionally composed urban population of both sexes and children. For the first time in PNG, an urban population in the full sense of the word emerged. A successful family is presented and it is demonstrated how similar strategies result in the husband as well as the wife being successful in the village as well as in town. In the second generation, however, the daughter loses her status after having adapted to a Western lifestyle.

Eric Venbrux examines the cultural aspects of self-management as performed by indigenous leaders in an Aboriginal society in Northern Australia, and proceeds from an ethnohistorical perspective. The central figure is John Tunkwaliti, a cultural broker who with great skill uses the system of the white people for his own purpose and who succeeds in obtaining subsidies for the construction of a new township with a golf-course, supermarket, tennis court, restaurant and so forth.

In 1990, a number of people from Tokelau, a tiny atoll in the South Pacific, living in the Wellington area in New Zealand came together to form a theatre group later called *Tokelau Te Ata*. Since then, the group has produced two plays, and in December 1993 members went on a tour of the three atolls of Tokelau to, as they said, 'bring the gift back home'. *Ingjerd Hoëm* describes this event, and discusses the creation of Tokelau drama within the context of current political changes taking place in Tokelau. The group is trying to articulate certain life-experiences that have not in their opinion been addressed previously within the forms of mainstream culture. Their doing so engendered a lot of tension and caused certain conflicts but, as the new cultural form fell into the category of entertainment, or a 'thing of no account', *mea tauanoa*, the objections did not become too serious. The author discusses how recent political changes in Tokelau have resulted in a perceived need for the articulation of new ways of 'being Tokelauan', and shows how some people attempt to bring about such visions, and the difficulties this entails.

Epilogue   .

Marilyn Strathern notes that the kind of knowledge anthropology produces is extolled in unusual contexts. Latour has recently decided that we were never modern and that Euro-American ways of thinking have always had more in common with the hybrid creatures of pre-modern imaginations than 'we' would care to admit. Now that the current perceptions of the world as plural, fluid and transgressive seem to be turning up hybrids everywhere, it is worth asking what these new parallels signify. Her contribution argues that Melanesians have never been pre-modern.

Note

1. The contributions in this volume are a selection of revised papers held at the Conference of the European Society for Oceanists, in Basel, in December 1994; a further selection is edited by Jürg Wassmann (1998b). I wish to thank Ingrid Bell and Norma Stephenson for translating and turning this introduction into acceptable English.

References

Antweiler, C. (1995). Lokales Wissen. Grundlagen, Probleme, Bibliographie. In: S. Honerla and P. Schröder (eds), *Lokales Wissen und Entwicklung. Zur Relevanz kulturspezifischen Wissens für Entwicklungsprozesse*, pp. 19–52. Saarbrücken: Verlag für Entwicklungspolitik.

Appadurai, A. (1988). Putting Hierarchy in its Place. *Cultural Anthropology* 3: 36–49.

—— (1991). Global Ethnoscapes. Notes and Queries for a Transnational Anthropology. In: R. Fox (ed.), *Recapturing Anthropology. Working in the Present*, pp. 191–210. Santa Fe: School of American Research Press.

Barth, F. (ed.) (1969). *Ethnic Groups and Boundaries: The Social Organization of Cultural Difference*. Boston: Little, Brown.

—— (1993). *Balinese Worlds*. Chicago: University of Chicago Press.

Bauman, Z. (1992). *Intimation of Postmodernity*. London: Routledge.

Benda-Beckman, F. von (1993). Scapegoat and Magic Charm. Law in Development Theory and Practice. In: M. Hobart (ed.), *An Anthropological Critique of Development*, pp. 116–34. London: Routledge.

Bloch, M. (1991). Language, Anthropology and Cognitive Science. *Man* 26: 183–98.

Borofsky, R. (1994). On the Knowledge and Knowing of Cultural Activities. In: R. Borofsky (ed.), *Assessing Cultural Anthropology*, pp. 331–47. New York: McGraw-Hill.

Bourdieu, P. (1977). *Outline of a Theory of Practice*. Cambridge: Cambridge University Press.

—— (1989). *The Logic of Practice*. Cambridge: Polity Press.

Brush, St. (1993). Indigenous Knowledge of Biological Resources and Intellectual Property Rights: The Role of Anthropology. *American Anthropologist* 95: 653–86.

Chamoux, M.N. (1981). Les Savoir-faire Techniques et leur Appropriation: Le Cas des Nahuas de Mexique. *L'Homme* 21: 71–94.

Chandler, N. (1996). The Figure of the X: An Elaboration of the Du Boisian Autobiographical Example. In: S. Lavie and T. Swedenburg (eds), *Displacement, Diaspora, and Geographies of Identity*, pp. 235–72. Durham and London: Duke University Press.

Clifford, J. (1988). *The Predicament of Culture: Twentieth Century Ethnography, Literature, and Art*. Cambridge MA: Harvard University Press.

Cohen, A. (1993). Segmentary Knowledge: A Whalsay Sketch. In: M. Hobart (ed.), *An Anthropological Critique of Development*, pp. 31–42. London: Routledge.

Comaroff, J. and Comaroff, J. (1992). *Ethnography and the Historical Imagination*. Boulder: Westview Press.

Connerton, P. (1989). *How Societies Remember*. Cambridge: Cambridge University Press.

D'Andrade, R. and Strauss, C. (eds) (1992). *Human Motives and Cultural Models*. Cambridge: Cambridge University Press.

Dasen, P.R. (1992). Schlusswort. Les Sciences Cognitives: Do they Shake Hands in the Middle? In: J. Wassmann and P.R. Dasen (eds), *Alltagswissen. Les Savoirs Quotidiens. Everyday Cognition*, pp. 331–52. Fribourg: Presses Universitaires.

Flick, U. (1995). Alltagswissen in der Sozialpsychologie. In: U. Flick (ed.), *Psychologie des Sozialen. Repräsentationen in Wissen und Sprache*, pp. 54–77. Reinbek: Rowohlt.

Fox, J.J., Bellwood, P. and Tryon, D. (eds) (1995). *The Austronesians: Historical and Comparative Perspectives*. Canberra: The Australian National University Press.

Frake, C.O. (1975). How to Enter a Yakan House? In: M. Sanchez and B. Blount (eds), *Sociocultural Dimension of Language Use*, pp. 25–40. New York: Academic Press.

Friedman, J. (1994). *Cultural Identity and Global Process*. London: Sage.

Giddens, A. (1984). *The Constitution of Society: Outline of the Theory of Structuration*. Berkeley: University of California Press.

Glazer, N. and Moynihan, D.P. (eds) (1975). *Ethnicity, Theory, and Experience*. Cambridge MA: Harvard University Press.

Goodenough, W. (1957). Cultural Anthropology and Linguistics. In: P.L. Garvin (ed.), *Report of the Seventh Annual Round Table Meeting on Linguistics and Language Studies*, pp. 167-73. Washington DC: Georgetown University Press.

Gupta, A. and Ferguson, J. (1992). Beyond 'Culture': Space, Identity, and the Politics of Identity. *Cultural Anthropology* 7: 6–23.

Handler, R. (1985). On Dialogue and Destructive Analysis. Problems in Narrating Nationalism and Ethnicity. *Journal of Anthropological Research* 41: 171–82.

Hannerz, U. (1996). *Transnational Connections. Culture, People, Places*. London: Routledge.

Harvey, D. (1989). *The Conditions of Postmodernity*. Oxford: Blackwell.

Hastrup, K. and Olwig, K.F. (1997). Introduction. In: K.F. Olwig and K. Hastrup (eds), *Siting Culture. The Shifting Anthropological Object*, pp. 1–16. London: Routledge.

Hau'ofa, E. (1994). Our Sea of Islands. *The Contemporary Pacific* 6(1): 147–61.

Hobart, M. (1993). Introduction: The Growth of Ignorance? In: M. Hobart (ed.), *An Anthropological Critique of Development*, pp. 1–30. London: Routledge.

Holland, D. and Quinn, N. (eds) (1987). *Cultural Models in Language and Thought*. Cambridge: Cambridge University Press.

Kahn, J. (1989). Culture. Demise or Resurrection. *Critique of Anthropology* 9(2): 5–25.

Keck, V. (1992). *Falsch gehandelt – schwer erkrankt. Kranksein bei den Yupno in Papua New Guinea aus ethnologischer und biomedizinischer Sicht*. Basel: Wepf.

—— (1993). Two Ways of Explaining Reality. The Sickness of a Small Boy of Papua New Guinea from Anthropological and Biomedical Perspectives. *Oceania* 63: 294–312.

—— (1994). Talks about a Changing World. Young Yupno Men in Papua New Guinea Debate their Future. *Canberra Anthropology* 16(2): 67–96.

Keesing, R.M. (1987). Models, Folk and Cultural Paradigms Regained? In: D. Holland and N. Quinn (eds), *Cultural Models in Language and Thought*, pp. 368–93. Cambridge: Cambridge University Press.

Lakoff, G. (1987). *Woman, Fire and Dangerous Things. What Categories Reveal about the Mind.* Chicago: University of Chicago Press.

Lave, J. (1988). *Cognition in Practice. Mind, Mathematics and Culture in Everyday Life.* Cambridge: Cambridge University Press.

—— (1993). The Practice of Learning. In: J. Lave and S. Chaiklin (eds), *Understanding Practice. Perspectives on Activity and Context*, pp. 3–32. Cambridge: Cambridge University Press.

Long, N. and Long, A. (eds) (1992). *Battlefields of Knowledge. The Interlock of Theory and Practice in Social Research and Development.* London: Routledge.

Malkki, L. (1995). Refugees and Exile: From 'Refugee Studies' to the National Order of Things. *Annual Review of Anthropology* 24: 495–523.

Marcus, G.E. (1993). Tonga's Contemporary Globalizing Strategies: Trading on Sovereignty Amidst International Migration. In: V.S. Lockwood, T.G. Harding and B.J. Wallace (eds), *Contemporary Pacific Societies. Studies in Development and Change*, pp. 21–33. Englewood Cliffs NJ: Prentice-Hall.

Moore, S.F. (1975). Uncertainties in Situations, Indeterminacies in Culture. In: S.F. Moore and B. Myerhoff (eds), *Symbol and Politics in Communal Ideology*, pp. 219–39. Ithaca: Cornell University Press.

—— (1987). Explaining the Present: Theoretical Dilemmas in Processual Ethnography. *American Ethnologist* 14: 727–36.

Murtaugh, M. (1985). The Practice of Arithmetic by American Grocery Shoppers. *Anthropology and Education Quarterly* 16: 186–92.

Olwig, K.F. and Hastrup, K. (eds) (1997). *Siting Culture. The Shifting Anthropological Object.* London: Routledge.

Ortner, S. (1984). Theory in Anthropology Since the Sixties. *Comparative Studies in Society and History* 26: 126–66.

Otto, T. (ed.) (1993). *Pacific Islands Trajectories: Five Personal Views.* Canberra: Australian National University, Department of Anthropology; Nijmegen: Centre for Pacific Studies.

Quinn, N. and Holland, D. (1987). Introduction. In: D. Holland and N. Quinn (eds), *Cultural Models in Language and Thought*, pp. 3–42. Cambridge: Cambridge University Press.

Rogoff, B. and Lave, J. (eds) (1984). *Everyday Cognition: Its Development in Social Context*. Cambridge MA: Harvard University Press.

Rogoff, B. (1990). *Apprenticeship in Thinking. Cognitive Development in Social Context*. New York: Oxford University Press.

Rosch, E. and Lloyd, B. (eds) (1978). *Cognition and Categorization*. Hillsdale NJ: Erlbaum.

Sahlins, M. (1991). The Return of the Event, Again: With Reflections on the Beginnings of the Great Fijian War of 1843 to 1855 between the Kingdoms of Bau and Rewa. In: A. Biersack (ed.), *Clio in Oceania: Towards a Historical Anthropology*, pp. 37–99. Washington: Smithsonian Institution Press.

Schank, R. and Abelson, R. (1977). *Scripts, Plans and Understanding. An Inquiry into Human Knowledge Structure*. Hillsdale NJ: Erlbaum.

Schröder, P. (1995). Lokales Wissen als konstruktives and kritisches Potential für die Entwicklungszusammenarbeit. In: S. Honerla and P. Schröder (eds), *Lokales Wissen und Entwicklung*, pp. 1–18. Saarbrücken: Verlag für Entwicklungspolitik.

Scribner, S. (1984). Studying Working Intelligence. In: B. Rogoff and J. Lave (eds), *Everyday Cognition: Its Development in Social Context*, pp. 9–40. Cambridge MA: Cambridge University Press.

Sørensen, B. (1997). The Experience of Displacement. In: K.F. Olwig and K. Hastrup (eds), *Siting Culture: The Shifting Anthropological Object*, pp. 142–64. London: Routledge.

Sperber, D. (1985). *On Anthropological Knowledge. Three Essays*. Cambridge: Cambridge University Press; Paris: Editions de la Maison des Sciences de l'Homme.

Strathern, M. (1995). The Nice Thing about Culture is that Everyone Has it. In: M. Strathern (ed.), *Shifting Contexts. Transformations in Anthropological Knowledge*, pp. 153–76. London: Routledge.

Tylor, E.B. (1958). *Primitive Culture*. New York: Harper Torchbooks. (First published in 1871.)

van Meijl, T. and van der Grijp, P. (eds) (1993). *Politics, Tradition and Change in the Pacific. Bijdragen tot de Taal-, Land- en Volkenkunde* (special issue) 149(4): 633–824.

Warren, M., Slikkerveer, J. and Brokensha, D. (eds) (1995). *The Cultural Dimension of Development. Indigenous Knowledge Systems.* London: Intermediate Technology Publications.

Wassmann, J. (1994). The Yupno as Post-Newtonian Scientists. The Question of What is 'Natural' in Spatial Descriptions. *Man* 29: 645–66.

—— (1995). The Final Requiem for the Omniscient Informant? An Interdisciplinary Approach to Everyday Cognition. *Culture and Psychology* 2: 167–201.

—— (1998a). Introduction. In: J. Wassmann (ed.), *Pacific Answers to Western Hegemony. Cultural Practices of Identity Construction*, pp. 1–34. Oxford: Berg.

—— (ed.) (1998b). *Pacific Answers to Western Hegemony. Cultural Practices of Identity Construction.* Oxford: Berg.

Wassmann, J. and Dasen, P.R. (in press). Balinese Spatial Orientation. Some Evidence of Moderate Linguistic Relativity. *Journal of the Royal Anthropological Institute.*

Westen, D. (1985). *Self and Society. Narcissism, Collectivism, and the Development of Morals.* Cambridge: Cambridge University Press.

Wicker, H.-R. (1997). From Complex Culture to Cultural Complexity. In: P. Werbner and T. Modood (eds), *Debating Cultural Hybridity. Multi-Cultural Identities and the Politics of Anti-Racism*, pp. 29–45. London: Zed Books.

Part I

Prologue

Chapter 1

Reflections on Knowledge in an Oceanic Setting[1]

Raymond Firth

I begin with a quotation from René Descartes, a chief founder of modern philosophy: 'That in order to seek truth, it is necessary once in the course of our life to doubt, as far as possible, of all things' (1929: 165). Descartes' enquiry into the principles of human knowledge led him to reject doubt as to his own existence and to affirm the existence of God. Although he accepted the authority of the Church, however, his ultimate desire was that his conclusions should be continually challenged by reason, of which the capacity to doubt is an essential component. To this I would add an opinion from Bertrand Russell on 'the vagueness and uncertainty that characterizes most of what we believe ourselves to know' (1948: 439), and the philosophical difficulties that arise from insufficient realization of the difference between different kinds of knowledge.

Such philosophers' views are relevant when we are dealing with *knowledge* and I think it important to examine such a basic concept in a sceptical frame of mind. I have been strengthened in this opinion by a recent Decennial conference of the Association of Social Anthropologists at Oxford (1993), where many papers were given about the *uses* of knowledge with hardly any enquiry into what was *meant* by the knowledge – or knowledges – spoken of.

Enquiry into the nature of knowledge has a long philosophical history. It goes back at least as far as Socrates, who is depicted by Plato as continually challenging assertions by people who met him that they knew what they claimed to know. Socrates himself had a very sobering view – that he himself did not know anything, and that his wisdom lay in his awareness of his own ignorance.

Hence his searching enquiry into the *meaning* of what was asserted to be known. So he asked such basic questions as: 'What is knowledge?' 'How do we get it?' 'Can we be sure that what we think we know is not just illusion?' 'What are the relations between knowledge and perception?' (Russell 1946: 157–8, Russell 1948; Guthrie 1950: 73–5).

These are questions that are still pertinent to serious enquiry, after 2,400 years, and in an Oceanic as well as in a Western context of study.

It is clear that the acquisition of knowledge involves mental activity, though it is not always clear what is the degree of consciousness involved. It is also clear that while much knowledge expresses itself in non-verbal action, a great deal of knowledge is expressed in the form of language. Problems connected with knowledge are by no means all linguistic. A person's command of skill in cooking, swimming, riding a bicycle – 'knowing how' to do these things – can be tested without linguistic communication by simply watching him or her carry out the activity. In Tikopia in 1929 I was much impressed as I watched a boy of nine years old prepare kava liquid for ritual libations to be poured to gods and ancestors by his grandfather, the chief. He did this without instruction at the time – though he would have been told on a former occasion; *nai iroa*, he knows already, it was explained to me. Yet in common activity of communication of knowledge (or purported knowledge) a resort to language is virtually essential.

Here two great sets of problems arise. The first set relates to what it is that is alleged to be known. What is the relation of an assertion about knowledge or a claim to knowledge to the state of affairs referred to? This assumes that there is a 'state of affairs' external to the presumed knower; that in colloquial terms there is a 'real world' distinct from the internal world of the knower. As I type this contribution in my study I assume that there are independent objects around me – shelves, books, pictures – which do not exist simply for me. Now it is possible that this assumption is an illusion, that my 'knowledge' of them is a reflection of my own imagination. Yet everyday experience of a relatively consistent kind leads me to think that this is not so, and that an 'as if' approach to reality yields results that can be anticipated. It is true that 'external' and 'internal' cannot be always very sharply differentiated but this does not mean that we live simply in a self-constructed world.

Assertions about knowledge are often thought to have a firm character, indicating a close correspondence between the statement of knowledge and the state of affairs about which the statement is made. This is often not so. The knowledge may be partial only; the state of affairs referred to may be different from that indicated. Take two common types of statement. 'I know that a train starts at nine o'clock every day from this railway station.' This item of knowledge may be valid in general but may be erroneous on any particular day owing to flood, an engine breakdown or a strike of railway workers. A more accurate statement would be 'I know that a train is due to start'. Again 'I know that the sun will rise tomorrow morning'. Here a valid phenomenon is referred to that is not subject to accident or to human intervention. But if literally interpreted the statement is not accurate. The sun does not 'rise'; the earth's rotation reveals it to a person in a given position. Some claims to 'knowledge' may therefore at times be inaccurate; they may be only approximations to the truth. So too a person's internal conception of what he or she 'knows' about an event or an activity may be imperfect or misconceived. Hence action based upon such putative knowledge may become ineffective.

Already we have been brought into the second great area of problems of knowledge, namely, those involving the language of expression. These problems are concerned with, among other things, what Susan Stebbing has termed 'the ambiguity of knowing'. According to an early view of Plato, knowledge is infallible as it is logically impossible for it to be mistaken. In this view, knowledge has the character of being absolute, eternal, immutable, and concerned with beauty itself, in its perfection. Statements of knowledge that may be fallible or approximate are then, in Plato's view, only 'opinion' (Russell 1946: 142).

But this is an idealistic conception of 'pure' knowledge, a logical relation. 'Knowing' as ordinarily used in English has several senses. The most obvious is the difference between knowing a person (or thing) and knowing a fact or event. This difference is expressed more overtly in German: *kennen* means to know a person, to be acquainted with or recognize him or her; *wissen* to know something, be aware of, understand it. In French a similar difference is expressed by *connaître* and *savoir*.

Philosophers through the ages have been much concerned with the different kinds of knowing and the ambiguities involved in use of the term knowledge but, although they have tended to deal with the same basic problems, their conclusions have varied widely. In recent times one of the most stimulating treatments has undoubtedly been that of Bertrand Russell. Apart from his historical survey of theories of knowledge held by philosophers of the past his distinction between knowing by acquaintance and knowing by description attracted much attention. The former takes place through direct awareness, the latter through knowledge of a property possessed. Such a distinction has not been universally accepted, however. From our point of view such difficult logical conceptions do not seem very relevant to Oceanic enquiry.

Yet it is of interest in all these philosophical arguments that use is made of the single abstract term 'knowledge'. Knowledge is regarded as a unitary concept, like honesty, courage, rectitude, justice. Some modern usage, however, at least in anthropology, has the term in the plural, 'knowledges'. I myself prefer the old-fashioned use of the singular term alone, as a universal. It is true that some universals such as truth and beauty have come to have plural usage too. (In English, some plurals of abstract terms have come to acquire peculiar meaning. 'Justices' as in Justices of the Peace applies to persons in a legal office; 'honours' applies to tokens or titles of esteem awarded to persons by the Crown or by academic or analogous bodies.) The use of plurals such as 'truths' or 'beauties' as concrete particulars in supplement to singular abstract universals is intelligible. But I think it needs careful scrutiny from a methodological point of view. The comprehensive and stimulating outline of this Basel Conference theme[2] states that 'knowing conveys the idea that the specificity of Oceanic *knowledges* permanently obliges us to re-scrutinize our own knowledges' (my italics). What is meant by this statement? What is gained by use of the plural forms? Does 'knowledges' refer to items or patterns of knowledge, as in the technology of Oceanic fishing, cooking or calendars? Does it mean types, forms or systems of knowledge or a more intangible kind, as exemplified in the language of personal relations and the ability to interpret them? Implications of this pluralistic usage can be far-reaching. They will include stories about island history, but will they involve a concept of different orders of knowledge represented by, say, spirit revelation as contrasted with ordinary observation? It is indeed not clear how far the use of the term 'knowledges' may imply differences of assumption about the nature of reality itself. Be this as it may, it seems to me that there are advantages in retaining the conventional usage of knowledge as a unitary universal and distinguishing types, forms, systems, items, patterns, bodies of knowledge, regionally and activity-wise, as empirically required, before going on to generalize about what is known in Oceania as a whole.

I have argued that, pragmatically, expressions of knowing in verbal forms are often approximate only, often matters of probability. The language of knowing, as an intellectual activity, is often close to that of belief, in which there is an assurance commonly due to an emotional component. Take a biblical example: when Naaman, captain of the host of the king of Syria, was cured of his leprosy, he said to Elisha the prophet 'I know that there is no God in all the earth, but in Israel' (2 Kings: V). The example is probably apocryphal but the phraseology of the religious statement is common.

Conviction that what is believed must be true, and is evident to the person making the affirmation, is of a very different order from knowledge resting upon the results of observation. It is claimed that knowledge is true belief; that there can be no false knowledge. But such claims to truth are not self-validating. What Ernest Gellner has described in another context as 'nonsense on stilts' (1974: 205) is an assertion of knowledge based upon inner conviction admitting of no doubt.

Let us turn to Oceania and touch a few relevant concrete topics regarding 'knowledge' there.

Knowledge of the natural environment is vital to a sense of identity. Oceania offers many varieties of environment, with strong contrast between Australian deserts, New Guinea mountain ranges and isolated, often remote, islands. Common to many island communities is recognition of the permanent presence of a circumambient ocean, a marine environment that has dictated adaptation to weather turbulence, travel and the business of making a living. Here is one of the great historical changes, as new technologies have entered to supplant those in traditional use and enforce new modes of behaviour. Replacement of canoe by motor boat has meant new patterns of fishing, gender alignment in travel, ownership of equipment, dances and songs. New economic, social and political environments have markedly changed fields of knowledge and senses of identity in the course of Oceanic history. One effect has been loss of traditional knowledge of myth and ritual and of religious ideology. Another has been loss of vernacular language, despite many recent efforts to retain and revive this traditional heritage.

Every student of Oceania is faced by the problem of categories – into what kind of classes are objects and relations of the environment placed by the people studied? Many categorizations are shared by the investigator and local people. Human beings seem everywhere to be separated from other living things and from inanimate objects. Basic relationships such as up/down or right/ left, near/far also seem to be common but much variation seems to occur in the cognitive arrangement of persons and things within the most general categories. In Tikopia, for example, with analogies elsewhere in Polynesia, different classifiers are used according to certain different kinds of objects specified. *Tino* is used in speaking of numbers of persons, *tau* for canoes, *pāpā* for leaf packages of food or other flat wrapped packets, but there are complications. *Pāpā* is a noun referring mainly to packages of grated vegetables; *tau* is a particle of many other meanings whereas *tino* as a noun means the body, of persons or animals. *Tauvaka rua* means ordinarily two canoes but *tino rua* means commonly not two persons but twenty (without mentioning persons at all!). In other words, although the Tikopia have a decimal counting system of some elaboration that is quite intelligible to a Westerner, they have some idiomatic usages of it which need to be specially learned. (A question of interest might be the extent to which modern education in arithmetic has tended to modify the idiosyncrasies of Oceanic counting systems.)

In an enquiry into knowledge and identity in Oceania two major pragmatic questions arise, in modern terms and on a historical basis. The first is 'how has knowledge been transmitted and acquired, both traditionally and by contemporary procedures?' Study of modern educational developments must not obscure the importance of less formal sources of knowledge, such as verbal and non-verbal imparting of information in family relationships or peer groups or nowadays in film and television viewing. The second great question concerns the distribution of knowledge, which is associated with questions of rank, gender and power. An obvious aspect of the modern situation is often a decline in the relative value of knowledge possessed by elders, especially by elder men. The advance of technology, more easily mastered by young men, the migration of many people away from their traditional cultural centres, the move from traditional pagan religions, usually locally based and controlled by elders, have all meant a radical shift in areas of knowledge, in the relative significance of different kinds of knowledge, and in the power given by knowledge most relevant to contemporary concerns. The male–female distribution of knowledge is particularly important here. It seems that in many contexts Oceanic women have lost ground in that so much of modern technology is male-operated and the modern wage system often offers so many more roles to men than to women. Yet women have had important roles in the traditional system. They also have their place in modern industry, if only mainly in clerical jobs. Some formidable Polynesian women have indeed been able to use their knowledge of men and affairs to great political and administrative effect. There is also a further element of a less concrete order. In a visit to an exhibition of Tibetan sacred art in London a couple of years ago I learned that in the Tibetan system of Tantric Buddhist thought the *possession* of knowledge is an attribute to the female element, whereas the *acquisition* and *interpretation* of knowledge is an attribute of the male element. This seems like another version of the classical male-active, female-passive roles, but in the Tantric system male and female are aspects of each other, so possession and use are ultimately fused. I do not expect anything quite similar to be discovered in Oceania but, when it comes to knowledge of human relations, Oceanic women may have a capacity that men cannot match. In some Oceanic communities women have been credited with mystic knowledge and mystical powers very different from those of men and feared by them. Investigation of the distribution of knowledge of a non-technological kind between the sexes/gender can be a significant aspect of Oceanic enquiry.

The relation between knowledge and perception offers interesting problems in the linguistic field. Have Oceanic communities any abstract conceptions of knowledge, expressed in language? It would seem so, but the different linguistic forms in which such ideas are expressed, some of them etymologically related, appear to embody a variety of sensory associations. I take examples from four Polynesian dictionaries to which I have easy access, namely Maori, Samoan, Tikopia, Tokelau.[3]

According to these dictionaries, the concept of knowledge occurs in all these languages, but though related in general terms, the languages show considerable variation in forms of expression. The expression of knowing in Maori is very different from those

in Samoan, Tikopia or Tokelau. The common Maori term *mōhio*
indicates 'know', 'understand', 'recognize', with an allied meaning
of being wise, intelligent. The corresponding Tikopia word is *iroa*,
with cognate Samoan and Tokelau *iloa*. The term *iroa* does not occur
in Maori, or at least only rarely and without any meaning of
'know'. The Maori dictionaries give a large number of terms for
'knowing', 'knowledge', with interesting links elsewhere in the
field of thought and understanding, according to the glosses. *Āro*,
to know or understand, is probably related to *aro*, a word of
many meanings, including 'mind', the seat of feelings, 'desire',
'inclination' – a suggestion that 'knowledge' may be related to
wish-fulfilment! *Hua*, glossed in some contexts as 'know', 'be sure
of', is given in a related semantic area as 'to name', implying that
if you can name someone you also know him. With the term *kite*
we approach a relation between knowing and bodily sensation.
In Maori, Tikopia and Tokelau this word represents visual
observation, with varying glosses of see, look at, watch, perceive,
discover. One might guess that an inferential meaning would then
be 'to know'. Yet this is not so either in Tikopia or Tokelau, and in
Maori the rendering of *kite* as 'know' is given only by Biggs and
not in the classic Williams dictionary. But what it notable is that
whereas knowledge of an empirical, pragmatic kind does not
appear to be described in terms of *kite*, a gloss for a kind of mystical
knowledge occurs in both Maori and Samoan. In Maori *kite* as a
noun is given as divination, prophetic utterance, while in Samoan
the cognate *'ite* in verbal from *'i'ite* is given as 'foretell', 'have a
hunch', 'a premonition', roughly equivalent to what in English we
would term 'second-sight'. To pursue possible Polynesian relation
between knowledge and sensation, take the term *rongo*. Generally,
this means to listen, to hear; a Maori gloss gives apprehension by
the senses except sight, and includes taste and smell. Now neither
Maori or Tikopia, nor Samoan (*logo*) gloss *rongo* as 'know'. In
Tokelau, however, *logo* (with velar-nasal *ng*) is glossed not only as
hear, be felt, but also as understand, know. A common Maori term
mātau, meaning to know, be acquainted with, understand, has
parallel connotations in Samoan and Tokelau, not in a specific gloss
of 'know' but as 'observe', 'notice', 'recognize'. Tikopia has no such
meanings. Conversely, Samoan, Tokelau and Tikopia all use the
term *poto* for a range of glosses including 'skilled', 'wise',
'intelligent', 'knowing'; in Maori *poto* simply means short.

I have taken this simple example of terms from Western

Polynesian vernaculars to bring out two points. One is that if one tries to understand Oceanic knowledge it is essential to examine vernacular concepts as expressed in language. 'Knowing Oceania' necessitates an enquiry into 'knowing *within* Oceania'. The second point is that whereas concepts of knowing comparable to Western ideas appear to be prevalent, these show a great deal of variation in their associations. The implication is, then, that 'knowing' in Oceania may not necessarily have the same meaning as for external observers. From this, a question arises – how far is a unitary expression for 'knowing Oceania' achievable at this stage?

An important problem in this field is 'how far do Oceanic languages allow of expression of belief, surmise, supposition as distinct from knowledge?' If we turn again to the Western Polynesian languages that I cited earlier we find that each language has quite separate linguistic forms for 'believe', 'suppose', 'surmise' and so forth from those used for know. (Only Tokelau uses *iloa* for believe and know.) As with the field of knowledge, there are a variety of expressions in vogue for 'belief', but with a range of associations concerning 'think', holding opinion, being in no doubt, mostly implying conviction. A common Maori term for 'believe', admitting as true is *whakapono*; this has a modern gloss of 'faith', presumably in the Christian sense.

Yet though belief may imply conviction of truth, there is room for recognition of difference between allegation and fact, based on checkable evidence. This comes out fairly well in the Tikopia data. The word *iroa* can be glossed as 'know' in English. *Iroa rei ona mātua ku lasi ko tona manava* – 'her parents knew that her belly had become large' – i.e. they observed she was pregnant. *Se kau iroa pe e tonu pe siei* – 'I do not know if it be true or not'. *Nga papalangi i mua e katakata ki nga Tikopia siei pe nia ratou iroa* – 'the white people (those from the far horizon?) of former times looked down upon (laughed at) the Tikopia, who knew nothing at all' (a modest deprecating statement by Tikopia expressing their early technical ignorance compared with Westerners).

With these uses of *iroa* may be contrasted those of *ati*, which emphasize imputation rather than evidence. Quite concretely, *ati* means to heap up, to accumulate but in a more abstract sense I have glossed it as 'suppose', 'allege', 'think', 'affirm', 'identify as'; to these glosses belief may well be added. *E ati te koroa nga āriki* – 'it is supposed to be a valuable of the chiefs'. *Ati mai koke kuou tenea seke pokouru* – 'you think/believe I'm a dunderhead' (literally, without a head). *Ko ratou i mua nga tāngata ka e ati e a tatou ki muri nei ko nga ātua* – 'they of olden times were men, but are alleged/ believed by us of recent times to have been spirits'. *Tikopia se kai, e ati e kona* – 'Tikopia don't eat it, believing it to be bitter/poisonous'. *Sa Namo e mataku, e ati kuou e fakateketeke* – 'the people of Namo are afraid, believing me to be angry' (a statement by the Ariki Taumako, who however, denied that he had been offended by their actions).

Some very subtle problems are involved in the relation between knowledge of persons, expressions of that knowledge in linguistic terms, and notions of personal identity. These may be illustrated by a simple comparison of personal pronouns in a Western context and that of an Oceanic community, say Tikopia. Differences in the grammatical categories of number, gender and case show that knowledge of persons is variously arranged in these two instances. In English, the personal pronouns in singular number are: I/me; you; he/she/him/her/it. The corresponding Tikopia pronouns are: *kuou*; *koke*; *(ko) ia*. In Tikopia there is no accusative case; nor is there any differentiation of gender. The plurals also show marked differences of category. In English they are: we/us; you; they/ them. This shows that the second person singular and plural are the same – 'you'. But as is known historically, 'you' is a plural, and the earlier singular was '*thou*'. In French and German this singularity has been retained. However, it expresses more than number; it also serves to indicate degree of intimacy between speaker and person addressed, and may involve considerable nuances in interpretation. To a person not well known, say, not a member of the family, the plural form is usually addressed, *vous* or *Sie*, analogous to the English usage. In Tikopia, as in many other Oceanic languages, the plurals are more complex. They include dual as well as regular plurals, and inclusive as well as exclusive. So, the first person indicative of more than one in number has four forms: *taua, tatou; maua, matou*. These categories are not unintelligible in English, but they are neater in Tikopia: you and I two; you and I more than two; he/she and I (not you); they and I (not you). Correspondingly, the second person has *korua* and *kotou*; the third person *raua* and *ratou*.

It is common in most languages, I would think, for pronouns often to carry a social, perhaps even emotional loading, and not merely to express formal characteristics such as number. Tikopia, for example, has what I have called a 'polite dual' analogous to the 'polite plural' of French and German. A close affinal relative in Tikopia such as a father-in-law or brother-in-law is addressed not as *koke*, you, but as *korua*, 'you two'. This is interpreted by the Tikopia as a sign of respect, and they have given rather fanciful explanations of the meaning of this usage (Firth 1936: 312).

My point here is that if one is seeking 'some central dimensions of the Oceanic specificity' one might start with notions of how persons are conceived, in various categories, which may give some clues to the ways in which the people relate to others and to questions of their identity.

I now turn to a matter of identity, of a personal kind, as manifest in the linguistic field, the important matter of personal names. As far as is known, members of every Oceanic society are involved in a system of personal naming, and such names are normally not only identifiers of particular persons but often also locate them as members of particular vernacular communities. The concept of proper name, applicable to persons or things, seems universal in Oceania, as the Western Polynesian *ingoa* (in Maori and Tikopia, written *igoa* in Samoan and Tokelau).

A feature of significance in probably every human society is that a personal name is not just a linguistic label, a means for identifying the person; it is commonly used also as some sort of classifier. In European societies a personal name is commonly a gender marker – William, John, Alfred are names for males; Jane, Margaret, Anne are names for females. Some personal names have male and female forms – Wilhelm, Wilhelmina; Charles, Charlotte. In English, at least a few names may be borne by either males or females – Evelyn, Lesley – but this is rare. In Oceania likewise some societies may use personal names as gender markers, but others such as Tikopia in its traditional phase did not. (Nowadays, as I mention later, modern Tikopia names are often gender aligned.) An important social usage in many Oceanic societies, I think, is the use of a personal name as a demonstration of social linkage. A person is named after a kinsman/kinswoman or a more remote ancestor. As Tikopia have said: *E ati saere ki a ingoa tatou puna; te ingoa matou sē fakaleku* – '(children) are called successively by the names of our ancestors; a name of our origin is not allowed to disappear.' Many children's names in Tikopia are given by their parents in memory of events in which the parents have participated. Other people may also be assigned mnemonic names as a token of esteem, to keep alive some sentimental memory. So,

when I was last in Tikopia in 1966 I was told that some time earlier
the name Makoimarae had been conferred upon me by elders as a
term of praise, reminding people of the occasion many years before
when I had danced in the sacred assembly ground as part of the
ritual of the 'Work of the Gods'. The name 'danced in the assembly
ground' conveyed a rich set of associations to the older men of
the community.

Each Oceanic society has its own framework of ideas pertaining
to the use of personal names. In Tikopia there is considerable
flexibility in the award and use of personal names. A Tikopia
personal name may be set aside without trouble and a new name
assumed by a person, with an expectation that the community
will accept this new designation without comment. In one sense,
personal names may be regarded very intensely as family or
individual property, as when in former times the names of
ancestors were jealously guarded by chiefs and lineage heads
because of their mystical value as powerful agents in prayers for
health and prosperity. More generally, Tikopia personal names
have been regarded as very much personal property, to be taken
up and put down at will.

Given this freedom in many respects, Tikopia has had a set of
very definite rules about the use of personal names. On marriage,
a person abandoned the ordinary use of his 'bachelor' or her
'mobile woman' name – which henceforth was used only by close
family kin – and took on a 'married' name. Traditionally, this
referred to the site of one of the family dwellings and so had an
ancestral flavour. Much variation was possible, and modern men
have tended to adopt household names of their own invention,
often referring to their own experiences abroad. Once married, a
man is known as Pa Rongomai (say) and his wife as Nau Rongomai
– terms for 'father' and 'mother' equivalent in the immediate
context to the English Mr and Mrs. It would be most impolite for
anyone except parent or sibling to address husband or wife by
their unmarried names, and I never heard such a breach of
etiquette.

Some Tikopia taboos on use of personal names are quite specific.
A man is forbidden to utter the personal name of his father, or of a
close agnatic kinsman in the same category. If such a name is asked
for, by say an inquisitive anthropologist, a man will either flatly
refuse to give his father's name or, if a rather distant 'father'
is enquired for, will get another man of a different order of

relationship to utter it for him – often in some embarrassment. A man is forbidden also to utter the personal name of his brother-in-law or father-in-law. There is also sensitivity about the use of one's own name. One is prohibited by custom from using the name of someone who bears the same name as oneself. *Ingoa* – 'name' – also means 'namesake', and one uses this term in calling to or referring to one's namesake.[4] Other people too conform to this usage. A person may say to me *tou ingoa ku au ki a kuou* – 'your namesake came to (visit) me' – without mentioning the visitor's personal name.

In the nineteenth and twentieth century the Tikopia link between personal name and personal identity underwent radical change. With economic and political, and religious intrusion from the west, the naming framework of ideas was altered in several respects. In the nineteenth century, as Tikopia men began to go abroad to work on whaling ships or on sugar plantations, they were often given short European names by their employers. Such names were sometimes adopted by the Tikopia themselves. In 1929 when I was first on the island an old man who had worked abroad many years earlier was generally known as Pen (Ben). In particular, as time went on, the proselytizing efforts of the Christian teachers made for marked name changes. When a Tikopia became a Christian he or she was given a Christian name as part of the baptismal ritual by the bishop. In early times, this Christian name was either Biblical – Samuel, Ishmael, Thomas, Ruth – or the first name or surname of a prominent Western Church dignitary – Alfred, Patterson. In later times many non-biblical Western names have been assigned as Christian names – Leonard, Marvin, Alice, Bessie. All these names are called *ingoa fakaokutapu*, 'names of baptism'. In the early times, traditional Tikopia names were known to Christians as *ingoa pouri*, 'dark names', in reference to the alleged lower moral standard of pagans as living in the darkness of ignorance of the true faith. Later, when the whole Tikopia population had become Christian, local Tikopia names have been known simply as *ingoa fakatikopia*, 'names of the Tikopia style'.

Complex relations between personal names and identity have now arisen. All Tikopia now have a 'Christian' (Western baptismal) name. With many of the younger unmarried people this is the only name they bear. By this token they are not only members of the Tikopia community by language and culture; they are also identified as members of a great external community, the Church of Melanesia in the Solomon Islands, and of a world-wide aggregation, the Anglican Communion. Many people, especially of the older generation, have a Tikopia form of personal name as well however, and when any Tikopia marries, he or she takes on a 'married name' of traditional style. So, when Tikopia take on the responsibilities of the married state there is a re-emphasis in naming terms in their indigenous cultural identity.

The modern naming system has allowed certain modifications in traditional kinship usage. I have referred to the convention whereby a man should not use the personal name of his brother-in-law. Mention of the name is still barred if it is of local Tikopia form, but citation of the brother-in-law's baptismal name is now allowed. In a sense, the baptismal name is regarded as being in a different custom-free category from the traditional Tikopia personal name, and the brother-in-law is given a new identity.

Many Tikopia now have dual identity. On the island of Tikopia itself or in the Tikopia communities now established elsewhere in the Solomon Islands Tikopia personal names or married names are freely used and fit in with indigenous social institutions. In the external community, on government service, at work on a plantation, in the Church of Melanesia, or in attendance at an overseas school or college, the named identity is different. In such circumstances a Tikopia man or woman is commonly known by the Western baptismal name. For further identification a Tikopia man may add an abbreviation of his indigenous name. So the Police Commissioner in Honiara, a Tikopia, was known to the Solomon Islands community at large familiarly as Fred Soaki. His personal name in the Tikopia community as a young man had been Soakimori (referring to the gift of a canoe). It has been recognized that Europeans cannot master the intricacies of the Tikopia language, hence such abbreviations of indigenous names have become common for external communication. In the Tikopia community itself, as a married man he is known as Pa Nukuriaki, a name completely unknown, I would think, to the general Solomon Islands society. Such dual identity in the personal name field is probably fairly common among Oceanic peoples. It is a question of whether such dual naming identity may give rise to problems of personal instability. However, I am inclined to think that most Oceanians cope fairly well with the practical aspects of dual identity and do not suffer from personality disorders or community disintegration therefrom.

An interesting twist to the problem of identity has recently been given by some Maori leaders in New Zealand. Because of miscegenation, a number of families of mixed blood have had European surnames, perhaps for several generations. In the past decade or so members of these families have reverted to an original Maori name in accord with the rising tide of Maori cultural nationalism. This has meant not a change of identity – they operate as before as members of the New Zealand community – but an emphasis on the Maori element in their make-up and their identification with claims to Maori rights and the preservation of Maori language and culture in its modern guise.

I return to the problem of relations between knowledge and identity. Over a whole range of particulars, knowledge is an essential component in a sense of identity with a group or community. The consciousness of sharing a language, some local technical know-how, acquaintance with and cooperation with neighbours and kin and much shared ability to interpret the activities of others give a powerful basis for recognition of a common identity. A common collective name is also a powerful symbol of identity, as the expression translated as 'we the Tikopia' has indicated in a variety of contexts in the Solomon Islands, but much recognition of identity lies in shared belief, not just in shared knowledge. Take for example, the Church of Jesus Christ of Latter-Day Saints, a religious organization that has a considerable following in many parts of Oceania. Members of this group exhibit a very strong identity, backed up by their overt expressions of belief in the Book of Mormon. This production, the work of the founder of the movement, Joseph Smith, and his collaborator, Cowdrey, purports to be a translation of hieroglyphic texts inscribed upon a set of gold tablets no longer in existence and which contained the sacred records of the ancient inhabitants of America and revelations supplementing those of the Bible. Mormons believe firmly in the authenticity of these records, as well as in special doctrines such as baptism for the dead and celestial marriage. Verification of all these beliefs is a matter of faith, not knowledge.

Here is a field where increase of knowledge may involve a threat to identity. For if a Mormon comes to think that the story of the discovery of the gold plates or tablets is fictitious, the sense of identity with other believing members of the movement is likely to be shaken. In a much broader context, knowledge of the true nature of social relationships in a community may lead to instability in the social structure. Members of the community who have shared in the general social solidarity may resent their relationship with those in power if modes of exploitation of which they had previously not been aware are exposed by investigation. In their 'grass-roots' studies anthropologists have sometimes discovered such exploitative situations, and the knowledge thus revealed may be unwelcome to those in power in the society. It is for such reasons that elsewhere I have labelled anthropology as the 'uncomfortable science' by analogy with a former description of economics as the 'dismal science'. The pursuit of knowledge is by no means always an approved enterprise.

The pursuit of self-knowledge also is not always reassuring in a search for self-identity. In the multicultural situations such as so often occur in modern Oceania, a person may be faced by the problem of what identity to adopt. Here the conviction of belonging to a particular local community, sharing its beliefs and behaviour, may be more important to an individual than exploring a deeper self-knowledge that can reveal inconsistencies and contradictions in attitudes that can inhibit action.

Finally, I raise the debatable question of the quality of knowledge that is presented by an investigator. When we offer an account of any Oceanic phenomenon, how far can this be regarded as a reasonably accurate description or is it to be taken as primarily an account of the investigator's own personality, temperament and commitment? Some years ago Edmund Leach, in characteristically challenging vein, put forward the proposition that 'all ethnography is fiction'. It was not really clear what he meant, but apparently he claimed not that the ethnographer is lying but that any ethnographical account is a constructed account, not a simple description of what has actually existed or occurred and is therefore quite unreliable if not inaccurate. In his view, the account is conditioned by and incorporates or indeed represents elements of the writer's personality to a degree that only a distorted version of the purported situation is given. (In writing this critique, Leach completely ignored his own *Pul Eliya*, a study of land tenure and kinship in Sri Lanka, published about twenty-five years earlier. In this admirable study he argued that the interpretation of the evidence was *his* interpretation but that 'the evidence "speaks for itself"'. This was a claim that he would later have disallowed.) This view that an ethnographic account is an internal, not an external reflection of reality, has had its analogies in historical and other studies, with well-known controversial argument. I have made some comments upon Leach's argument elsewhere (Leach 1989; Firth 1989), so here I make only a few remarks upon the general issue, as it affects Oceanic studies. That any historical, geographical or anthropological account is to some extent constructed by an author and reflects aspects of his/her personality and experience can be agreed. More than fifty years ago this was recognized by anthropologists, though they considered it to be a marginal, not a central, issue in their ethnography. I, for instance, on the last page of We, the Tikopia (1936: 599) wrote that an anthropologist should not be bound by the conventions and values of the time, that the claim of absolute validity usually made for them sprang *inter alia* from confusion with the universal of what in reality was a set of moral ideas produced by particular economic and social circumstances:

> This is not to say that the scientist himself may not have his own personal predilections, based on his upbringing and social environment, his temperamental disposition, his aesthetic values . . . The greatest need of the social sciences today is for a more refined methodology, as objective and dispassionate as possible in which while the *assumptions due to the conditioning and personal interest of the investigator must influence his findings* [my emphasis now] that bias shall be consciously faced, the possibility of other initial assumptions be realized and allowance be made for the implications of each in the course of the analysis.

What I wrote in 1936 referred to the general methodology of the ethnographer, not specially to the construction of an ethnographic text, but the same principles apply.

In the argument about identification of ethnographic text with author's personality, it might be claimed that in the 'participant observation' of the working anthropologist, the observation is merged with or totally conditioned by the participation. I doubt if many Oceanic anthropologists would argue this way. The Tikopia were insistent that in my attendance at their ceremonies and rituals I was a participant, not just an onlooker; I had to behave as a member of a group, take part in gift exchange, dance as one of them. Yet I did not become a Tikopia, nor did I assimilate their behaviour to my own Western models. My own reflective, critical faculties were brought to bear on what I saw, heard, smelt, and the records of my notebooks were supplemented by photographs and, later, tape recording. In writing my ethnography I was able to incorporate many examples of discussions with Tikopia in which they confirmed or modified my representations of their institutions or beliefs. A statement that Oceanic ethnography is fiction would therefore seem to me to be meaningless. An ethnography is a complex construct in which personal elements of authorship enter in but in which the major contribution is a depiction of what has been observed by the author as a working investigator. What is commonly overlooked in criticisms of the accuracy of an ethnography is that the ethnographer has not only observed and participated in what is described but also had to use the knowledge so gained for prediction as to future behaviour. For the ethnographer to be able to move freely in the community she/he must be able to interpret correctly the local rules of behaviour and successful adaptation to the community's way of life has required a great deal of accurate observation and correct inference. All such experiences, including memory of sharp correction from local people when inferences were not adequate, lie in the back of the construction of an ethnography. I believe, then, in the reality of an external world, open to sensory observation and the collection and interpretation of evidence about it.

Notes

1. I am indebted to my wife Rosemary and to my philosopher colleague Roger Montague for helpful comments on a draft of this article.
2. The general theme of the Basel Conference of the European Society for Oceanists was 'Knowing Oceania: Constituting Knowledge and Identitites'. Sir Raymond Firth could not personally participate, due to age and health concerns and the anticipated strenuous journey from England to Switzerland. His contribution was read by Michael O'Hanlon and discussed by Christine Jourdan, Ton Otto, Meinhard Schuster and Andrew Strathern.

3. Cf. Biggs (1981) and Williams (1985) for the Maori language; Milner (1966) for the Samoan, Firth (1985) for the Tikopian, Tokelau Dictionary (1986) for the Tokelau language.
4. My linguistic colleague J.R. Firth was delighted to hear of this Tikopia custom, and thereafter used to write to me 'Ingoa!' (namesake).

References

Biggs, B. (1981). *The Complete English-Maori Dictionary.* Auckland: Auckland University Press.

Descartes, R. (1929). *A Discourse on Method.* Translated by J. Veitch. London: Dent. (Everyman's Library 570.)

Firth, R. (1936). *We, the Tikopia: A Sociological Study of Kinship in Primitive Polynesia.* London: Allen & Unwin.

—— (1985). *Tikopia–English Dictionary: Taranga Fakatikopia ma Taranga Fakainglisi.* Auckland: Auckland University Press. (In typescript facsimile.)

—— (1989). Fiction and Past in Ethnography. In: E. Tonkin, M. McDonald and M. Chapman (eds), *History and Ethnicity,* pp. 48–52. London: Routledge. (ASA Monograph 27.)

Gellner, E. (1974). *Legitimation of Belief.* London, New York: Cambridge University Press.

Guthrie, W.K.C. (1950). *The Greek Philosophers. From Thales to Aristotle.* London: Methuen.

Leach, E. (1989). Tribal Ethnography: Past, Present, Future. In: E. Tonkin, M. McDonald and M. Chapman (eds), *History and Ethnicity,* pp. 34–47. London: Routledge. (ASA Monograph 27.)

Milner, G.B. (1966). *Samoan Dictionary.* London: Oxford University Press.

Russell, B. (1946). *History of Western Philosophy and its Connection with Political and Social Circumstances from the Earliest Times to the Present Day.* London: Allen & Unwin.

—— (1948). *Human Knowledge. Its Scope and Limits.* London: Allen & Unwin.

Tokelau Dictionary. (1986). Apia: Office of Tokelau Affairs.

Williams, H. (1844/1975). *A Dictionary of the Maori Language.* Wellington: Government Printer.

Part II

Embodied Personhood

Chapter 2

Body, Being and Identity in Ambonwari, Papua New Guinea

Borut Telban

Ambonwari in East Sepik Province, Papua New Guinea is, with over 400 people, the largest of eight Karawari-speaking villages. Karawari language is classified as a member of the Lower Sepik family, which belongs to the large group of Papuan languages (Foley 1986, 1991; Telban n.d.1). About 2000 people speak Karawari.[1]

Ambonwari social structure resembles that of Iatmul (Bateson 1932, 1936/1958; Stanek 1983; Wassmann 1991) though with some distinct social institutions; there are 12 totemic clans and 35 patrilineages (including six with no present members) in Ambonwari. Each clan holds the name of at least one men's house, though not all of them are built or exist as structures. Residence is patri-virilocal. The kinship system of Ambonwari is a variety of the 'Omaha' system.

The concepts that are most important in Ambonwari's conceptualization of their collective and personal identity are: first, *kay* (way, habit, manner; ritual; being) associated with *konggong* (path; marriage) and *mariawk* (speech, discourse, thought; story, myth), and second, personal spirit and *wambung* ('insideness'), which represents knowing, understanding and feeling – the centre that I call 'heart' (Telban 1993, 1994, 1998). Though it is an aspect of *kay*, 'heart' is always able to transform *kay* through self-transformation. It is my contention in this article that the concept of *kay* and those concepts with which it articulates closely – 'heart', speech and paths – are the means by which Ambonwari represent their lifeworld both as an enduring structure and as an ongoing process. Linking institutional and individual practice *kay* temporalizes both.

It is primarily grounded in embodied processes that it temporalizes in relation to both a past and a future that are mythic, closed and necessary, yet historic, open and contingent.

I shall begin the chapter with a linguistic discussion before proceeding to some village practices with a view to giving some ethnographic content to the notion of *kay* and its relation to 'body'.

The Semantics of *kay* and its Relation to 'Heart'

The verb *kay*, which is probably the most frequently used verb in the language, captures several meanings: to be, to exist, to live, to remain, to stay. But *kay* is also used as a noun.[2] It has the following meanings: being, habit, way, fashion, manner, as well as ritual, custom, law. People speak of the habits of animals, the manner in which plants blossom, sleeping postures and eating manners, or the ritual of initiation and the ways of the village (traditions, customs) as *kay*. Every individual in the village has his or her own *kay*, which may be either accepted (*kay yapakupan*, 'good manners') or rejected (*kay maman*, 'bad manners'). People talk about 'the way of dying' (*mar kay*), menstruation (*sunggwin kay*, literally 'the way of the moon'), or initiation (*iman(bas) kay*, lit. 'the way of the men's house(s)'). The way of the ancestors (*kupambin kay*) refers to all those diacritical practices associated with ancestors – for example, the *kurang* ceremony (known as *naven* to most anthropologists since Bateson), the ways people use dance decoration or beat the slit drums, and including such mundane activities as processing sago or trapping pigs. When used in an unqualified sense, 'the way of the ancestors' refers to the most important ancestral ritual male initiation or sometimes to the rites of first menstruation. It is as though only these two rituals, but especially male initiation, concern Ambonwari existence or being in its totality.

Having stressed, as Ambonwari do, 'the way of the ancestors', I would not want to lose sight of the fact that ancestral *kay* has its life in *kay* itself – that is, the ancestral way is the crystallization of the life-world, its themes and orientations as they present themselves to those who live it, but for that reason it cannot contain within itself the grounds of its own existence. *Kay* represents those grounds. Accordingly, I referred to ritual practices whose character as bodily *kay* is obvious.

I wish to emphasize the interrelationship between *kay* and 'heart'. The 'way of the village' (*iminggan kay*) has its origin in the past (*kupambɨn kay*, 'the way of the ancestors'), but people's 'heart' and their *kay* together sustain, perpetuate, and modify it. For the most part 'the way of the village' and those esteemed institutions brought under the term *kupambɨn kay* 'go without saying', as Bourdieu might put it. 'Heart' is an aspect of *kay* in its most fundamental sense and when circumstances dictate new departures are undertaken. On the other hand, it would be wrong to view 'the way of the ancestors' as lacking real meaning for Ambonwari, as an ideological cloak under which the real business of social life is hidden. On the contrary, 'the way of the ancestors' is the locus of those values and orientations that give life its shape and to the extent that people, through 'heart', can objectify and set aside the dictates of ancestral *kay* in particular circumstances, those same values and aims rationalize their departures from it.

Hunting and Fishing

Ambonwari recognize and define these practices according to the way they are performed and according to the tools they use. Such a 'classification' breaks down generalizing notions such as fishing and hunting into more precise units of the activities themselves.

People fish with traps, hooks, nets, arrows fitted with a bicycle inner tube that are used as a sort of spear-gun, ordinary spears and bush knives, and occasionally by poisoning the creeks. All these fishing practices are acquired during childhood and become an important part of the common 'way of doing things'. Thus, people may refer to these practices as 'the way of catching fish' (*aria awur kay*) when they use hooks; 'the way of pulling out the fish' (*aria awkwiyar kay*) when they use fish traps; 'the way of putting fish inside' (*aria apɨr kay*) when they drag a hand-net or a basket through the water; and 'the way of shooting fish' (*aria wandɨr kay*) when they use pronged spears or homemade arrow-guns. Like fishing, hunting practices also fall under the general aspect of *kay*, more precisely 'the way of finding meat' (*kumɨndɨ kay*).

Everyone has to find meat in whichever way they can but it is the mastery of different ways of performing the activities of fishing and hunting that becomes habitual and thus characteristic of an individual Ambonwari. It is proficiency in using particular tools or weapons that brings recognition. Based on past experiences it formulates someone's expectations about the future; the acquired *kay* always relates 'before' to 'after' and past to future. To put it in Ambonwari terms: a man who did not acquire in the past the practice of making a pig trap 'the way of pulling out' (*awkwiyar kay*), does not make it at all and thus has no hunting expectations in the future concerning this way.

People inside and outside the village are differentiated according to the ways or manner they perform their activities. For example, Ambonwari remark about differences between themselves and neighbouring Imanmeri concerning canoe-making and fishing, arguing that because Imanmeri are hill people (*kambo*) they do not make good canoes. Ambonwari think that especially the final shaping of a canoe is done better in their village, but this might simply be a case of local chauvinism. More obvious is the difference in fishing during the dry season. While Ambonwari women make fishing baskets (*simbang*), Imanmeri women make fishing nets in a round frame (*yuway*), though both are held in the hands while fishing. Ambonwari women who have good relationships with Imanmeri women can obtain a few of these nets, but they are not made in Ambonwari village and are rarely seen there.

I have already mentioned that the human 'body' is seen through its activity. It is defined by *kay* (the way of doing things) and extended to the things that are used in particular activities.[3] The 'life' of things such as small canoes, stools, paddles, spears, adzes for pulverizing sago, axes, bush knives, hand drums, mats, baskets, body decorations and so on is derivative in that it depends on the life of humans. Most of this equipment is handled only by those who own it and the identities of these things are determined by the people who use them. A thing becomes 'something' only when a person uses it. Ambonwari employ the same verb *sa-* with the meanings of 'to use' and 'to hold'. A typical round stool, for example, becomes a part of the person who sits on it, absorbs his 'dirt' and is not supposed to be used by anyone else. While being used, a thing 'gives something' to its user. At the same time, its usefulness and the way people use it gives a thing its character: thus the term for 'something' is *kanggining* or *k(a)-anggin-ing* ('should-give-ness'). A paddle, for instance, gives its user the ability to move a canoe on the river; its usefulness gives existence, identity and value to the paddle. We could say that the essence of *kay* (habit) 'which is not performed but "acquired" by mastering an activity

. . . lies in its use-value' (Ricoeur 1966: 281, 283). A paddle and a person become one in terms of *kay*, the way of paddling a canoe.[4]

Taboos

The symbolic aspects of food become visible through its prohibitions before, during, or after particular activities and events. As the human 'body' is defined by ways of doing things and as this notion is extended to the objects which a person uses, it is understandable that people do not touch those things that could have undesirable consequences for their 'bodies' or the 'bodies' of those with whom they are in frequent contact (a child, a wife, a husband). Likewise, people do not want others to interfere with their *kay*.

One can often see in the village that the owner of a coconut or betel palm has wrapped some leaves around its trunk to prohibit others from taking the nuts. Whenever people plant tobacco they leave a sign of prohibition on their plantation. Signs are specific to every clan. They put these signs inside the 'v' of a split stick which they thrust into the ground. To disregard these prohibitions would be to interfere with the *kay* of the owner.

There are prohibitions related to fishing and hunting activities. Ambonwari make fences or barricades on the flooded bank of the river in the same place as their ancestors did. People refer to prohibitions as 'very ancestral' (*pan kupambi*) or 'the way of grandparents' (*arkin kay*). By observing them they can expect a successful catch with the approval of spirits. For this reason, all those who are going to eat the catch from the traps placed in the barricades are not allowed to eat eel beforehand. People say that if they disobeyed this rule, which they inherited from their ancestors, the eel's fat that they had eaten would seal the entrance of the trap and fish would not go inside. If we recall that the 'body' of a person is 'connected' to those things he or she uses (the traps in barricades in this case), then we can easily comprehend the avoidances that people impose on themselves for a successful catch. Another instance when prohibitions apply is in the use of fish poison. Because of the direct contact between the 'body' and the poison, in the act of beating the poisonous vine, the man who beats the roots is not supposed to have had sexual intercourse the previous night, to have had 'wet dreams', or to have a pregnant wife. Women cannot beat the vine if they are pregnant or menstruating.

Hunters in general do not eat the meat of the pig that they have killed with a spear because this would make a man's spirit lazy. It would result in unsuccessful hunts in the future. Hunting with a spear brings the hunter and his victim close together. The hunter 'gives his strength to the pig', as Elias, one of the most successful hunters in the village, puts it. To eat such a pig would mean to eat his own strength – i.e. to eat himself. This is a good example of how people understand *kay* as being extended not only to the things which a hunter uses (a spear, for example) but also to the game or a human victim.[5]

If one looks at the taboos on consumption, where every single prohibited food carries its own symbolic meaning, one might surmise that their purpose is to protect and preserve the 'body' of a person. First of all one does not eat one's own 'body', and because people have their own distinctive habits (*kay*) they also have many distinctive taboos. Another aspect of prohibitions refers to the interrelationship between one's 'body', the food that one eats, the things that one uses in a particular activity, and the activity itself. As all of them are part of a person's *kay*, he or she has to consider the effects of one upon the other (for example, 'I do not hunt the morning after sleeping with my wife'). In a period of transition (pregnancy, initiation, first menstruation ritual, or even fishing and hunting with traps), *kay*, which is in a state of becoming, is vulnerable to the influence of the habits and manners of some other 'body'; thus, those *kay* and things that could have a negative influence have to be avoided. Likewise, in any activity with a dubious outcome, such as hunting or fishing with traps, the practice is in process until completed – whether the outcome is successful or not. The fact that taboos differ between individuals and groups, and that new taboos might be tried out before becoming habitual, also suggests the openness and experiential nature of *kay*. Taboos represent a strategy needed to bring an activity successfully from a beginning to an end.

Healing Practices

Given what has been said so far about the intimacy of *kay* and those things and persons identified with it, it comes as no surprise that sicknesses of children, for example, are attributed to the wrongdoings of their parents. Through their close 'bodily' relationship (both in terms of skin and *kay*) the parents' *kay maman*, wrongdoings in this case (literally 'bad habit'), is easily transmitted to children who are an extension of their parents' *kay*. The sickness of either a child or an adult is then manifested through unusual practices, through the impairment of their usual *kay*.

The main sign that someone is sick is that her or his *kay* is not as it should be. A person's breathing is different from usual, his or her skin is hot or cold, she or he sleeps more, and these people do not perform their usual activities. People say that a person is 'with sickness' (*min mari ngandikin*), that is not only that she or he 'has sickness' but that sickness is embodied with a person. Sickness 'has taken hold of a person' (*min mari yan sarinyan*). By holding and 'using' a person, the sickness and person become one; they share, or better, they are the same 'body'. To get better a person has to remove 'sickness' as a part of the 'body'. Only in this way will people rehabilitate their previous *kay*.

In healing ceremonies, the specialist tries to find the cause and remove the objects that are the embodiment of sickness. A healer tries to restore the *kay* to its previous condition. As *kay* of an individual incorporates a different collective *kay* the sickness also becomes a collective issue (of household or lineage, for example), incorporates past and present relationships, including with their own familiar spirits. The wrongdoers then have to 'cut themselves off' from the practice that caused the sickness by following practices such as payment of compensation, seclusion, washing, food presentation, and so on. Ambonwari people often say that they have to look after their skin properly, which includes their acts. In regard to sickness we can make some common observations: a healthy 'body' is defined by its visible healthy skin and its activity; a sick 'body' is defined by unhealthy skin and its aberrant activity. Thus, a healing ritual is concerned with the extraction of invisible stones, shells, teeth, bones and thorns from beneath the unhealthy skin, the restitution of *kay* by identifying the cause of sickness in wrongdoings and finally by addressing the spirits of the household, lineage or clan that share collective identity with the sick person.

The focus of healing ceremony as well as ritual in general is *kay*: either its transformation or its presentation. In either case what matters is that embodied *kay* is not something that one simply possesses (like knowledge), but something that one *is* (Bourdieu 1990: 73).

The Significance of *kay*

Kay (being, habit, way, manner) relates to the whole realm of practice: from mundane food gathering to the most important ritual. For Ambonwari, it includes both the collective and the idiosyncratic; moreover, it denotes not just the practice as such but the manner in which it is carried out too. Only through its way does a practice achieve its specificity.

The way of sitting, the way of cooking, the way of eating, the way of arguing, or even the manner in which adolescent girls walk (Telban n.d.2), or gestures of support (Lewis 1990), or techniques of fighting (Harrison 1993: 35, 38–40) are all embodied habits acquired and recognized by those who share the same 'way of the village' (*iminggan kay*). The 'lived body' (*kay*), not just the visible 'skin', manifests itself through the way acts are performed.

Ambonwari do not have a term for any kind of physical body removed from the totality of human existence. Terms are given to individual organs, bones, body fluids and so forth with considerable anatomical accuracy. People refer to the 'body' in its active, behavioural state by *kay* and by *arim* (skin). Thus, it may be said, that 'body' has meaning for Ambonwari people only through the external appearance of skin and the way it is observed to act. We could say for Ambonwari that their 'body is in the world as the heart is in the organism' (Merleau-Ponty 1962: 203). 'Body' has to be understood through the ways (*kay*) of its actions, which are not to be distinguished from its presentation. Following such a conceptualization of the human 'body' in Ambonwari, we can readily comprehend Leenhardt's puzzle concerning the Canaque body when he says that it has neither an existence of its own nor a specific term to designate it (1979: 164). When Leenhardt provoked his old friend Boesoou by saying that foreigners had introduced the notion of spirit to the Canaque way of thinking, Boesoou objected: 'We have always acted in accord with the spirit. What you've brought us is the body' (1979: 164). Leenhardt's discussion shows that it is not a conflict between different perceptions but rather a conflict between different cosmologies: one with a notion of abstract physical body and the other in which such a notion does not exist. Likewise, a person's 'body' in Ambonwari cannot be conceptually 'removed' (abstracted) from the person.

Through socialization – which has to be seen as an active process, a process, moreover, that is an aspect of *kay* and *wambung* ('heart') – every person is subjected to the collective village practices, habits and manners, in short, 'the way of the village'. For Bourdieu, practical belief is not adherence to a set of instituted doctrines or beliefs nor even a 'state of mind', but rather a state of the body (1990: 68). A recent study of 'bodily social memory' by Connerton also argues that 'habit cannot be thought without a notion of bodily automatisms' (1989: 5; see also Foucault 1979: 135–70). However, the Ambonwari evidence suggests to me that these bodily automatisms should not be construed as atemporal: they are themselves the product of a definite history implicating both a human 'body' and a specific social history.

In the Ambonwari case habits locate *kay* in relation to a past, but what of the future? In fact, *kay* is temporally 'thickened', to use Husserl's term (1964), for it is constituted as a temporal horizon embracing a past – sedimented as habit – and a future inscribed in the projective aspect of practice. To illustrate this point ethnographically, I need only refer to the prohibition signs placed around valuable plants, such as tobacco and betel nut, as discussed above. Underlying this practice is the notion that preventing the realization of a person's project is *ipso facto* an infringement of that person. In Ambonwari a person is constituted not only by a definite past but equally by a projection of that person's being in their plans and projects. An even more striking illustration of the simultaneously 'retentive' and 'protentive' (Husserl 1964) nature of *kay* is afforded by certain aspects of mortuary practices. Upon the death of a child, especially a first-born son, a man destroys all belongings that are associated with the child's *kay*: tools, growing plants, even the house that the father occupies but which the boy would have inherited. With the extinction of the boy's *kay* all those things linked to it must also perish.

To look briefly at the gender of *kay* one could say that only brother and sister share generational *kay*, household *kay*, lineage *kay*, clan *kay*, and can cosmologically be merged, by collapsing the generational difference: father, son and grandson all 'become' one, all the clansmen identify with mythological ancestor. At some point even the sexual differences disappear ('making' sister into a younger brother), into 'oneness', while at the same time securing the continuation of generation (cf. Mimica 1988; Strathern 1988; Telban 1994, 1998). This is the reason, I suspect, why the men's houses and canoes in Ambonwari and elsewhere in the Sepik basin are androgynous objects. Despite the fact that she dealt with a matrilineal society, Annette Weiner's arguments about brother–sister relationship (1977, 1982) seem to be applicable also to the patrilineal Ambonwari. Among other things she argues that 'an incest prohibition separates women sexually from their brothers, but, paradoxically, women as sisters remain essential for the regeneration of the relations between their brothers and ancestors' (Weiner 1982: 62).

As *kay* is not a physical body, gendering of it – in a common way – is impossible. In Ambonwari cosmology, male and female *kay* are social categories attached to differences on the skin, but not, however, the consequence of these differences.

Conclusion

In this chapter I have concentrated on *kay*, the term most intimately involved in the conceptualization of life as it is lived in Ambonwari. *Kay*, seen as an embodied, but not unchangeable, process is already characterized by specific temporality that encompasses ancestral, historical and personal time. Though I have stressed the 'bodily' nature of *kay* throughout the essay, I have sought to make it clear that *kay* is not the Ambonwari term for a physical body. It would be more accurate to comprehend this term as 'being', provided its essential condition is understood to be an active corporeality that may or may not be instantiated in material flesh (compare, for example, the *kay* of living people and that of spirits). *Kay*, as we have seen, refers to the most secular habits of an individual as well as to the most complex collective ceremonies and rituals. *Kay*, being temporal in itself, relates present with past and future. In such a way, *kay* is not simply a being but a process of continuous becoming. The most inclusive variant of *kay* is *iminggan kay* which represents the collective identity of Ambonwari village. *Iminggan kay*, like the *kay* of an individual, is not an unquestioned and unreflexive state but a process that encompasses transformation. Through their 'heart', which is an aspect of *kay*, that is, through understanding, people continually confront and (re)produce their own *iminggan kay*.

The concept of *habitus*, as known through the work of Mauss and elaborated by Bourdieu, is thus evoked by the many dimensions of *kay* I have charted in this chapter, such as its relationship to 'body', habits, the importance of collective past and its social origin. However, there is a difference between the two: an important dimension of *kay* is 'insideness'. It is a crucial dimension that reflects upon and through its own transformation, transforms *kay*; *habitus* has no such element. In short, as I have stated earlier, through 'insideness' *kay* is transformed; but since 'heart' itself is an aspect of *kay*, 'insideness' is the means of *kay*'s self-transformation. Although 'heart' is socially produced, it is nevertheless the means by which existence itself comes into question and cannot therefore be seen purely as habit; this means that *kay*, of which 'heart' is a part, should not be seen as such either. This interpretation brings me closer both to Gell, who questions Bourdieu's identification of 'knowing' with 'doing' and his treatment of 'cultural knowledge as a set of dispositional propensities of socialized agents' (Gell 1992: 274) and to Connerton who regards the term 'disposition' as misleading, in that it 'suggests something latent or potential, something which requires a positive stimulus outside ourselves for it to become actively engaged' (1989: 94).

It was my intention to emphasize that not only Cartesian dualism of Western philosophical tradition but the concepts of 'mind' and 'body' themselves are Western inventions. It seems that recent studies which emphasize 'body' and embodiment simply try to shift our attention away from the enduring stress on cognition, mind and the like. I could say that Ambonwari in their conceptualization of human existence rather emphasize being, whereas at the same time they have no concept of 'body' as such. The point of the possible connection between two cosmologies (Western scientific and Ambonwari) lies either in the practices that beings perform or in addressing the existential being.[6]

If we look at the possible translations of *kay* and our knowledge about habits or ritual we cannot deny the relationship between *kay* and the Western concepts of embodiment or physical body. However, *kay* includes also other aspects of human existence, such as custom, past, mythology, society, individuality and so on. It includes most of those things that are grouped under the concept of culture. In *kay*, however, there is no dichotomy between nature and culture. Moreover, *kay* rejects such a dichotomy making it unproductive for understanding human existence. Following Merleau-Ponty, Csordas correctly argues that the body is always already cultural (1994a: 20 n.2) and that 'cultural meaning is intrinsic to embodied experience on the existential level of being-in-the-world' (Csordas 1994b: 270).

The 'psychological' and 'physical' aspects are in Ambonwari merged into 'oneness'; thus, one thinks and feels with flesh[7] and one 'materializes thoughts and feelings' (the importance of spells and magic). This is an ongoing process. 'Heart' is not only understanding, memory, emotion; it is also flesh and internal organs, pith of a sago palm, stone or wood of the carved spirits. Yet, there is no word for 'body'. Ambonwari could not talk in such a way as Stoller (1994: 639), following Connerton (1989: 72), says that 'in *cultural memory*, "the past is, as it were, sedimented in the *body*"' (italics mine), but would talk rather about being (*kay*) with its past (*kupambin kay*) and its present (*iminggan kay*) collective dimensions. These dimensions of being are not static but influence and change each other in a continuous process of becoming.

Notes

1. This chapter is a kind of a short though 'thick' analysis of Ambonwari conceptualisation of 'body' and being, the topic that has been in its expanded and more elaborated form discussed in my PhD dissertation and my book (Telban 1994, 1998). I thank Don Gardner and Michael Young who were generous with their comments. I gratefully acknowledge the generous support of the Australian National University through its Scholarship Stipend, Tuition Fee Scholarship and other funding. I also thank the Slovene Research Association for a grant awarded to me before I went to Australia, and the Royal Anthropological Institute of Great Britain and Ireland for a Radcliffe-Brown Memorial Fund/Sutasoma Trust award which enabled me to complete my PhD thesis after my ANU funding had expired. The Slovene Ministry of Science and Technology awarded me a small grant, which also helped me survive during the final stage of my writing. I am thankful to the organizers of

the Basel Conference and to the Open Society Fund – Slovenia for enabling me to attend the conference.

Throughout the chapter I use the phoneme /ɨ/ which is heard as /a/ in 'about' or as the vowel in 'sir'; whenever /g/ follows /n/ it indicates eng, nasal /n/ with /g/ inaudible.

2. *Kay* might be translated 'standing presence' in a similar way to Classical Greek *parousia* which meant 'being' (Heidegger 1959/ 1987: 61).

3. The extension of lived body to tools is not alien to some genres of Western philosophy, such as phenomenology (Heideggerian equipment, for example) and existentialism. Thus, Sartre wrote:

> My body always extends across the tool which it utilizes: it is at the end of the cane on which I lean and against the earth; it is at the end of the telescope which shows me the stars; it is on the chair, in the whole house; for it is my adaptation to these tools . . . A body is a body as this mass of flesh which it *is* is defined by the table which the body looks at, the chair in which it sits, the pavement on which it walks, etc. . . . The body is the totality of meaningful relations to the world (1956: 428, 452).

Phenomenologists and existentialists, such as Sartre and Merleau-Ponty in particular, have contributed to the notion of lived body as against the Cartesian dualism of the Western philosophical tradition which treated the body as an object of knowledge. Sartre distinguished three ontological dimensions of the body: for-itself, for-others, and for-itself as an object for others. In his distinction of body as being-for-itself and as being-for-others Sartre addressed Cartesian dualism of mind and body in the following way: being-for-itself must be both wholly body and wholly consciousness; consciousness 'cannot be *united* with a body'. In the same way, being-for-others is wholly body with no consciousness there to be united with the body. 'There is nothing *behind* the body. But the body is wholly "psychic"' (1956: 404). It is not the aim simply to reject Cartesian dualism, however, but to recognize temporality and engagement of the 'body', the flow of past, present and future, and of inter-bodily relationships and reciprocity. '[O]ur body is not only what has long been called "the seat of the five senses"; it is also the instrument and the end of our actions' (Sartre 1956: 422). Thus, the definition of 'body' should avoid static abstract or absolute conceptualizations and rather see it in terms of actions, activities, movements, operations (cf. Merleau-Ponty 1962). Such a definition of lived body leaves space for the recognition of many different possibilities among different people, different societies, and different periods in history.

4. Using something y to do x is expressed by a construction: x-ing-with-y. Such a construction, involving the 'postposition' (Foley 1991:107) *ngandïk* 'with, together' suggests an intimacy between a person and a thing used that is absent from English constructions.

5. Gilbert Lewis also noted that a Gnau man would not eat anything that he had shot: 'by shooting it he has put something of himself into it', that is, his blood (1980: 174).

6. The scientific concept of physical body along with Christianity, that is 'the hard facts of organic existence, of the ineffable chain of biological being, had come to determine the place of human beings in the world' (Comaroff 1993: 308). Human sciences such as biology emphasize the mechanistic, physical and universal notion of 'body' whereas psychology seeks to explain 'mind' (for a critique see Scheper-Hughes 1992). In many non-European societies, however, monism and holism, which highlight the unity of 'mindful body', appear either as a conception of harmonious wholes (where microcosm reflects macrocosm and vice versa) or as a yin/yang type of complementarity (Scheper-Hughes and Lock 1987).

7. For corporeal knowing see Stoller (1994) and Taussig (1993).

References

Bateson, G. (1932). Social Structure of the Iatmul People of the Sepik River. *Oceania* 2: 245–91, 401–53.

—— (1936/1958). *Naven*. London: Wildwood House.

Bourdieu, P. (1990). *The Logic of Practice*. Cambridge: Polity Press.

Comaroff, J. (1993). The Diseased Heart of Africa: Medicine, Colonialism, and the Black Body. In: S. Lindenbaum and M. Lock (eds), *Knowledge, Power and Practice: the Anthropology of Medicine and Everyday Life*, pp. 305–29. Berkeley: University of California Press.

Connerton, P. (1989). *How Societies Remember*. Cambridge: Cambridge University Press.

Csordas, T.J. (1994a). Introduction: The Body as Representation and Being-in-the-World. In: T.J. Csordas (ed.), *Embodiment and Experience: The Existential Ground of Culture and Self*, pp. 1–24. Cambridge: Cambridge University Press.

—— (1994b). Words from the Holy People: A Case Study in Cultural Phenomenology. In: T.J. Csordas (ed.), *Embodiment and Experience: The Existential Ground of Culture and Self*, pp. 269–90. Cambridge: Cambridge University Press.

Foley, W.A. (1986). *The Papuan Languages of New Guinea*. Cambridge: Cambridge University Press.

—— (1991). *The Yimas Language of New Guinea*. Stanford: Stanford University Press.

Foucault, M. (1979). *Discipline and Punish: The Birth of the Prison*. New York: Vintage Books.

Gell, A. (1992). *The Anthropology of Time: Cultural Constructions of Temporal Maps and Images*. Oxford: Berg.

Harrison, S. (1993). *The Mask of War: Violence, Ritual and the Self in Melanesia*. Manchester: Manchester University Press.

Heidegger, M. (1959/1987). *An Introduction to Metaphysics*. New Haven: Yale University Press.

Husserl, E. (1964). *The Phenomenology of Internal Time-Consciousness*. Bloomington: Indiana University Press.

Leenhardt, M. (1979). *Do Kamo: Person and Myth in the Melanesian World*. Chicago: Chicago University Press.

Lewis, G. (1980). *Day of Shining Red: An Essay on Understanding Ritual*. Cambridge: Cambridge University Press.

—— (1990). Gestures of Support. In: N. Lutkehaus et al. (eds), *Sepik Heritage: Tradition and Change in Papua New Guinea*, pp. 255–65. Bathurst: Crawford House Press.

Merleau-Ponty, M. (1962). *Phenomenology of Perception*. London: Routledge & Kegan Paul.

Mimica, J. (1988). *Intimations of Infinity: The Mythopoeia of the Iqwaye Counting System and Number*. Oxford: Berg.

Ricoeur, P. (1966). *Freedom and Nature: The Voluntary and the Involuntary*. Evanston: Northwestern University Press.

Sartre, J.P. (1956). *Being and Nothingness: An Essay on Phenomenological Ontology*. New York: Philosophical Library.

Scheper-Hughes, N. (1992). Hungry Bodies, Medicine, and the State: Toward a Critical Psychological Anthropology. In: T. Schwartz, G.M. White and C.A. Lutz (eds), *New Directions in Psychological Anthropology*, pp. 221–47. Cambridge: Cambridge University Press.

Scheper-Hughes, N. and Lock, M. (1987). The Mindful Body: A Prologomenon to Future Work in Medical Anthropology. *Medical Anthropology Quarterly* 1(1) (n.s.): 6–41.

Stanek, M. (1983). *Sozialordnung und Mythik in Palimbei, (Iatmul, Mittelsepik)*. Basel: Wepf.

Stoller, P. (1994). Embodying Colonial Memories. *American Anthropologist* 96(3): 634–48.

Strathern, M. (1988). *The Gender of the Gift: Problems with Women and Problems with Society in Melanesia*. Berkeley: University of California Press.

Taussig, M. (1993). *Mimesis and Alterity: A Particular History of the Senses*. New York: Routledge.

Telban, B. (1993). Having Heart: Caring and Resentment in Ambonwari, Papua New Guinea. *Bulletin of the Slovene Ethnographic Museum* 54(3): 158–77.

—— (1994). Dancing Through Time: Temporality and Identity in a Sepik Cosmology. PhD dissertation. Canberra: Australian National University.

—— (1998). *Dancing Through Time: A Sepik Cosmology*. Oxford: Oxford University Press.

—— (n.d.1.). The Grammar of Karawari, East Sepik Province, Papua New Guinea. Unpublished manuscript.

—— (n.d.2.). Fear of Being Seen and Fear of the Unseen in Ambonwari, Papua New Guinea. Paper presented at the Institute of Social and Cultural Anthropology, University of Oxford, January 1993.

Wassmann, J. (1991). *The Song to the Flying Fox: The Public and Esoteric Knowledge of the Important Men of Kandingei about Totemic Songs, Names and Knotted Cords (Middle Sepik, Papua New Guinea)*. Boroko: The National Research Institute.

Weiner, A.B. (1977). *Women of Value, Men of Renown: New Perspectives in Trobriand Exchange*. St. Lucia: University of Queensland Press.

—— (1982). Sexuality among the Anthropologists: Reproduction among the Informants. In: F.J.P. Poole and G.H. Herdt (eds), *Sexual Antagonism, Gender, and Social Change in Papua New Guinea*, pp. 52–65. *Social Analysis* special issue 12.

Chapter 3

On the Acquisition of Knowledge: Teaching Kinship through the Body among the Tiwi of Northern Australia

Andrée Grau

> The anthropologist seeks to distinguish what derives from being human from what derives from being born into a particular group of humans in a particular time and place (Keesing 1976: 1).

> Human behavior and biology are inextricably intertwined, with each affecting the other in important ways (Haviland 1990: 2).

The general aim of anthropology, it can be argued, is to describe in the broadest possible sense what it means to be human. Such a perspective implies, in theory at least, an investigation into both the biological and the socio-cultural foundations of human life. In practice, however, greater emphasis has been laid on the latter than on the former, even when dealing with subjects such as the 'body' and 'dance', both ideally suited to engage in a discussion on the dialectic between the biological and the socio-cultural. This chapter will investigate various possibilities of looking at dance both as a social construction and as a biological phenomenon with some evolutionary significance.

The Social Construction of Dance and the Body

Anthropologists specializing in dance all start with the premise that the making of dances is not simply an exercise in the organization of movements but a symbolic expression of cultural organization that expresses, in part, the values and the ways of life of the human beings who create them. As nothing can be understood outside the cultural, historical and physical contexts that make it possible, dance must be seen as a social fact made by people for other people, in the sense that it depends upon associations between people for its transmission and meaning. Without cultural agreement among at least some human beings on what is perceived there can be neither dance nor dance communication.[1]

Similarly the body in general, and the dancing body in particular, cannot be understood as a constant amidst cultural flux. Rather, it is perceived as having a history, in the sense that it behaves in different ways at particular historical moments. It is shaped, constrained, and invented by society. Human beings live in a socially constructed world and the body can be seen as a metaphor for society as a whole. A central theme in Mary Douglas's seminal work on the body, for example, was that the social body constrains how the physical body is perceived and experienced (1966, 1970). More recently, Paul Connerton attributed great importance to 'body memory'. He distinguished between two types of social practice: 'incorporating practice' and 'inscribing practice' (1989: 74–5). A smile or a handshake, for example, are incorporating practices. They are messages people send by means of their own bodily activity. The transmission occurs only during the time that their bodies are present to sustain that particular activity. Inscribing practices, on the other hand, are practices that do something to trap and hold information, long after the human organism has stopped informing. The alphabet, for example, is a typical example of an inscribing practice. Connerton asserts that the transition from an oral culture to a literate culture is a transition from incorporating practices to inscribing practices.

In my own work, comparing Western theatre dance and Tiwi dance, I have shown how the dancers' bodies can be seen to symbolize the world view of their respective societies (Grau 1997, n.d.). Western theatre dancers are typical examples of a world where the body, by being perceived as a machine with parts that can break down, be repaired (and even replaced) independently, is divorced from the mind and made into *something* rather than *somebody*.[2] In this world the body/self has become primarily a performing self of appearance, display, and impression manage-ment, and dancers' bodies are perceived by their owners as *instruments* that can be stretched, bent, starved or whatever depending on the technique involved. Performance artist, Nigel Charnock, for example, when talking about his work, recently argued: 'Dancers are 85% masochistic. I look down on my body like it's a separate thing. I'll do anything to it. Throw it against walls, whatever. If I feel pain I think: Yes I am here. I am alive' (in Terry 1995: 18).

Among the Tiwi, on the other hand, the body is not only socially and collectively constituted but also cosmologically constituted. Dancers' bodies literally embody the Dreaming, the unifying concept representing both the formative and creative period when the foundations of human life were established, as well as a parallel dimension to historical time, a sort of ever-present cosmic memory accessible through ritual activities and essential for the continuation of life. For them there is neither separation between the body and the self, nor separation between the body and the world at large. Bodily, social, ecological and spiritual worlds are all interconnected and part of a single cosmological universe given signification through the dancers' bodies, which embody land, social relationships, and spiritual beliefs.

Looking at the enculturation and socialization of human beings one sees the transformation of the body from a genetic product into a social and symbolic entity. Early in childhood individuals learn how to present their bodies through styles of walk, talk and dress that are on the whole predictable and acceptable to the people around them. This process continues throughout their lives, for the body is constantly affected by social, cultural, and economic processes. As they develop, their bodies bear the indisputable imprint of their social backgrounds. Bourdieu, for example, demonstrated how different social classes produced different bodily forms, with the dominant classes tending to be less concerned with producing a large, strong body than with producing a healthy, slim body better suited to a world in which economic practice is constituted more by the presentation of the self than by manual/physical work (1978, 1984).

What is important is not just that the lifestyles of women and men from different social backgrounds become inscribed in their bodies but that these bodies 'fit' people for different activities. Social differences then become incorporated as 'natural' differences, and are recognized falsely as such. This 'naturalness' is rarely questioned because the cultural conceptualizations of the body become merged with the reality of bodily perceptions and experiences. They are so ingrained in the collective psyche that they seem inherently natural and basic.

Critique of the Social Constructionists' View

As a social anthropologist I am without doubt a 'social constructionist' yet I feel that the paradigm taken to its most extreme 'Foucaultian perspective' is leading us to a dead end, especially, for example, when the argument goes that as the body cannot be known apart from specific systems of knowledge it is not only given meaning by discourse, but it is wholly constituted by discourse, to the extent that it vanishes as a biological entity.[3]

Thinking of some of today's theoretical discourse, I cannot help being reminded about some aspects of positivist science, which claimed, for example, that a single scientific method could be used to investigate all domains of reality, including human life; which aimed to produce a knowledge about reality that would be true for all people in all times and places; and that assumed that if other people described the world differently from the scientific observer, their perception was in some way distorted.

Having worked not only among the Tiwi but also among the Venda of South Africa, the logocentricity underpinning so much of today's theoretical thinking disturbs me. Like Dissayanake, I am uncomfortable, for example, with Derrida's statement that 'from the moment that there is meaning there are nothing but signs. We think only in signs' (quoted in Dissayanake 1992: 217) and I agree with her when she argues that 'contemporary knowledge about the brain, about child and animal behavior, or human mentality in cross-cultural perspective . . . makes this assumption at least debatable' (Dissayanake 1992: 217). There is no doubt that post-modern, post-structuralist theories could only have emerged in hyperliterate societies (it is no accident that many of the more extreme proponents of post-modernism are *literary* critics). Hyperliteracy has permeated most of contemporary Western thoughts, producing an almost obsessional preoccupation with language, particularly the relationship between language and thought, and language and reality. There is nothing wrong with that – indeed the pursuit is worthwhile – but again I would agree with Dissanayake when she argues:

I doubt that many philosophers spend much time doing mechanical repairs. And it seems obvious that they do not stay at home with young children either, or they could never have come up with their assumption that you cannot think, you cannot have meaning and experiences, except in terms of language. Look at the toddler who has only a tiny vocabulary, yet can figure out (think) how to solve problems with her toys (which shape goes where in the puzzle, which ring goes on the spindle), how to quietly drop her peas on the floor so she can have a cookie, how to engineer a second or third good-night kiss (Dissanayake 1992: 216).

Infants transmit clear messages without verbal language. They are fully competent in using alternative, non-verbal modes of communication. Although they have to acquire the language and cultural conventions of their societies, infants are nevertheless fully equipped with their own 'supra-culture' that transcends the limitations of time, space and cultural convention. The anthropologist John Blacking, with whom I worked for many years, called these 'angelic qualities'. Through our research work, Blacking and I felt that these non-verbal modes were later used by older children and adults in self-consciously structured forms of music and dance. This allowed them to communicate 'spiritual' reality and also to relate to it. If this was the case among the Tiwi and the Venda, we argued, could not music and dance then be taught in such a way in our society too, so that it would help children to develop their angelic qualities through the exploration of non-verbal, 'performative' modes of thought?

It is evident to me, trying to make sense of the Tiwi data for the past fifteen years, that the social construction analysis is insufficient to interpret it. What is needed is an analysis that would see the body as both receptor and generator of social meanings.

The Body and Dance as Biological Phenomena

Human beings are affected by both biological and social forces. Biology, one can argue, sets parameters within which history moves, and to ignore the biological foundations of dance, to fence off the social from the biological, in my view, can only succeed by impoverishing history.

One must not forget, however, that the participation of history and biology is not symmetrical. As Connel argued in his discussion of patriarchy:

> Historicity implies a historical process, a social dynamic. Biology enters the constitution of the major categories of patriarchy; but [it enters] a social dynamic. There is such a thing as a biological dynamic, i.e. organic evolution. But the space of historical transformation is vastly greater than that, and dominates its effects (Connel 1983: 60).

Organic evolution may not seem as directly significant[4] as social dynamic, it is nevertheless there and must not be ignored. Human evolution has provided us with species-specific capacities for such phenomena as language, intellect and imagination, upright stance, tool making and manipulation, and extended childhood and parenting. Bodies are not just social constructions. They are also biological entities. It is through our bodies that we make contact with the entire spatio-temporal world that surround us. As Marcel Mauss argued in 1934, the body is at the same time the original tool with which human beings shape their world, and the original substance out of which the human world is shaped. The position of our body in space, the amount of space we occupy, the spatial distance between us and objects, for example, are all existential givens of which we have unverbalized tacit awareness. Human cognition is a holistic phenomenon that involves perceiving, thinking, feeling, and acting in the world and each cognitive domain shapes the others. What we perceive triggers thoughts and feelings and suggests possible actions. At the same time, how we think, feel and act shapes our perceptions.

George Lakoff and Mark Johnson (Lakoff and Johnson 1980; Johnson 1987), for example, recognized the importance of 'embodied' imagination when they demonstrated how many of the metaphors that structure our experiences are derived from bodily-based image schemas such as containment, balance and force. These patterns are constrained by the logic of bodily experience and are projected metaphorically across various domains of experience. When we speak, for example, of someone being upright, as enjoying a high standing, as being balanced, or falling upon hard times, our oppositional concept of up and down arises out of our bodily experience of verticality. Although people differ in individual metaphor-making and metaphor-recognizing abilities, language itself is full of hidden metaphors that allow us to understand and experience one thing in terms of another. Contemporary neurophysiologists describe the activity of human thought as an activity that involves the transformation of represented information from one form to another. Their way of thinking about thinking not only accounts for abstract rational thought but also acknowledges that other quite normal but non-verbal transformation can be considered as types of thoughts. Howard Gardner, for example, has proposed a theory of multiple intelligences, giving a list of seven different types of intelligence: bodily, musical, linguistic, logical-mathematical, spatial, inter-personal and intrapersonal (Gardner 1983).[5] Every individual possesses all of these mental capacities, and under normal circumstances each of these intellectual regions will develop to some degree as most domains of activity require the joint mobil-ization of many intelligences. Spatial thinking, for example, is an important mode of thought for all living creatures. Although space is largely visually perceived, even with our eyes closed we are aware of the muscular, kinaesthetic feeling of our position in space, whether, for example, we are vertical, tilted, or resting horizontally. Spatial awareness is so ingrained in our psyche, so much part of our being-in-the-world that we are rarely aware of the degree to which we perceive and act in our everyday lives on the basis of concepts of objects, persons, and events that are in large part constructed out of spatial features and relations. Western dancers may have a much more developed spatial intelligence than non-dancers, but this awareness tends to be limited to their immediate space, whereas in many Australian Aboriginal societies, including Tiwi, dancers are physically aware of their whole geographical environment, as, in ritual, they regularly have to 'face' sacred places that may be many miles away.

Each socio-cultural environment provides different encourage-ment and support towards different types of intelligences. In our Western science-oriented world, for example, the term 'intelligent' is reserved for talking about rational-logical thinking. 'Skilled' or 'talented' rather than 'intelligent' would be used for people with excellent knowledge and control of their bodies. A student of mine at the London Contemporary Dance School told me that when her ballet school merged with the local grammar school to provide a broader education for its students, the dance students were systematically put with the low achievers in class. This clearly illustrates the belief held by many in our society that people who go into dance cannot be intellectually very bright.[6] In contrast anthropologist David MacKnight, talking about the Lardil of Mornington Island, commented that among them 'the best dancers are the best intellectuals' (n.d.). This hold true for the Tiwi too and bodily intelligence is very much part of their everyday reality. An approach that incorporates looking at dance as a category that is both biological and social and looking at the dialectic between the two, could provide a starting point for going beyond the limitations of both naturalistic and social constructionist views. Such an approach, however is not easy. Any discussion of a biological foundation of dance, because of its universalist tendency, is extremely unfashionable today, but I feel that we have to investigate the possibilities of new ways of thinking that such a perspective can give us.

My work in the anthropology of performance has been greatly influenced by the late John Blacking, mentioned earlier. I worked with him from 1976 to the time of his death in January 1990. When I first met him he had just published a rather controversial article on the subject of dance and evolution. In it he argued that 'the evidence of the forms and functions of music and dance in different societies can throw considerable light on relationships between [human beings] biological evolution and cultural development' (Blacking 1976: 5). This idea remained with him for the rest of his life and resurfaced on regular occasions in different forms. In 1984, for example, he argued that dance encompasses both:

1. the enormous range of movement styles which members of different societies conceptualize as being significantly different from their everyday, practical movements and liable to stimulate transcendental experiences and,

2. an innate, species-specific set of cognitive and sensory capacities which human beings are predisposed to use for communication and making sense of the environment (Blacking 1984: 6).

and in 1988:

There is little doubt that 'music' and 'dance' are species-specific behaviours that are part of the human biogrammar and that as primary modelling systems of communication they preceded speech in human history. Thinking in motions, a mode of thought characteristic of the operations of the right hemisphere of the brain, appears to be phylogenetically as well as ontogenetically (in the behaviour of infant children) older and more basic than thinking in concepts. The earlier species of human being, *homo erectus* and *homo sapiens neanderthalis*, had cultures and cultural traditions that were passed on from one generation to another, but they did not have speech as we know it. Verbal language is not a prerequisite of human thought (Blacking 1988: 3).

In an interview given four months before he died, Blacking reiterated his belief that 'the origins of culture are to be found in music, in dance, and in performance' (Blacking 1990: 199). As dance is contained within the body, one can argue that, with song, it is the most elementary artistic process. Blacking believed that they were 'a special kind of exercise of sensory, communicative and co-operative powers that is as fundamental to the making and remaking of human nature as speech' and that they 'can be understood as primary adaptations to the environment; with them, [humankind] can feel towards a new order of things and feel across boundaries' (1987: 60).

To me these ideas are important and need to be explored further. Although Western societies have for centuries manifested the tendency to view thinking as rational, orderly, and critical, and to believe that abstract concepts can only be elaborated, learned and taught in an intellectual way, it is important to realize that this is really only one kind of thought, and that its predominance is by no means universal. The following discussion will show how the Tiwi used the body and dance for elaborate abstract thought.

Dance and Body Intelligence among the Tiwi of Northern Australia

Mortuary rituals have always been at the core of Tiwi cultural life and dance and the body are at the core of these rituals. Through the dancers the Dreaming is embodied and the three parallel worlds of the Spirit Children, the Living, and the Dead, usually kept at bay, can interact. The body is the primary medium through which an incredibly complicated and abstract system of kinship becomes part of an individual's knowledge. My discussion will

focus on a group of ten dances that belong to that section of the
Tiwi dance repertoire that is owned by everybody. This group of
dances can be labelled the 'kinship dances', a term first used by
Jane Goodale (1971: 300–2), because they show a specific kinship
relationship between the dancer and the person for whom the
dance is performed. Among the Tiwi most dance performances
are dedicated to someone, dead in the context of mortuary rituals,
alive in the modern contexts of celebrations for weddings,
birthdays, or graduations.

My argument will be that dance plays a significant role for
kinship in three important ways:

1. It teaches the system to the youngsters by encoding it into their
   bodies.
2. It allows people to remember not only contemporary but also
   past kinship relationships between individuals.
3. Through dance, kinship theories are elaborated through the use
   of bodily intelligence.

On my first day at Pularumpi, on Melville Island, I was made
aware of the very close connection the Tiwi made between dance
and kinship. When I mentioned my interest in dance I was told
'you dance like this (with your fists clenched opposite your mouth)
for your mother', 'like this (with the hands underneath your
breasts) for your daughter', and 'like this (holding your leg) for
your brother'. As the weeks went on, I discovered quickly that
kinship was important throughout the Tiwi dance repertoire, not
only in terms of dance ownership, but also in terms of organization
of dance events: responsibility for organizing, choreographing,
composing, and paying for specific performance events depended
on kinship. Similarly the order of performance during a single
dance event depended on kinship. I also realized that the system
of kinship dances was much more complicated than had been
suggested on my first day, that some of these dances were
physically almost indistinguishable unless one was constantly
aware of them in movement terms and kept checking what the
movements meant (Jane Goodale, for example, identified six
kinship dances against my ten), and that it obviously needed a
detailed study.

My first step was to work out an 'ideal' kinship dance system,
asking questions of the type 'how do I dance if such and such a

relative dies?' I then compared this model with what happened in practice, being especially attentive to the instances where practice did not fit the system, since one has to be careful with the very notion of prescriptive models.[7]

The Kinship Dances of the Tiwi

The Tiwi saw themselves as all being related through kinship. Consequently every individual always had one kinship dance to perform at every dance event. Every time someone died, everybody in the society changed status from the time of death to the time of the final mortuary ritual. The name of the bereavement status of the dancers became the label for the dance, as performing specific dances was part of prescribed bereavement behaviour. The modern contexts of parties for birthdays and so on were modelled on the mortuary rituals, and the same terminology for labelling status of performers and dances was used even though no bereavement was involved.

The kinship dances can be divided into three categories: patrilineal, affinal, and matrilineal dances. I will first give an overview of the whole system, showing who the performers of each dance are and giving a brief verbal description of the movements of the dances. Then I will comment on them and discuss the kinds of insights an understanding of Tiwi kinship from a dance perspective can bring.

It is interesting that, for the Tiwi, certain relatives were seen as being associated with certain body parts: the legs represented a certain kind of sibling; the cheek, another; the abdomen, a woman's children or a man's sisters' children; the shoulder, the in-laws, especially a man's mother-in-law; the groin, a man's children or a woman's brothers' children; the big toe, the husband. In this way Tiwi truly embodied their social world. When individuals felt a pain in their bodies, for example, they immediately interpreted it as a warning of illness or even death of specific relatives.[8] This relationship between body parts and specific individuals was clearly articulated in dance. Many of the kinship dances consisted of holding the specific body part with both hands while performing prescribed feet movements.

Patrilineal Dances

The *mamurapi turaa* can be seen as the dance of the Spirit Children. One was *mirauni/mirama turaa* if one called the deceased *ringani* (F; FB; step F; MZH, and sometimes by extension men of the same matrilineal clan as one's father or of one clan of one's father's semi-moiety), *tinganinga* (FZ), *timinti* (SWB, ZHF, HF) and *timintinga* (SW, ZHM, HM, MBW). Before Tiwi men and women could be born into the human world they first had to be dreamed and found by their father as Spirit Children. At the death of their father, or of any individual belonging to that unit, they emphasized that relationship: they were not human beings any more, but once again Spirit Children, carrying a spear and being mischievous towards their fathers, hiding and playing tricks on them. The dancers either performed carrying a spear or pretending to throw a spear.

The *krimirika* dance concerned the Spirit Child and its grandfathers. One was *krimirika* if one called the deceased *amini* (FF, MF, FMB, FZS) or *amo* (FM, FFZ, MFZ, FZD). Men were often helped by their fathers and fathers' fathers when looking for their children, especially, I was told, in more recent times when fathers are much younger than in the past and not yet very knowledgeable in traditional matters.[9] Again the dance was about the Spirit Child carrying a spear and being mischievous. The only difference from the *mamurapi turaa* dance was that the left hand was kept 'on the heart' during the performance.

The *krimirika* was opposed to the *kiakiae* dance where the dancer carried his/her grandchild who had died. One was *kiakiae* if one called the deceased *mawanyini* (SS, BSS, BDS, ZSS, MBS, DS – male speaking) or *mawana* (SD, BSD, BDD, ZSD, MBD, DD – male speaking). The movement of the dance showed in an abstract way the deceased as a child being carried by the dancer on one shoulder, in a typical Tiwi fashion. *Krimirika* and *kiakiae* were two aspects of the same relationship and were very close. Indeed for some Tiwi the two were synonymous and on some occasions they interchanged them. Others, however, were adamant that they were distinct dances showing precise kinship relationships.

The *mutuni* dance was performed by the patrilineal 'siblings' of the deceased. One was *mutuni* if one called the deceased *ingkalapini* (paternal half brother belonging to a matrilineal 'clan' other than one's own), *ingkalapa* (paternal half sister belonging to a matrilineal 'clan' other than one's own) or if one was *aminiati* (plural *aminiatuwi*) with the deceased, that is if one shared one *amo* (FM, FFZ, MFZ, FZD) or one *amini* (FF, MF, FMB, FZS). *Aminiati* was the only kin term which implied equality between the people who used it. All the individuals who comprised the *mutuni* group were considered the 'same'. During the *mutuni* dance the performers held their cheeks with their hands.

The *wunantawi pulanga* dance where the father found and made his child was opposed to the *mamurapi turaa* dance. One was *wunantaka/wunantani pulanga* if one called the deceased *murani* (BS, S – male speaking) or *muraninga* (BD, D – male speaking), brother including one's *aminiatuwi* (see *mutuni*). The dance was about the making of the child. The dancers held their groin (*pulanga*) and sometimes their genitals, making the sexual connotation fairly obvious.

Affinal Dances

The *impala* dance was concerned with the relationship between an individual and his in-laws, and especially the relationship mother-in-law / son-in-law. One was *impala* if one called the deceased *ampirinua* (WM, BWM, DHZ – female speaking) or *pinua/pinyiwini* (DH – female speaking; WMB, ZDH – male speaking). In the relationship between body part and kin, a man's mother-in-law was the shoulder and the movements of the dance emphasized them. For a man this relationship was probably one of the most important of all his social relationships and he was obligated to his mother-in-law throughout his life.

The *amparuwi* dance was performed by the deceased's 'spouses'. One was *amparu* if one called the deceased *apunainga* (W), *apunai* (H), *inyimunga* (BW, WZ, HZ) or *inyimini* (ZH, WB, HB), brothers and sisters including one's *aminiatuwi* (see *mutuni*). One was also *amparu* if one's spouse or potential spouse *paputawi* (see below) died. In this case one was a 'long way *amparu*' and could be selected as a worker to perform the mortuary tasks; or if one was promised to the deceased (even if one later married somebody else), or even, in some cases, if one had been a lover of the deceased.

In many ways a Tiwi woman was subordinate to her husband. She was not subservient to him: as a food-gatherer and rearer of children she was fairly independent from him and the Tiwi saw the relationship husband/wife as one of co-operation, but she was not equal. It was interesting, then, to note that in the spouse dance men and women performed in exactly the same way, the men changing from their 'masculine' style of feet movements (both feet on the ground on the beat) to the 'feminine' style (one foot away from the ground on the beat), the dance thus showing a relationship of equality. The dance was about a fight between the dancer and the ghost of the dead person, the ghost may have been reluctant to leave the world of the living for the world of the dead and it was the role of the *amparuwi* to chase him/her away.

Matrilineal Dances

The *mamurapi pularti* could be seen as the matrilineal 'counterpart' to the patrilineal *mamurapi turaa*, the dance of the Spirit Children, discussed earlier. One was *mirama/mirauni* if one called the deceased *naringa* (M, stepM, MZ, FBW), *ilimani* (MB) or *nirinua* – if older than ego (DH – male speaking, WF, BWF, FZH). The dance was about being fed by the deceased. The dancer put one or both hands on or close to the mouth in a drinking movement.

The *wunantawi pularti* could be seen as the matrilineal 'counterpart' to the *wunantawi pulanga* dance where the dancer found and sired the child. One was *wunantaka/wunantani* if one called the deceased *mwaringa* (D – female speaking, ZD), *mwarti* (S – female speaking, ZS) or *nirinua* – if younger than ego (DH – male speaking, WF, BWF, FZH) sister including one's *aminiatuwi* (see *mutuni*). The movement of the dance showed the dancer being pregnant with the deceased, having labour pains, breastfeeding the deceased, or/and nursing him/her.

The *paputawi* dance was performed by people who were full consanguineal, or matrilineal clan, or semi-moiety, siblings with the deceased. One was *putaka/putani* if one called the deceased *impunga* (EZ), *impoka* (YZ), *iuwini* (EB), *iuwani* (YB), *maningao* (MM, MMZ), *angimani* (MMB, EB if much older than ego), *intamilinga* (DD – female speaking, ZDD), *intamili* (DS – female speaking, ZDS), *umpuruteri* (SWM, DHM) or *umpurutrini* (SWF, DHF). The members of this group, in contrast to the *aminiatuwi*, were not all considered the 'same'. There were differences in status between them, mainly due to age. They were nevertheless very closely associated and dancers performed the same dance for their matrilineal relatives in their own, in the second ascending and in the second descending generation levels, even though they called them by different kin terms. In the relationship between body parts and kin, an individual's *paputawi* were represented by the leg; this was emphasized in the movement of the dance, the dancers performing holding their legs.

Comments on the Kinship Dances

The Tiwi recognized both patrilineal and matrilineal principles of descent and belonged to descent units of both types. This was well illustrated in the kinship dance system. Looking at the dances one sees that, although the kin terms stressed a speaker's own and related matriclans (there were twelve terms used for people in those clans as distinct from eight terms for patrilineal relatives) the dances stressed the patrilineal side of the family. There were five patrilineal dances, three matrilineal dances, and two dances associated with relatives acquired through marriage.

Four dances were reciprocal – the person for whom the dance was being performed would have danced in the same way if the roles had been reversed. In these dances one sees that the *mutuni* emphasized the patriline of the deceased, the *paputawi* stressed his/her matrilineal affiliations, and that the *impala* and the *amparuwi* recognized his/her affinal affiliations. Six dances were non-reciprocal dances – the person for whom the dance was being performed would have performed a different dance if the roles had been reversed. The units *mamurapi turaa/wunantawi pulanga* and *krimirika/kiakiae* emphasized the patriline and the meeting between Spirit Children and their fathers and fathers' fathers. When men and children found each other the children received part of their identity in receiving their Dreamings. The unit *mamurapi pularti/wunantawi pularti* on the other hand emphasized the matriline and the link to the ancestresses, the daughters of Pukwi, the Sun-woman, who created the Tiwi world and from whom every Tiwi is descended. Through their mother Tiwi received their matrilineal clan, the other side of their personality.

The organization of the final ritual followed a specific order of performances. However the system did allow a certain amount of flexibility in that not all categories of personnel may have had available members at the time, either because people were not around or because they simply did not exist. Usually the order was: first the patrilineal relatives, then the in-laws, then the matrilineal relatives, and last the *amparuwi* – people who were in the category of widows/widowers.

Looking at Tiwi kinship through the performing arts, gives a dimension different from those previously given by other anthropologists. It has been said, for example, that in Tiwi society an individual looked to his/her matrilineal kinsmen in the field of physical welfare but that in spiritual matters and in ritual obligations she or he looked towards her/his patriline (Brandl 1971: 229). From the perspective of the kinship dances this observation needs to be qualified: it is true that the patrilineal dances were mainly concerned with Spirit Children, but the movement of the respective dances also showed the physical making of the child, as well as physically caring relationships. Similarly although the matrilineal dances were about the physical welfare of individuals, in that they dealt mainly with pregnancy and motherhood, they were reaffirming the links with Pukwi and the Dreaming. In addition, they were often accompanied by songs related to specific Dreamings and the spiritual associations between individuals and their land.

It is interesting to compare the discussions given by different writers of the patrilineally organized sibling group, the *aminiatuwi*. Hart argued that members of this unit maintained exclusive rights to a geographical area validated by the presence of the grave of the common fathers' father in the area, and that only those individuals descending from an important man (a man who had enough wives to produce enough grandchildren to enforce their claim and demonstrate their existence as a localized social group) belonged to such a group (1930: 173–5). Goodale disagreed with this view of the *aminiatuwi* being a non universal social group. For her, it was a patrilineal sibling set, 'conceptually parallel to the matrilineal sibling set so that members of such a set were considered as being "one person" by kinsmen outside the set' (1971: 97). However she saw it as being 'overshadowed by the matrilineal system of affiliation' (1971: 98).

My own analysis brought another emphasis. Documenting the *mutuni* dance I was told that it 'marked' a relationship between equal individuals related through someone important, *amini* or *amo* (*amini* and *amo* are also masculine and feminine adjectival suffixes meaning 'big'). Looking at who performed the *mutuni* dance together, my data also showed clearly that the sex of the linking relative was not always male as had been argued by Hart and Goodale, though it usually was. The importance of this group was reflected throughout the Tiwi ritual life. During the annual Kulama yam ceremony men had to compose and perform over three days a song cycle; at one stage the songs had to be about people who had died during the year, at another they were about pretending to be women. In all the songs I studied, covering six Kulama, these people always belonged to the same *aminiatuwi* set as the performer. I was told that the performers were 'making them important'. During mortuary rituals members of the same *aminiatuwi* set as the deceased were decision-makers as well as choreographers and composers.

Discussion and Conclusions

What is to me particularly interesting in the kinship dances is that, through them, every Tiwi experienced all the social roles of the society, even those that were impossible to execute or socially unacceptable. I have discussed elsewhere (Grau 1993b), for example, how, in dance, individuals could somehow change gender, in the sense that in dance being a mother, a father, or a grandfather had nothing to do with the gender of the performer. Men and women both found Spirit Children even though in every day life women were not even supposed to know what the Spirit Children looked like; in dance one could be a spouse or potential spouse to both men and women regardless of one's gender; and both men and women were pregnant, gave birth and nurtured the baby.

Thus not only did the Tiwi have a system where men and women generally had valued complementary roles but they also had the opportunity through performance somehow to 'become' the other, therefore experiencing the whole world rather than just the one limited by their gender or age. Within the kinship dance system they also had the opportunity to experience other impossible roles such as being Spirit Children, or being parents to much older individuals, thus imagining reality as well as reflecting it. Through the kinship dances, one could argue, reality was transcended, the performers dancing through the three parallel worlds of the Unborn, the Living and the Dead.

Through dance the Tiwi could also manipulate the social reality. Depending on how one looks at a genealogy, looking at the relationship between two individuals via the mothers, via the fathers, or via the spouses, one can have different results about what role an individual should or could take in the dancing. Sometimes, in such cases, the dancers performed all the dances associated with their roles. Sometimes they chose to perform one role only, thus emphasizing a specific relationship. Occasionally they manipulated the system to avoid performing the dance that genealogical connections prescribed them and performed another dance related to the message they wanted to send. I have described elsewhere, for example, a woman using dance in such a way as to protect her daughters from men she did not want them to marry (cf. Grau 1994, 1995a).[10]

The kinship dances were truly kinship in action. It established and re-established kinship ties between individuals past and present through bodily practices and bodily intelligence. As Schultz and Lavenda argued 'our understanding of the world does not come merely from mind, but rather from coming together of mind, emotion, and body. By performing our ideas, our ideas become real' (1990: 177). This statement is well supported by an analysis of Tiwi dance.

It is important that we attempt to look at the integration and working together of mind, body and emotion, rather than constantly looking at the body as a kind of readable text upon which social reality is inscribed, as a creature of representation, an object of understanding or an instrument of the rational mind, a kind of vehicle for the expression of a reified social rationality. It is time to ask, in Thomas Csordas's words, why not 'begin with the premises that the fact of our embodiment can be a valuable starting point for rethinking the nature of culture and our existential situation as cultural beings?' (Csordas 1994: 6). It is only through the exploration of the dialectic between the biological and the cultural foundations of human life that the ultimate goal of anthropology – making sense of the human condition – will be realized.

Notes

1. For recent overviews on the field of the anthropology of human movement/anthropology of dance see Grau (1993a), Kaeppler (1991), Williams (1986).
2. Although many Western theatre dancers also use a number of techniques to help them with their work, such as Pilates, Feldenkreiss, or Alexander, where body and mind are integrated, and there are Western philosophies, such as Rudolf Steiner's anthroposophy, which do not endorse the dichotomy, the idea of the body as machine is prevalent. It can be traced all the way back to classical Greece, but it became especially strong from the Enlightenment onwards when the foundations were laid down of both modern science and of Western theatre dance with the establishment of the Académie Royale de Danse in 1661.
3. Foucault, in his *History of Sexuality* had proposed that the notion of 'sex' does not exist prior to its determination within a discourse in which its constellations of meanings are specified. Following this argument bodies have no 'sex' outside discourse in which they are designated as sexed. In Foucault's terms: 'The notion of 'sex' made it possible to group together, in an artificial unity, anatomical elements, biological functions, conducts, sensations, and pleasures and it enabled one to make use of this fictitious unity as a causal principle, an omnipresent meaning; sex was thus able to function as a unique signifier and as a universal signified' (1984: 154).

   I have no problem with that. This notion is indeed useful, for example, to argue against the idea that the natural body is the basis on which individual identities and social inequalities are built, or to support the argument that gendered identities are fractured, shifting, and unstable (indeed the division 'sex-gender' used in the social sciences becomes highly challengeable from such a perspective) but I cannot come to terms with this idea of a vanishing body, as I do not think one can ignore people's experiences of their bodies. I agree that the body is shaped and perceived through discourse, but it is not reducible solely to discourse (see Shilling (1993: 79–81) for a critique of Foucault's vanishing body).

4. It is quite possible that organic evolution seems insignificant in comparison to social evolution because the time scale is so vast. It deals in thousands of years rather than a few generations and our minds cannot quite comprehend it.

5. This idea of the integration of different modes of experience is not new. At the turn of the century, for example, the philosopher Rudolf Steiner proposed a theory based on twelve senses linked to the activities of willing (senses of touch, movement, balance, and life/metabolism), feeling (senses of smell, taste, sight, and heat/cold) and thinking (senses of hearing, language, thought, and self/other). In this approach movement is seen as a way of awakening perception and thinking. In Steiner education, for example, the body is involved as a way of learning: when children encounter writing, for example, the teacher takes them through the gestures and movements of the vowels and consonants. At the age of 9–10 when they are seen to encounter a new self-consciousness, specific exercises are introduced to meet and foster this process. Movement helps to retain a living quality in subjects that demand abstract thinking, such as when geometry appears on the curriculum. Forms are experienced through the body; geometrical exercises become progressively more complicated and lead not only to increased spatial awareness, but also to the ability to visualize and carry out an intention with precision. These exercises are used because they are said to develop the adult's capacity for clear and mobile thinking and thus as enhancing their freedom of choice.

6. Katherine Healy, principal dancer with the Vienna State Opera Ballet, for example, explored the image of the 'dumb dancer' (1994).

7. My particular interest in anthropology is to look at the tension between human creativity on the one side and social norms on the other, looking at both the coherence and non-coherence of cultures. In that I share Emily Schultz's and Robert Lavenda's view that central to anthropology is 'the ambiguity of experience and the resolution of that ambiguity through the human capacity to create meaning' (1990: xix).

8. This ability was somewhat uncanny. I can recall a number of times, spending a day out in the bush with people gathering food, when someone suddenly complained about a pain and talked about his/her worries about a certain relative, and then

hearing about the illness or the death of this person when returning home at the end of the day.

9. Missionaries from the turn of the century onwards had at first forbidden, then openly discouraged, marriage between old men and young women as was the norm in the past. By the time of my fieldwork most couples consisted of partners of the same generation.

10. The dance floor was also a space where the agendas of competing constituencies could be articulated and confronted with one another and where the heterogeneous aspects of the society could be sorted out (see Grau 1995b).

References

Blacking, J. (1976). Dance, Conceptual Thought and Production in the Archaeological Record. In: G. Sieveking, I. Longworth, and K. E. Winston (eds), *Problems in Economic and Social Archaeology*, pp. 3–13. London: Duckworth.

—— (1984). Dance as Cultural System and Human Capability: An Anthropological Perspective. In: J. Adshead (ed.), *Dance: A Multicultural Perspective,* pp. 4–21. Guildford: University of Surrey.

—— (1987). *A Common Sense View of All Music.* Cambridge: Cambridge University Press.

—— (1988). Dance and Human Being: Strengthening Children's Individuality and Angelic Qualities for Adaptation to Cultural Convention. *Proceedings of Fourth Conference of 'Dance and the Child International' (DaCI),* vol. 3, pp. 4–15. Worcester Park: DaCI Publications.

—— (1990). Interview with Keith Howard, Translated into French, published under the title 'Un Homme Musical: Entretien avec John Blacking', *Cahiers de Musiques Traditionelles* 3: 187–204.

Bourdieu, P. (1978). Sport and Social Class. *Social Science Information* 17: 819–40.

—— (1984). *Distinction: A Social Critique of the Judgement of Taste.* London: Routledge.

Brandl, M. (1971). Pukumani: The Social Context of Bereavement in a North Australian Tribe. (Unpublished PhD thesis.) Nedlands: University of Western Australia.

Connel, R. (1983). *Which Way is Up?* London: Allen & Unwin.

Connerton, P. (1989). *How Societies Remember.* Cambridge: Cambridge University Press.

Csordas, T. (ed.) (1994). *Embodiment and Experience: the Existential Ground of Culture and Self.* Cambridge: Cambridge University Press.

Dissayanake, E. (1992). *Homo Aestheticus: Where Art Comes From and Why.* New York: The Free Press.

Douglas, M. (1966.) *Purity and Danger: An Analysis of the Concepts of Pollution and Taboo.* London: Routledge & Kegan Paul.

—— (1970). *Natural Symbols: Explorations in Cosmology.* London: The Cresset Press.

Foucault, M. (1984). *History of Sexuality, An Introduction,* vol I. Harmondsworth: Penguin.

Gardner, H. (1983). *Frames of Mind: The Theory of Multiple Intelligence.* New York: Basic Books.

Goodale, J. (1971). *Tiwi Wives: A Study of the Women of Melville Island, North Australia.* Seattle and London: University of Washington Press.

Grau, A. (1993a). John Blacking and the Development of Dance Anthropology in the United Kingdom. *Dance Research Journal* 25(2): 21–32.

—— (1993b). Gender Interchangeability among the Tiwi. In: H. Thomas (ed.), *Dance, Gender, and Culture,* pp. 94–111. London: Macmillan.

—— (1994). Dance as Politics: The Use of Dance for the Manipulation of the Social Order among the Tiwi of Northern Australia. *Proceedings of the Seventeenth Symposium of the Study Group on Ethnochoreology, International Council for Traditional Music,* pp. 39–44. Nafplion: Pelopponesian Folklore Foundation.

—— (1995a). Dance as Part of the Infrastructure of Social Life. In: J. Baily (ed.), *John Blacking: the Belfast Years,* pp. 43–59. Berlin: International Institute for Traditional Music.

—— (1995b). Ritual Dance and 'Modernisation': the Tiwi Example. In: G. Dabrowska and L. Bielawski (eds), *Dance, Ritual and Music. Proceedings of the Eighteenth Symposium of the Study Group on Ethnochoreology, The International Council of Traditional Music,* pp. 89–96. Warsaw: Polish Academy of Sciences.

—— (1997). Dancers' Bodies as the Repository of Conceptualisations of the Body, with Special Reference to the Tiwi of Northern Australia. In: I. Rauch and G.F. Carr (eds), *Semiotics Around the World: Synthesis in Diversity. Proceedings of the Fifth*

Congress of the International Association for Semiotic Studies,
Berkeley 1994, pp. 929–32. New York: Mouton de Gruyter.
—— (n.d.). Social Practices, Bodies, and Human Evolution:
Dancer's Bodies as World Views. Unpublished paper presented
at the Bodily Fictions Conference, Brunel University College,
8–10 September 1995.

Hart, C.W.M. (1930). The Tiwi of Melville and Bathurst Islands.
Oceania 1(2): 167–80.

Haviland, W. (1990). *Cultural Anthropology.* New York: Holt,
Rinehart, Winston.

Healy, K. (1993). Expanding Minds. *Dance Now* 2(4): 10–17.

Johnson, M. (1987). *The Body in the Mind: The Bodily Basis of Meaning,
Imagination, and Reason.* Chicago and London: University of
Chicago Press.

Kaeppler, A. (1991). American Approaches to the Study of Dance.
Yearbook for Traditional Music 23: 11–21.

Keesing, R.M. (1976). *Cultural Anthropology: A Contemporary
Perspective.* New York: Holt, Rinehart, Winston.

Lakoff, G. and Johnson, M. (1980). *Metaphors We Live By.* Chicago
and London: University of Chicago Press.

MacKnight, D. (n.d.). Untitled Paper on Dance Among the Lardil
of Mornington Island. Presented at the Fourth Goldsmiths
Anthropology of Dance Colloquium 'Reflections on the Body',
1994.

Mauss, M. (1934). Les Techniques du Corps. *Journal de Psychologie
Normale et Pathologique* 32: 271–93.

Schultz, E. and Lavenda, R. (1990). *Cultural Anthropology: A
Perspective on the Human Condition.* New York: West Publishing
Company.

Shilling, C. (1993). *The Body and Social Theory.* London: Sage
Publications.

Terry, St. (1995). Body Exploitation. *The Big Issue,* September 25 –
October 1: 18–9.

Williams, D. (1986). (Non)anthropologists, the Dance, and Human
Movement. In: B. Fleshman (ed.), *Theatrical Movement: A
Bibliographical Anthology,* pp. 158–215. Metuchen NJ and
London: The Scarecrow Press.

Chapter 4

Cannibalism and Compassion: Transformations in Fijian Concepts of the Person

Christina Toren

Hierarchy, Equality and Personhood

In a recent historical-cum-ethnographic analysis of the history of chiefship in the *vanua* of Sawaieke, central Fiji, I argued against the prevailing view that Fijian social relations are fundamentally hierarchical. Rather, social relations in general and chiefship in particular are constituted in terms of complementary and opposing concepts of equality and hierarchy, such that neither can become, in Dumont's (1980) terms, 'an encompassing value'. This radical opposition between equality and hierarchy, Hegelian in form, pervades Fijian daily life and informs, for example, sexual relations, kinship, chiefship and concepts of the person.

That hierarchy in Fiji is *not* an encompassing value is apparent in the words of Hocart's Lauan informant: 'In Fiji all things go in pairs, or the sharks will bite' (Hocart 1952: 57). Here 'sharks' denote the ancestor gods manifest in that form or chiefs as dangerous and warlike persons. The saying emphasizes the duality of 'all things', but what is most important here is the antithesis that is captured by this duality. In other words, 'things' have to be related to one another in a reciprocal form that allows hierarchy and equality to be *at one and the same time* implicated in that relationship. This is because, in Fiji, the fundamental concept of social organization is 'the household', which by definition depends for its continuity on the existence of other households. People relate to one another as kin, but while kin relations *within* the household are axiomatically hierarchical – husband above wife, older sibling above junior sibling – kinship *across* households references the equal relationship between cross-cousins. Further, *all* exchange relations are competitive and ultimately those of balanced reciprocity even while the rituals of chiefship render them as tributary and apparently unequal.

If hierarchy is not and cannot be an encompassing value for Fijians, neither can competitive equality achieve the ascendancy, for equal relations always implicate their opposite value. The logic of Fijian social relations is always a twofold logic where hierarchy and equality are in tension with one another and dependent on one another for their very continuity. The rituals of chiefship are explicitly understood to promote prosperity, but they do so by virtue of projecting onto the collectivity – the *vanua* (country) – an image of the hierarchical household; this image implies the necessity for its own transformation because marriage is not possible within, but only across, households; in other words one has always to posit the existence of at least two households 'attending on each other' (*veiqaravi*, literally 'facing each other'). So Fijian chiefship *has* to be dual, *has* to be made up of land and sea, of the executive powers of the land chief and the ritual precedence of the paramount; only thus can it project an image of the hierarchical household as existing *alongside* other households in the relation of balanced reciprocity and competitive equality that makes marriage possible. In other words, the logic of Fijian chiefship is such that it can promote prosperity only if it is dual (see Toren 1994b).

The present contribution takes up where this previous paper left off; it is a preliminary attempt to trace historical transformations in respect of this continuing radical opposition between hierarchy and competitive equality. It examines certain aspects of pre-colonial ideas of person and self with respect to *mana* (literally 'efficacy') as the immanent power of the ancestors made material in the fertility of the land and the acts of living persons, especially of chiefs. It argues that one's existential efficacy as a person, one's selfhood, ultimately resided in what one could be seen to consume, and that anger and courage, shame and fear can be understood as the experiential dimension of any person's own effectiveness *vis-à-vis* others. This chapter focuses on data concerning death, birth and sacrifice to suggest that, in conceiving of the person as consumer, nineteenth-century Fijians created a subject/object relation between the self and lived experience.

Death as Self-Sacrifice

To be unable as an adult to provide for oneself implied that the *yalo*, passions, were too weak to sustain life. Thus little effort was made to feed or give drink to persons who had no appetite for it or who were unable to get it for themselves. Missionaries and colonial administrators found it abhorrent that Fijians routinely described as already dead, *mate*, one who was, from a European point of view, merely ill and likely to recover if properly treated; indeed such a person might be buried while still alive or, if of no status, thrown into the river or sea or abandoned in the bush. The missionary Williams, in his 1858 publication, made the following observations:

> . . . the aged, when they find themselves likely to become troublesome, beg of their children to strangle them. If the parents should be slow to make the proposal, they are anticipated by the children . . . a repugnance on the part of the sound, the healthy, and the young, to associate with the maimed, the sick, and the aged, is the main cause of the sacrifice . . . exposure, burying alive, and the rope, are the means generally used . . . there is truth in what the people allege, as one reason for their anxiety to get rid of their sick. The malignity of the afflicted ones does not seem to be diminished by their bodily weakness; for when left alone, they will lie on the mats of their friends, and leave saliva in their drinking vessels, or even in their food, that they may thus communicate the disease to the healthy members of the household . . .

These actions on the part of the malignant ill do not denote a germ theory of disease. To spit on the personal belongings of a dead person removed the *tabu* on their use by others, thus the actions of the ill suggest that they might evade death if only they could assimilate themselves to the living, change places with them. By the same token the healthy one is threatened, perhaps marked out for death, by virtue of being made to ingest, or in some other way assimilate, the substance of his or her sick kin.

Other accounts suggest that to recognize for oneself that one's life was no longer viable allowed one to seize control of one's own death and direct the obsequies, even where that death had been initiated by others. Thus Wilkes (1985: 94, orig. 1845) recorded that: 'It is among the most usual occurrences, that a father or a mother will notify their children that it is time for them to die, or that a son shall give notice to his parents that they are becoming a burden to him.'

He goes on to describe an eye-witness account by the missionary Hunt of an old lady walking to her own grave 'as gay and lively as any of those present, and apparently as much pleased' and after describing her strangling by her sons and interment, goes on to say that: 'Mr Hunt, after giving me this anecdote, surprized me by expressing his opinion that the Feejeeans were a kind and affectionate people to their parents, adding, that he was assured by many of them that they considered this custom as so great a proof of affection that none but children could be found to perform it' (1985: 95–6).

The published literature and archives record numerous other cases of self-sacrifice by the old, and by wives who asked to be strangled on the deaths of their husbands, even after they had been 'reprieved' by missionaries.

Williams tells us that,

> The process of laying out is often commenced several hours before the person is actually dead. I have known one take food afterwards; and another who lived eighteen hours after. All this time, in the opinion of a Fijian, the man was dead. Eating, drinking, and talking, he says, are the involuntary actions of the body . . . the soul having taken its departure (1858/1982: 183–6).

'Spirit' or 'soul' is a translation of the Fijian *yalo*, but Fijian usage, while it refers to the immaterial substance of the person that continues after death, also suggests that the passions are definitive of human life. Thus *yalo* is used in very many compounds to indicate human qualities; for example *yalo qaqa*, determined, courageous, *yalo ca*, bad-tempered, *yalo kaukaua*, aggressive, *yalo lailai*, timid, *yalo katakata*, angry (literally 'hot spirited') and so on. These passions of the *yalo* are, I suggest, what binds one to life.

Half a century after the period to which Williams and Wilkes were referring, the 1896 Report of the Commission on the Decrease in the Native Population remarked that: 'Instances are known where a Fijian, ill of some chronic malady, has fixed the date of his death two or three weeks before its occurrence, and died on the appointed day . . . a mother with a sick child expects its death, and her expectation is invariably realised' (Report of the Commission 1896: 70).

Elsewhere the report notes that

> Wilful neglect of the sick seems to be a large factor in the excessive
> mortality... The whole village will turn out to cut firewood for
> a sick man, but no one will put the wood within his reach or
> systematically make up the fire. If a fowl is killed to make soup, the
> sick man will be given a few mouthfuls, and the neighbours will come
> in and consume the remainder ... to keep the food for the use of the
> patient would be considered inhospitable ... 'When sick' says another
> writer, 'they turn from their own food with disgust, and during the
> epidemic of influenza numbers begged rice, biscuit, tea and sugar
> from the European settlers, being unable to eat their ordinary food'
> (Report of the Commisson 1896: 165).

Taken together, these sets of observations suggest that the old, the
sick, the weak while they might accept food when it was given,
could not depend on its being so; neither could they ask it of their
kin. To have to ask one's kin for food to support life was to give
up one's subjecthood, to become entirely an object – one's view of
oneself being predicated on the view of the kin who fed one. This
suggests further that *all* consumption was the site of a struggle to
convert eating as a passive activity in which one was fed, and thus
the object of others' actions, into an activity in which one was the
subject of one's own actions and, in the case of cannibalism, so
entirely an agent that one was able to consume others and cause
them to be consumed.

Birth and Establishment of the Passions

The loss of the *yalo* before death, suggests the material separation
between the passions and the body. The *yalo*, it seems, was
established in the newborn child some time after birth. So Fison
tells us that: 'An old chief ... defended the practice of infanticide
by the following curious argument ... "A newborn child is scarcely
a human being. Its spirit [*yalona*] has not yet come to it."'

I have no explicit data on when the *yalo* came to the newborn
child, but ceremonies for the firstborn suggest that the *yalo* become
established by virtue of the child being fed. Ratu Deve Toganivalu,
writing in 1912 of the pre-Christian customs of Bau says that on
the day of the birth the father made a feast for the woman's kin

called *tunudra* (literally 'heating blood'); female kin on both sides were appointed to carry the child for ten days in their arms – *kevekeve*; female kin slept in the house with the woman and child for ten days – *mocemoce*; they sang and played jokes on one another to celebrate 'the new child', as the firstborn was called.

> After the child is born he is given to drink the juice of candle-nut fruit . . . that he may vomit away the bad drink which he had in the womb. [Then] ripe coconut is chewed and the milk squeezed out of it, then a piece of barkcloth is soaked in this and given to the child to suck. After this the wet-nurse is sent for to suckle the child for four days, then it is put to drink to its mother . . .
>
> After two days . . . a dish of water is brought and a stone which has been roasted hot: the stone to be put in the water to warm it, to wash the flesh of the child; a feast is made for his washing . . . *tavudeki* . . .
>
> The women appointed to nurse are forbidden to take up their own food. Another person puts their food into their mouths up to the end of the ten days. The mother of the child remains lying down and is wrapped up in barkcloth . . . Her food must not be prepared with sea-water, and the relish with it is taro-tops . . . [she] keeps hidden inside the barkcloth covering, the child is also covered with barkcloth . . . They appear for the first time when the ten days are ended. The inside of the house becomes very hot, as all the doors are shut, and it is crowded with the women 'mocemoce' and 'kevekeve' (Toganivalu 1911).

On the tenth night another feast was prepared and after it most of the women left, though some remained until the hundredth night, also marked by a feast, after which the child could be taken outside. 'And if a new child like this is taken into another house, the owner of the house will present a whale's tooth . . . or he will promise a piece of land or a house site to the child' (Toganivalu 1911).

The birth ceremonies suggest that this first child's *yalo* was established by virtue of the way it was made to become, as it were, the agent of acts that were performed on it. First it had to be made to distinguish food from non-food; only then could it be put to a wet-nurse and, after four days, to its mother. It ate of its mother, but she could eat only such land food as might not be inimical to the child – *kakana dina*, true food, root vegetables boiled only in fresh water, and their leafy green tops. It seems the child had to be assimilated fully to the land of which it was a product before it could be allowed even indirect contact with sea. In being kept 'hot' and carried for the first ten days, the child was implicitly attributed with the agency that the passions make possible – the child made the women carry it and care for it; this is apparent in the way that the women became passive objects of the child's desires, so they might not feed themselves but had to be fed. Further, the child was separated from its mother who became the object of its oral passion; she lay hidden under the barkcloth while her own substance became its food. Neither child nor mother should be seen by a woman whose pregnancy had just become apparent, lest their newly achieved separation be threatened by this woman's continued containment of her own child in the womb 'and then the mother's breasts become dry, or the child die'. The actions of the women caretakers, who themselves ate the feasts provided by the father's kin, impressed upon the child its personhood and thus its relation to its kin and the land, the *vanua*, of which it and they were a manifestation. The ceremonies rendered the passions of the first-born more salient than those of its later-born siblings who, throughout life, would owe respect to the eldest and, by virtue of being obedient, of 'listening to' what the eldest said, make his or her words *mana*, effective. The mark of this efficacy of the eldest is apparent in the way 'the new child' can compel tribute from the owners of any house it enters. In later life, when little fingers might be lopped off the hands of children as a mark of mourning for a dead chief, the eldest child was exempted from this sacrifice of its bodily integrity (Cargill 1839–40: 77).

Consuming the Sacrifice That is Death

Until today, eating together is definitive of kinship; consumption is the summation of the cycles of production, exchange and tribute that constitute relations across households and more inclusive groups. Thus to refuse to eat is a denial of the kin relations in which one's personhood is bound up. Jackson's narrative of the year 1840 tells of,

> a tall young man, about twenty years old . . . somewhat ailing, but not at all emaciated . . . I . . . asked him where he was going . . . he answered that he was going to be buried. I observed that he was not dead yet, but he said he soon should be dead when he was put under ground. I asked him why he was going to be buried? He said it was

three days since he had eaten anything, and consequently he was getting very thin; and that if he lived any longer he would be much thinner, and then the women would call him a 'lila' (skeleton [thin]), and laugh at him. I said he was a fool to throw himself away for fear of being laughed at . . . he told me I knew nothing about it, and that I must not compare him to a white man, who was generally insensible to all shame, and did not care how much he was laughed at (Jackson 1967).

Jackson goes on to describe how the young man walked to his grave, followed by his parents, sister and other relations: 'His father then announced to him . . . that the grave was completed, and asked him, in rather a surly tone, if he was not ready by this time. The mother then *nosed* [i.e. sniff-kissed] him, and likewise the sister.'

The young man asked for a drink of water, which his father fetched with the remark that the young man was as much trouble in death as he was in life; the young man then said he would rather be strangled than smothered in the grave.

His father became excessively angry, and, spreading the mat at the bottom of the grave, told the son to die 'faka tamata' (like a man [a person]) when he stepped into the grave . . . and lay down on his back with the whale's tooth in his hands, which were clasped across his belly. The spare sides of the mats were lapped over him so as to prevent the earth from getting to his body, and then . . . earth was shovelled in upon him as quickly as possible.[1]

Here shame and anger are juxtaposed as dimensions of one another. The young man was ashamed of himself, of his own person; his shame was a transformation of an anger whose only object could be himself; he made this plain in willing his own death. The young man's reference to women laughing at him leads me to speculate that his refusal to eat was caused by thwarted desire – *dodomo*, whose root is the same as that for throat, sexual desire in a man being expressed as a desire 'to eat'; in sexual intercourse the woman is the man's food, he eats and she is consumed. So, till today, thwarted desire combined with a loss of appetite is a sign that one is 'lovesick'; this is a serious condition for it turns a man's desire in on itself. So one who is humiliated by a refusal may give up eating. Shame, unlike anger, is self-consuming for it can have no external object.

This becomes plain when we compare the father's passions with his son's. In wilfully choosing to die, in refusing to eat, in being as much trouble in death as in life, the young man shamed his father, because in doing so he at once denied and usurped his father's authority. In insisting on his son's self-sacrifice, however, the father converted his own shame into anger, making another its object, and in so doing asserted his own personhood.

The young man, Jackson tells us, was 'nosed' by his mother and sister before he lay down in his grave. Till today, mortuary ceremonies or *reguregu* (literally 'sniff-kissing') evoke an idea of consumption by smell. The corpse is laid out on the floor of a house in the honoured place above, and just before the coffin is closed and removed for burial, the close kin of the dead come one by one, press their noses against the cheek or forehead of the corpse and sniff deeply, taking into themselves its sweet rotting smell. This ceremony implies that, in the past, death as a radical conversion of substance was pivotal to the cycles of consumption and exchange between the people and the land. The intangible substance of the dead was consumed by their living kin and their tangible substance was buried on ancestral land or in the foundations of houses.

Every death was a sacrifice; to cease to consume or to be unable to compel others to feed one was a sign not only that one's *yalo* was no longer effective, but that the land demanded the sacrifice of death and the return of its own substance from those who could no longer make it produce. So, once begun, the process of death could not be interfered with – which explains why those who fell from a canoe into the sea were not saved by their fellows and were caught, sacrificed and eaten if seen by people who were not their own kin, and why missionaries found it so difficult to reprieve people whose kin were on the point of strangling them or burying them alive. Only when they began to offer whales' teeth as what they saw as 'payment', but which Fijians understood as the substitution of one sacrificial object with another, did missionaries begin to succeed.

Vanua may refer to a land or place, a confederation of villages, or the people who occupy them. People are holders and users (*i taukei*, owners) of land, but this birthright is grounded in an idea of people as materially belonging to the land, so being an owner does not allow one to alienate it, though in the past one might gift land to kin, for example as part of marriage exchanges. Ultimate ownership of the land rested with the ancestors who formed and shaped it; their *mana*, immanent in the land, was made material in the fertility of land, people and paramount chief. The people (*lewe ni vanua*, literally 'flesh of the land') were the land's very substance; they gardened and fished, consumed the products of their labour and exchanged them in terms of a balanced reciprocity between land and sea. At the same time they rendered certain relations hierarchical through the transformation in ritual of balanced reciprocal exchange into tribute and thus constituted husbands as heads of houses and certain heads of houses as chiefs.[2] The sacrifice of death broke the cycle of exchange and tribute between people, and between people and the land, for the dead were removed from those exchanges between kin to become objects of consumption. Consuming the food products of the land fuelled the living and created the heat of sexual desire that produced children; just so the land's eventual consumption of the dead constituted the ancestral *mana* that drove the entire process.[3]

Sacrifice and Cannibalism

To refuse to eat is a denial of kinship, but cannibalism (*veikanikani*, literally 'eating one another') is an annihilation at once of kinship and personhood, and as such it is the most powerful of Fijian tropes. So it is instructive to compare consumption by smell of the sacrifice that is death in one's own place, with the cannibal sacrifice and its consumption.

Nineteenth-century missionaries in Fiji were at one in describing Fijians as 'great cannibals', but their squeamishness was such that they declined to leave us many details. The fullest accounts are written mostly by sailors. Jackson's 1840 *Narrative* tells of an encounter between men sent by Tui Cakau, paramount of Cakaudrove to aid a lesser chief, Tui Mativata, in responding to the challenges of the men of the island of Male, who relied on the safety of their inaccessible mountain village 'to commit great depredations on the mainland, taking off women as prisoners, and killing the men for food'. He tells how the invading war party and the defenders of Male taunted each other and how three of the Male men were thus enticed down the path and killed.

As soon as we were close enough to distinguish the natives on the mountain we saw that they were 'bole' (challenging) by their antics and beckoning to us with their hands . . . we made out their speech of defiance to be, that they were extremely tired of waiting for us, especially as they had anticipated this visit so long . . . Each party continued for some time this kind of banter to each other, till three of the Male people ventured halfway down the path and dared any or all to come up. As they were shaking their 'masi' (or waist-belts) behind them in the most deriding manner, all our party that had muskets fired and killed the three . . .

The dead bodies were set up in a row on their hinder parts, with a pole rove through their legs, just under their knees, to keep them in a sitting posture on the bows of the canoe. We then pushed off . . . The drums then were kept beating all the way. We soon reached Mouta . . .

The bodies, which were painted with vermilion and soot, were carefully handed out, and placed in the . . . square, between the king's house and the bure. Then an old man advanced up to them, and laying his hand on each (everybody being present, and not a sound to be heard), he began by talking to the bodies in a low tone, asking each, while he held one of their hands in his own, 'Why he had been so rash in coming so far down the hill? that he was extremely sorry to see him in such a predicament; and whether he did not feel ashamed of himself now that he was obliged to encounter the gaze of such a crowd, and especially when he reflected on the challenging antics he had been cutting such a very little time ago?' . . .

The old orator commenced his bantering in a low tone, but kept raising it as he became more excited, and waxed warm with his eloquence, till at last he had to call out as loud as his lungs would admit. To finish off with success he kicked the bodies down as they were sitting up in such formal order, and then ran off, the air ringing with the shouts and bursts of laughter of the spectators; while the bodies were dragged along by one leg, or an arm, or any other part that could be first caught hold of, over stones, through sloughs, or anything else, the more obstructions encountered the better for the general amusement.

Only then were the dead bodies taken to the temple to be offered to the ancestors and the high chief as their living instantiation.

Implicit in this account is an opposition between the anger that fuels courage and the shame that is the mark of fear. *Bolebole* or challenging was an intrinsic aspect of this kind of fighting. The mutual taunting was explicitly understood to arouse anger in both parties. It further suggests that, pending the outcome of the fight, the two sides had to be regarded as independent of one another and thus as equals. The taunting of the living before the fight mirrored the taunting of the dead after it; indeed both the challenging before the fight and the behaviour of the orator are suggestive of the joking that is appropriate between people who, as cross-cousins (potential marriage partners or siblings in law) are one another's equals irrespective of rank, seniority or gender.

If the orator's mockery of the dead began on this joking note between equals, it ended on one that showed the dead to be degraded slaves, for whatever their status in their own *vanua* (land or country) and irrespective of whether they were taken dead or alive, those captured in war were by definition *kaisi*, without status; precisely because they and their gods were seen to be ineffective. Thus the conquering of one *vanua* by another in warfare might annihilate the efficacy of its original ancestors and render their descendants *kaisi*, often translated as 'slaves'.

People taken captive were presented as tribute to the victorious party's paramount chief. As *kaisi* or descendants of *kaisi*, they might be sacrificed to form the living rollers over which a chiefly canoe was first launched, and on such occasions as the building of a chief's house when they were buried upright and alive, clasping in their arms its corner posts. Cannibal sacrifices not only followed warfare, but were required as gifts for a high chief's allies – the chiefs of other confederations – and routinely marked ritual occasions such as the celebration of high status visitors. Thus the 'the flesh of the land' – but of land that was not one's own, for one did not eat close kin – was directly consumed by the high chief and his peers.

These data refer primarily to the great chiefdoms of Bau, Rewa, Cakaudrove and to some extent to Lakeba, which between them carved up central, northern and eastern Fiji. The escalating terror practised by these chiefs in the eighteenth and early nineteenth centuries can be understood as a deliberate attempt to render hierarchy absolute and thus secure their status as paramounts in a situation where the political economy of daily life rested on competitive equality between houses, between *yavusa* (groups of houses closely related by descent or marriage) and between *vanua* (lands or countries).

The tension between hierarchy and equality given respectively by relations between kin *within* the household and kin relations between cross-cousins as affines *across* households can be historically related to the nature of chiefship. High chiefs are associated on the one hand with relations within the household and on the other with affinity. By virtue of drinking the installation *yaqona* a high chief becomes the leader of the *vanua* whose image in *yaqona*-drinking ritual is that of 'the household' writ large. At the same time, in both myth and history, the first high chief is represented as a foreigner from over the sea who married a daughter of the indigenous land chief and was later installed by him as paramount. But the high chief and his descendants rule thereafter only by consent of the landspeople; so the *mana* that lies with the land chief as head of the clan who 'makes the chief' is crucial.

In *yaqona*-drinking the paramount is seen to take precedence over and to be above others just as, within the household, a man is seen to take precedence over and to be above his wife. *Yaqona*-drinking in part constitutes the *mana* (literally 'effectiveness') of chiefs for it is the medium of their embodiment of the efficacy of their ancestors, which is immanent in the land and the source of fertility and abundance. The perceived subordination of wife to husband itself depends on the ritual transformation of the equality of cross-cousins into the hierarchy of marriage and is effected not only in the marriage ceremonies themselves, but on a daily basis in the conduct of every meal (Toren 1990: 52–64). The exchange relations between spouses are complementary and balanced; but at meals the wife sits below her husband, serves him, and eats only when he has finished. The ritual transformation of balanced reciprocity across households into tribute to chiefs that takes place on a daily basis in *yaqona*-drinking has the appearance of being fully effective only in the ceremony of the installation. Nevertheless the land chief whose *mana* allows him to install the paramount retains his own efficacy undiminished.

His installation made a chief at once the object of sacrifice and the sacrifice itself; in drinking the installation *yaqona* he died as a man to be reborn as a living god 'with all the ancestors at his back' (Sahlins 1983; Toren 1990: 100–18). His sacrifice rendered the *yaqona* root he received as tribute a medium for the conversion of immanent and dangerous ancestral *mana* into a material form whose effects could be known by the lesser chiefs (married men) who drank after him.

Drinking *yaqona* together and eating the bodies dead captives were the two activities that distinguished married men collectively as chiefs, *turaga*, and young men as warriors; for neither women nor *kaisi* were allowed to partake. Women's involvement in cannibal sacrifice consisted in their deriding of the dead.

This was a great day at Bona-ra-ra . . . This tribe had not only been successful in their attack upon their enemy, but had succeeded in securing the slain . . . I noticed that a very particular interest was taken in one of the dead savages, and there were none present who talked louder or expressed more vehement gestures, or savage feeling, than an old woman . . . [S]ome time previous this tribe had made war with the Andre-getta people, and the son of this old woman was a young chief in the fight and was slain; and it was believed that this individual had killed him . . .

This old female savage went to her hut and brought all the property of her late son; such as sleeping mats, tappa, i-fow carlic, angona-dish, and some other little furniture which make up the necessaries of a chief's dwelling. The angona bowl was placed near the head of the dead savage; a bamboo of water was brought and laid by his side, when several young men after well rinsing their mouths were employed in chewing and preparing a bowl of angona. After the drink was made ready this old savage after a short speech from the priest . . . took her small dish full of the liquor and presenting it to the lips of the dead savage bade him drink. No sooner was this done than a general yell ran through the tribe - 'Amba cula boy thu-ie', [*A bakola boi ca*] he is a stinking dead man. She then dashed the liquor in his face and broke the dish in pieces upon it. She then took up her bamboo of water, and removing the tuft of grass from the end placed it also to the mouth of the dead man and again bade him drink. A repetition of the same ceremony was gone through with, when she poured all the water upon his face and then broke the bamboo in pieces upon his head, and told the men to take it to cut him up with . . .

The head of the savage on whom this ceremony commenced was first cut off and laid aside, then the furniture that was brought by the old woman was broken up and placed around it; the fire set to it so that the whole was entirely consumed about the head, and rendered thereby in a fit state for cleansing . . . (Endicott 1845/1923: 58–62).

The evocative power of this 1845 account by the sailor Endicott resides in its references to a deliberate and ferocious mockery of the *yaqona* ceremony. In its full and proper form, the ceremony entails the offering of a full *yaqona* plant to the chiefs as *sevusevu*, an offering that requests that they recognize and accept one; then the drink is prepared by squeezing the ground root in water to extract its essence, and the first bowl is served to the highest-status

chief present, his drinking of it being acknowledged by a clapping
of cupped palms by all persons present; in some areas it is also
acknowledged by a shouted formula. The ceremonies of welcome
to a visiting chief from another *vanua* (land or country) also entail
the presentation of mats and whales' teeth and a feast of pig and
root vegetables.

In the description given above, the *tanoa* in which *yaqona* is made
and from which it is served was placed 'near the head of the dead
savage', which suggests that he was made to preside as chief; the
old woman (mother of a chiefly son supposed to have been killed
by the dead man) takes the bowl of *yaqona* that is served to her
and offers it to the dead man – as she should do to one who was
of higher status than herself; but he is dead, and so she dashes the
drink in his face and in place of the acknowledgement proper to a
chief's drinking there is the shout, 'he is a stinking *bakola*'. The
term *bakola* or *bokola* refers not to any human corpse but specifically
to a corpse that is to be eaten. *Yaqona* is a psychoactive drug and
to be drunk on it is to be *mate ni yaqona*, literally 'dead of *yaqona*'
and each bowl was followed by a drink of fresh water. In this case
the fresh water too is dashed in the face the dead man in mockery
of its reviving qualities and the bamboo in which it is contained is
broken against his head and its pieces sharpened to become the
knives that will carve up his body.

The dead man himself becomes the feast that is offered to follow
this *yaqona*-drinking. He is to be consumed just as (one assumes)
was the old woman's son, whose personal belongings become fuel
for the fire that burns off the hair and singes the flesh of the dead
man's head.

Endicott tells us that Fijians were eager to bring home the bodies
of slain enemies, but it is recorded too that they were equally eager
to secure the bodies of their own slain so that they might be
accorded a proper burial. The eating of enemies helped constitute
the *mana* of chiefs but I argue this was not because, in eating, they
consumed their enemies' strength as such, but because they
annihilated it by virtue of this demonstration of their own efficacy.

Women and Consumption

Few accounts are explicit, but many make it plain that women
abused and mutilated the bodies, and especially the genitals, of

dead captives and that the songs women sang on the occasion of the bringing home of bodies were fiercely sexual. I noted above that in sexual intercourse a woman is a man's food and elsewhere I have shown how women are not allowed explicitly to be subjects of desire, but this does not mean that they are denied agency, for they are represented as deliberately causing men to desire them. Thus the routine anger displayed by younger married men towards their wives, usually said to be caused by jealousy, is the overt dimension of the covert shame they feel in the face of their desire. In their abuse of the bodies of the slain, women were able openly to demonstrate the pretensions of men either to arouse or satisfy them and to challenge the living men who looked on to show what *they* could do. The women's actions showed not only that they were *not* consumed in sexual intercourse but suggested that it was they who ate men, for men's genitals are explicitly likened to yams, taro and suchlike – that is to the 'true food' that men are obliged to produce for their wives and that form the staple element of any meal, and sex is understood to be depleting for men whereas it is not so for women. Thus women could not be allowed to eat the flesh of human sacrifices, for they consumed men on a daily basis; by the same token when men ate human flesh, they might by these means convince women that they were indeed their consumers.

Cannibalism and Compassion

In Fiji the antithesis between hierarchy and competitive equality pervades production, exchange and even tribute. Consumption is at once the end and the beginning of these processes and in pre-colonial Fiji was the privileged site of existential agency. This is apparent not only in the sacrificial and consumptive processes of birth, death, and cannibalism but in stories and myths where eating is an act that is *mana*. For example, the first Takalaigau (title of the paramount of Sawaieke *vanua*) initiated the process that eventually made him paramount by taking up a challenge to eat the head of a *saqa*, a fish reserved to chiefs. Most important in this battle to establish agency in and through consumption were the everyday facts of eating. In every meal in every household husbands ate before their wives the best food in the largest portions; parents ate better than their children; older siblings ate better than younger ones – thus Hocart tells us that a younger son was referred to as his elder brother's 'after eater'. Certain foods, such as turtle and the fish *saqa* were tabooed to commoners – a prerogative of chiefs; of seasonal crops nothing could be eaten until the first fruits had been presented as tribute; moreover, whenever they wished to amass certain foods in quantity chiefs routinely declared them *tabu*, forbidden. Yet other foods were tabooed because they were identified with the ancestors of one's own clan or *yavusa*. Even chiefs could not be unambiguously superior to others, for they too had their peers; and they could not eat their own kin lest their teeth should fall out. Thus, as the locus of relations with others, any given person was implicated as much in competitive consumptive practices as in hierarchical ones. To be able to eat largely and well without shame constituted one as the existential subject of one's own actions rather than as the object of others' – to be fat, *levulevu*, excited admiration. In causing others to feed one, one might experience the act of eating as an agent. This was so even although it was also the case that to give food from one's own dishes to others was to cause them to be fed – an act that marked one's superiority. A child might bestow desirable tidbits on one younger than itself, even while it compelled nurture from its elders; a paramount chief might compel tribute from the people but, to retain his position, had to redistribute it and see it consumed. So consumption itself was *the* arena of competition. Was one the feeder of others or the fed? The sacrificer or the sacrificed? The eater or the eaten? Eating was at once the most banal, the most highly elaborated, and the most subtle of the material acts in which hierarchy could simultaneously be constituted and potentially subverted.

Today nearly all ethnic Fijians are Christians, the majority being Methodists. The early European missionaries, the first of whom arrived in Fiji in 1835, recorded in their journals and day-books a desperate and, for the first ten to fifteen years, largely unavailing struggle to turn the Fijians away from their gods. They could not credit that the people attended on their chiefs as living instantiations of ancestral *mana* and thus as gods, but they knew that success could come to them only through the conversion of paramount chiefs. In 1854 they finally persuaded the powerful Cakobau to convert (he did so as a matter of political expedience) and tens of thousands of conversions followed in his wake. Meanwhile, missionary time had not been wasted, for they had already secured some following by teaching people to read and write, using religious texts as the medium of instruction. They preached against war, polygamy, wife strangling, the burial alive of the old and sick and, of course, against cannibalism – *veikanikani*, literally, 'eating each other'; they instilled in people a fear of the afterlife and of the day of judgement, taught them to pray that the Christian god might pity them and told them they might avert his wrath and be saved (*vakabula*, literally 'made to live') if they acknowledged their sins and repented. They transformed the old gods and the ancestors into devils, *tevoro*, and those who converted ceased to attend on them, that is to make sacrificial offerings. Gods and chiefs were *mana* only to the extent that they were directly attended on and when, with conversion, people came to attend on the Christian god, the ancestors and the installed chiefs who were their instantiation, came under his aegis. God enjoined *veilomani*, mutual compassion – literally, loving or pitying one another – on his followers and so Christianity significantly undermined the *mana* of chiefs, who could no longer assert themselves as consumers *par excellence*.

To understand how conversion might have an impact on consumption and what implications this might have for mutual compassion, consider the following extract from Cargill's journal:

> [25 December 1839] Gross ignorance still characterizes some of the converts to Xianity. One old man in relating his experience said that he was very happy because he could now eat with impunity certain articles of food wh. he formerly considered sacred & worshipped as gods; & stated that for this deliverance his gratitude and love to the Lord were such that he wished to have the privilege of carrying him on his back that he might not touch the ground & be thereby defiled! Gross darkness still envelops the faculties of his soul (Cargill 1839–40).

It seems to me that, on the contrary, the old man understood very well how being freed to eat formerly tabooed foods made him existentially more an agent. That his augmented agency might be the cause of his wish to show gratitude to the Christian god who had shown compassion for him demonstrates how compassionate love coerces a response whereby it becomes a function of hierarchical relations. God's merciful love allowed the old man to eat freely and he, by virtue his continued attendance upon God, would be able to compel continued freedom, and thus assert himself as an agent.

Conversion did away with cannibalism and other sacrificial practices, depriving chiefs of their consumptive power to demonstrate their own *mana* in the annihilation of the *mana* of others. Other chiefly perquisites such as *lala*, tributary labour, were curtailed by the British colonial authorities to whom Fiji was ceded by the chiefs in 1874. Still other changes were wrought by the importing of indentured labourers from India whose descendants today form half the population of Fiji; by the introduction of taxes that forced people into commodity relations with respect to the colonists and partially so with one another and, with independence, by the institution of centralized democratic government based on the Westminster model. Fijian villagers today depend on a mixed subsistence and cash-cropping economy, are for the most part devout Christians, routinely have a secondary school education that allows many to become fluent speakers of English and regularly vote in their parliamentary representatives.

Nevertheless, production, exchange, tribute and consumption are still recognizable as transformations of pre-colonial processes and, as such, still distinctively Fijian. Eating together still defines the household and drinking *yaqona* defines the collectivity; relations within household are still axiomatically hierarchical and relations across households are of competitive equality which, in *yaqona* drinking, is transformed into tribute to chiefs. Both within and across households, consumption in all its forms, and eating in particular, is still the site of a competition to demonstrate agency and, at the very least, to avoid being the passive object of others' actions. Today, however, the consumptive process as an aspect of hierarchy is linked not to cannibalism, but to compassion, to *veilomani*, to mutual love or pity. To be able to compel compassion from the other threatens the hierarchical pretensions of pity with competitive equality. So the evident assertion of the subject's superiority in giving food, clothing, labour or whatever is undermined by the receiver's asserting control as at once the implicit initiator *and consumer* of the gift. Thus one often hears people say of others, of their parents, their older siblings, their mother's brothers – of persons to whom they are subordinate – 'they give me everything I want' and if one asks why, one is told 'because they love/pity me'. It is by virtue of this compassion that what is given *can* be consumed without implying the possibility that the consumer might ultimately have to become the sacrifice.[4]

In pre-Christian Fiji, cannibalism and compassion were inimical to one another since the former connoted annihilation and the latter connoted kinship. Moreover, in the Christian afterlife, all the dead would rise again – a truly terrifying prospect for those whose attempt to annihilate others would then be undone. So the missionary Hunt writes in his journal:

> February 12, 1844. Last Monday a number of people from Gau were brought to our house . . . by degrees we got fully into the subject of religion . . . Namosimalua told them that those who had eaten men would vomit them up again at the day of resurrection. The idea of their vomiting the bodies of the poor wretches they had eaten was quite calculated to produce effect, as to the correctness of it I can say but little. It is certain, however, that these dead among the rest must rise and it may be that their eaters may appear to themselves to vomit them. The idea was I believe quite original. It is perhaps one among many of the notions that one can neither believe nor confute.

Notes

1. The reliability of reported speech in Jackson's *Narrative* leaves something to be desired; for example the young man said the women would laugh at him because he was *lila*, which means 'thin', not 'skeleton', and in this case the term could possibly refer to fear of a wasting illness of the same name said to have been epidemic at the end of the eighteenth century. Further, to die *faka tamata* is to die 'like a person', or like a human.
2. For a detailed description of these processes in contemporary village life, see Toren (1990: 50–64, 90–118, 238–44).
3. For an analysis of Fijian ideas of land, see Toren (1995).
4. For an analysis of the way that compassion and desire are represented by Fijians as constitutive of kinship, of hierarchical relations within household and competititve equality across households, see Toren (1994a).

References

Cargill, D. (1839–1840). Journal. Manuscript. Sydney: Mitchell Library.

Dumont, L. (1966/1980). *Homo Hierarchicus: The Caste System and Its Implications*. Chicago and London: University of Chicago Press.

Endicott, W. (1923). *Wrecked Among Cannibals in the Fijis*, Salem MA: Marine Research Society.

Hocart, A. M. (1952). *The Northern States of Fiji*. London: The Royal Anthropological Institute. (Occasional Publication No. 11).

Hunt, J. [n.d.]. Private Journal. Manuscript. Sydney: Mitchell Library.

Jackson, J. (1853/1967). Narrative of His Residence in the Feejees. In: J.E. Erskine, *Journal of a Cruise among the Islands of the Western Pacific*, Appendix A. London: Dawsons of Pall Mall.

Report of the Commission appointed to Inquire into the Decrease of the Native Population. (1896). Suva: Government Printer.

Sahlins, M. (1983). Raw Women, Cooked Men and Other 'Great Things' of the Fiji Islands. In: P. Brown and D. Tuzin (eds), *The Ethnography of Cannibalism*, pp. 72–93. Washington, Society for Psychological Anthropology.

Toganivalu, R.D. (1911). The customs of Bau before the advent of Christianity. *Transactions of the Fijian Society for the year 1911*.

—— (1912). Ai tovo mai Bau ni sa bera ni yaco mai na lotu. *Na Mata*, (January 1912): 9–17.

Toren, C. (1990). *Making Sense of Hierarchy. Cognition as Social Process in Fiji*. London: Athlone Press. (London School of Economics, Monographs in Social Anthropology 61).

—— (1994a). Transforming Love: Representing Fijian Hierarchy. In: P. Gow and P. Harvey (eds), *Sex and Violence. Issues in Representation and Experience*, pp. 18–39. London: Routledge.

—— (1994b). All Things Go in Pairs or the Sharks Will Bite: The Antithetical Nature of Fijian Chiefship. *Oceania* 64: 197–216.

—— (1995). Seeing the Ancestral Sites: Transformations in Fijian Notions of the Land. In: E. Hirsch and M. O'Hanlon (eds), *Anthropology of the Landscape*, pp. 163–83. Oxford: Clarendon Press.

Wilkes, C. (1985). *United States Exploring Expedition. Togataboo, Feejee Group, Honolulu*, Vol. III. Suva: Fiji Museum.

Williams, T. (1858/1982). *Fiji and the Fijians*. (Ed. G.S. Rowe). Suva: Fiji Museum.

Part III

Changing Life Histories

Chapter 5

A Twist of the Rope

Andrew Strathern

Life-History as a Genre

'Life history' is an ambiguous genre, covering a multitude of possibilities and examples by means of a hyphenated etic category (Langness and Frank 1981). Yet if the current vogue of studies on personhood or the self is to emerge from the realm of abstracted generalities into the embodied contexts of time and change, there will clearly be a need to incorporate life-history materials into our accounts (Marcus and Fischer 1986). This is not to argue for some hypothetically universal construct of 'the individual' that we can apply cross-culturally (Dumont 1986; M. Strathern 1988; Harris 1989; A.J. Strathern n.d.). It is rather, in the first place, to relate local ideas about personhood and individuality, in a broad sense, to local cases of life experience, especially when these cases are narrated by people themselves. Here again, the task is by no means simple. 'Ideas of personhood' that we create for the people we study may themselves be derived ultimately from 'cases'; ideas as discourse themselves influence cases; narrations are selected and translated as well as presented in some initial framework that influences them. To whom is the narrator talking and how does the talk end up as a book? All these are questions to which the only overall answer we can give is 'it depends'. And the only overall observation about the putative genre that we can make is that the idea of a narrated life history is not likely to be one previously existing in the roster of narrative types recognized by the people with whom the anthropologist is working (unless it has earlier been introduced by an anthropologist).

What then to do with such a project? The first step is to dissolve
the category analytically so as to reconstitute it in practice. Life
history is not a unitary category, yet the narrations collected under
its rubric do tell us much about the cultural contexts we study
and inevitably, through their particularity, pose problems of
generalizing. In addition, the forms such narratives adopt tell us
about the ideas of what makes a narrative and how narratives are
variably attached to or detached from temporality in people's
consciousness (Brumble 1988). What goes into such narratives also
reflects strongly the degree and type of intimacy that holds
between narrator and anthropologist – or even the perceived
power balance between them, as when at the end of his autobiographical dictation into my tape recorder in 1975 my friend
Ongka instructed me to ensure its publication, partly so that there
would be a book of the film in which he had recently starred for
Granada TV. His instruction here was in line with the comments
he made about me in the film *Anthropology on Trial*, produced in
the 1980s: 'In the place of the white men Andrew is the professor,
but here at my place Mbukl I hold that title!' In the imaginary
global competition between Ongka and myself for prestige Ongka
saw it as most important that products stamped with his own
personality and name should appear alongside my own – always,
of course, facilitated by me, just as my own writings in earlier years
were shaped by what I had learned through living in Ongka's
shadow among the Kawelka (A.J. Strathern 1979a).

The Narratives of Ongka and Ru

My own purpose in soliciting his story from Ongka and similarly
at a later point from Ru, a friend closer to myself in age (A.J.
Strathern 1979a, 1993c) was rather straightforward. At the end of
my first book on the *moka* exchange system of Mount Hagen in
Papua New Guinea (A.J. Strathern 1971), I had speculated about
future patterns of change: would the leaders in Hagen in the future
make another turn in the 'rope of *moka*' or would they unravel it
altogether? My own answers to this self-posed question have
appeared in a series of publications since 1971 (A.J. Strathern 1976,
1977, 1979b, 1982a, 1982b, 1984a, 1984b, 1993a, 1993b) but I had
wished to gain a glimpse at least of the viewpoints of my chief
mentor and my chief companion, Ongka and Ru, and 'life-history'

seemed as good a vehicle as any to seek this outcome. At the same time I had no wish to impose a narrow format. I wanted the narrations to appear largely as their authors themselves wanted them to be, though admittedly in response to my invitation. In a real sense, their narratives were told in the first place to me, but the notion of a readership in the outside world was also very much a part of their horizons. Produced very differently – Ongka's spoken in Melpa over three days on ten C-60 cassettes, Ru's written laboriously in Tok Pisin over a period of two months – each narrative took a very long time to emerge into a consideration of contemporary changes and an evaluation of these. Ongka bemoaned the gradual attrition of the basis for *moka* in women's productive labour; and both men described the imaginary realm of the 'red box' money cult with its projected transformation of rubbish into wealth by a kind of ritual processing (see A.J. Strathern 1979–80). Neither, however, made my etic notion of 'social change' the *Leitmotiv* of his account, and in retrospect I understand their choices better. Given a chance to tell 'their histories,' they gave me just that: history as constituted by their memories, experiences, and current concerns, their local knowledge, their *petits récits*: 'social change' emerges almost incidentally.

My purpose in this contribution is to draw a contrast between these two narratives in terms of two different understandings of 'the person' in Hagen, or rather two different understandings of male leadership roles. Ongka's account instantiates the 'achievement' orientation, Ru's the picture of the leader as 'mediator', the one who solves moral problems by reconciling people to one another. My point is that *both* schemata are important, in spite of the greater prominence given to the former in the literature on 'big-men' (including that written by myself). Both schemata have been equally challenged and rendered problematic by historical forces that have found their focus in events since the 1980s. My discussion here is intended therefore both to redress an imbalance in ethnographic focus relating to the past and to carry forward my own reflections on 'change' into another set of speculations about the future: another point where I ask if the 'rope' will be turned, or twisted, or perhaps unravelled (cf. Gewertz and Errington 1995).

The Ethos of Leadership: Collectivity and Individuality

A commonality joins these two versions of leadership, that of the Melpa concept of *noman*. *Noman* defines the person, either in its variability or its uniformity (A.J. Strathern 1981, 1994b; M. Strathern 1981, 1988). It is the measure of comparison and evaluation and of speculation between people. Its imputed presence or absence defines immaturity and maturity, normality and deviance. A leader should have a strong *noman*, yet strength of this kind need not result in or be attached to leadership status. Strength can manifest itself in quite different ways; for example, by assertion or restraint. The point is, however, that the criteria here are what we would call 'mental' rather than 'physical' (misleading as this dichotomy is in the broader cultural context). The criteria are not physical (beauty, size, ability to fight); nor do they depend on lineage (descent, succession, blood). They have to do with personal capacities that are essentially biographical, cumulative, emergent and are therefore connected with a life-span. In that sense they are aspects of embodiment.

There is another commonality also. Leadership always implies a connection with exchange in the life-worlds of either 'achievers' or 'mediators'. The moral meanings of exchange may differ, but exchange is still constitutive. We have learned that this constitutive feature does not necessarily hold throughout the Highlands, for example, in the so-called 'great-man' cases (though the big-man and great-man categories have also been shown to fold into each other) (Godelier and M. Strathern 1991). It certainly is, however, constitutive in Hagen. Achievement means success in *moka* exchange; mediation means settlement of conflict by exchanges. The two forms therefore also fold into each other, and collaborative ties between those who specialize in one or the other can build up over time. In a recent article I applied Ray Kelly's concept of a collaborative elite set to some 'great-man' cases (A.J. Strathern 1994a). The same concept can be applied to big-man cases also. Big-men *in practice* do not stand alone within and between their local groups, nor are they simply in competition with one another. They build cooperative alliances, they sponsor younger men, they rely on each other to act for them, they rally round in a time of crisis or disturbance such as occurred when Ongka was physically attacked by younger co-clansmen in October 1985 (A.J. Strathern 1993a: 85–166).

Given this wider point, it is still worthwhile to draw at least a partial contrast in the performative ethos of leadership exhibited by Ongka and Ru in their autobiographical accounts and to note that the contrast is not simply a textual effect or one elicited by myself, but is deeply inscribed in their life careers. It is not simply that the two men differ as personalities or as individuals in our sense, although such differences are certainly present and perceived clearly by their associates. Rather these differences in temperament are linked to role-perceptions and ideal aims in life. Nor is it the case that Ongka is to be seen as simply 'more individualistic' than Ru, perhaps because he obtained more power and influence in his time than Ru has done. Ru also has had highly 'individualistic' phases in his earlier years (when he suddenly became successful as a 'businessman', drank a good deal of beer and had numerous unorthodox liaisons). Ongka, too, is not to be characterized just as an individualistic entrepreneur in the old-fashioned anthropological terms of the 1960s. Over the years he has gained a considerable aura as a leader in collective concerns, as was made abundantly clear in speeches made on his behalf after the 1985 assault on him (A.J. Strathern 1993a: 108, speech made by M., an old leader of a clan linked by marriage to Ongka's). In his declining years, he has retired from exchanges and joined a new collectivity through baptism into the Catholic Church. Summarizing here, we can say that Ongka highlights his individuality against a background of implicit collectivity in life; Ru foregrounds collectivity against a background of increasing individualism in his social milieu.

Ongka's Speeches

A good deal of Ongka's account is ethnography in a standard sense, seen from his own standpoint and knowledge, but essentially a description of aspects of his lifeworld as he has known it (for example the coming of the white men, childhood games, his first marriage, war histories and experiences, personal conflicts – in which Ongka always wins – magic and divination, 'cargo cult,' and his links with the Jimi Valley area). It is in Chapter 13, on the *moka*, that Ongka shows his ethos most clearly, beginning with the sentence 'now let me talk again about how I make *moka*'. He switches into a style of self-assertion about his own agency in the sense of his own centrality as an actor and decision maker, not simply doing things for his group but creating those group activities by his own efforts, his agency as the builder of a conduit, not just the conduit itself (on this issue see M. Strathern 1988):

> I have given war-compensation payments to many different clans, starting a long time ago . . . I have added extra numbers of pigs over and above the ones solicited for in many cases . . . On these occasions I wore special decorations . . . I made these *moka* gifts along with the men of my own clan, the *Mandembo*, at different times and in different years . . . We did all this many times, until it was all completed and I was tired of it . . . I myself became a *boss-boy*, a *tultul*, a *luluai*, and then a Local Government Councillor . . . The times had changed, and I thought to myself that I would take off my bark belt, my cordyline-sprig rear covering, and my apron, and I would follow the new ways (A. J. Strathern 1979a: 117).

This disquisition is a prelude to the description of the 1974 *moka* to his allies among the Tipuka tribe in which he himself predominated as a planner, organizer, and manager. He saw it at the time as his last big show because he felt that the modern generation of young women was no longer fit or willing to do all the hard work needed to raise pigs, but he wanted to make a large gift to honour the local Member of Parliament (MP) who was a sister's son of one of the Kawelka clans and had been attacked in revenge for a motor accident earlier. Ongka phrased the event therefore within the interlocking frameworks of kinship and politics as well as a criticism of contemporary ways, but he took the opportunity, by his own account again, to recite his achievements, done on behalf of the group as he put it. For example, he had hired a tractor to come and re-fashion the old ceremonial ground at his place Mbukl and thus save the labour of his clansmen (A.J. Strathern 1979a: 121).

In accordance with idioms of the 1960s and 1970s, when outside objects and cash were pulled into the sphere of *moka*, Ongka emphasized that they bought a Toyota truck to give away to their ally, the MP, as well as the by now conventional beef cattle in addition to local pigs. He stressed further that his largest named pigs, all called after his own locality-places, Rut and Poklök, were the ones he put at the head of the ceremonial line of pigs stretching from the sacred cordyline tree, thus claiming pre-eminence of prestige. In his formal speech, Ongka adopted both the collective singular ('we' as I), the collective collective itself (we), and the singular singular ('I' as himself), blending these together and running them into one another. He made a personal narrative of finality by lamenting times past and saying that he now ends the *moka*, it becomes like a funeral gift which the MP is to take to the Parliament and himself transmute into a new phase of history as a younger leader who is able to raise money in modern ways. Not content with making the gift as an offering, he also presents it as a challenge:

> If you are strong,
> Later you will make returns to me,
> And I shall eat the returns and become old . . .
> Have you the strength?
> If you bring back strength with you
> From the Parliament,
> Show it to me, let me see it . . .
> Before, when Australia was here
> I worked alongside the white men,
> They helped me and I helped myself.
> Now it is up to you MPs.
> What you will do I do not know.
> Eat my gifts and go.

Finally, Ongka explains that he addressed the crowd: 'This is my show, I am making it here at my place Mbukl, on my own ground. If anyone is willing to come forward and take the knotted cordyline from me [in acceptance of a challenge to do as well], let him do so . . . No one took up the challenge. So I finished my show after very many years of planning' (A.J. Strathern 1979a: 125–8).

The tone is agonistic and nostalgic at the same time, Ongka is inscribing himself on history as a self-invented unique case that simultaneously captures an ideal value of prestige-hunting by action and assertion. The meanings are moral and political, the intent is personal and self-affirmatory or aggrandizing. Ongka wants to transcend the collaborative elite set and create his own myth. The film *Ongka's Big Moka* and his autobiography with his name as title (my device to indicate double authorship) certainly have helped to expand that myth to global level. These two opportunistic projects, then, represent simply an extension of Ongka's speech-lines:

I worked alongside the white men,
They helped me and I helped myself.

Ru: The Production of an Autobiography

Ru's project followed in the pathway of Ongka's. I translated
Ongka's story largely at his own behest, and gave him also $A1,000
(in lieu of a visit to England) from my savings as a recognition
and because no royalties were ever generated from the book. Ru
is some twenty years younger than Ongka, an almost exact
contemporary of mine. I worked with them both from the
beginning in 1964 and on two separate occasions have built
fieldhouses beside Ru's settlement places rather than with Ongka.
Ru got the idea that he would like to have a film and a book as
Ongka had, and my own aims in setting out to fulfil his wishes
were that the book should contribute to the project of polyphony
that had begun to penetrate ethnographic consciousness and was
much on my mind when I was at the Institute of Papua New
Guinea Studies in 1981–6, and that the film should be produced
as a part of the Institute's overall programme of cultural
conservation at the national level. These products, therefore, were
intended to 'belong' more obviously to the people themselves than
had happened the first time (Ongka's book was published in
London, and his film by Granada TV in Manchester). The ideology
was thus post-colonial, and I insisted that the royalties contract
for his book be made out to Ru, not myself, as I had learned that
huge claims of royalties supposedly made from the *Ongka* book
were circulating among the Kawelka and had aroused hostility
and suspicion: ironically enough, since in fact I had paid £400 for
printer's corrections, given Ongka $A1,000, and myself received
simply ten free copies of the book.

So much for the background to production. Ru set to work
sitting at a desk beside me in my office in Port Moresby, laboriously
writing his text in capitals in Tok Pisin on carbon notebooks, after
an abortive attempt to emulate Ongka with a direct narration onto
cassettes. Like Ongka he used a fairly linear style of narration,
beginning with early marriages, but a different moral tone enters
his reflections. Except when he discusses with some moving
sentimentality the death of his first wife, Ongka tends progressively to adopt a 'hard' line. He married wives; if they misbehave,

he tells them to be off. Enemies attack him physically or by sorcery: he outwits them, finds out, pays them back. Ru, by contrast, shows a continuous concern for the opinions of other people. For example, when describing how he made a consolation payment to the father of a girl who had come to live with him but he could not quite take on in marriage because she was Catholic and his own family was then Lutheran (Lutherans and Catholics are not supposed to intermarry) he says that he suggested to the father there should be no hard feelings between them. The father agreed and they shook hands. Ru adds:

> I could have sent the woman back without anything, but I realized that when she returned she would marry a man from another place again and she would tell them my story and they would admire what I had done. Later, if her new husband beat her or was angry with her and spoke crossly she would feel sorry and think 'Oh, before I was married to a good man, and now you're a bad one', then she would remember me (A.J. Strathern 1993c: 6).

This kind of imaginative second-order attainment of prestige through sympathy is quite distinct from the standard picture of the big-man who makes his 'name' simply by excelling in *moka*. I doubt if the refinement would have emerged other than in an extended self-account.

Ru, in general, is much concerned with reciprocity and gratitude between himself and his parents. Today in 1995 he awaits with sadness and trepidation the death of his aged father, presaged by the demise earlier in 1994 of an uncle of his, Rumba. He spoke to me of the serious trauma that occurs after the death of one's mother, as I visited him following the death of my own mother in 1992. Throughout his life history he shows much concern about the moral context of relationships in his complex polygynous family. He mediates conflicts over the distribution of brideprice payments (p. 7). He reports speeches of praise at marriages (p. 16) and also in his earlier *moka* partnerships when his recipients told him he was a good man, for giving quickly and generously (p. 17). He criticizes clansmen who are intransigent in disputes with their wives, beat them and have to pay compensation (pp. 29–32). He stresses and records carefully the division of items from all payments (for example p. 34). He discusses at length and with some humour his efforts to secure a wife for one of his less prepossessing clanmates and added a hard-won cassowary to the gifts made for her, enabling him to claim a return gift when the wife later bore a child (p. 80). In Chapter 13 (pp. 59–62) he outlines the reasons for a particular affinal *moka* paid to a wife's brother Wamndi, which developed out of the sickness of a child and a dispute between sister and brother. Ru's wife, Mberem, had a daughter, Saina, who fell ill with diarrhoea and hospital medicine did not help her, so the child's mother's brother Wamndi came and offered a pig as a sacrifice because his sister was angry with him for not giving her the head of a pig killed previously and the sickness had resulted from her anger. Ru received Wamndi's gift, killed the pig and shared its meat, using this as a lever to repay him later. Small gifts, courtesies, and acts of support followed, all within the context of illnesses, sacrifices, and brideprice gifts until eventually he was able to make a generous return. The speeches he reports are full of appreciative remarks going backwards and forwards (for example p. 62), and the operative term is to be thought 'a good man' (*wuö kae*), not just a 'big man' (*wuö nuim*). For Ongka, the proposition would be phrased in the reverse order of priority.

A high spot of Ru's account is the chapter on the *Amb Kor* or Female Spirit cult that was completed in 1984 (but was still unfinished when he originally wrote his story; the film also is still not completed). Ru presents his leading role in this cult performance as a result of his encounters with the Spirit herself. He is in general less sceptical and perhaps more imaginative than Ongka in religious terms (one could compare their accounts of the 'red box' money cult to show this point, although both acknowledged the cult to have failed). Ru's emphasis is on the collective obligation and opportunity to perform the cult and thus through its ritual secure fertility and male progeny for himself and his group (at the time he had numerous daughters but only one son). Although he undoubtedly did gain prestige from the ultimate performance, it was still phrased in terms of an act of homage to the Spirit, a kind of sacral collectivization focussed on the Spirit rather than the secular collectivization focussed on himself that is projected in Ongka's account of his big *moka*.

Ongka's self-image is thus global and relatively uni-dimensional; Ru's is more local, even domestic and multi-dimensional, involved with the expression of the emotion of sympathy (*kaemb*) and the mediation of disputes that are triggered by anger so that they result in such sympathy if possible. Ru's self-presentation therefore corresponds more to a 'relational' model of the person Ongka to an 'individual' one, a point that is perhaps interesting given the current analytical discussions on these matters (cf. A.J. Strathern 1994b).

Violence and Change

Ongka's politics and Ru's morality have equally been shaken in a post-colonial world to which violence has returned. Ongka 'retired' from politics after he was attacked from within his own clan in 1985 and when, in the succeeding years, the Kawelka were embroiled in an escalating spiral of warfare with their old enemies the Minembi and Kombukla (A.J. Strathern 1992). This fighting was made much the worse by the introduction of guns, a process that distorted the patterns of killing and compensation for killing. Ongka in 1991 announced that at least if he no longer took part in the raising of pigs and money for ally payments he might no longer be a prime target for retaliatory killing by the Minembi, and his entry into the Catholic Church was intended as a signal that now he would leave the fray. (The Church tends to deal – or not to deal – with issues of fighting by simply saying that its members must stay out of the warfare process.)

For his part Ru has found it increasingly hard to ground his own life in clan and sub-clan morality. Many of his neighbours are 'jealous' of him, he says, for his (very limited) success in money-making through small business projects over the years. Old issues are brought up and are made the occasion for inflated demands on him. Tensions surround his friendship with me since I am known to send him money at times to help him with his obligations and needs. Capitalist relations of production have indeed eroded the base of clan morality or exposed its frailties in a new way. When Ongka observed the beginnings of this process in 1974 he spoke of it as the breakdown in men's control over women's labour for *moka*. Ru echoes this sentiment (A.J. Strathern 1979a: 117; 1993c: 83). In August 1994 in a later interview he went further and himself argued that the fabric of mutual concern or sympathy in his area was tearing apart and he chose as his exemplification of this proposition the fact that younger people were now failing to rally round and give to their dead a proper burial, funeral feast, and 'cement' over their graves. He declared that some of the younger men would rather go on gambling at cards and wasting their money rather than making a contribution to the funeral of their kin. There is an interesting and poignant shift of gears here. *Noman* defines the person, as I have indicated. When Ongka wanted to commemorate his love for his first wife, he described how he buried her with care. Love is shown at death if not before; it objectifies itself in its own loss. But Ongka did not, in the mid-1970s, foresee a possibility that burial customs could be threatened as he felt *moka* customs were. In 1994 Ru enunciated this fear, using it to stand for his feeling of outrage that the younger generation now growing to maturity would not have the knowledge or the inclination to follow custom even in such a deeply felt arena as that of burying their dead. Ongka's laments in the 1970s were self-reflecting and focussed on the likelihood of big-manship not being viable in future. As Ongka grows old and contemplates his own death, Ru grows indignant with the generation of his own sons and prepares himself to witness not simply the passing of the *moka* but the passing of what he defines as something tantamount to humanity itself, while opposing that process vigorously in a renewed effort, at the end of 1994, to help organize a massive sacrifice of pigs for the collectivity of those who have died within the tribe in the last few years. Enacting the memory of the dead has thus become, for him, the latest ideological schema for the performance of a kinship-based morality and its associated definition of personhood, seen now as a hostage to history. It is not just 'the rope of *moka*', then, that he sees as twisted, or frayed, but 'the ties that bind' between generations within the clan itself. Younger people do not see things in this way. They see the older people as irritatingly in control still, and sometimes as manipulative. They are seeking their freedom, but do not know what that will be.

Imported Culture, Altered Knowledge: The Context of Religious Change

Generational conflicts and discrepancies are nowadays also played out in the realm of varieties of the introduced religion of Christianity. Lutheran and Catholic missionaries entered the

Hagen area hard on the heels of the initial explorers in the early 1930s (for example, Mennis 1982; Connolly and Anderson 1987) followed by Seventh-Day Adventists in the 1950s and a plethora of fundamentalist and charismatic sects from the 1970s onwards, notably ones belonging broadly to Pentecostalist traditions of speaking with tongues and making prayers for the sick to heal them. With the advent of these sects conflict between Churches, as well as competition between them, has become overt and pervasive. The competition is for adherents and a major counter in the process is the threat that the millennium is approaching and only those baptized in the 'proper' way and possessing the correct version of the truth will be saved. Rumours regarding the end of the world have been rife in Hagen since at least the mid-1980s, and have fed on the turbulent and strained conditions of life in a tribal society exposed since independence in 1975 to a combination of capitalism and patronage-based politics that has conspired to erode and transform every facet of institutional and personal life. Inter-group fights, political riots, gang activities, car thefts, and changing patterns of sexual activity are all taken as portents that the end times are near, and tremendous consternation arises.

Ongka has responded to these new circumstances by joining the Catholic Church, into which he was baptized in 1991. He explained to me that he wished to have a reason to opt out of compensation payments for killings since these exposed him to animosities and the risk of himself being killed. He rejected the 'new-fangled' extravaganzas of the charismatic Churches, predictably preferring the order and hierarchy of an old established Church into which many members of his own sub-clan had also been baptized. Ongka believes that the communion bread that he receives regularly at Catholic services will also enable him to enter into heaven because it drives out or expels remaining bits of sin in his body. He has selectively taken pieces of knowledge belonging to Church traditions and fashioned them according to his needs.

Ru's situation is more complex. He is an active polygynist (as Ongka was in the 1970s – now he stays with just one wife, although two others live in the vicinity) and he is very concerned about the problem of how to retain his wives and still perhaps join one of the Churches. Rue has also been a staunch traditionalist. He believes firmly in the existence and powers of ancestral ghosts and greatly regrets also the passing of the Female Spirit cult that he successfully introduced in his sub-clan in 1983–84. Nevertheless, he recognizes that his wives are all church-goers and that they expect him eventually to convert too. In this situation he rather reluctantly concedes that he might be induced to join one of the Pentecostalist-style sects (the Christian Revival Crusade) since this sect appears to allow polygynists to enter into baptism with all of their wives. The local pastors of the sect appear to have made their own interesting adaptation of biblical ideas and have arrived at an excellent recruiting device, matched only perhaps by the SDA's rule that girls belonging to their Church can be married without bridewealth, providing the husbands are also of the SDA Church. Lutherans and Catholics cannot offer such adventitious special benefits; however, younger Catholics at Kuk have for some time engaged in nocturnal seances and musical sessions in which the participants sing in tongues (to local melodies); and the Lutherans have for many years run sessions at the family or household level known as *sutmang* in which confessions of wrong-doing or grievances are made and if possible resolved between kinsfolk, along lines similar to those conducted in the indigenous religious system. The Lutherans have also adopted the Pentecostalist practice of building small 'fellowship' houses in particular settlement where neighbours can gather for prayer or worship in the evenings. A complex process of diffusion is thus in train, beginning with introduced ideas ('imported knowledge') and ending with a variety of local forms that then evolve in their own directions. Ongka and Ru are participants and spectators more at the edge than at the centre of these processes, which may hold the key for the positive aspects of social organization in the future, although they are also the cause of new forms of factionalism and a growing 'self-Orientalism' about the past (Carrier 1995).

Conclusion: Narrative and Embodiment

It would be incorrect, as I have already noted, to end with a simple dichotomous picture of Ongka as the 'individualist' and Ru as the 'moralist'. I have been concerned largely with the self-accounts or self-representations of these two men and have noted that the re-runs of their performances that they themselves enact in their narratives do lend themselves to such a contrast. In historical practice, however, both men have exhibited both individualistic and relational sentiments, as when Ongka articulates the collective ideologies of fighting and at the same time describes how he personally beat people who opposed his will; or Ru describes with pride how he became an entrepreneur by establishing a tradestore but also discusses how he went out of his way to help clansmen obtain brides. Rather than setting up a true dichotomy my aim has been to show that there are tendencies in these accounts that move in one direction or another in mutual tension. Another point is also of interest here. Brumble, in his study of American Indian autobiographies, has made an interesting contrast between the narratives of Don Talayesva and Gregorio as produced by their amanuenses/ethnographers, the Leightons and Simmons. He argues that Talayesva is portrayed as concerned with the development of his own personal identity over his lifetime, while Gregorio is not, and he suggests that Simmons worked hard to elicit such 'human details' from Talayesva as would conduce to that picture, whereas the Leightons worked just as carefully *not* to influence Gregorio in this or other ways (Brumble 1988: 98–117). In my own case, I tended to follow the Leighton pattern, but it is important to note that my life has been itself intertwined with those of both Ru and Ongka in the wider life of the Kawelka people, so the distinction becomes less clear. In any case, my overall conclusion about portraits of the 'self' is rather different from Brumble's. Ongka and Ru are like Gregorio in not giving a developmental/personality-oriented slant to their narratives, but they are still portraying *themselves* in embodied, local, historical contexts and their style in doing so curiously anticipates and matches the contemporary interest within anthropology in the concept of embodiment *itself* (A.J. Strathern 1996).

Finally, let me note that the appeal of and to embodiment is only a means of opening up a new series of debates or considerations rather than a way of making a conclusion. In following practice theory with its emphasis on communication, experience, situatedness, negotiation and the like, we shift in a sense from nouns to verbs; while in the portmanteau of 'embodiment' we turn a verb back into an abstract noun. Crucial to the use of the term 'embodiment' is the idea of process encapsulated within result, and result as the anticipation of further process – Heidegger's *Dasein*, in fact, representing both the 'thrown-ness' (*Geworfenheit*) that comes from the past and the 'pro-ject' (*Entwurf*) that aims at the future (Gadamer 1979: 113). The idea of the body or embodiment, thus constituted, stands not only for 'being in the world' but also for the historicity and facticity of that being. Embodiment implies that the body endlessly becomes the ground of being as it absorbs the inscription of meanings and acquires motivations from the larger contexts in which people move in time and space. It also implies that there is, in Bourdieu's terms, a dialectic of embodiment and objectification, in which embodiment stands for the immanent and the creative and objectification for the explicit, separated, cultural product (Bourdieu 1977). If autobiographical life history as a genre has something potentially important to tell us, it is because it represents a moment in which the teller makes the transformation from his or her own embodiment to a self-projected objectification. As what is told is a history, both embodiment and objectification cease to be static and become instead the dynamic counters or instantiations of human temporality. The kinds of narratives that are 'projected' in this way can indeed form clues as to the wider constructions people make of their life worlds as processes. Here it is interesting that the theme of 'the development of personality', related closely to the *Bildung* and *Bildungsprozess* theme in European philosophy (for example, in the works of Gadamer and Habermas, see Wallulis 1990), tends not to appear. The child may indeed be the father of the man; but in the accounts of Ongka and Ru, for example, like that of Gregorio, childhood is presented as no more than a brief preface to the adult life-worlds of marriage, custom, and history in which their personhood is seen as produced.

References

Bourdieu, P. (1977). *Outline of a Theory of Practice*. Cambridge: Cambridge University Press.

Brumble, H.D. (1988). *American Indian Autobiography*. Berkeley: University of California Press.

Carrier, J.G. (ed.) (1995). *Occidentalism. Images of the West*. Oxford: Clarendon Press.

Connolly, B. and Anderson, R. (1987). *First Contact. New Guinea's Highlanders Encounter the Outside World*. New York: Viking Penguin.

Dumont, L. (1986). *Essays on Individualism. Modern Ideology in*

Anthropological Perspective. Chicago: University of Chicago Press.

Gadamer, H.G. (1979). The Problem of Historical Consciousness. In: P. Rabinow and W. Sullivan (eds), *Interpretive Social Science*, pp. 82–140. Berkeley: University of California Press.

Gewertz, D.B. and Errington, F.K. (1995). *Articulating Change in the 'Last Unknown'*. Boulder: Westview Press.

Godelier, M. and Strathern, M. (eds) (1991). *Big-Men and Great-Men. Personifications of Power in Melanesia*. Cambridge: Cambridge University Press.

Harris, G. (1980). Concepts of Individual, Self, and Person in Description and Analysis. *American Anthropologist* 91(3): 599–612.

Langness, L.L. and Frank, G. (1981). *Lives. An Anthropological Approach and Biography*. Novato CA: Chandler and Sharp Publishers Inc.

Marcus, G. and Fischer, M.M.J. (1986). *Anthropology as Cultural Critiques*. Chicago: Chicago University Press.

Mennis, M.R. (1982). *Hagen Saga*. Port Moresby: Institute of Papua New Guinea Studies.

Strathern, A.J. (1971). *The Rope of Moka*. Cambridge: Cambridge University Press.

—— (1976). Transactional Continuity in Mount Hagen. In: B. Kapferer (ed.), *Transaction and Meaning*, pp. 277–87. Philadelphia: Institute for the Study of Human Issues.

—— (1977). Contemporary Warfare in the New Guinea Highlands: Revival or Breakdown? *Yagl Ambu* 4: 135–46.

—— (1979a). *Ongka. A Self-Account by a New Guinea Big-Man*. London: Gerald Duckworth.

—— (1979b). Gender, Ideology and Money in Mount Hagen. *Man* n.s. 14: 530–48.

—— (1979–80). The 'Red Box' Money Cult in Mount Hagen 1968–71. *Oceania* 50: 88–102, 161–75.

—— (1981). Noman. Representations of Identity in Mount Hagen. In: L. Holy and M. Stuchlik (eds), *The Structure of Folk Models*, pp. 281–303. London: Academic Press. (ASA Monograph No 2).

—— (1982a). The Division of Labor and Processes of Social Change in Mount Hagen. *American Ethnologist* 9(2): 307–19.

—— (1982b). Tribesmen or Peasants? In: A.J. Strathern (ed.), *Inequality in Highlands New Guinea*, pp. 137-57. Cambridge: Cambridge University Press.

—— (1984a). *A Line of Power*. London: Tavistock.

—— (1984b). Ein Bruder ist das halbe Leben: Konflikt und Wandel in einer Melpa Familie. In: H. Medick and D. Sabean (eds), *Emotionen und materielle Interessen*, pp. 253–81. Göttingen: Vanderhoeck and Ruprecht.

—— (1992). Let the Bow Go Down. In: B. Ferguson and N. Whitehead (eds), *War in the Tribal Zone*, pp. 229–50. Santa Fe: SAR Press.

—— (1993a). *Voices of Conflict*. Pittsburgh: Ethnology, University of Pittsburgh. (Ethnology Monographs No 14).

—— (1993b). Violence and Political Change in Papua New Guinea. *Pacific Studies* 16(4): 41–60.

—— (1993c). *Ru. Biography of a Western Highlander*. Port Moresby: National Research Institute.

—— (1994a). Between Body and Mind: Shamans and Politics among the Anga, Baktaman and Gebusi in Papua New Guinea. *Oceania* 64(4): 288–301.

—— (1994b). Keeping the Body in Mind. *Social Anthropology* 2(1): 43–53.

—— (1996). *Body Thoughts*. Ann Arbor: University of Michigan Press.

—— (n.d.) Whither the Interpretive Turn? Person, Individual, and Self in Melanesianist Paradigms. Manuscript.

Strathern, M. (1981). Self-Interest and the Social Good: Some Implications of Hagen Gender Imagery. In: S. Ortner and H. Whitehead (eds), *Sexual Meanings. The Cultural Construction of Gender and Sexuality*, pp. 166–91. Cambridge and New York: Cambridge University Press.

—— (1988). *The Gender of the Gift*. Berkeley: University of California Press.

Wallulis, J. (1990). *The Hermeneutics of Life History. Personal Achievement in Gadamer, Habermas, and Erikson*. Evanston: Northwestern University Press.

Chapter 6

Biographies of Social Action: Excessive Portraits

Lisette Josephides

Finding the Talk

An unusual if not downright ungrammatical title requires explanation. This chapter[1] is concerned with explicit knowledge: with how a social group acknowledges the actions of persons as a part of the accepted conventions of their common world. It thus gives accounts of strategies of action by which social knowledge is made explicit. A single act of recognition provides little security; acknowledgment must be renegotiated constantly. 'Social action' is clearly key here, but why 'biographies'? Because I am concerned with the kinds of biographies that could be constructed in terms of the activity just described. The term 'biography', however, is too closely associated with life histories of a different kind; so I introduce two other terms, portraits and stories. Their substitution results in a more grammatical title, but they still require definition.

Portraits and Stories

Kewa portraits and stories are collages made up of my representations of people's self-accounts, their accounts of others and my observations of their talk and actions. They are not folk models, indigenous metanarratives that anthropologists collect to give insightful glimpses into people's own understandings of their culture (cf. Narayan 1989). Their excessiveness makes them seductive and distinguishes them from theories whose value resides in their explanatory power. I call them portraits when I am referring to the pictures they present of Kewa people and their culture (what they communicate); I call them stories when I am concerned with what went into their making (how they were constructed and how they communicate). Following on these definitions, the present chapter has two aims. The first is to put together a narrative that brings Kewa people to life through their own words and actions. This is the objective of the two stories to which I must limit myself: they communicate active attempts to construct a social self with its relations. In the process, they show how knowledge of social arrangements is made explicit and thus enable the elaboration of an epistemological point about the effectiveness of social action. This elaboration implicitly questions a conventional theoretical orientation towards some key concepts that we use to describe social determination. For the Kewa at least, 'institutions' such as mediated conflict settlement and local court hearings do not operate as essentially different cultural forms from everyday strivings to achieve specific social ends.

My second aim is methodological. The crafting of the stories inevitably brought up issues to do with the conduct of fieldwork and the writing of ethnographies. I begin by taking up these questions under the headings of observation and solicitation, stories, portraits, and representation.

Observation and Solicitation: The Visible, The Explicit, The Constructed

Kewa stories bring together in continuous accounts various daily interactions as they are made socially visible: narratives of self and other, eliciting strategies and responses, fights, disputes, jokes, gossip. While I don't conceal my presence or at times even my sentiments as I record these stories, my aim is to describe a local discourse. An argument in favour of observation and description in ethnography may seem unnecessary; after all, ethnographers have always observed and described. It is nevertheless worth making, in view of the much-debated shift in modern ethnography. Barbara Tedlock (1991) characterizes it as a move from participant observation to observation of participation. Participant observation is associated with Malinowski's 'scientific ethnography', at once empathetic and distancing and resulting in a dual product: the monograph centring on the other and the memoir centring on the self. Observation of participation, on the other hand, produces 'a single narrative ethnography, focused on the character and process of the ethnographic dialogue' (Tedlock 1991: 69). Tedlock goes on to state that 'there currently exist a new breed of ethnographer who is passionately interested in the coproduction of ethnographic knowledge, created and represented in the only way it can be, within an interactive self/other dialogue' (1991: 82).

I share that passionate interest, but perhaps I'm a hybrid: I also want to argue for the value of observing life as it is lived and recording talk as it is spoken.[2] This does not require distancing and should not give rise to reproaches of setting oneself up as a transcendental observer (Tyler 1986: 126). It simply acknowledges that the ethnographer's presence need not, indeed should not, be foregrounded at all times. Granting that the ethnographic encounter is cooperative and collaborative and creates new contexts, different levels of co-production must also be recognized: Some acts of observation are less constructive than others of what is observed. All ethnographies are founded on a 'dialogical production of discourse' but they also record a local discourse that is not, strictly speaking, concerned with the communicability of the ethnographic process (Manganaro 1990: 11).[3] The recording of a local discourse is the aim of my essay; it brackets its textuality and the conditions of its own production.

This aim calls for a distinction between accounts that the ethnographer solicits for specific purposes and the unfolding of everyday activities in which the ethnographer barely has a role. Thus it qualifies suggestions that it is the ethnographer's task 'to discover the conditions under which informants can talk' (Gal 1991: 191). Gal's remarks refer to the interview context. There of course she is right; informants, especially women, may speak more freely in private, or when the ethnographer does not present them with a blueprint of assumed domains of experience for each sex. A more active (or proactive) strategy would, I think, be problematic. It would imply that we should actively create the conditions that will enable our informants to reveal themselves and their cultures to us. In that case, however, an understanding of the social significance of much talk would have to take into account the special circumstances in which it was elicited. If we create special contexts for informants to speak, they will say things they would not otherwise have said. Contexts may become scrambled, leading to misjudgments about the social relevance of certain talk, and the extent to which certain perceptions inform action in specific situations. For these reasons, I consider people's talk only in the context of how it becomes operational in real life situations.[4] In the story of 'Persons' I watch how Rarapalu negotiates her position. I don't contribute in any significant way to the forum in which she speaks and acts. In the portrait 'Eliciting Talk', on the other hand, I become the conduit for Busi's elicitations. However, responses other than mine determine whether his self-construction has been successful. Clearly the texts of these observations may never 'speak for themselves', but need to be 'contextually situated, socially implicated' (Keesing 1985: 32). My method of contextualization is to bring in more talk and action, perhaps from a different context or person. This is not a dialogic exchange between the ethnographer and the informant, or even a polyphony on which I draw to construct a more inclusive picture of Kewa culture (Devisch 1993: 9; see also Clifford 1988: 43ff). Rather, I want to elicit the strategies by means of which Kewa create the discourses of their world.

Observation and description guide my broader theoretical interest. I don't analyze action in order to discover what it hides or mystifies (as in Josephides 1985); rather, I bring to view the social processes by which explicit knowledge is constituted via the efficacy of social action.[5] To some extent, my findings interface with Marilyn Strathern's. In *The Gender of the Gift* (1988), Strathern engages an extensive body of ethnographic materials to develop a theory of action that discovers the mechanisms that create Melanesian sociality. By contrast, I confine myself to the mechanisms that make social knowledge explicit. Appropriately, my materials are intensive and localized, allowing me to trace a particular theory of action rooted in actions as performed and recounted. The stories and portraits exhibit an excessiveness which breaks up any attempt to give a single narrative of 'Kewa culture'.

Stories

The term 'story' serves as the anglicized form of ιστορια (*historia*), which refers to a narrative but also to the process of finding out. 'Narrative' denotes a mode of communication quite different from explanation. In the sorts of exchanges recounted here, the act of finding out elicits a specific, desired response. We may say, then, that the stories narrate and elicit. In this section I consider the related questions of how stories communicate, and what sort of communication they are.

I shall let Walter Benjamin pave the way. In his essay 'The Storyteller', he distinguishes between stories and information as forms of communication. Information is already 'shot through with explanation'. The art of storytelling, on the other hand, is 'to keep the story free from explanation as one reproduces it' (Benjamin 1968a: 89). The story, not its explanation, must tell the story. Benjamin illustrates these points through a telling of a story from the Greek historian Herodotus. It recounts how the Egyptian king Psammenitus, vanquished by the Persians, retains a dignified self-control while being submitted to various humiliations but breaks down when his old servant is paraded as a prisoner in front of him. Herodotus relates the events and actions with the greatest accuracy but he does not force psychological connections on the reader. This, says Benjamin, is what gives the story power, its ability after thousand of years to arouse interest and encourage speculation and identification (1968a: 89). In his words

> From this story it may be seen what the nature of true story-telling is. The value of information does not survive the moment in which it was new. It lives only at that moment; it has surrender to it completely and explain itself to it without losing any time. A story is different. It does not expend itself. It preserves and concentrates its strength and is capable of releasing it even after a long time (1968a: 90).

As a form of communication, storytelling reveals its message through a variety of retellings 'that slow piling one on top of the other of thin, transparent layers' (1968a: 93). Benjamin reminds us that storytelling is a web, one story tied to another, as in the tradition of *A Thousand and One nights*.[6] The connection and interdependence of the Kewa stories – in fact as seamless webs of life – reveal the commonalities in people's lives, despite my emphasis on personal agency. We shall see in the story of 'Persons' that Rarapalu and her antagonists are bricoleurs in the same spare parts yard, engaged in constructing definitions of institutions such as marriage, and defending their interpretations of the social meaning of action in specific situations.

Benjamin is dealing, of course, with the more conventional stories of the storyteller; nonetheless, his insights into how stories are constructed and how they communicate have a relevance for my Kewa hybrids. Implicitly, Benjamin merges construction and communication in the storyteller's mode of '[sinking] the thing into the life of the storyteller, in order to bring it out of him again' (1968a: 91–2). No mere narrator, the storyteller, like the Ancient Mariner, is personally involved in the story.[7] The story communicates as a lived narrative, teeming with the redundancies and *non sequiturs* which abound in life, since life as activity does not require that everything have a point or be carried to a conclusion. Paralleling the storyteller's appropriation ('[sinking] the thing . . .'), the Kewa actor interprets other people's actions and shows their causal relation to her or his own actions. (Rarapalu explaining why she left Waliya, how she understood his decision to remarry; Busi's reading of men's relations and alliances on the settlement.) In the context of people's lives, the stories communicate as direct action. But action is always more than just action; it places itself within a discourse and provides a metadiscourse for itself. (Rarapalu explained the meaning and intention of her actions, and placed the explanation within a discourse of marital practices.)

When I, as an ethnographer, retell people's stories – now alloyed with my contextualizations – I expect them to communicate as stories in Benjamin's sense. I contextualize them to make them clearer, not to restrict their sense to the Kewa or Kewa culture. They are not culture-bound, as Psammenitus' story is not tied to one historical context. Plucked from their cultural context, their content can still touch us: the interplay between personal strategies and social meanings; the personal dangers, stakes and commitment; the frustration of failure; the intertwining of social and psychological needs; the need for alliance; the suspicion that things might be different, that something crucial is concealed, that individual actors are unfair, that power may cover uncertainty, that personal relations – how we attach others to us – make all the difference to our lives; how social knowledge is created and made explicit; how discourses are formed and enter into struggle; that we can't understand everything, or predict how things will turn out.

If Benjamin's argument convinces us, stories are less vulnerable than theories to the vagaries of fashion. This is not to suggest that they make no theoretical points. How I put the stories together, how I use them to develop an argument for the relevance of this kind of ethnography, implies a critique of other methods of presentation and contains assumptions about relevance, interest and legitimacy. It needs to be said that I did not construct the stories as an architect, who first made a plan of Kewa culture in her head and then selected the blocks to build it. The process was at once more serendipitous and constrained. The random process of selection (what incidents I readily remembered and what first caught my eye while reading through my fieldnotes) was controlled by the structural requirements of narrative, which would not allow me to use an incident that displayed no logical or aesthetic links with its surroundings. If it would take too long to construct a framework to make an incident part of my story, I was forced to discard it. Yet within these constraints – which may be seen as the requirements of intelligibility – the stories do tell a story: the story of people's own discourses in shaping their cultural context.

Portraits

The portraits that appear in this chapter are not of individual life histories. I have referred to them as pictures of Kewa people and their culture. Their make-up and excessiveness allows them to escape criticism directed at accounts of life histories as a Western genre (Kondo 1990; Seremetakis 1991; Abu-Lughod 1993; Behar 1994).[8] Ruth Behar defines this genre as one that deals with the revelation of the 'real truth' of inner life; while her own study of Esperanza, a Mexican woman, was an 'account of physical suffering, martyrdom, rage, salvation' (Behar 1994: 273). It will be evident that my portraits do not reveal such inner truths. Nor is my aim to investigate individual personalities, or the mechanics of personality function in general (Watson and Watson-Franke 1985: 98). The portraits depict real social actions in which strong actors undoubtedly emerge; but their emergence becomes socially visible as a struggle to establish an approved self.[9]

In his discussion of stories solicited from Kwaio women, Roger Keesing questions the extent to which these accounts 'constitute direct evidence of how our narrators actually live, and experience, their lives'. He argues instead that they are 'normative statements about how women should feel and act' (Keesing 1985: 58). Indeed, it is easy to see Kwaio women's stories as 'moral texts'. I would argue that, in addition, they make personal claims. They could be read like the Yukon native elders' stories collected by Julie Cruikshank. Cruikshank was aware of the symbolic qualities of these narratives, but she also saw how the women elders used them: as 'metaphors for explaining their experience' and interpreting everyday life (Cruikshank 1990: 341). Her conclusions inverted Keesing's because her model, as she explained, took seriously 'what people say about their lives rather than treating their words simply as an illustration of some other process' (1990: 1). This is precisely the point. In telling their stories, people do not only or even necessarily reproduce a metadiscourse on a shared culture; they also give personal accounts of their own experiences and perceptions. The portraits communicate these experiences as images that can be seized only as they '[flash] up at the instant when [they] can be recognized'. Recognition is crucial. Like the historical past, every image 'that is not recognized by the present as one of its own concerns threatens to disappear irretrievably' (Benjamin 1968b: 257).

Writing and Representation

Much as I argue that my accounts present Kewa people's own discourse, I am of course their storyteller here. What sort of storyteller am I? Noting Benjamin's distinction between stories and information, Ruth Behar is concerned that, as anthropologists, we do not turn the stories we collect into disposable commodities of information (Behar 1994: 13). In a poignant analogy she compares Esperanza's idiomatic expression of cutting out the serpent's tongue to her own activity of snipping at Esperanza's story until it could be contained within the pages of an academic book. How far is it possible to avoid cutting out the other's tongue and still write something that will arrest the attention of academics and like-minded persons?

At issue here is the possibility of a strategy that allows the subjects of our studies to 'narrate their understanding of the world', to be thinkers, cosmologists, storytellers (Behar 1994: 270; cf. Tsing 1993). Behar mentions two styles of ethnographic narrative, the novelistic documentary or testimonial (such as Rigoberta Menchu's story edited by Burgos-Debray 1983) and the dialogical style of oral storytelling that builds in interruptions and offstage events. Mine is the second style. It includes the context-ualization, open-endedness and multi-layered meaning that makes a story excessive. Does it thereby escape what Susan Lanser (1992: 60) has called authorial hegemony? Lanser is discussing literature, but ethnographers have no less of an interest than novelists in 'negotiating authoriality' (1992: 60). Dramatic truth and aesthetic validation are important for novelists; as 'authorial intrusions' are too crude to work dramatically, they must be built into the novel. Accordingly, the author's comments are validated by being woven seamlessly into the texture of the narrative (1992: 61). This interweaving, however, is exactly what ethnographers are at pains to disentangle, to make the intrusions visible and evident. Legitimacy rather than dramatic truth or aesthetic validation dogs the ethnographer. In the stories that follow I keep my own reflections for a final section. There is no pretence in this that I did not write the rest of the story; as a reminder, I deliberately leave in some traces of myself and my responses ('Waliya mumbled self-pityingly in his beard'; 'Rimbu was visibly shaken'), but it refers back to earlier comments on observation and description, and underscores my strategy to take seriously people's intentionality as agents by attending to the creativeness of their elicitations.

Kewa stories are actions for creating social realities, not information about some other process. In my observation of everyday interactions the path of unfolding events constantly bifurcates, as actions lead to other events, revealing new impli-cations and entailments. Recent ethnographic critiques of linear, structured accounts – seen to flatten cultures and homogenize individuals – recognize this vibrant complexity. However, to 'let the story tell the story' leads to an unwieldy ethnography that constantly slips from the ethnographer's grasp and escapes conventional scholarly enquiry. Nevertheless, the pursuit fascinates the ethnographer, who – to paraphrase Coleridge – cannot choose but follow. Will the story captivate the reader? The storyteller can only hope so.

The Portraits

'Why a play format?' is a question that may legitimately be posed to my mode of presentation. My motive is simple: the play format was the most economic way to present this sort of information. It allowed me to introduce characters in a shorthand way, give background contextualization efficiently, present people's talk in a readable fashion, and keep separate some of my own speculations and conclusions. In short, it made the stories clearer and more evocative.[10]

Many of the self-accounts I collected recount situations dealing with new contexts (plantation life, modern literate education and conversion to Christianity) in which the narrator was conscious of developing an active and innovative agency in the formative field between conventional and social change. The two stories I selected for this essay are not entirely of that kind. They occur in a village setting and concern ostensibly traditional matters. However, they explore different agency and intentionality in eliciting strategies essentially not different from those used in the new contexts.

Persons: Constructing the Self and its Relations, a Story in Three Acts

Characters

Rarapalu	A woman from Samberigi, south of the Kewa area; she speaks a different dialect.
Waliya	Her husband, a Kewa of Yala clan living in Yako-paita.
Karupiri	Waliya's second wife; Mapi's kinswoman and a Yala.
Mapi *Rusa* *Kalepea* *Lepo*	Kewa magistrates in Sumbura village court. Mapi is a Yala, Rusa (court chairman), Kaleapa and Lepo belong to other clans.
Ipa	A kinsman of Waliya and Mapi. Formerly a government translator between Kewa and Tok Pisin.
Yasi *Pataroli*	Two young unmarried kinsmen living with Waliya.
Kiru *Michael*	Two married kinsmen of Waliya.
Rimbu	A Yala big man, kinsman of Waliya.
Rorea	Village pastor, a Kewa from Erave.

Village women: Giame, Kiru's wife Liame, Rarapalu's niece

Village men: Giame's husband Yandi (Pataroli's older brother), Rarapalu's niece's husband, Koipa, big Sipi, Yembi, Pombo, Wasa.

The action takes place between 1980 and 1981 in Yakopaita and Sumbura in the Kagua district of the Southern Highlands, Papua New Guinea. The characters belong to the Kewa-speaking group (circa 50,000). They are patrilineal, patrilocal gardeners and pig herders known in the literature for their egalitarianism, ceremonial exchange and pig killing feasts, achieved 'big man' status, sexual antagonism, and a rich mythic corpus (Josephides 1985; LeRoy 1985).

The story so far: Rarapalu had been married to Waliya for four years. Rumour had it that she had had twenty-five husbands. Village women described her as an outsider with different customs and language, ignorant of proper behaviour and a trouble to her husband. Soon after the pig kill in Aka (a Yala village) Rarapalu's natal group in Samberigi began preparations for a pig kill. Her brother's children sent word that they would give her 160 kina (Papua New Guinea currency), so she arranged to take one pig and go with Waliya's clan brother Kiru. Instead, she decamped the night before. Kiru followed her to Samberigi, where, according to him, she turned down two proffered pearl shells and said she had finished with Waliya.

When Waliya took out summons against her she sent word that she was in hospital in Erave. Waliya complained he had paid double for her. He gave her former husband eleven pearl shells, two kina in cash, and a pig worth 120 kina, and her kinspeople five pigs (really six, but the sixth was compensation for beating her once and the magistrates said it couldn't be counted) and twelve or fifteen pearl shells. She was notorious 'up and down the highway' for never lasting more than two or three months with a man. I asked why he married her, knowing her prodigious reputation and apparent childlessness. 'It's women's power', he said, 'she decided to come and I couldn't shift her.' Then his Church would not allow divorce.

Waliya told his story over a period: Rarapalu preferred to keep her goods and money in the house of Yembi, whose clan originated in Samberigi; he tolerated this because she was a good worker. At the time of the Aka pig kill he gave Pombo a small pig which Rarapalu thought should go to her kin. That was when she left. Three months later she sent word that she would return if he made

an appropriate gift, but he wanted a new wife. Rorea the pastor
told him he could divorce her because of her desertion, but his
kinsmen were preparing for a pig kill and could not help with
brideprice.
Nonetheless Waliya showed brideprice for Karupiri, a widow
with no children. It was accepted and distributed, but the pastor
now said that though the sin was with Rarapalu, she had to
remarry or die before Waliya could remarry. Rarapalu chose this
time to return. A preliminary hearing took place in Yakopaita, with
Mapi presiding.
Now read on.

Act 1, Scene I
The public pre-hearing in the open ground in Yakopaita

Mapi   For a long time this man lived like a widower. His
             pigs had to be farmed out. Yandi's [and Pataroli's]
             mother went to live with him so she could look after
             the pigs. Then he married this woman [*To Rarapalu*]
             Another woman came to your house, didn't you
             think of that? There are many widows about. You
             broke the law of Jesus, and the man found his way
             to us. Your husband and brothers-in-law are sitting
             here waiting to hear what you have been doing. We
             are listening.

Rarapalu   He didn't give me pork so I went. He only gave me
             a bone from the pig he killed. I thought I would eat
             one side and give the other side to this woman's
             children. [*To Waliya*] You little possum, you didn't
             think of giving more; you butchered a pig and gave
             to your own kin first. I put the little pig bone over
             the fire and just sat there. I looked after your baby
             pig, you should give me ten kina, I said. I said this
             over and again, but he didn't give me the money. I
             ate some of the pork, but I got sick. Then I looked
             up and saw the pork had gone from the shelf. I asked
             him what he'd done with it and he said but you
             didn't want to eat it. I said I would have eaten it,
             and he gave me the pig's neck. The old woman
             [Pataroli's mother] was staying here, so I went home
             [*To Samberigi*] and stayed there.

Pataroli's mother gave me a pearl shell. She didn't put it into your hand, she put it in mine. I gave you this shell, but you gave me no pork when you killed pigs. I heard about the pig kill in Samberigi on Saturday, so I went and planted a mound of sweet potatoes. I was hungry for pork so I went home. Then my brother's wife came and sat with me and talked about what I should do. She and my brother saw Kiru, and they told him it was not right for me to work in another man's coffee business [Waliya was not treating her like a wife]. A new law states this. 'If he brings you something, you can go back to him.' That's what my brother's wife said.

I would have come with Kiru, but my brother was too angry. Kiru said let's go and you'll receive shells, but I am just one person. What could I do? I said to Kiru it was not right for me to work in another man's business. They didn't make gifts to my brothers and father. I saw Wasa and sent word that they should bring me my things. For five months I was very sick. I sent word: 'five months I've been ill, come and fetch me.' I was really sick; Wasa came and saw me – the whole Kamerepa clan came and saw me.

Mapi Five months you were sick. Five months you were angry. Ten months you stayed away.

Rarapalu My sister-in-law was angry. I saw many people and sent word. I was about to pay ten kina to fly to Erave [hospital] from Samberigi but missed the plane. I was too weak to walk. My brother killed a pig and gave me [traditional] medicine. When I got better I sent a letter to Waliya. He is lying when he says he didn't receive it. He didn't let me know he was getting married. I was angry because of the pork and later I was sick. I would stay with the new wife too, but he doesn't want me. [*To Waliya*] I looked after the pigs but you married again. This pig Giame gave to Karupiri is mine. The gardens are all mine. You shake and make noise. But I say you can't marry two women. It would be good if you could marry this woman and go to heaven. My talk is done. When you talk, remember Jesus who came to earth and died.

[*Waliya replies that the letter was written in the Samberigi dialect and he did not understand it, that it arrived only the previous week, and that she sent it only because she wanted to return.*]

Mapi	Rarapalu is claiming pigs and gardens. Should she have them?
Waliya	She took all her things to her house. She said she didn't want to leave anything in my house.
Ipa	She didn't say she wanted to leave you. She still likes you.

[*Waliya says Rarapalu must go, she warns him he will pay for it in heaven. Mapi quips that she should have thought of this when she left her work and neglected her coffee gardens. He informs her that a new law states that deserting wives will not taken back. He asks if she would leave Waliya if he did not ask for brideprice to be returned. She answers she would go only if he compensated her. Mapi says they would see about her chickens, her bags and clothes. Waliya interjects that he has thrown her clothes away. He repeats he won't have two wives. Ipa asks with whom she will stay.*]

Mapi	They all said she'd gone. I can't lie; I'll have to say it's the woman's fault. We've ruined the hearing here. But on Tuesday we'll have a good hearing.

[*Waliya protests that she can't sleep in his house in the meantime; Ipa repeats this and adds that she can't go to the gardens or look at Waliya's new wife. Rarapalu insists on seeing her chickens; Rimbu offers to give her her things but Waliya says only he can do that. Mapi says she can't have her things because she is at fault. Rarapalu has the last word: 'They are mine, I'll take them.' Privately, Rarapalu tells me that Waliya's excuse for divorcing her was nonsense; for a long time he hadn't liked her. He had thrown her clothes down the toilet. Also privately, Waliya tells me it's true he doesn't like her, but she was his wife and a good worker so he never considered sending her away before she left.*]

Act I, Scene II
The hearing in Sumbura village court two days later. Kalepea, Lepo and Mapi presiding, Rusa chairing. Mapi begins with a résumé of the case.

Mapi	So you have heard it. She says we didn't give him the summons, we didn't send word to her and the lad did not come for her. She couldn't tend the gardens and pigs while she was away. So one piglet turned feral and we had to kill it and cook it, another he left with us and comes to feed it, and the sow we keep for him. When she left we had to farm out the sow and her litter. He made the gardens over to his new wife. The day before yesterday Rarapalu came back and they talked. We've seen this fashion of coming and going. Now they'll talk again, and we'll decide the case.
Rusa	[*To Waliya*] Are you suing this woman or is she suing you?]
Waliya	She heard what I had done when I spoke up there [at the prehearing]. Let's not go to court, I said. Let's share things out now. I married a new wife when she didn't come. Now she can go back.
Mapi	Now he is telling the woman to go, but she won't listen.
Waliya	I didn't want two wives. It was her decision to go. When I killed pigs I gave her one bone [side], another I gave away and a third I cooked. I gave a bone to her brother. I cooked the head, the stomach, and the fat, and I put it by for her. She didn't eat the pork, she went off in a huff and stayed away ten months. What do you make of this?
Kalepea	Are you the cause of this hearing, or the woman?
Mapi	Tell us right away, are you tired of this woman?
Rusa	[*To Rarapalu*] What were you thinking of when you returned after spending ten long months away? When you went we wrote again and again. Did you consider well before you came back?
Rarapalu	I didn't go because I wanted to leave, really I didn't. I went because I was angry over pork. Then I heard they were killing pigs at home, so I went. In ten months my anger finished and I wanted to return, but my father and brothers were angry and said I shouldn't go. Many people saw me when I lay sick, but they didn't tell Waliya. I was too sick to come myself. I saw Rorea and sent a letter with him. In

	the letter I asked him to come and fetch me in three weeks. [*To Waliya*] In three weeks you married another woman. The letter I sent you tore up, threw it away and married another woman. I cried when I heard he had left me. You know this man's talk is the talk of a man who has left his wife.
Rusa	What you are saying is that for five months you were sick, and for five months you were angry. I planted the banana a year ago, yesterday I bound it and ate the fruit [one year is a long time]. You lived like a single girl; no law says a married woman can go and stay in another place. Did you think of this when you stayed away? Anger lasts for one month, the second month the angry ones return home. Another month and another and another is too many months to stay away. Now, one year later, it's like coming to a stranger's house. You've come like a feral pig from the bush.
Rarapalu	I was sick and stayed away because I thought he would come and fetch me. I was picking coffee.
Rusa	I say that a married woman can't stay away a whole year.
Mapi	A married woman, my wife, goes away. We kill pigs and cook them, the smell wafts to her and she wants to eat, so she returns.
Rusa	Now he has married again so you must find another partner. Look for him here.
Rarapalu	I didn't stay away because I was looking for a partner. Before we were married he carried my umbrella, he carried my radio backwards and forwards. Pigs, gardens, all sorts of things we gave him, but he didn't reciprocate.
Rusa	I understand your talk. You talk in God's sight. I say that for one year you did not live like a married woman so it's truly finished, you are not a married woman. You left your husband a long time ago, and hearing about this or that, about his new wife, or because your own kin were angry with you, you came back. [*To Karupiri*] If he says it's alright to have two wives, will you agree? [*To Rarapalu*] If he says 'I don't want two wives', what will you do? If he won't

	look after you you will have no name, you can't keep his name. You will be like a widow.
Rarapalu	I'll stay. He is my husband, I'll stay.
Waliya	I never wanted to marry two women. I only thought of her as my wife. If I thought otherwise I would have finished with her long ago. Everything I had in my house is gone now. I thought she was my wife, but she ate everything and left. Now I married a woman and everything is gone [in bride-price].
Rusa	They said you were in Mendi so I told Waliya to pay our fares there. I tried to find a way to see you but I couldn't. If I had come I would have gaoled you in Mendi.
Rarapalu	Wasa said you would come and fetch me. I was in hospital [in Samberigi] while you were strolling about in Mendi. Wasa said 'You are still in this hospital!'
Rusa	And if you had died while you were away this man wouldn't have got compensation for you. You left him for five months; a long time you stayed away, seven or eight months or a year. You lived like a single woman and he like a bachelor, so he married again. The village magistrates in Ialibu have made a new law which says you must pay compensation to your husband. We have not adopted this law, otherwise you would have had to pay two or three hundred kina to this man, for one year you would have had to pay one thousand kina.
Mapi	If we applied the Ialibu law we would ask you to pay compensation.
Rusa	You are not this man's wife, he is not your husband. He is Karupiri's husband.
Rarapalu	He is lying, this woman doesn't want us to live together either.
Kalepea	This man says you are not his wife, your father and brothers live a long way off. If a car ran you over here, who would receive compensation?
Rarapalu	It's his fault.
Lepo	He says you are not his wife.
Rarapalu	He is lying, he is my husband.

Lepo	This witness went and stayed away. She stayed for a year, you are witnesses to that.
Rarapalu	You talk about this new law, but there is an old law. In the old days, if a woman was angry and went away they would follow her. But now they don't do this. I didn't say I went because I was tired of you.
Mapi	[*Reflecting*.] It's true that this was the law in the old days. My father told me but I didn't listen.
Rarapalu	Here you've had magistrates for a long time and the new law is in force, but down there [in Samberigi] we don't have the badge [of the village magistrate] yet, so we don't have this law. [*Rarapalu is arguing a legal point but Rusa gives her short shrift*].
Rusa	This man says he doesn't want you. I can't divorce you now. Come on Thursday for your divorce, and you'll get the torn paper. That's all. If you run aground somewhere or work in the area, you'll die with no compensation.
Mapi	If you die we'll say we already told you: you are not Waliya's wife.
Rarapalu	I didn't stay in other men's houses. I've come to stay at this man's house.
Rusa	She is lying. She went and stayed away a year, she comes back a year later and says this, I can't believe her.
Mapi	She forces him to abandon God's work. When you went away you closed this road. There is no way to reinstate you.

[*The magistrate and others express their regrets but insist she'll have to accept the divorce and go.*]

Rusa	Come and take your paper on Thursday. You can't keep your name. If you are killed by a car here, you don't have a name. You have no place here. You will run around like a feral pig, there is no way for you so you will return home. He has rejected you. He can't do God's work while he keeps you as well as the other woman. You were finished a long time ago; you'd better take notice.

Rarapalu	I didn't just stay away ten months. I was ill, very ill. Everyone heard this, he is the only one who won't hear.
Rusa	You went and didn't come back. You were sick? These ten months you stayed away, who told you to follow this law?
Rarapalu	I was waiting for him to come.
Rusa	You are lying. You've come here to lie to everyone.
Rarapalu	If I am lying, he who is the cause of everything will see.
Lepo	No man can take her to his house now. If another man wants her he'll have to go and get her from her home. You must go home. Go directly back to your place, no man of Yala or Perepe clan can marry you. Go home I say. This woman must go to her place, if another man wants her she can't think of it. She must go home. Her father and brothers, her kinspeople must be told and they will listen. If there is trouble her people will hold us responsible. You will go to your home. You haven't thought about your father and brothers.
Mapi	We'll cut this talk short now.
Ipa	The woman looked after the house up there, tended the pigs and gardens we've all eaten from. We are very sorry.
Lepo	This woman who tended the pigs and made the gardens is not your responsibility. Her husband looked after her, and he can get rid of her. The man who is the cause of her being here is tired of her, he wants to leave her. If you want this woman to stop here, you must marry her.
Ipa	I was just talking.
Lepo	Many cases wait – you go. Come back on Thursday.

Act II. Dénouement in Yakopaita

Rarapalu had to leave, despite the misgivings of some clansmen who said that Mapi would be answerable if the new wife did not work well. Eight months later, Waliya fetched her back for that reason. He had a legal right because no wealth had changed hands, but now he complained that both women squandered their time in squabbling. Karupiri beat him too, but not very hard. She only used the tip of the stick, so he said he didn't mind. One day Waliya put in Karupiri's room some coffee he had picked and Rarapalu had washed. She flew at him: it was her coffee, why did he put it there? If it was his coffee, as he argued, he should have put it in his own room. She carried on until the morning, when Karupiri reported she was not her wife and did not have to listen to all this. They started to throw plates and saucepans at each other until Yasi threw Rarapalu out of the house. She grabbed Waliya and tore off his shirt, he responded by knocking her down and beating her on the head. When Liame separated them, Rarapalu turned on Pataroli's mother. She couldn't get inside the house where Karupiri was hiding because Pataroli was guarding the door, so she started throwing stones. An audience from Yakopaita, Puliminia and Aka had gathered. The fight ended when Rarapalu left to take out a summons against Yasi ('you only threw me out, not her'), and against Karupiri and Waliya for unfair treatment. Yasi said to me 'Waliya always distributes everything fairly. Karupiri doesn't nag or fight, only Rarapalu keeps on and on and on day and night'. Rimbu blamed Waliya for not providing adequate housing, as in the old polygynous days.

Some days later I woke up to the sound of Rarapalu's voice. The fights continued for three days until the court sent both women to gaol. Waliya gave Rarapalu thirty kina to bail herself out, but instead she banked the money. Later he gave Michael fifty kina and sent him to Kagua to bail out both women – Rarapalu with the thirty kina from the bank, and Karupiri with the fifty. Rarapalu would not withdraw the money, so only Karupiri was released. Later Mapi paid thirty kina bail and Rarapalu returned home, bringing the other thirty kina which she now took out of the bank. (This money, together with a pearl shell, was presented to Mapi at the time of the pig kill. Both Waliya and Rarapalu claimed agency for this action.)

Four months later Rarapalu was again the focus of a dispute. Her niece from Samberigi had given her a pig and two shells. Waliya had killed the pig. He now argued that since Rarapalu had eaten the pig, he did not have to reciprocate. The niece and her husband were called to the longhouse where the facts were laid out. At the time of the pig kill Waliya had given Rarapalu a bloody nose in a quarrel over sago. She sued him and expected to receive compensation. Waliya argued that he had to keep the disputed pig for this fine, or go to gaol. If Rarapalu wanted her niece to get the pig she should withdraw her charges against him. Several people pressed this solution on Rarapalu. Rarapalu resisted this solution very strongly. The summons and the pigs came on two different roads, she argued. Waliya had to compensate her for her blood; the other matter concerned a loan that had to be repaid. No one supported Rarapalu. The niece said nothing; her husband was conciliatory. As a lone man without kin in a possibly hostile village he would have experienced sufficient uneasiness. At one stage Rarapalu stood over Waliya and repeated in a loud hiss: 'Two pearl shells! Return the two pearl shells!' (This referred to their joint gift to Yembi at the time of the pig kill.) It looked as though she might strike him. Giame and some young girls present did not talk. Other men there were Rimbu, Kiru, Koipa, and Sipi. Supposedly Rarapalu's protector, Sipi did not take her part.

Moods were mercurial. One minute Rimbu was shouting and Rarapalu was on the verge of tears, the next everyone was in fits of laughter (though Rarapalu laughed less than the others). After Rarapalu, Rimbu and Yadi did most of the talking, while Waliya mumbled self-pityingly into his beard. Over and over again they asked Rarapalu to 'throw away the paper' (recall the summons), sometimes as if they considered it a huge joke and sometimes in deadly earnest. The niece's husband was careful to laugh a lot. Eventually niece and husband left, *sans* pig. Rimbu said that when the case came to court he would testify how Rarapalu constantly entangled her husband in costly litigation. Bowing under this pressure, Rarapalu eventually agreed to 'tear up the paper' and the niece returned to take the pig. (Rarapalu later attempted to put the torn summons together, but was laughed out of court.)

Two weeks later Rarapalu took Waliya to court because his pig spoiled her garden. The magistrate (Kalepea) dismissed the case. The gardens, he said, belong to both of you, as husband and wife. The pig also belongs to you both. So how can you bring a case to court because your pig spoiled your garden? Who is to compensate whom? Straight after the hearing Rarapalu and Waliya fought over this case. He complained: 'It's my pig and my garden.' Like the magistrate, he was arguing that there was no case to answer, but he suggested a different property relation.

Rarapalu left soon after this. Four years later I learned that she was living with another man. She and Waliya were not properly divorced, so he attempted to have her and the man summoned to court, but they failed to turn up and he has not had the time or money to pursue the matter. Waliya married a third wife two years after Rarapalu's departure. When I asked when he got this wife, he laughed self-consciously: 'I didn't get her, she herself moved into my house.' She and her sister were visiting a kinswoman in the area, and she took a fancy to Waliya. So she moved in with her sister (who later married Kiru). After a while he wanted to send her back with the present of a pig and twenty-four kina, but her brothers told him this would be foolish: the woman was a good child-bearer (she had two children by a previous marriage). Waliya said that his main worry was to beget his replacement. So he gave an initial brideprice of one sow, five pearl shells and twenty-four kina in cash. More brideprice followed from time to time, especially when their two children were born. Karupiri and the second wife do fight, he said, and that is why he didn't want another wife at first. But they are not always fighting.

Act III. Reflections in Yakopaita, Port Moresby, London and St Paul
Throughout the story we heard Rarapalu insist that Waliya was her husband, while the court argued she was not his wife. She gave personal reasons for leaving him: he did not value her as his wife or acknowledge her place in his relations and affections. She saw her flight as a positive step which offered him the opportunity to make up these deficiencies. Each side gave a different meaning to Rarapalu's action. The court ruled that to leave a husband is always reprehensible and has inescapable consequences. Rarapalu claimed that her flight had a cause and agency related to her perception of proper marital relations. In the end, her failure to tie in Waliya personally decided the issue. All her actions and strategies can be seen as pleas that he should acknowledge and value her.

Rarapalu's childlessness was never mentioned in the court hearings. Privately people referred to it as a disadvantage, but publicly several men, Waliya included, claimed it did not matter as long as a woman was a good worker. Rarapalu never demanded that the second wife should go; her grievances always concerned unfair, preferential treatment. Yet from her story and other women's stories emerges a picture which showed that a wife always experienced her husband's remarriage as a repudiation. Whatever Waliya did for his second wife, Rarapalu saw as preferential treatment. Her reaction seemed an objection to polygyny itself.

Rarapalu's arguments were always attempts to place herself as a person within certain social relations. She operated in a preexisting situation with whatever cultural materials were available, but her actions entailed a redefinition of those materials and her relationship to them. Anthropologists often describe the decisions of socio-political institutions as authenticating a culture's practice. They are the 'final word', whereas daily strivings appear as prevarications or corrections. Here we see, on the contrary, that those strivings and the pronouncements of the village court are not related as essentially different levels of discourse, but, rather, they are different strategies for making claims about relations. A judgement in court is not a final decision or an impartial consensus at which one arrives by following the correct cultural rules. It may be couched in the language of finality and objectivity, but it remains a claim of social reality that seeks wider support. It certainly left a space for Rarapalu to act out her own understanding of marital relations and their entailments, and develop an argument about the sort of wife she was.

Eliciting Talk, a One-act Portrait

Characters

Busi	A young schoolboy
Rimbu	a Yala big man
Hapkas	his brother
Wapa	father of Rimbu and Hapkas
Papola	Wapa's sister's son
Lari	Rimbu's wife
Payanu	Wapa's wife
Yandi	
Kiru	} Rimbu's kinsmen
Waliya	
Wasa	

Act I Scene I
It is evening in Yakopaita. I hear shouting from Rimbu's house. I
see Busi at the water tank by my house and ask him what is going
on.

Busi   Rimbu and Hapkas are fighting again. You know,
Hapkas is not Wapa's son. When Payanu came to
marry Wapa she was pregnant, and had Hapkas
here. Whenever they have an argument, Rimbu tells
Hapkas to go back to where he came from. Their
argument tonight is over a pig. Hapkas gave a large
pig to Rimbu, but Rimbu gave him back a small one.
He promised Hapkas that when he exchanged the
big pig the two of them would share the proceeds.
Rimbu exchanged the pig in the recent marriage
exchanges in Aka, but Hapkas is angry and wants
his pig back right away. He says he will go off and
live in Popa [ancestral mountain settlement] by
himself.

Busi went on to say that another three kinsmen had fallen out with
Rimbu and would not participate in this pig kill. Papola had fought
with Lari over the ownership of a banana tree which she had
planted, but he and his wife had tended. Papola also received
taunts for living at his mother's place; he'd been so incensed he
said he would kill his pig here and then rather than save it for the
pig kill. He had to be placated with money and shells. Rimbu had
also argued with Yadi and Yadi had been on the point of removing
to his own land when Rimbu begged him to stay. Another
misunderstanding was with Wasa, who was not given food at a
small feast in Yakopaita so he left carrying a stone, to remind him
of his decision not to kill pigs in Yakopaita. There were so many
unoccupied longhouse doors [so few committed pig killers] that
no pig kill would ever take place in Yakopaita. The whole of the
previous day Hapkas had been taunting Lari with invitations to
take up an unoccupied door. The way things were going only
Rimbu, Kiru and Waliya would be left to kill pigs. Kiru had vowed
to move away directly after the pig kill. Waliya was not involved
in the fights only because he lived further off.

Act I Scene II

The following day I sought Rimbu's confirmation of Busi's account. Rimbu was visibly shaken; nobody had ever told him Hapkas was not Wapa's son, so it had never occurred to him to tell Hapkas to go back to his place. Nor had he ever said this to the other men. If he had, his clansmen would have sued him for usurping absolute rights over common land. Papola and Yadi would have left long ago, if he had hinted at such a thing. Why should they stay to be insulted? And why should he have wanted them to go? (A measure of a man's success is his ability to attract others to him.) As for the argument over the pig, it was true that Hapkas's was bigger than his, but Rimbu had not really wanted to swap; he had done it at Hapkas's insistence. He had not told Hapkas they would share whatever proceeds accrued from the exchange of the large pig. Hapkas hadn't wanted Rimbu to exchange the large pig because he wanted it to stay in the settlement, but the arguments so far had been trifling. Wasa withdrew from the pig kill because Rimbu, tired of his attempts to have the event brought forward, told him to take himself off.

Wapa's response to Busi's allegations was short: 'A bad wind has blown into Yakopaita, and people make lying [crazy] talk.' Payanu had come to him from another man, but her baby had died and she had just started menstruating, so she couldn't have been pregnant. Rimbu then gave a different account of the previous day's argument – one that had to do with residence and the problems of undesirable closeness.

The following day, Busi received a public arraignment, which reduced him to tears. The previous night he had denied telling me these things, so now he was called to answer questions in the presence of people from the two settlements, Yakopaita and Puliminia. At first he tried to speak to me in English; but I answered in Tok Pisin that he should speak in a language everyone understood. He said no one had given him the information concerning Hapkas's paternity, he had just 'heard it'. (He did not say he had made it up.) When he began to cry I tried to get him into the house, but Rimbu said no, I should not worry about him. 'It's our fashion to cry when we have no answers. Grown men would do the same. Busi must bear his shame and learn to think before he speaks.' One man remarked that Busi should go back to his own place if he intended to talk in this way, but the other men were not unkind. Busi did not even hide afterwards. 'This is just a boy so it doesn't matter', one man said. 'But if a grown man had said such things we'd had something to worry about; we'd have gone to court.'

Act I Scene III Reflections
The reaction to Busi's talk is an interesting aspect of this portrait. Wapa's and Rimbu's denials expressed shock and a quiet anger. Payanu, Hapkas's mother, was not cited or consulted. Questioning her would have been an insult. Rimbu appeared confused, like a character in search of a scriptwriter. Busi had said unsayable things, irrespective of their truth or falsity. Why did he say them? Was something being covered up? There was an uncertainty in the air, as if everything may be other than it appears, but there was also a perverse sort of confidence, as if what may be covered up is not necessarily more powerful, more true, or more real than the social arrangements that are made visible.

In another respect Busi had said the unsayable. He gave voice to decisions in the village, and he did it just before a pig kill. His was like the talk of a trickster or an agent provocateur, or the foolhardy youth who provokes an enemy clan when his own clan is not ready to fight.

The portrait brought out the meaning of 'eliciting talk'. However much Kewa may claim never to know what is inside somebody else's head, it is everyone's constant endeavour to discover the other's intentions. Talk always elicits, probes, provokes responses. It is used to find out from others, to make explicit, to test the ground, sow seeds. Busi's revelations to me were experimental, a line and a bait. He was trying his hand and agency at social construction by creating an important and informative self in relation to me, and testing the waters with the grown-ups in the area. Possibly he elicited and provoked more than he had anticipated, but he was not unduly concerned; he was learning to play this game of constructing his social reality and had made others aware of it.

Conclusions

The portraits I have offered are texts 'necessarily bound within the parameter of discourse' (Manganaro 1990: 15). But whose or what discourse? Though the portraits exist within anthropological discourse because I have placed them there, they also portray a local discourse whose meaning and inventiveness should not be subsumed within the discourse that describes them. I have been engaged in the exercise of tracing what Kewa actions do. Though the portraits show that 'cultural interplay is itself semiotic' (Manganaro 1990, after Geertz), I am less interested in the culture reader's interpretations of these signs (how I came to understand their culture) – or even in grasping 'the native's point of view' (how they understand their culture) – and more in how Kewa use these signs in the process of creating their social lives and culture. Each portrait exceeds my 'summing up' comments or reflections; they, rather than the portraits, are 'illustrative', selecting one strategy for elaboration. Explanation is unable to follow each avenue opened up by the strategies that the story reveals. A reader may decide to follow a different actor's strategy, and thus develop a different narrative. In this sense, my approach is a reversal of theoretical strategies that use stories as illustrations.

I consider action, stories, and gossip, as eliciting strategies that demand recognition and response, sometimes forcefully and aggressively, at other times subtly and insidiously. A good part of Kewa semiotic cultural interplay consists in attempts to make meanings explicit. There is a Kewa form of veiled speech, *siapi*, which is not simply an alternative language, readily understood by initiates; its meaning must be worked out on every occasion of its use. Though *siapi* requires explanation, attempts to understand it often come in the from of action, or by means of eliciting talk. Eliciting talk in this case is an attempt to elicit both meaning and intent. It would be unwise, however, to be complacent about what is made explicit; *siapi* offers its users several avenues for redefinition and retreat. Thus, when Kewa, perceiving the unpredictability of social encounters, say 'we don't know what's in other people's heads', they mean that they must wait for the meaning of their actions to be manifest in their efforts on others (cf. Strathern 1988). Action demands to be acknowledged, but the form of its acknowledgement cannot be known in advance.

The portraits, picturing specific accounts of Kewa social reality, allow the delineation of a particular theory of action that is not deduced from a set of norms derived from an uncovered structure. Rather, it emerges from action itself as it is performed or recounted. My intention was to give an account of what might motivate this action. A major motivation was the acknowledgment of one's social self. When we view the portraits in this light, we see that people did not merely respond to situations; they responded to their implications for the perception of the self. Their actions, then, subverted so many generalizations about social action and cultural institutions.

Notes

1. Background work for this contribution was undertaken while I was recipient of the British Economic and Social Research Council's award number R000231053. I wish to thank the ESRC for its support.
2. In similar language, Condominas (1977: xix) described his purpose 'to render reality as it was lived while being observed'.
3. I hope I may be excused from rehearsing the arguments in the pioneering collection, *Writing Culture* (Clifford and Marcus 1986).
4. For a discussion of talk in Melanesia from a different perspective, see Brison (1992).
5. I am grateful to Rena Lederman for her perceptive phrasing.
6. Lévi-Strauss (1963) stresses the importance of different versions of myths for an adequate analysis. LeRoy (1895), in his study of Kewa tales, emphasizes 'intertextuality'.
7. In a nice analogy in his *Mimesis and Alterity* (1993), Taussig links the ethnographer to the Ancient Mariner, both compelled to tell their stories.
8. Abu-Lughod (1993: 31) writes that her accounts in *Writing Women's Worlds* are not presented in the form of life stories, because this format would have shown persons as isolated individuals, a self-presentation quite foreign to the Awlad'Ali Bedouins. Seremetakis (1991: 7) writes that Maniat women do not present their biographies 'in the form of confession, or journalistic profile, or as an objective collation of facts'.
    Kewa men and women did not tell their stories in the same style. Some gave generic accounts whereas others were more

personal. They told their stories because I asked them, because they wanted to try something out, or because they found it an interesting and creative exercise. Women tended to talk more about courtship, marriage, women's work, the coming of government (in the from of rice, clothes, money, pacification) and conversion to Christianity. Men tended to talk of wars, pig kills, plantation labour. It is part of men's experience to know about wars and part of women's to know about garden and marriage; all of these are important for livelihood.

It is worth keeping in mind that traditional Kewa contexts for self-accounts do exist. One is the composing and singing of *temali*, dirges in which the singer describes (or bewails) the predicament that hindered her/him from sufficiently honouring the deceased, or the respective positions of the deceased and the singer (which debases the singer); or praises the deceased for good services to the singer. Though the songs are formalized, they often contain (auto)biographical detail (see Josephides 1982: 43ff). Another context is that of conflict resolution. Here personal, self-righting claims are more urgent, and the presentation of self *vis-à-vis* the other tends to be antagonistic rather than humbling (the other, in this case, being very much alive). Exchanges in fights also provide personal information. In a fight with a co-wife, a woman will often give details about her predicament, enumerate the proper actions of wives and workers, and evaluate her own and the cowife's respective positions.

9. In *Interpreting Women's Lives*, members of the Personal Narratives Group write 'each life provides evidence of historical activity' (1989: 6). I would paraphrase: 'each life provides evidence of cultural activity'.

10. I tried other mixed genres, which proved cumbersome. Reading Visweswaran's (1994) *Betrayal: A Play in Three Acts* emboldened me to use the play format.

References

Abu-Lughod, L. (1993). *Writing Women's Worlds*. Berkeley: University of California Press.

Behar, R. (1994). *Translated Woman: Crossing the Border with Esperanza's Story*. Boston MA: Beacon Press.

Benjamin, W. (1968a). The Storyteller. In: W. Benjamin, *Illumin-ations*, edited and with an introduction by Hannah Arendt. New York: Harcourt, Brace & World Inc.

—— (1968b). Theses on the Philosophy of History. In: W. Benjamin, *Illuminations*, edited and with an introduction by Hannah Arendt. New York: Harcourt, Brace & World Inc.

Brison, K. (1992). *Just Talk: Gossip, Meetings and Power in a Papua New Guinea Village*. Berkeley: University of California Press.

Burgos-Debray, E. (ed.) (1983). *I, Rigoberta Menchu*. London and New York: Verso.

Clifford, J. (1988). On Ethnographic Authority. In: J. Clifford, *The Predicament of Culture*, pp. 21–54. Cambridge MA and London (England): Harvard University Press.

Clifford, J. and Marcus, G. (eds) (1986). *Writing Culture*. Berkeley, Los Angeles and London: University of California Press.

Condominas, G. (1977). *We Have Eaten the Forest: The Story of a Montagnard Village in the Central Highlands of Vietnam*. New York: Hill & Wang.

Cruikshank, J. (1990). *Life Lived like a Story*. Vancouver: University of Columbia Press.

Devisch, R. (1993). *Weaving the Threads of Life: The Khita Gyn-eco-logical Healing Cult among the Yaka*. Chicago: University of Chicago Press.

Gal, S. (1991). Between Speech and Silence: The Problematics of Research on Language and Gender. In: M. di Leonardo (ed.), *Gender at the Crossroads of Knowledge*, pp. 175–203. Berkeley, Los Angeles and London: University of California Press.

Josephides, L. (1982). Kewa Stories and Songs. *Oral History* 10(2).

—— (1985). *The Production of Inequality: Gender and Exchange among the Kewa*. London: Tavistock.

Keesing, R.M. (1985). Kwaio Women Speak: The Micropolitics of Autobiography in a Solomon Island Society. *American Anthro-pologist* 87: 27–39.

Kondo, D. (1990). Orientalism, Gender, and a Critique of Essen-tialist Identity. *Cultural Critique* (Fall 1990): 5–29.

Lanser, S.S. (1992). *Fictions of Authority: Women Writers and Narrative Voice*. Ithaca: Cornell University Press.

LeRoy, J. (1985). *Fabricated World: An Interpretation of Kewa Tales*. Vancouver: University of British Columbia Press.

Lévi-Strauss, C. (1963). The Structural Study of Myth. In: C. Lévi-Strauss, *Structural Anthropology*. New York: Basic Books.

Manganaro, M. (ed.) (1990). *Modernist Anthropology*. Princeton NJ: Princeton University Press.

Narayan, K. (1989). *Storytellers, Saints and Scoundrels: Folk Narrative in Hindu Religious Teaching*. Philadelphia: University of Pennsylvania Press.

Personal Narratives Group. (1989). *Interpreting Women's Lives*. Bloomington: Indiana University Press.

Seremetakis, N. C. (1991). *The Last Word*. Chicago: University of Chicago Press.

Strathern, M. (1988). *The Gender of the Gift*. Berkeley, Los Angeles and London: University of California Press.

Taussig, M. (1993). *Mimesis and Alterity: A Particular History of the Senses*. New York and London: Routledge.

Tedlock, B. (1991). From Participant Observation to the Observation of Participation: The Emergence of Narrative Ethnography. *Journal of Anthropological Research* 47: 69–94.

Tsing, A.L. (1993). *In the Realm of the Diamond Queen: Marginality in an Out-of-the-Way Place*. Princeton NJ: Princeton University Press.

Tyler, S. (1986). Post-Modern Ethnography: From Document of the Occult to Occult Document. In: J. Clifford and G. Marcus (eds), *Writing Culture*, pp. 122–40. Berkeley, Los Angeles and London: University of California Press.

Visweswaran, K. (1994). Betrayal: A Play in Three Acts. In: *Fictions of Feminist Ethnography*. Minneapolis: Minnesota University Press.

Watson, L.C. and Watson-Franke, M.B. (1985). *Interpreting Life Histories*. New Brunswick: Rutgers University Press.

Part IV

Local Recasting of Christianity

Chapter 7

'Praying Samoa and Praying Oui-Oui': Making Christianity Local on Lifu (Loyalty Islands)

Anna Paini

Works by Barker (1990a, 1990b, 1992, 1993) on the comprehension of the modalities of conversion and on Christian practices of Pacific islanders, specifically within the Maisin group (PNG), have shifted the focus of anthropological studies on Christianity in Melanesia from a critical understanding of evangelization processes to a more dynamic examination of indigenous involvement with Christianity. In the wake of Barker, I shall attempt to explore some changes in the relations between indigenous and European Christian discourses and practices among the inhabitants of a Christianized village on the west coast of Lifu, the largest and most populous island of the Loyalty archipelago, a group of coral atolls east of the Grande Terre, the main island of New Caledonia.

This chapter is in two parts. First, I portray the interaction of Lifuans with foreigners, mainly missionaries, and the different modalities of evangelization of the Catholic and Protestant missions, primarily in relation to the language of evangelization. The process of choosing religion by Lifuans and differences and similarities between Catholic and Protestant rhetoric of conversion are then considered. Village–mission relations are at the heart of this analysis. This section deals more specifically with the Catholic community of Drueulu, my particular case study. In the past this village mission was run by the Catholic Marist Fathers, and Drueuluans still form a mainly Catholic enclave in a Protestant island. In the conclusions I consider the non-antithetical relation between religion and *coutume* (custom), one the one hand, and its continuing renegotiation on the other are underscored.

The sources used here[1] to depict Lifuan interactions and responses to outsiders in general, and to missionaries in particular, are early colonial narratives as well as oral accounts I gathered from elderly women and men. I have been drawn to these narratives to look for clues and traces that could facilitate an understanding of Lifuans' selective engagement with the Westerners' presence, ideas, and commodities. I have not attempted any kind of reconstruction of the past, heeding Bronwen Douglas' warning against 'reinvent[ing] the past as cause of a later present, teleologically designated as effect' (Douglas 1993: 2). Douglas remarks that it can be 'seductive' for an ethnographer who has questioned the monolithic essentialistic, timeless representation of alien societies, to draw on historical sources as an island of safety. The questioning of the production of knowledge applies to our ethnographic representations as much as to these colonial narratives. I have approached these missionary texts aware that they were informed by a colonial agenda, that they represented the 'natives' as a homogeneous group and that my reading is constructed from a specific historical and intellectual location.

My reading of Lifuans' interaction with the outside world focuses on Kanak[2] as active agents in this process, although I will argue that there were gender/sex,[3] generational, and social differences. I will consider how this society has reworked foreign images and messages in local forms and contexts. Christianization and colonial forces did not neutralize local religious and social practices. I believe that many related but contingent factors facilitated and constrained these engagements. Yet I do not want to downplay the role of the missionaries in the establishment of the Code of Law in Lifu,[4] nor minimize the role of the French army in the initial establishment of the Catholic Mission on the island. This is clearly stated in some of the early Marist missionaries' correspondence: '*Si on ne nous repoussait pas violemment, c'est que l'on était intimidé par la présence d'un navire de guerre.*'[5]

In analyzing the articulation between Christian and indigenous elements I do not resort to the term 'syncretism'. Clark (1989) finds this notion inappropriate and proposes that of 'synthesism'. He presents the latter as concerning 'the process by which the cult "present" is constituted through a dialectical relationship with the past, and gives a sense of the possibilities emergent out of a structural transformation' (1989: 186). Shaw and Stewart (1994) have instead challenged the connotation that 'syncretism' has taken in the discipline and propose a more dynamic reconsideration of it. The authors in fact distance themselves from the way syncretism has been used as a category and shift their interests to *processes* of religious synthesis and . . . *discourses* of syncretism' (1994: 7; emphasis in original). Considering the etymology of the term and its changing historical contextualization, they emphasize the prejudice attached to the term within anthropology, too often considered as opposed to anything that is 'pure', 'authentic'. Shaw and Stewart are perplexed by the fact that the alternative 'creolization' has recently gained favour among anthropologists, while ironically the same term in linguistics has had a very troubled history of negative connotation.

My choice not to use the term 'syncretism' should not be considered as an 'antisyncretic' stance (Shaw and Stewart 1994: 3) but rather underscores the desire not to convey the idea of two static categories (the old and the new belief system) in conjunction but rather to stress their dynamic articulation and recombination in new forms.

Selective Engagement with the Outside World

Although the Kanak of New Caledonia do not generally perceive being Christian and following *la coutume* in antithesis,[6] the articulation between custom and Christianity is different from the Grande Terre. This is due to the specific intersection of colonial, missionary and indigenous interests and engagement in the context of Lifu.

By 1841 the Loyalties were constantly visited by sandalwood traders;[7] missionaries, bêche-de-mer traders, the French colonizers, and labour recruiters soon followed (Shineberg 1967: 29). Missionaries thus were not the only mediators with the outside world; traders and labour recruiters also played a role, though again their interests intersected differently in the Grande Terre and in Lifu. These animosities and rivalries were differently configured in Lifu (see below), because of the absence of settlers and the presence of a Protestant mission often accused by the Marist Fathers of spreading anti-French and anti-Catholic rumours (Palazy to Favre, July 1858, APM/ONC 208; Montrouzier to Favre, 1 January 1859, APM/ONC 208).[8] In spite of French annexation the Marists often complained that their endeavours were jeopardized by the anti-clerical policy of the colonial authorities. Interactions with foreigners were taking place not only in Lifu, but away from home as well. Lifuans and other Loyalty Islanders were hired as crew on vessels, mainly British. As Howe stated, '[they] played a major role in maritime commerce in New Caledonia waters and beyond' (1977: 15). They were also recruited to work on Queensland sugar cane plantations.[9]

European travellers to the Loyalties in the second half of the nineteenth century remarked on the readiness of the islanders to adopt Western technology and material culture. The chiefs had concrete houses to show to their European visitors, wells for fresh water, roads cut through woods and coral, horses and carts to transport commodities for exports. Lifuans were responsive to Europeans using selected material commodities in a display of prestige and power. However, concrete houses were reserved to receive foreigners, and chiefs still slept in their huts (Howe 1977: 111). Moreover, what visitors perceived as an emblem of adaptation to Western civilization belonged only to a restricted number of people – chiefs, missionaries, teachers, traders. Furthermore, the use of these European commodities assumed a different meaning in the Lifu social context.[10] A more complex balance of continuity and change thus prevailed than is indicated in the colonial narratives which describe the outright adoption of European goods and ways.

In presenting the interaction of Kanak with foreigners it is important to specify how these engagements were historically and contextually located and structured in terms of the specificities of Lifuan social structure (cf. Thomas 1989; Jolly 1994). Here I consider only some elements relevant to the issues under question.[11] The three chiefdoms into which the island was and is divided seemed to have been larger and more stable political entities when compared to the numerous smaller chiefdoms of the other two Loyalty Islands at the time (Jouan 1861: n.118). Normally hereditary chiefly positions and status were more ascribed than achieved, unlike big-man systems.[12] The use of Miny, a respectful language,[13] today known only by a few elderly people, used in addressing chiefs and high ranking people, was considered a further clue to this stratified system (Howe 1977: 6). Nevertheless Lifuans conceived authority in a fluid way.[14] A rigid European notion of hierarchy contrasted with a flexible Kanak concept, which focuses not on individuals but on relations. Furthermore this organizational principle was not perceived by Kanak in opposition to the notion of reciprocity. This still holds true (see Douglas 1994). In Kanak society, the chief is not usually the first occupant of the land. He has received authority over the people, but not over the land. In fact the first inhabitants maintain the prominent role of *trenadro*, 'masters of the soil' and the associated connections with spirits and the ancestors (Leenhardt 1947; Guiart 1954; Bensa 1986, 1990b). This stratified but fluid system still presents multiple counterbalances to the power of the *anga joxu* (high chief).[15] In the past in Drueulu a check to despotism was represented by *Hneumëte*, which should not be confused with the Council of Elders, a body created by the colonial administration. Social relations thus were ruled by several intersecting hierarchical principles based on ranking residential seniority and itinerary (first occupants/foreigners/refugees/integrated), on the distinction of chiefs/subjects,[16] and on kinship seniority (senior/junior). The relationship senior/junior is a pervasive metaphor for social relations in Lifu. What is specific to this principle of seniority/ juniority is the parallel in terms of respect and privilege between first and last born: the youngest male member of a lineage is called *qatr* (elder). This principle still influences contemporary interaction and operates in daily life. I recall a raffle organized by the Protestant women's group of Lifou in 1990 in which the first and the tenth and last prize were both a hand-made straw mat of the same value. This tendency to counterbalance the power of the eldest with that of the youngest suggests that the notion of hierarchy and rank is not rigid and is always subject to qualification.

The Church and the State

As Kohler reminds us, until recently a plaque on the façade of Noumea's Roman Catholic cathedral claimed that the country was given 'to God and to France' (Kohler 1988: 145), yet relations between the French administration and the missions were tense and complex throughout the second half of the nineteenth century. French governors in the colony and the missions in Lifu competed for influence among the local population. Such tensions were expressed sometimes by their supporting one denomination against the other and at other times by asserting colonial power over the Kanak as in the imposition of *corvées* in Lifu from 1864 to 1870.[17] Even the military intervention in Lifu (1864)[18] was aimed more at imposing French power than at protecting the Catholic Mission (Howe 1977, Chapter 6). This was clear in the ban imposed by Governor Guillain on both London Missionary Society (hereinafter LMS) and Marist missionaries against teaching, preaching or distributing religious literature (Rivierre 1985). This replicated the dispute between state and Church that was taking place in France at the time.

Imposing a colonial order and converting people to Christianity were two overlapping ways of claiming exclusivity for one's Truth. Both projects were validated by the shared dogma of ontological differences between Europeans and other human beings. They originate from the assumptions of a binary opposition of superior/inferior that engendered the conviction that conformity with Western civilization and Christianity had to be achieved: to domesticate the exotic and to normalize it in a European order of things, be it moral, economic, social, religious (cf. Said 1979: 60). Not only was the convergence of missionary and government interests not evident throughout the colonial history of the country but missionaries and state agents differed in the way they activated their projects and accomplished their ends. Unlike government authorities, the missionaries lived with the people, in some cases achieved a vernacular competence, and developed a relativistic view of the indigenous society, which emerges from their texts.

In the nineteenth century the Protestant Church in Lifu was British and not French, and the French Marists remained a minority whereas the Catholic Church had the monopoly on the main island. By the time France annexed Lifu in 1864, Protestant and English influence was strong. The first missionaries to set foot on the Loyalties belonged to the LMS.[19] They reached Lifu in 1842, one year before the Catholic Marists arrived on the Grande Terre. In 1860, out of a population of 6,000 converts the Marists had only 750 followers (Howe 1977: 45). Being a religious minority, a characteristic that has never changed, put them in a different position from their counterparts on the main island.

In contrast to the situation of the Grande Terre, the program of Christianization was not strongly opposed by indigenes in Lifu, from the outset. In fact, while in other parts of New Caledonia (as in case of Balade) islanders became hostile to missionaries who failed to meet their expectations of balanced reciprocity, in Lifu people generally maintained good relations with the missionaries. I am not implying that Christianity in Lifu was simply a question of positive accommodation, but rather that all these facets should be taken into account in order to gain a more diversified representation of indigenous engagement with outsiders than that which emerges from the generalized opposition colonizer/ colonized (cf. Kohler 1988). As Keesing stresses: 'We are as prone to reify and oversimplify and essentialize about the other, dominant "side" in struggles for power as to romanticize and spuriously collectivize the subordinate "side"' (1992: 6).

The environment was another feature that shaped the colonial history of Lifu, as it did in the rest of the Loyalties (Henningham 1992: 13). A coral atoll with approaches by sea but difficult access to the shores, and lacking rivers or streams, Lifu was of no use for European settlement. 'Colonisation is out of the question, as there is not an acre of land on the island upon which a plough can be used', wrote MacFarlane (1873: 4). This meant that the French government's programme of a settler and penal colony that was implemented on the main island and on the Isle of Pines was not applied here or in other parts of the Loyalties. Moreover, Lifu offered no prospect for nickel or other mining as the Grande Terre did. Furthermore, the policy of *cantonnement* (confinement) which began in 1876 on the main island was never implemented on Lifu. Thus the struggles for land that marked the history of colonial confrontation on the main island (1878 and 1917) were absent here.[20] Still, in 1887 the *Code de l'Indigénat* (Native Regulations) applied to the whole of New Caledonia. These regulations imposed a special legal code on the Kanak, defining their status, restricting their mobility, imposing a head tax and forced labour.

Praying Samoa and Praying Oui-Oui

The rivalries between the colonial and the religious order were amplified in Lifu in the dispute between the Catholic and the Protestant Mission.[21] As the first LMS 'teachers' were from Polynesia, in the Marist texts Samoa or *hmi Samoa* (praying à la Samoa) became synonymous with Protestant Lifuans, whereas *hmi oui-oui* (praying the French way) came to be used by Lifuans to mean Catholicism (Gaide to Favre, Mars 1864, APM/ONC 208).[22]

I turn now to the missionaries' rhetoric of conversion. A parallel reading of Catholic and Protestant texts yields contrasting accounts, although they converge in stressing the highly structured social system and what they considered the motives for people's religious choice and alignments. In the presence of a more profoundly hierarchical system, on Lifu, conversion was perceived more as a chiefly choice than a personal one made by ordinary individuals. As in Polynesia and Fiji, missionaries and traders gained security by winning the support of a chief (Shineberg 1967: 26; 1971: 112; Sahlins 1986: 33). 'At the introduction of Christianity this [chiefly rule] was of immense service; for having secured the favour of the king, you were not only safe, but the gospel became popular, and multitudes attended the services who would not have dared to be present, if the king had expressed his disapprobation' (MacFarlane:1873: 22).

Choosing religion became a strategy in the political arena, a novel strategy in reinforcing or breaking from an allegiance. While the high chief Bula from the southern chiefdom of Lösi had aligned himself with the Protestant teachers, a more complex situation was present in the northern chiefdom. In fact the high chief of Wetr, Ukeinesö, was challenged by the chief of Xepenehe, Waehnya, who had aligned himself with the Protestant Church. The political confrontation has been interpreted as the chief motive for Ukeinesö's calling for the Marist missionaries. A mutually advantageous relationship was established: the missionaries seeking places where authority was vested in powerful chiefs,[23] and the chiefs accepting them in order to enhance their political and military prestige. The Fathers could clearly resort to this argument to justify their lack of success compared with the Protestants:

> [L]e plus grand nombre ont pris autrefois l'hérésie, uniquement parce que leurs chefs se faisaient samoa, la religion à Lifu est une affaire de chefferie plutôt que de conviction; je connais des villages entiers où l'on s'assemblait et l'on disait: nous ne pouvons plus demeurer païens, prenons donc une religion, et pour contenter tout le monde un vieux faisait le partage et disait: toi tu vas te faire catholique avec le chef, toi, samoa avec tel chef, etc. et voilà le seul motif de l'élection.[24]

A close reading of this text, however, seems to confirm a greater complexity and flexibility than that implied by the chiefly choice.

The respect for customary allegiance as the motive for the religious choice of Lifuans, emphasized by indigenous narratives, seems to emerge in this Marist text as well. Thus the accounts (discussed further on) pertaining to Gaica (the area of my field work), where the high chief Zeula chose Catholicism after Protestantism had spread among the people living within the chiefdom. This apparent contradiction can be understood only if one keeps in mind that social relations in Lifu are not informed by just one encompassing hierarchical principle but several intersecting ones.

As Barker points out, to focus on the notion of conversion 'is deceptively simple. It may imply no more than a change in religious affiliation.' (1990a: 10). Except for the period of civil war in which Fao (the first LMS teacher) had to leave the island,[25] Lifuans did not offer open resistance to the new foreigners. In Lifu, unlike the Isle of Pins where missionaries were blamed for an epidemic and the sick were hidden from them (Douglas 1989: 29), people regarded baptism favourably. Often baptism was requested by people who were dying; polygynists would give up all their wives but one and ask to be baptized (Fabre to Poupinel, 4 May 1860, APM/ONC 208).

The readiness to receive foreigners was not something new to the interactions with Europeans and not something to ascribe only to chiefly choice. Written and oral accounts stress the place that 'foreigners' had in indigenous thought and society. Immigrants and strangers had been previously accepted and integrated into the local community in the Loyalty Islands (Howe 1977: 35). This fluid way of conceiving and dealing with foreignness allowed people to recast their identity without completely forgetting their origins. In oral histories Kanak still emphasize fluid rather than rigid boundaries. The integration of foreigners is stressed as part of the Kanak way of hospitality even if defined within indigenous cultural boundaries. This flexibility of relations obtained across indigenous social fabric. It allowed people to dissent, to split from a previous allegiance, to move away and to become integrated within another chiefdom by assuming a specific role and named position. Even the widespread practice of adoption can be considered within this framework of changeable boundaries.[26]

The first teachers who came to Lifu were not Europeans but Polynesians; in fact Fao was from Rarotonga. His Polynesian origin, the fact that he was selected by the chief Bula as his *enemu* or special friend (MacFarlane 1873: 27) and used the vernacular language in spreading the Gospel – all these factors were conducive to facilitating the spread of Protestantism throughout the island.

Language as a Tool to Spread the Gospel and as an Element of Cultural Identity

In Lifu, unlike the Grande Terre, people spoke one language throughout the island and Protestant missionaries always made use of Drehu in their work. The importance of Drehu as the language of communication on Lifu seemed to have been acknowledged even by the French. The colony's official newspaper *Le Moniteur de la Nouvelle-Calédonie* on 3 July 1864 published Governor Guillain's order declaring martial law in Lifu both in French and in Drehu. This bilingual official document is even more revealing if one considers that it was published after the order dated October 1863 by the colonial government banning native languages from schools and demanding that all teaching be done in French (Rivierre 1985: 1693).[27] In Lifu this order was implemented in May 1864 when the island was annexed forcing the closure of the missionary schools and of the Theological School, which had opened in Xepenehe (Whitehouse n.d.: 33).

Protestants were largely responsible for translating the scriptures. By 1871 most of the Bible had been translated and printed in the vernacular. The importance of learning the vernacular emerges from MacFarlane's own account as well. Reflecting on his experience as a LMS missionary on Lifu, he remarked that, though a few young men spoke 'broken English', he felt that 'especially amongst a people like this, *language is power*' (1870: 73, emphasis in original) and started to acquire Drehu. Catholic priests did little in this field, sometimes because of lack of support from their General House. Generally speaking Catholic evangelization in New Caledonia did not stress the use of the vernacular, yet from the correspondence of the Marists based on Lifu a more diversified picture emerges. Father Gaide in 1868 noted that: *'Voilà bientôt deux ans que nous avons envoyé notre catéchisme traduit en Lifou pour le faire imprimer en France, et nous n'en avons encore reçu aucune nouvelle.'*[28]

In 1870 Father Fabre wrote to a fellow-member in Toulon again drawing attention to his superiors' lack of interest in the issue. He complained that already three years had gone by since he had sent his Lifu translation of the catechism to be printed, but the importance of such a tool to facilitate catechizing was ignored by his superiors.

It is interesting to note that both Gaide's and Fabre's comments are found in letters addressed to family members or friends and not to Church superiors. By 1894, according to the LMS census, 2,453 out of 5,659 Lifuan Protestants could read. If the concern for learning the local language is present in the correspondence of the Catholic Fathers, however, their eagerness to show that their followers had became acquainted with the French language also emerges, and in the following years all Catholic teaching was carried out in French. This had a twofold effect: men and women who had become Catholic became familiar with written French but less skilled in written Drehu; the contrary was true for Protestant men and women. People in Lifu are very aware of these differences. The way they explain the lack of French of some elderly women or their unwillingness to speak it, is 'because they are Protestant' or 'because they have married into a Catholic family but they came from a Protestant village'.[29] These same women, however, not only speak Drehu confidently, but read and write it as well.

The influence of the LMS meant that English was then the dominant European language;[30] French did not become predominant until well into the twentieth century (Howe 1977: 128). Today many English loan words are found in Drehu, which has also borrowed a number of English voiced consonants; numbers, names of months and other lexemes (Moyse-Faurie 1983: 7, 20). The use of Drehu in teaching and preaching meant that important distinctions in Christian theology, such as the concepts of a monotheist religion, were translated into indigenous categories of belief in the ancestors and in spiritual powers.[31] The Christian god became *caa haze* (the ancestor); soul was presented as *u* (spirit); faith as *lapaun* (which means also to trust) and miracle *iamamanyikeu*,[32] used as well to refer to the spirit of the dead returning among the living. This difference in the use of the written language in the Church is reflected in the religious words used in speeches on ceremonial occasions. Protestants make use of words introduced by the missionaries in translating the Bible in Drehu – *faipoipo* for marriage, *baselaia* for chiefdom, for example – whereas Catholics tend to use the French equivalent more, though the tendency to slip French words into Drehu is present in both groups.[33] The importance for the Protestants of being able to express themselves in their own language was stressed by an elderly man of Drueulu much involved in the local Catholic Church:

Je crois qu'il y a eu un effort chez les Protestants. Tout de suite ils se mettent à traduire la Bible. Il n'y a que les Protestants qui savent parler le Drehu. C'est la manière d'évangéliser. Chez les Protestants tout de suite ils apprennent la langue. Tandis que nous il y a quelques pères qui traduisent, mais c'est pas général. Ils [les Protestants] ont une fierté d'avoir une religion à eux, à cause de la langue. Nous parlons français, nous parlons un langage étranger. Pour eux c'est pas une religion étrangère c'est la religion à eux. C'est bien plantée dans la langue.[34]

The use of Drehu, a clergy composed of Kanak pastors, the fact that Fao was constantly mentioned in the big church gatherings – these are factors that combine to make people feel that their religion is something that belongs to them and not something imposed from the outside. The use of the vernacular is not just considered an element of difference between the two denominations in the past, but is rendered as an essential element of Drehu identity today. It should also be pointed out that teaching in the Theological School is in Drehu, which has become the language of Protestantism on the main island as well.

Making Christianity Local

Today Lifuans consider the Catholic and the Protestant Churches as the 'real religions' and do not perceive them as opposed to their heritage. 'Sects' are perceived as dangerous, however, and in Drueulu Jehovah's Witnesses have been forbidden to preach on the grounds that they disrupt community life.[35] Since 1960 the Evangelical Church in New Caledonia and the Loyalty Islands has been independent of Paris, and in 1966 the Catholic Church in New Caledonia ceased to be a mission and became an Archdiocese within the Roman Catholic Church. Unlike the two Evangelical Churches[36] in which the clergy is fully indigenized, in 1989 the Catholic Church had only one young Kanak priest in the whole country. An elderly catechist from Drueulu whom I had asked to comment on this stated that the seminary in New Caledonia is not operating anymore, whereas the Protestant *Ecole Pastorale* (Theological School) established in Xepenehe (Lifu) in 1862 is still functioning as a Church training school for the whole country. Further, the same man stressed celibacy as the *problème fondamental* (key problem) that explains the lack of an indigenous catholic clergy. The celibacy required by the Catholic Church is not advocated by the Protestant Church, which on the contrary requires that students entering the Theological School be married. This is a very important difference in a society that places great emphasis on being married and having offspring. The catechist's statement indicates a tension between the Catholic requirement of celibacy and Kanak cultural assumptions but also hints at differences in the integration of Christianity into indigenous categories. However, other aspects help us to understand better how Kanak deploy indigenous and Christian commitments (I have discussed how commonalities work *vis-à-vis la coutume* at greater length elsewhere, Paini 1993).

The rhetoric of conversion provides a key to interpreting how Lifuans have managed to reconcile apparently contrasting value systems. These oral narratives are cast in an idiom that does not speak of the abuse of colonial power, an abuse that does emerge in other narratives. Rather they deploy indigenous categories of thought. They all stress customary allegiance and the role of the chief in deciding his subjects' alignment with one or the other mission, yet Catholic and Protestant rhetoric of conversion differs:

> *La chefferie de Wetr avertie par Ouvéa de ne pas prendre la religion qui est en train de se propager à Lifou. Il faut attendre deux missionnaires en robe longue. Il [grand chef de Wetr] a vite envoyé un message à Drueulu au grand chef Zeula de ne pas embrasser la religion prêchée par Fao. Le grand chef a accepté alors que les sujets étaient tous Protestants. Il a accepté par respect. Le grand chef de Wetr n'a pas envoyé n'importe qui, il a envoyé Isamatro.*[37]

Although the Protestant versions ascribe conversion to customary allegiances, they are always framed as a prophecy (see below). This, I argue, reflects the different kind of indigenization process that has taken place in the two Churches. '*Le vieux Walewen (Wetr) avant sa mort a appelé ses enfants: quand la chose viendra du fond de la case il faut la prendre parce que c'est une petite tortue; si elle vient de devant la porte faites attention: c'est une murène.'*[38] Even though Lifuans usually do not speak of the location of the hut in normative terms, this narrative implies that the entrance should face west. The Catholic missionaries arrived at Eacho, on the west coast of Lifu, whereas the first Protestant teachers landed at Mu, on the east coast.

These oral accounts have many levels of interpretation. I will concentrate on two of them. The first concerns how Kanak present themselves to the outside world. They do so by stressing similarities and minimizing internal differences. People reconcile biblical teachings with indigenous customs by framing their religious choice in terms of indigenous rules. Allegiance to each was fortuitous. As a Protestant put it: *'Nous sommes devenus catholiques et protestants par accident de l'histoire, mais nous faisons partie du même clan.'*[39]

Even the tensions that emerge between the two groups when people related accounts of the past are today mitigated by giving for example a 'reconciliatory' interpretation of the arrival of the missionaries. The interpretation given to me by a young Kanak pastor was not in terms of counterposing Protestantism which landed on the south-east of the island, to Catholicism which arrived from Ouvéa to the West, as the accounts told by the elderly usually imply, but:

> *Ce qui arrive de l'ouest c'est le serpent et si vous l'enlevez un jour il va vous manger; et le serpent qui nous mange ce n'est pas le Catholicisme mais l'Etat. Les deux religions sont arrivées avec deux symboles différents: Fao a amené la Bible, les catholiques le drapeau qui était aussi le symbole de l'Etat. Le Catholicisme est emprisonné dans cette affaire à cause de l'Etat.*[40]

His reading of the prophecy is not cast in terms of opposing denominations and his meta-narrative is quite consciously an attempt to reconcile Christianity and custom, so that in a period of political tension, the two discourses become compatible. This tendency to separate the colonial state and the mission and reconcile customs with Christianity emerges in Catholic accounts as well. The interpretation Paul Zöngö offered clearly differentiates between indigenous engagement with different imported values: *'Les danses, tout ça c'est défendu. Tout ce qui regarde la coutume c'est païen. Moi je regrette beaucoup qu'on a beaucoup perdu. On était en temps de colonisation. C'est difficile de dire, mais même les missionnaires, on vivait dans le régime. Il faut le dire.'*[41] Thus Christianity does not represent the outside world. Christianity and custom are both of the essence of internal identity. What is foreign is the mission as an alien institution.

This brings us to the second level of interpretation: the different way of relating the past to the present among Catholic and Protestant women and men. If their narratives reconcile Christian and indigenous thought, when it comes to commentaries related to past daily practice and morality different attitudes obtain. In the past Lifuan Catholic women distinguished themselves from Protestant women by cutting their hair short. A friend told me she remembered when at Wanaham (the landing area in Lifu) women would identify other women as coming from Hnathalo, a nearby Catholic village, by their hair style. An elderly woman very clearly stated the reasons behind strict missionary impositions on behaviour: *'Les règlements étaient sévères pour les catholiques surtout à Drueulu où il y avait deux religions et on devait toujours montrer la différence.'*[42]

Younger women today are virtually unaware of this difference between Catholic and Protestant women as the following anecdote illustrates. When I asked Kamaqatr[43] to recall this experience, I phrased my question in a way that implied girls had to cut their hair at a certain age. Kamaqatr did not understand my question. When I reformulated it, she replied with a tone of voice that implied I had simply not understood, that it was something that had been imposed on all Catholic women and as such there was not a question of age or status difference. Kamaqatr explained that women stopped cutting their hair when the priest residing in Hnathalo (Northern Lifu) allowed them to do so. She could not remember his name, and turned to a younger woman for help. Her suggestion was welcomed with: *'wanahmatra, kalo hilo ka catrehnin xötrei he lai'* – 'come on, he was the one that went down strongly [in the sense of enforced] with hair cutting'. It is interesting to note that nowadays women who cut their hair short are thought to be following a Western style, although Protestant missionary descriptions of indigenous hair styles portrayed Lifuan women in the second half of the nineteenth century as having short hair and, unlike the men, devoting little time to hair-dressing (Hadfield 1920: 138).

Women and men acknowledge that there has been a change in the religious discourses of both Churches and that now they are invited to work together in religious matters; but again this was not the case in the past: '*C'est bien maintenant c'est pas comme avant; ka catr ekö la i[t]re hmi.*'[44] Paul Zöngö explained to me how the animosity of the past and the collaboration of the present were promptly endorsed by Drueuluans, well aware that antagonistic behaviour, as a sign of belonging to a particular Church, was determined by the presence of missionaries. Cutting hair signalled hostilities between Churches.

Both men and women agree that these differences were not relevant in customary work. It is as if there were two spheres of action – religious and customary – clearly separated, both in terms of physical space and social systems: one revolving around the mission and the other around the chieftainship. Even the space for the dead was divided along confessional lines. In the old cemetery people were separated by religion. Today, instead, Catholics and Protestants lie side by side, though still according to clan affiliation. Two elements distinguish their religious commitment and their social allegiance: the presence or absence of the cross and the clan-designated plot within the cemetery. Another plot near the entrance is reserved for young children, whereas high chiefs and their wives are buried within the separate chiefly compound.

People are well aware that islanders have always been divided by different allegiances; they do not recall a peaceful past abruptly interrupted by the arrival of the missionaries but they do cast the disputes of the past and those that were imposed by the missionaries in a different idiom. Again Catholics have emphasized this much more than Protestants: '*Les vieux faisaient la guerre, mais c'était une guerre officielle à We entre les deux grandes puissances [Wetr et Lösi]. Mais là entre catholiques et protestants c'est à cause de la religion.*'[45]

Representation of the Village and the Mission

Drueulu is one of the four villages of the district of Gaica, the smallest of the three districts into which the island of Lifu is divided, and is today the second largest village of the island with 1,100 inhabitants. Because of extensive migration to Noumea, only

half of the population lives in the village.[46] Today the local economy
relies less on primary productive activities (gardening and fishing)
and more on welfare payments, salaried jobs (mainly in the public
sector) and remittances and commodities from employed relatives
in Noumea. In contrast with the other two villages in Lifu, which
are seats of chiefly residence, Drueulu is bi-denominational. Mu,
situated in the Protestant district of Lösi, is inhabited by Protestants
and Hnathalo is a Catholic enclave in the Protestant district of
Wetr. Catholics represent a minority of the population in Lifu but
in Drueulu they constitute the majority and include the chief's
family.

The village of Drueulu in the past had only a Catholic mission,
although both Catholic and Protestant Churches were present in
the village. Whereas Protestants refer to the pastor's house and
nearby terrain as *Eika*, a Greek word meaning 'people living in
the same house', Catholics still refer to the former mission as *la
Mission*, even though the physical space of the Mission and of the
village do not operate as two distinct spaces.[47] Today, in the absence
of Catholic clergy, this is even more the case. The catechists are
people who have important roles and functions in the social
structure and they are married.

Nowadays the Catholic primary school is run by local lay
teachers, one man and three women in 1992. In the last few
years more children coming from Protestant families have been
attending this school whereas when I started fieldwork in 1989
the line between attending one or the other primary school was
rather rigidly defined. In the absence of a Protestant school in the
village Protestant children went to the Public elementary school,
which has Kanak and white teachers.[48] Prior to the Second World
War, the school and the Church were part of the Mission, though
within village boundaries they formed a distinct environment.
Both girls and boys separately attended this school. While the boys
school was a daily school, the girls attended a boarding school.
Elderly women today have very bitter memories of that period.
Culpability was and is still considered by people in their own
terms. Someone who behaves individualistically is not conforming
to the indigenous moral code. Nuns were thus considered selfish:
'*Y a pas donné à [nous] quelque chose par les soeurs. C'est pas bon,
longtemps, bonnes soeurs ont fait à nous. Sont là qui mangeaient comme
ça, mangeaient toutes seules; quand y a les restes à manger pour les
autres, y donnaient aux cochons mais pas manger à nous. C'est vrai.*

C'est bon maintenant.'[49]

The representation of the Catholic mission as a space ruled by self-interest is present in most of the Catholic narratives relating to that period. The bitterness of past experience made even a man who is deeply involved in the Church express strong feelings of disapproval: *'quand on m'a envoyé à l'école j'avais quinze ans, on ne savait pas même un mot en français, mais c'est défendu de parler le langage par les vieilles soeurs.'*[50]

These accounts of the selfish behaviour of the missionaries within the institutional framework in contrast to the sharing and reciprocity stressed as part of past and present Kanak identity, should not be considered only as factual recounting but also as a rhetorical device to evidence 'a behavioural ethic which exists in the absence of actual equity and redistribution' (Thomas 1989: 113). People no longer experience life in the mission and in the village as they did in the past, when the physical and constant presence of nuns and a priest made the boundaries between the two environments so rigid and where different moral codes prevailed. The mission was the place where French had to be spoken, where sharing did not take place; it was a place ruled by different moral tenets. Today this difference is perceived differently. The mission is a space that can be used for community purposes: people gather to worship as well as for more social occasions.

The indigenous categories and the imported ones were not just two different sets of ideas – they entailed 'oppositional conceptualizations of morality, of mental and physical health, and explanatory models of human action' (Macintyre 1990: 88). Missionaries strongly objected to certain cultural practices – doing away with nakedness, polygamy, cannibalism, idolatry were amongst the goals of the mission as was the destruction of the *hmelöm*, the bachelors' house.[51] Missionaries also imposed their ideas of sanitation, clothing, health, family values, motherhood. Education was central to their work. The Marists and the Protestants established boarding schools. Education was considered to be the core of civilization and thus of true conversion.

The missionaries in Lifu elaborated a discourse on gender relations, unlike the French state's colonial policy in New Caledonia, which hardly dealt with relations between the sexes.[52] As the collection of articles on domestic life in the Pacific edited by Jolly and Macintyre suggests 'it was missionaries who articulated the need to reform the family and who actively intervened to promote such changes' (1989: 7). Drueuluan women's narratives clearly distinguish what was forbidden by the Church and what was forbidden by customary practice. The Catholic perception is that Church standards were set outside the village's domain, though narrated as something belonging to the past; Protestant narratives tend to minimize the foreignness of the imported religion. When asked if any particular behaviour was expected of a menstruating or lactating woman, Awaqatr, a Catholic woman, commented: '*C'est défendu de rester avec ton mari: c'est la coutume.*'[53] Well aware that Christian morality had different assumptions from local values, and that the mission sisters were concerned with raising 'good wives' by separating girls and boys from the rest of the community in a sex-segregated boarding school until suitable marriages could be arranged, she added: '*C'est défendu de se refuser au mari . . . c'est l'église qui a dit ça.*'[54]

Women's attitudes to sexuality and motherhood, however, still do not conform to missionary teachings. This provides an illustration of the fact that the missionary discourse on motherhood, family values and domestication was imposed while the missionaries were a daily presence in people's lives but was later dispensed with. It was only superficially accepted by women.[55]

The indigenization process at a general level has occurred only within the Protestant Church. This has meant that local men are responsible and have authority both in customary and religious domains, which are crucial to defining their identity. During my fieldwork I perceived gender relations as being more asymmetrical in the Protestant community (see Paini 1993). The choice of the first Kanak woman, who had entered the Theological School of Lifu as the wife of a student, to become a student herself was opposed by part of the clergy. When she was ordained pastor in Lifu in April 1992, the first Kanak woman pastor, the ceremony was low key. Thus any analysis of the renegotiation of exogenous and endogenous cultural values must take into account gender/ sex, age, status, and other differences; for example, the fact of being a religious majority (Protestants) or minority (Catholics). In the Catholic community of Drueulu, the absence of any religious authority has meant that local catechists are taking charge of the community, although within a national structure that is white dominated and highly hierarchical but not locally present. Thus authority within the community is more diffused, less centralized. During meetings of the parish committee women take part in the decision-making process, although customary rules are never forgotten.[56]

Whereas Catholics distance themselves from the way the mission schools operated, a Protestant from Lifu saw the Protestant boarding school for boys as a substitute for the *hmelöm*, where all the young men except the sons of the high chief stayed until they reached the age of marriage, and were taught to fight, to dance, and to become full members of their society. Protestants differently articulate their arguments in closing the distance between their traditions and the foreignness of Christianity. Though they acknowledge the differences of the past, there is more continuity in their narratives between the old and the new, the past and the present.

When I asked a Lifuan friend how he reconciled being Kanak and being Protestant, he answered: *'le concept, la notion de Dieu . . . les Kanak n'ont pas eu besoin de l'arrivée des Européens pour savoir de quoi il s'agit. Les Kanak c'est un peuple religieux, écologiquement religieux.'*[57]

The notion of God is not considered foreign, brought by outsiders, but rather it is viewed as part of Lifu's heritage. Precolonial indigenous religious beliefs are not perceived as having being supplanted, but rather as anticipating Christianity.

However, in examining their way of explaining events, sickness, death and other practices something more complex emerges. In everyday life people interact using indigenous categories. Their way of explaining events rests on explanations rooted in their beliefs. The Christian cosmology has been informed by local cultural assumptions. Church attendance and ritual have not displaced traditional beliefs in the intervention of spirits and human agencies in the world. Sickness and death are still perceived both by Catholics and by Protestants primarily as something brought about by human intervention. As Barker argues, speaking of custom in terms of unchanging morality and blaming the missionaries for ending particular practices 'are complementary aspects of a single ideology that legitimate changes within ostensibly unchanging moral truths' (1993: 210).

They may have marginalized or rejected some practices but they still hold to an indigenous view of human and spiritual agencies. I found a strong attachment to these explanations on my second trip to Lifu (1991–2) in a period when the arrival of many French white-collar workers employed by the newly decentralised administrative services[58] was perceived by people as a threat. Discussions I had with some French teachers working in Lifu supported my observations. Several deaths occurred in the village in a short period of time, mainly among the Catholics. Both young and old were searching for an explanation. The motive was found in the destruction of the old church building, the work of their forefathers, which was replaced in the early 1980s by a new one, built with the money collected by the people of the village through the sponsoring of fêtes (*kermesses*) and other events. The old church was said to be very dark: people entered it timorously. The new church is full of natural light and people do not feel intimidated anymore. They lack respect for this sacred space: they talk, dogs enter during Mass, and so on. This argument was rejected during a Sunday homily by the local catechist. At the end of the service some Catholics commented that he was brave to make such a strong public statement, though a woman ironically retorted back that something would probably happen to him.

Both Catholics and Protestants organize fêtes to raise funds for Church projects but, as they point out, it is they who manage the money and decide how the money should be used. The Catholics, for example, have built the local church, a large hall for meetings, and have recently restored one of the buildings that used to be the mission school for the community. The whole community takes part in these fêtes. Even people with very little money will buy food in order to contribute to the fund-raising. These fund-raising activities might be seen as immorally exploitative for the money used to build brick churches or halls is collected from people who live in small, unhealthy corrugated sheet-iron houses. One should bear in mind that the Committee, composed entirely of men and women of the village, independently initiates activities, sets its own goals and directly manages the money raised. The goods thereby purchased, from sports equipment to kitchenware, are for the use of the whole community, though kept either in the Catholic or the Protestant Church. Usually money goes to fund a big project, such as the church hall, or to pay back debts incurred to accomplish it. In May 1990 the Catholics of Drueulu raised CFP 1.168.000 (FF 64.240)[59] during a three-day *kermesse*. These fêtes are also occasions that bring the members of the community together and give young people, especially girls, an opportunity to spend longer hours outside the household with others of their own age.

These feasts are seen as 'work', in the indigenous sense of the word. The autonomy of local Church activities and practices is stressed all the time. It was the reason given by the Catholic community of Drueulu living in Noumea for refusing to enter into the *Conseil pastoral du diocèse* (Pastoral Council of the Diocese) in 1990. A member of the group commented that because the aims of the two organizations (their committee and the Council) were the same, they would not gain anything by joining the new structure; rather, they were afraid of losing *le pouvoir de gérer nos choses* (the power of managing our affairs).

Today many social meetings are opened with gift-exchanges and a prayer; this is more prominent amongst the Protestants. Customary exchanges always take place even in the case of religious ceremonies, but they only occur once people have departed from the physical space of the Church. Thus, while on the one hand people's accounts emphasize a shift in the perception of boundaries between the village and the mission, on the other some sort of separation still exists. As social and political conditions change with the implementation of the Matignon Accords, not only have men resorted to custom as a language of resistance but the boundaries between religion and custom are been redrawn.[60] In the face of new changes these boundaries are being readdressed in terms of practices by some high-ranking men who see their power and authority under threat. The encounter of the imported and the local religion must be considered but it must be contextualized. As long as White presence was minimal in Lifu, the new religious discourse was shaped according to indigenous rules; but now that the social and political conditions are changing a new balance between custom, religion, and political authority must be negotiated. People thus resort to indigenous categories to explain and accommodate unforeseen or unexpected events.

During the year, the liturgical calendar is followed. When the *chefferie* planned the yearly social activities, it was taken into consideration; for example, weddings in the period of my field-work were scheduled between May and September[61] so they would not interfere with the yam season, the beginning of school, Christmas, Easter, or the yearly Protestant Convention (a formal gathering of Lifuan Protestants) – periods when the community is busy with other events.

Conclusions: Constellations of Heterogeneous Elements

Lifuans' religion should be considered as an indigenous strategy for thinking about the world and for defining oneself within that world. As Barker (1992) suggests for Oceania, and Mbembe (1988) for Africa, the indigenous symbolic sphere has not been supplanted, but rather it has readjusted. What Mbembe calls the *génie du paganisme* (borrowing the term from Marc Augé) is alive and well and is not regarded as being in opposition to monotheistic religions but rather as one of the many forms religion has taken. The Gospel was accepted by local agents as a strategic way, subject to renegotiation, for gaining economic, or political advantages.

There was a notable lack of questioning of liturgy and theology even by the students of Bethania, the Protestant Theological School in Lifu where I spent a week. It was interesting to compare the tension between the metropolitan view of Christianity of a young French minister teaching theology, and his wife, with that of the Kanak teachers and students. The couple criticized Kanak for accepting obsolete religious customs and not trying to challenge them. They were looking for the same kind of change that swept through much of the Western Protestant and Catholic Churches after Vatican II; instead they were confronted with what they perceived as complacent, old-style practices. To their disappointment, even pro-independence Kanak did not even contemplate a new theological dynamic. Similarly, in the Catholic Church in Lifu, continuity seems to be the rule. The point of view of the young Pastor, however, does not take into account the admonishment of Mbembe (1988) who argues that liberation theologists stress the bias of Eurocentric interpretations of the Gospel which, they argue, must be read from the people's point of view, but they do so without questioning the universality of the message.

Although some degree of overlap and synthesis of Christian and customary elements occurs, a degree of separateness is still maintained. For example, although the customary gift-exchange is often carried out following a Sunday Mass, it never takes place within the Church building, but only after the physical space of the Church has been abandoned: this practice underscores the fact that some kind of demarcation between the Church building and the rest of the village exists, although it is not a matter of separation between Christian and secular activities. I recall during the month of May when people would gather for a week to pray, each evening at a different compound: once they had entered the hut, just before praying, people would carry out customary gift-giving. In this case the two activities were not physically separated. The difference was in the physical place chosen: a hut and not the Church. This is why I refrain from using the term syncretism to refer to Lifuan reworking of Christianity – its symbols and icons. What these practices and commentaries tell us is that there has been not a displacement of one system by another but rather the mutual accommodation or coexistence of local, Christian, and newly synthetized elements. Boundaries remain but their degree of overlap shifts in time.

It is not a case of Christianity replacing traditional beliefs, nor of compartmentalization of discrete religious systems (see Keesing 1992). Nor is it either a case of Sunday Christians, Monday Sorcerers (Kahn 1983). Religion unites people, yet it does so not in terms of a celestial ideal and not in opposition to custom. Thus a more accurate way to represent the religion practised by people in Drueulu is as a complex of 'constellations' of indigenous, Christian, and synthetic elements in constant flux (Barker 1990a: 11). Although it may seem paradoxical, having just employed a celestial metaphor, it is a commitment rooted in daily village communal practice.

Acknowledgements

I wish to acknowledge the support of Research School of Pacific and Asian Studies, Australian National University, for carrying out doctoral fieldwork in 1989–90 and 1991–2 in New Caledonia. My deepest thanks go to the Kanak women and men of Drueulu and to the whole village community who received my daughter and me. Further, my gratitude goes to the late Roger Keesing, and to Margaret Jolly and Michael Young for their invaluable help in the process of bridging between cultural values and ideas as well as between languages. This chapter is dedicated to the late Paul Zöngö.

I feel the need to explain the use of quotation in this chapter as well as the use of French/Drehu. In Lifu people speak the vernacular language, Drehu, and French which, although it is the colonizers' language, is the lingua franca in communication among

Kanak from different linguistic areas. As my fluency in French progressed much faster than in Drehu, I relied more on it for long conversations and intensive interviews. Sometimes I would ask questions in French and people would reply in Drehu. In writing my PhD thesis I was confronted with several issues of 'translatability', how to deal with the language – be it oral or written – of the original utterances. French is a second language for Kanak, whereas I had to deal with a source language (French) and a target language (English), neither of them my mother tongue. Lifuans speak French while imposing Drehu patterns of grammar and world-view, yet it has not developed into a Creole but is rather considered by most speakers of Standard French as 'broken French'. Because of the lack of social legitimacy of this variety of French which is connected with the social status of the speakers, I was confronted with the question of how to present these texts. Some French researchers warned me against the risk of making the people appear to talk *petit-nègre*. However, once having recognized the issues at stake – that a language which does not conform with the Standard language is not recognized as such but instead is patronised and deprecated – I decided not to edit but to give a verbatim transcript of the parts of interviews I was using. Having to render in anthropological Anglo-American categories concepts I had spoken about with people in a different language presented a further problem. In the field I was not so struck by these differences because French and Drehu seem in some cases to overlap. For example, the range of contexts in which Drehu uses *u* is similar to the French *esprit*. I am not implying a closer mapping of French into Drehu; for instance there is no semantic equivalent to *qene nöj* (custom) which French glosses as *la coutume*. Despite the inevitable distortion in both cases, it is somewhat different to render *u* in a language that centres the human being on a notion of 'body/soul' or 'body/spirit' rather than 'body/mind'. I am not arguing that one language makes the task easier, I simply want to problematize the issues involved and not 'rely uncritically on concepts such as "mind"' (Wierzbicka 1992: 26). Looking at another society through a particular language prism makes a difference. Too often we tend to overemphasize differences between Western/non-Western languages and to downplay diversities within Western languages.

Each quotation is followed by the name of the author or interviewee and then the date on which the oral or written

narratives were produced. I indicate archival documents with
unknown author or incomplete date with a question mark. I have
decided to use the full name of the interviewees. The women and
men I have worked with would be pleased to find themselves
mentioned in this essay.

Notes

1. The ideas expressed here are based on a larger work, my PhD
   dissertation, 1993. The material was gathered in 1989–90 and
   1991–2 during eighteen months' fieldwork in the area. I have
   also consulted the Marist correspondence in the Archivio dei
   Padri Maristi (hereinafter APM) in Rome, the London Missionary Society (hereinafter LMS) published and unpublished
   material relevant to Lifu, and writings of later French Protestant
   missionaries to Lifu. I have also relied on early interpretations
   of the social scene by European traders, naval and colonial
   officers, and researchers (see Paini 1993).
2. Following Bensa (1990a) I use the term 'Kanak' in its invariant
   form. The word has an interesting history both in terms of its
   changing connotations over time and its spelling. It is an
   Hawaiian word that came to be used in a derogatory way to
   refer to indigenous people of Melanesia. Whereas nowadays
   in countries like Papua New Guinea 'Kanak' is still a derogatory
   term, in New Caledonia the indigenes have inverted this
   connotation substantially, transforming it into a symbol of
   positive cultural identity. The independence movement has also
   chosen a spelling that replaces the French form of *canaque*; but
   it should be noted that in early French documents the word is
   spelled with a 'K'. O'Reilly (1953) argues that 'Kanaks' was used
   by travellers, officials, and people from Noumea generally, but
   it was not used by missionaries who used terms such as
   islanders, indigenes, pagans, Caledonians, or the name of the
   place they came from, *mais jamais on parle de Canaques* ('but they
   never spoke of Canaques') (1953: 205).
3. Beyond the debate about differentiating biological sex from
   cultural/historical gender, what I believe is that despite the
   varieties of historical/cultural configurations, women and

men are always embodied differently as sexed subjects and therefore as knowing and speaking subjects (see Paini 1993, Chapter 1).

4. From MacFarlane's accounts (1873, Chapter 10) emerges his role in setting up the Code of Law in Lifu in 1862 but also the strategical ends of the *anga joxu* (high chief) Bula to enhance his power.

5. 'If they did not drive us back violently it is because they were intimidated by the presence of a warship' (Palazy to Favre, July 1858, APM/ONC 208).

6. Jean Guiart has criticized my use of the term *la coutume* (Paini 1992, discussion following). He rightly argues that the term today is widely used by white settlers in New Caledonia with derogatory connotations (see also Guiart 1992b). In fact it is perceived by them as an obstacle to economic development and change. However, I use the term because the Lifuans have adopted it (along with *qene nöj*, which is widely used) and also because it is the term Kanak use everywhere in the country, side by side with the vernacular term of each area. The term 'tradition', as Guiart suggested, would still leave us with a polysemic concept. Furthermore, the two notions partially overlap but do not coincide.

7. The Loyalty Islands were never a 'closed society'; long before European invasion, interaction was taking place with islander groups from the east who had drifted westward and with groups from the Grande Terre (Guiart 1963: 643; Howe 1977: 13).

8. ONC stands for Oceania Nova Caledonia; dossiers marked 200 Historia; 208 general correspondence (missionaries' files).

9. For more details see Paini (1993, Chapter 4, The History of Lifuan Mobility). See also Corris (1970), Howe (1978), Saunders (1980), Moore (1985).

10. For example the use of money within customary exchanges, see Paini (1992).

11. I have dealt with these questions in greater detail elsewhere (Paini 1993). For an in-depth analysis of the social structure of the whole island of Lifu, see Guiart (1963, 1992a).

12. Howe (1977) and Douglas (1982). See also Douglas (1979) for a discussion of ascription and achievement viewed not as polar opposites but as a matter of emphasis in particular contexts (1979: 4). For a more recent debate on Austronesian concepts

of hierarchy, see Jolly and Mosko (1994).
13. See Tryon (1967: Introduction). For a more detailed account of Miny, see Lenormand (1990).
14. The clash of a different set of values attached to the notion of authority by Kanak and French colonizers emerges in considerations of the hierarchical indigenous organization, implemented by the colonial administration all over the country regardless of the specificity of each area. Authority was vested in *grands chefs* (high chiefs), and *petits chefs* (literally small chiefs), who were legally appointed as responsible for territorial entities – districts and tribes in the case of Lifu. The difference lies in these territorial entities being clear-cut, bounded space and not having contested borders as the *chefferie* boundaries are (see Guiart 1992a, Chapter 3).
15. In the use of the Drehu orthography I follow Sam (1980) and Unë and Ujicas (1984).
16. This translation does not convey the whole meaning implied in the *tixe/jin* relation.
17. This is not the *code de l'Indigénat* which will come in twenty years later and apply to the whole country.
18. Cf. the different accounts of these events: the Protestant version given by MacFarlane (1873) and the Catholic ones found in Gaide to Rougeryon, 17 August 1864 (APM/ONC 208); in Fabre to Poupinel, 3 December 1864 (APM/ONC 208), and in *Notes Historiques sur Lifou* (APM/ONC 200).
19. The inter-denominational Protestant London Missionary Society, founded in 1795, began work in Tahiti in 1797 and then moved westward. It arrived in Maré (Loyalty Islands) in 1841 and in Lifu a year later. The organization remained in the Loyalties for more than fifty years, before being replaced at the end of the nineteenth century by the *Société des Missions Evangéliques* (Society of Evangelical Missions) of Paris (R. Leenhardt 1980:178).
20. For an overview of the colonial situation on the main island, see Bensa (1990); more specifically on land alienation, see Saussol (1985).
21. In the 1850s the Melanesian Mission based in New Zealand also had interactions with Lifuans.
22. Here I follow the Marist's orthography 'oui-oui' or 'ui ui' (Palazy to *le Supérieur Général*, July 1858, APM/ONC 208) instead of the Drehu *wiwi* (Tryon 1967).

23. Montrouzier complained that the Marist Fathers had been called in by a chief whose authority had been undermined (Montrouzier to Yardin, 8 September 1858, APM/ONC 208); this explanation could justify the difficulties of implanting the Catholic mission in a mainly Protestant area.

24. '[I]n the past many had taken up heresy only because their chief had become Samoa; religion in Lifu is more an affair of chiefly loyalty than one of faith. I know entire villages where people gathered and said: "We cannot stay pagan, let us take a religion", and in order to please everybody an elder divided the people and said: "You are going to be a Catholic with the chief, you, Samoa with another chief", and so on, and this is the only reason for their choice.' (Gaide to Favre, March 1864, APM/ONC 208).

25. On the civil war in Lösi, see MacFarlane (1873: 37), Ray (1917: 243), Howe (1977: 38), Dauphiné (1990: 8), Guiart (1992b: 3).

26. These strategies were and still are used to counterbalance chiefly authority and to minimize inherent structural tension, but present sociopolitical changes suggest that boundaries are becoming more rigid (see Paini 1992).

27. This meant the imposition of French as the lingua franca everywhere in New Caledonia. Since then French has became the medium of instruction.

28. 'Almost two years have gone by since we sent our Lifu translation of the catechism to be printed in France, but we still haven't received any news' (Gaide to his family, 30 July 1868, APM/ONC 208).

29. Protestant men have had more opportunities to leave their village than Protestant women, and therefore to learn French or Bislama.

30. This familiarity with English was due to the influence of the LMS missionaries and also to opportunities for travelling and working in nearby countries where English was spoken. In 1859 Father Montrouzier wrote that several indigenes, including the chief Bula, had spent time in New Zealand with an Anglican minister where they were taught English and instructed into the Christian doctrine. They were asked to reciprocate by teaching Drehu to the local missionaries (Montrouzier to Favre, 1 January 1958 APM/ONC 208).

31. On the relevance of the process of translation in the conversion process in the colonial context of Vanuatu, see Jolly (1996).

See also White (1992) and Burt (1994).

32. This religious vocabulary is taken from a list written by P. Dumas, pastor at the Theological School of Bethania, Lifu, from 1980 to 1983.

33. It is interesting to note that in Lifu and in Maré the LMS teachers and missionaries did not use the indigenous word for 'territory' but have introduced the Greek word *baselaia*. In the A' jië translation of the Bible by Leenhardt – based on a previous translation done by Loyalty Islander teachers – *mwâciri*, the indigenous term for 'territory', was incorporated into the religious domain. Today it is used both in religious and customary contexts (Michel Naepels, personal communication, September 1993, Canberra).

34. 'I believe that among the Protestants there has been an endeavour. They start to translate the Bible immediately. Only the Protestants can speak Drehu. It is their way of evangelizing. Among the Protestants they learn the language straight away, whereas us [Catholics] there are some priests who translate but it is not the rule. They [Protestants] are proud of having their own religion, because of the language. We speak French, we speak a foreign language. For them it is not a foreign religion, it is their own religion. It is rooted in the language' (Paul Zöngö, recorded interview, December 1989).

35. The arrival of new religions or 'sects', regarded as 'heretical religions' (as most Lifuans call them), is a recent phenomenon, which, as one man commented, coincided with the Kanak demand for independence. Here I do not deal with them.

36. In 1958 the *Eglise Evangélique Libre* (Free Evangelical Church in New Caledonia and the Loyalty Islands) was born out of a split within the *Eglise Evangélique en Nouvelle-Calédonie et aux Iles Loyauté* (Evangelical Church in New Caledonia and the Loyalty Islands). The latter was to adopt this name in 1960 after becoming autonomous from the Society of Evangelical Missions in Paris. Membership in both Churches, respectively 5,000 and 25,000, is made up almost exclusively of Kanak (Wapotro, October 1989). For an overview on religious institutions in New Caledonia, see Kohler (1981).

37. 'The chief of Wetr was warned from Ouvéa to reject the religion that was spreading in Lifu. They should wait for two missionaries dressed with a gown. He [high chief of Wetr] quickly sent a message to Drueulu, to the high chief Zeula,

not to espouse the religion preached by Fao. The high chief
accepted even though the subjects were all Protestants. The
high chief of Wetr did not send just anybody, he sent Isamatro
[*Atresi*]' (Paul Zöngö, recorded interview, December 1989).

38. 'Old Walewen (Wetr) before his death called his children: when
the thing will come from the back of the hut you must take it
because it is a small turtle. If it [the thing] comes from the
front you must be careful: it is a muraena' (which in some
versions becomes a serpent).

39. 'We became Catholics and Protestants by historical accident,
but we all belong to the same clan' (Billy Wapotro, October
1989).

40. 'What comes from the west is the serpent and if you pick it up
one day he will eat you up. But the serpent that eats us up it is
not Catholicism: it is the State. The two religions came with
two different symbols: Fao brought the Bible, the Catholics
the flag which was also the symbol of the State. Catholicism
is caught up in this question through the State' (K. Cawidrone,
May 1992).

41. 'Dancing and other practices were forbidden. Everything
connected with custom was considered pagan. I enormously
regret that we lost so much. We were in times of colonization.
It is difficult to say, but even the missionaries, we all lived
under the system. It must be said' (Paul Zöngö, recorded
interview, December 1989).

42. 'Rules were strict for the Catholics, especially in Drueulu
where there were two religions and one always had to mark
the difference' (Awaqatr, January 1992).

43. *Qatr* is a suffix meaning 'elderly'.

44. 'Now it is okay; it is not like it was in the past: before it was
too rigid' (Kamaqatr, recorded interview, April 1992).

45. 'The elders made war, but it was an official war in We between
the two great powers. But between Catholics and Protestants
it was because of religion' (Paul Zöngö, recorded interview,
December 1989).

46. Source: Etat Civil de We, 1 January 1990.

47. In Lifu village settlement patterns were imposed by missionaries; people gathered to live around the church or the temple.
See Guiart (1992a), but cf. Howe (1977).

48. I chose to put my daughter in this school not only because I
did not want to be strongly identified with the Catholic

community, coming from a Catholic background and living
with a Catholic family in the village, but mainly because of
my personal views *vis-à-vis* denominational and state-run
school systems. As I got to know how the school was run I
realized that I had brought to the field ideas about Western
Christianity that had not been replicated in Drueulu. The
Catholic school was more dynamic than the State one, which
was very rigid and conservative. This is also one of the main
reasons given by the teachers to explain why more parents
from the village are sending their children to the Catholic
school. The Catholic school of Drueulu, though part of a larger
institution DEC (*Direction de l'Enseignement Catholique*), has
become in my view an indigenous institution.

49. 'The sisters never gave us anything. In the past the good sisters
were not nice to us. They were there eating, eating, all by
themselves. Their leftovers were given to the pigs not shared
with us. Indeed, that's the truth. Now it is good' (Kamaqatr,
recorded interview Drehu/French, April 1992).

50. 'When they sent me to school I was fifteen; we didn't know a
word of French, but it [was] forbidden to speak our language
by the old nuns' (Paul Zöngö, recorded interview, December
1989).

51. Hadfield portrayed this building also as the locus of public
life. The *hmelöm* and the houses of the chiefs stood out from
the other dwellings (Hadfield 1920: 40–1).

52. For a compelling account of European colonization and
consequential forms of gender relations in French Indochina
and the Dutch East Indies in the early 1900s, see Stoler (1991).

53. 'It is forbidden to stay with your husband: it is custom!'

54. 'It is forbidden to refuse your husband: the Church said that!'
(Awagatr, October 1991).

55. I have discussed these questions elsewhere (Paini 1993,
Chapter 6).

56. Although it is a structure where people are elected, when a
member of the Church committee died in 1989, he was
replaced by his eldest son: the criterion followed was more in
line with succession rules of local social structure.

57. 'The concept, the notion of God . . . Kanak did not have to
wait for the arrival of Europeans to know what it was about.
Kanak are a religious people, ecologically religious' (Wapotro
1990).

58. I am referring to the decentralizing process implemented by the Matignon Accords (see Paini 1992).
59. The rate of exchange between the New Caledonian currency (CFP) and the French Francs (FF) has fixed parity: 100 CFP equal to 5.5 FF.
60. The yam feast of 1990 has emphasized this distinction (see Paini 1992).
61. In the last few years the calendar has changed slightly .

References

Archivio dei Padri Maristi, Rome. ONC/200, ONC 208.

Barker, J. (1990a). Introduction: Ethnographic Perspectives on Christianity in Oceanic Societies. In: J. Barker (ed.), *Christianity in Oceania*, pp. 1–24. Lanham: University Press of America. (ASAO Monograph No.12).

—— (1990b). Mission Station and Village: Religious Practice and Representation in Maisin Society. In: J. Barker (ed.), *Christianity in Oceania*, pp. 173–96. Lanham: University Press of America. (ASAO Monograph No.12).

—— (1992). Christianity in Western Melanesian Ethnography. In: J. Carrier (ed.), *History and Tradition in Melanesian Anthropology*, pp. 144–73. Berkeley: University of California Press.

—— (1993). 'We are *Ekelesia*': Papua New Guinea. In: R. W. Hefner (ed.), *Conversion to Christianity*, pp. 199–230. Berkeley: University of California Press.

Bensa, A. (1986). Sans couper les racines. *La Lettre de Solagral* 45: 7–14.

—— (1990a). *Nouvelle-Calédonie: un paradis dans la tourmente*. Paris: Gallimard.

—— (1990b). Terre kanak: enjeu politique d'hier et d'aujourd'hui. *Etudes rurales* juillet–décembre, 127–8: 107–31.

Burt, B. (1994). *Tradition and Christianity. The Colonial Transformation of a Solomon Island Society*. Chur: Harwood Academic Publishers. (Studies in Anthropology and History No. 10).

Clark, J. (1989). God, Ghosts and People: Christianity and Social Organisation among Takuru Wiru. In: M. Jolly and M. Macintyre (eds), *Family and Gender in the Pacific*, pp. 170–92. Cambridge: Cambridge University Press.

Corris, P. (1970). Pacific Island Labour Migrants in Queensland.

Journal of Pacific History 5: 43–64.

Dauphiné, J. (1990). *Lifou (1864). La prise de possession.* Nouméa: C.T.R.D.P.

Douglas, B. (1979). Rank, Power, Authority: A Reassessment of Traditional Leadership in South Pacific Societies. *Journal of Pacific History* 14: 2–27.

—— (1982). 'Written on the Ground': Spatial Symbolism, Cultural Categories and Historical Processes in New Caledonia. *Journal of the Polynesian Society* 91: 383–415.

—— (1989). Autonomous and Controlled Spirits: Traditional Ritual and Early Interpretations of Christianity on Tanna, Aneityum and the Isle of Pines in Comparative Perspective. *Journal of the Polynesian Society* 98: 7–48.

—— (1993). Anthropological Discourses and Clio the Temptress: Appropriation and Subversion in Disciplinary Contexts. Paper presented at the Symposium 'Regional Histories in Oceania', ASAO Annual Meetings, Hawaii.

—— (1994). Hierarchy and Reciprocity in New Caledonia: An Historical Ethnography. In: M. Jolly and M. Mosko (eds), *Transformations of Hierarchy, Structure, History and Horizon in the Austronesian World,* pp. 169–93. *History and Anthropology.* Special issue vol 7.

Dumas, P. (n.d.). List of Religious Drehu/French Words. Unpublished. Lifou: École Pastorale, Bethanie.

Guiart, J. (1954). *L'organisation sociale et coutumière de la population autochtone de Nouvelle-Calédonie.* Nouméa: ORSTOM.

—— (1963). *Structure de la chefferie en mélanésie du sud.* Paris: Institut d'Ethnologie.

—— (1992a). *La chefferie en mélanésie.* Paris: Institut d'Ethnologie.

—— (1992b). Progress and Regress in New Caledonia. *Journal of Pacific History* 27(1): 3–28.

Hadfield, E. (1920). *Among the Natives of the Loyalty Group.* London: Macmillan.

Henningham, St. (1992). *France and the South Pacific.* Sydney: Allen & Unwin.

Howe, K. R. (1977). *The Loyalty Islands. A History of Cultural Contacts 1840–1900.* Canberra: Australian National University Press.

Jolly, M. (1994). Hierarchical Horizons. In: M. Jolly and M. Mosko (eds), *Transformations of Hierarchy, Structure, History and Horizon in the Austronesian World,* pp. 377–409. *History and Anthropology.* Special issue vol. 7.

—— (1996). Sacrifice, Holy Spirits and the Swollen God: The

Marists in Northern Vanuatu, 1887–1934. In: P. Van der Veer (ed.), *Conversion to Modernities: The Globalization of Christianity*, pp. 236–62. New York: Routledge.

Jolly, M. and Macintyre, M. (eds) (1989). *Family and Gender in the Pacific*. Cambridge: Cambridge University Press.

Jolly, M. and Mosko, M. (eds) (1994). *Transformations of Hierarchy, Structure, History and Horizon in the Austronesian World*. *History and Anthropology*. Special issue vol. 7.

Jouan, M. (1861). Notice sur les Iles Loyalty. *Le Moniteur Impérial de la Nouvelle-Calédonie et Dépendances* nos 117, 118.

Kahn, M. (1983). Sunday Christians, Monday Sorcerers: Selective Adaptation to Missionization in Wamira. *Journal of Pacific History* 18: 96–112.

Keesing, R.M. (1992). *Custom and Confrontation*. Chicago: University of Chicago Press.

Kohler, J.M. (1981). Religions. In *Atlas de la Nouvelle-Calédonie*. Paris: ORSTOM, plate 27.

—— (1988). The Churches in New Caledonia and the Colonial Order. In: M. Spencer, A. Ward and J. Connell (eds), *New Caledonia. Essays in Nationalism and Dependency*, pp. 145–74. St. Lucia: University of Queensland Press.

Leenhardt, M. (1947). *Do kamo*. Paris: Gallimard.

Leenhardt, R. (1980). *Au vent de la Grande Terre*. Published by the author, Paris.

Lenormand, M. (1990). *Le Miny: langue des chefs de l'île de Lifou*. Nouméa: EDIPOP.

MacFarlane, S. (1873). *The Story of the Lifu Mission*. London: Nisbet.

Macintyre, M. (1990). Christianity, Cargo Cultism, and the Concept of the Spirit in Misiman Cosmology. In: J. Barker (ed.), *Christianity in Oceania*, pp. 81–100. Lanham: University Press of America. (ASAO Monograph No. 12).

Mbembe, A. (1988). *Afriques Indociles*. Paris: Karthala.

Moore, C. (1985). *Kanaka. A History of Melanesian Mackay*. Port Moresby: Institute of Papua New Guinea Studies and University of Papua New Guinea Press.

Moyse-Faurie, C. (1983). *Le Drehu. Langue de Lifou*. Paris: Selaf.

O'Reilly, P. (1953). Le Français parlé en Nouvelle-Calédonie. *Journal de la Société des Océanistes* 9: 203–28.

Paini, A. (1992). Kanak Women Negotiating their Identities in a Changing World. Paper presented at the First European Colloquium on Pacific Studies, Nijmegen, 17–19 December.

—— (1993). Boundaries of Difference. Geographical and Social

Mobility by Lifuan Women. (PhD thesis). Canberra: Research School for Pacific and Asian Studies, Australian National University.

Ray, S. (1917). The People and Language of Lifou, Loyalty Islands. *Journal of Royal Anthropological Institute of Great Britain and Ireland* 47: 239–332.

Rivierre, J.C. (1985). La colonisation et les langues. *Les Temps Modernes* 464: 1688–717.

Sahlins, M. (1985/1986). *Isole di Storia*. Torino: Einaudi.

Said, E. (1978/1979). *Orientalism*. New York: Vintage Books.

Sam, Drilë. (1980). *Lexique Lifou-Français*. Nouméa: CTRDP.

Saunders, K. (1980). Melanesian Women in Queensland 1863-1907. *Journal of the Pacific History* 4: 26–44.

Saussol, A. (1985). La terre et la confrontation des hommes en Nouvelle-Calédonie. *Les Temps Modernes* 464: 1612–22.

Shaw R. and Stewart, C. (1994). *Syncretism/Anti-Syncretism. The Politics of Religious Synthesis*. London: Routledge.

Shineberg, D. (1967). *They Came for Sandalwood. A Study of the Sandalwood Trade in the South-Pacific 1830–1865*. Melbourne: Melbourne University Press.

Shineberg, D. (ed.) (1971). *The Trading Voyages of Andrew Cheyne 1841–1844*. Canberra: Australian National University Press.

Stoler, A. (1991). Carnal Knowledge and Imperial Power: Gender, Race, and Morality in Colonial Asia. In: M. di Leonardo (ed.), *Gender at the Crossroads of Knowledge. Feminist Anthropology in the Postmodern Era*, pp. 51–101. Berkeley: University of California.

Thomas, N. (1989). *Out of Time, History and Evolution in Anthropological Discourse*. Cambridge: Cambridge University Press.

Tryon, D. (1967). *Dehu–English Dictionary*. Canberra: The Australian National University.

Unë, E. and Ujicas, R. (1984). *Langue Drehu. Propositions d'Ecriture. Aqane troa cinyihan la qene Drehu*. Nouméa: Bureau des Langues Vernaculaires, CTRDP.

White, G. (1992). *Identity Through History: Living Stories in a Solomon Islands Society*. Cambridge: Cambridge University Press.

Whitehouse, J.O. (n.d.). The Loyalty Islands to 1896. Canberra: Pacific Manuscripts Bureau.

Wierzbicka, A. (1992). *Semantics, Culture, and Cognition. Universal Human Concepts in Culture-Specific Configurations*. New York: Oxford University Press.

Chapter 8

Appropriating the Other: A Case Study from New Britain

Monique Jeudy-Ballini

Relations between native and white people in Melanesia have often been studied with regard to the reinterpretations, manipulations and appropriations of knowledge, techniques, objects or religious beliefs by the Melanesians.[1] The many studies dealing with the so-called 'cargo' or 'messianic cults' illustrate this tendency or bias. The appropriation of local representations by foreigners, however, is rarely dealt with.

This chapter seeks to show that appropriation is not a unilateral process; nor it is a process that pertains only to the relationship between native and white people. These two issues will here be examined principally on the basis of Sulka ethnography,[2] complemented by further ethnographical material on other New Britain populations. It will thus appear that the 'other' that is appropriated is not only the missionary for the Sulka; it is also the Sulka for the missionary, and the Sulka for the Sulka.

Difference and Identity: The Original Unity

The Sulka live in the province of East New Britain (Papua New Guinea); they number about 2,000, and inhabit two main areas several hours' walk from each other. In the Wide Bay coastal area, the original Sulka territory, the first permanent missionary station was established in 1930 by Catholic missionaries of the Order of the Sacred Heart. They had no competitors before the arrival of representatives of other religious denominations in the 1960s. Catholic German missionaries had visited the area as early as the end of the last century. At that time, however

> The archbishop objected to the sending of missionaries as long as the
> government would not first agree to establish a police station in the
> area. The government refused to do so. So neither priests nor
> government officials went to Wide Bay. The archbishop did not want
> a mission to be established in a such a remote and dangerous area. It
> was inconceivable to sow the Gospel seed among savages excited by
> blood and death . . . (Schneider 1932: 50).

However, one could infer from later missionary literature that
such 'sowing' would in fact have seemed 'inconceivable' for
another reason: the 'Gospel seed' had been sown among these
'savages' before the arrival of the first missionaries . . . This point
can be developed by means of a few examples illustrating the way
local representations were interpreted by the missionaries dealing
with Sulka culture, or with the cultures of their close neighbours,
the Baining and the Mengen.

The Ten Commandments

The Baining Example

Let us first of all consider how Father Carl Laufer understood the
Baining 'rules of life'. According to this member of the Order of
the Sacred Heart, the cultural or theological and moral norms
inculcated in the youth during initiation closely paralleled Biblical
teaching. He thus proposed to sum these norms up 'in accordance
with the model of the Ten Commandments' (1946–49: 524–5).
Several years later, Theo Aerts, obviously concerned with ration-
alizing Laufer's description, summarized it in the following way:

> The Central Baining rules of life, when arranged in the same order as
> the Ten Commandments, run as follows:
>
> • The first commandment of Moses, that one shall have one God,
>   is accepted in full. There is no specific prohibition against
>   worshipping or accepting other gods, but in practice there is only
>   one God; all the others are rather symbols.
> • The second commandment, that one shall not take the name of the
>   Lord in vain, holds force absolutely in the Baining religion. The
>   name of Rigenmucha ('The one who always was there') is called
>   holy and is not to be uttered . . .

- With our third commandment we have to let the parallel drop. The Bainings have no regular rest day or holy day.
- Our fourth commandment, that one shall honour one's father and one's mother, is completely analogous to the Baining teaching.
- The fifth commandment – you shall not kill – is kept in various modalities. The Bainings regard killing within the family and within the tribe as a very serious crime . . . while the killing of non-Bainings is called war and may be tolerated.
- The sixth commandment – you shall not commit adultery – is taken by the Bainings more seriously than by Westerners . . .
- Our seventh commandment, you shall not steal . . . on this point the Bainings have an absolute injunction from Rigenmucha to respect the right of property. They have, however, two kinds of property right – the personal, and the tribal .
- The commandment about not bearing false witness, our eighth commandment exists among, and is respected by, the Bainings . . .
- The ninth commandment: 'You shall not covet your neighbour's wife' does not seem to exist. Perhaps to the Bainings' way of thinking the sixth commandment is enough, and they do not trouble their heads about what precedes the actual act, namely desire.
- The tenth commandment – about the neighbour's house or field – is equally absent. A probable explanation about this is, of course, that a great many of the bigger things that might give rise to envy are either communally owned or communally made (Aerts 1978: 61–3).

The Mengen Example

Father Tim O'Neill was a missionary from the same order as Carl Laufer and lived among the Mengen for some ten years. He writes:

> The people's idea of right and wrong falls plumb within the Natural Law and the Ten Commandments: Man must honour Nutu; he must obey authority; he must not kill a person without good reason; he must not interfere with other people's mates; he must not steal; neither may he tells lies or defame a person, for if a person loses his good name the only honourable course left to him is suicide . . . 'but he who steals my good name . . .' Moses and Shakespeare would have felt quite at home in Salumpuna [a Mengen village] (O'Neill 1972: 46).

The Sulka Example

Father Joseph Meier, who worked among the Sulka from 1910 to 1914, also belonged to the Order of the Sacred Heart. He reports that an 'old pagan' man said to him:

> You need not tell us that we should take good care of our relatives
> (fourth commandment), that we should not kill anybody (fifth
> commandment), that we should not commit adultery (sixth command-
> ment), that we should not steal (seventh commandment), that we
> should not lie (eighth commandment). These things are not new to
> us; we are fully aware of them, although we act against them frequ-
> ently. I am an old man now. When I was a boy, I was taught these
> lessons by my relatives who had not learned them from any white
> man, but knew them all by themselves. For at that time they had as
> yet no knowledge of people with a white skin; they had not seen any,
> and still less had come in contact with them (Meier 1945: 34–5).

In the eyes of these missionaries, Christian morality – of which
Baining, Mengen and Sulka customs represent, as it were, a sort
of reminiscence – would thus be a form of innate cultural
knowledge among these peoples. Now, an unlearned local cultural
wisdom that is also regarded as universal inevitably raises
questions about its common source. Laufer felt that there could
be no doubt that its origin was (the Christian) God himself.

The Supreme Being

Laufer postulates the existence of a Supreme Being, identified as
the God of Scripture, within both the Sulka cosmological
representations (Laufer 1955) and those of the other peoples he
visited in New Britain: the Tolai, Baining, Mengen, Arowe, Kilenge,
Bariai, and Kove (Laufer 1950a, 1950b, 1952a, 1952b; cf. Janssen
1975). Referring to Father Joseph Meier, he writes that among the
Sulka '... his capable catechist, E Kamnge ... told him, after
painstaking comparison and careful consideration, that he had
often thought their E Nut and the Christian God were, in fact, one
and the same person' (Laufer 1955: 55–6).[3]

Having posited the identity of the Sulka ancestral founder
and Biblical God, Laufer's concern was to comprehend native
institutions as their meaning, in his eyes, was linked to what (or
who) had primordially caused them to exist. 'That tribal morality
is grounded in the Supreme Being E Nut is not explicitly stated
by the natives, and has likely been forgotten by them nowadays.
But all the tribal rules must have had a beginning and an origin,

otherwise it would be impossible to understand them' (Laufer 1955: 58). The implicit reasoning is here that Sulka silence on this matter stems from a form of cultural amnesia. The deeply Christian character of 'tribal morality' could not derive from mere human invention. This 'morality', viewed by Laufer as the equivalent of the Ten Commandments, must therefore be understood as a survival of the tribal organization's divine origin.

In this connection, Laufer elevates E Nut to the status of Supreme Being, assuming that *das Höchste Wesen E Nut* rules over the other divine beings of the Sulka cosmology, such as the spirits of the dead and the ambivalent *o kol* spirits. Thus, he conjectures that the ancestral spirits live in the Supreme Being's company. To be sure, Laufer admits, this is never stated by the Sulka; but such a belief, he contends, 'would be quite consistent with their logical mind' (Laufer 1955: 63). Laufer deals in a similar way with another category of spirits – *masalai* (pidgin) or *o kol* (Sulka), which are said to inhabit various parts of the local topography (especially ponds, boulders, caves and waterfalls) and are feared for their aggressiveness to humans. Laufer conceives of them as agents of God's repressive power; He send them 'to punish humans for their violation of the tribal moral code of life' – that is, to the missionary's mind, their violation of the Ten Commandments (Laufer 1955: 63).[4]

From his perspective, the final challenge consists in assigning a place in the Sulka cosmology to other characters of religious importance. The totemic ancestors are particularly threatening because their autonomy and status as founding heroes might allow them to compete (or even supplant) the Supreme Being. Laufer solves the problem by positing the priority of the latter. The Sulka, he writes, 'descend from an original couple, created by the Supreme Being. However, there are also many myths that assign different origins to the moiety system, as well as to the numerous totemic clans that they comprise. This is an indication that the sociological differentiations within the tribe are more recent' (Laufer 1955: 57).

In the Beginning . . .

By first postulating a Supreme Being, then subordinating the spirits to Him, and finally considering the myths about other cultural heroes as the result of cultural decay, Laufer is able to uphold the notion of an original local monotheism.[5] Thus, cultural changes that an anthropologist would no doubt interpret as the unfortunate effects of Christianization conversely appear, to the missionary, as resulting from an unfortunate process of paganization. In both interpretations, however, change involves an undesirable loss (cultural amnesia or decay) when compared with the supposed original state of the culture – that Golden Age when the natives were still behaving like genuine Christians, or like genuine pagans.

According to the missionary, indeed, the founding ancestor whom the Sulka call Nut, the Mengen Nutu, the Baining Rigenmucha, and so on, is in fact the Christian God. However, neither the Sulka, nor the Mengen, nor yet the Baining realize this, for their original knowledge deteriorated as time passed. Now, a similar conception prevails among the Sulka. They regard the cultural hero that the Mengen call Nutu, the Baining Rigenmucha, and so on, as in fact none other than their own primordial ancestor Nut, but neither the Mengen nor the Baining are conscious of this, for their original knowledge deteriorated as time passed. Just as pagan people are in fact Christians without knowing it, so the Baining and the Mengen are in fact misguided and amnesic Sulka, Sulka blind to their 'Sulkaness' – in a word, Sulka who have gone astray. The truth and authenticity of cultures lie in their past. In the beginning was unity, when the pagans worshipped the same god as the Christians, and when the Baining, Mengen and other peoples worshipped the same Sulka ancestor.[6]

Cultural diversity, as it is conceived of both by missionaries and by the Sulka, is attributed to deviance, confusion, distortions. It is a sort of accident in the course of history; or, more precisely, the intrusion of history upon mythology, the falsification of myth by history. It thus appears as a form of decay. In much the same way, anthropologists, when confronted with intra-cultural diversity, distinguish between 'authentic' data pertaining to 'tradition' and less 'authentic' data ascribable to a process of 'acculturation' or 'syncretism'.

The appropriation of the other is grounded upon his alleged ignorance or unconsciousness, on the idea that the other does not realize who he really is (or was), and what he really does (or did). Such ignorance is meant to have redeeming value. When it is ascribed to a foreign culture, continuity and discontinuity, identity and difference, similarities despite deviation, are made thinkable.

Amnesia is postulated so that difference can be explained as the result of change; what the other no longer is today, he once was. He is thereby credited with the innate capacity to return to his original 'authenticity'. The pagan was not always pagan. For the missionary, this means that he has an internal disposition favouring the acceptance of Christian truth. He is, in other words, inclined to salvation from his otherness, his past being, in a way, the missionary's present. The task at hand, then, is less to convert him (to a truth foreign to him) than it is to call him back to his own truth – which is none other than the missionary's own, as well.

What native people and missionaries thus supposedly have in common is the result of God's visit to the local populations. As another missionary of the Sacred Heart Order put it: 'It was Laufer's primary anthropological and missionary concern to show that God has been in Papua New Guinea before the white man entered these islands. To prove this was not easy' (Janssen 1975: 19). He goes on, quoting further from Laufer's writings: 'I would like to repeat . . . a word from John V. Taylor, a missionary in Africa: "When we approach a person of another culture and of other religions we have first of all to lay off our shoes, because the place we enter is holy. Otherwise . . . we might forget that God has already been in this place before us . . ."' (Laufer, Die Religiöse Ideenwelt der Baining, P.M., IV, nd: 275, quoted by Janssen, 1975: 19).

Missionary literature shows that this concern was by no means Laufer's alone. Some decades later, Harold Turner sums up the consensual view in the following way: 'missions did not bring God to Melanesia. God made Melanesia and the Melanesians and has never left them. The Biblical God, Father, Son and Holy Spirit, was here before missions, and before Christianity . . . Theology in Melanesia has to articulate how God was present and active in Melanesian religions' (Turner 1978: 19).

The Biblical God went to Melanesia before the missions did.[7] For the missionaries arriving there long after Him, the problem was (and still is) a hermeneutical one: to grasp how the 'pagan religions', unwittingly and, so to speak, despite themselves, testify to this 'first coming'. This project of reinterpretation involves identifying as similarities between paganism and Christianity anything in the former that can be regarded as a sign of 'morality' or 'rationality'; considering these similarities as survivals from the past; and in viewing the rest – differences and inconsistencies – as fallacies resulting from cultural amnesia. In order to posit, as Laufer does, the principle of continuity between 'Christians' and 'pagans', one must assume a historical discontinuity within pagan society. In this regard, missionary work consists of awakening the Christian lying dormant within the pagan – in making pagans realize that they are not what they think they are. Appropriating the other means leading him to cast aside his acquired otherness and thus reappropriate his own original sameness: his unchanging, though underlying, identity.

Identity and Difference: The Power of Disbelief

We shall now see how, among the Sulka, the symmetrical strategy of appropriation is used to show that Christians (including the Catholic missionaries) are in fact pagans. I will examine the example of the Sulka who have joined the Seventh-Day Adventist (SDA) Church in order to demonstrate how the other, can just as well be a Sulka for another Sulka.

Comprising approximately one-tenth of the overall population, the SDA Church today outnumbers all the other religious groups among the Sulka, except the *Katolik* (Tok Pisin for 'Catholics'). According to the minimal definition most common among the non-SDA, what principally characterizes the Adventist movement are the many prohibitions observed by its members. The SDA are known as those who must refrain from eating specific foods (pork, fish without scales, crustaceans), smoking, drinking alcoholic beverages, chewing betel nuts, feasting and performing traditional ceremonies, dances or songs.

To distinguish themselves from the Adventists, non-SDA refer to themselves as *Katolik, Katolik* being also the generic name given them by the SDA.[8] For both SDA and *Katolik*, the latter are those who are allowed to do all the things the SDA are forbidden, and which are not forbidden by the Catholic Church, 'those who observe the custom' as opposed to 'those who observe the Bible', that is, the SDA. In the *Katolik*'s eyes, the SDA are free-thinkers of sorts, a reputation they have acquired through the acts of defiance they commit against places and objects held by the *Katolik* to contain magical powers. The Adventists, in fact, attribute an experimental and demonstrative value to this provocative behaviour.

SDA and Magic

Joining the Adventist Church implies renouncing the use of magic.[9] Renunciation of magic usually consists of rendering the magic 'cold', that is definitively inefficacious. Magic's 'coldness' results from its being publicly disclosed. The magical spells, often first revealed in the course of an initiation ritual or a marriage feast, are then set to music. Repudiating magic is thus a form of ritual sabotage. These spells increase the collection of ritual songs performed during the masked ceremonies and handed down from one generation to another. A great many songs are known to be old magic, so that the custom is in a way being continually bolstered by the repudiation of the custom.

For those undertaking it, renunciation of magic is felt to be a great hardship, because it is inconceivable that any human activity be successful without its assistance. The children's, pigs' or garden's development; the ability to find a spouse, cure a disease, accomplish work or organize a feast . . . these are all essential matters, and none can come to be without both human will and industry and the help of magic.

'For everything: magic, magic, always magic', an elderly *Katolik* stated emphatically. 'Provided one believes in it', would add an SDA. From the Adventist point of view, what is effective in magic is that it be presumed to be so. Magic is thus defined as a self-validating belief: it gives proof of itself if it is believed and can therefore be described as a belief in the efficacy of believing. Successful magic demonstrates the strength of belief. Conversely, each instance of failure of magic is accounted for by invoking disbelief as its cause. We have here a good example of an 'etiology of failure' (Fredrikson 1991), disbelief causing impotence, and impotence being the negative condition of failure. Powerful for some while ineffective for others, magic thus cannot be detached from the subjectivity of those who wield it.

A man who was approximately fifty years old, the only one of his family to have become a member of the SDA Church, illustrated this causal relation in the following way:

> When I was young, an old man taught me how to kill men with magic, as the killer-sorcerers do. He taught me this magic, which is pronounced on a stone that one then throws at a man, a pig, or any other thing you want to kill. I wanted to test it on a tree, so I

pronounced the magic on a stone and I threw the stone at a tree. Then I waited, as I expected the tree would wither. But the tree did not wither, because I did not think it would do so. I did not believe that. I had said to myself: 'Is this possible or not? I am going to try first.' And nothing happened. I threw the stone, then I waited, waited, waited. . . . but nothing happened, for I did not really believe that something would happen. The tree did not wither, and today it is still at the same place, still growing . . . You see, if you believe in magic, magic has power, because of your belief. If you don't believe, magic is nothing. This man who taught me this magic, he does believe in it and if he tries, of course it will work!

Regarding his refusal to use magic in his daily life, he said: 'Magic is nothing. . . . I now garden like that, without magic, and the food grows by itself. The curing magic too is nothing. When a man is sick, how would magic be really able to enter his body, so as to cure him?' (Jakob Sako, Guma village).[10] The same informant complained that his chronic stomach ache was caused by his enemy's sorcery. When asked how sorcery could enter his body, he answered that it was because his enemy believed in sorcery . . .

In the eyes of those who have renounced the power of magic, the superiority of the *Katolik* is due to their faith in it. This is especially the case when harmful magic is used against SDA. As we began to see a moment ago, the misfortunes SDA suffer they regularly attribute to *Katolik* magic. On the other hand, the occurrence of failure is properly speaking only a concern for the *Katolik*; for the SDA, it on the contrary a posteriori validates their professed disbelief. We shall see that in some circumstances the converse situation obtains: belief is construed as credulity, and far from representing strength, it is a source of weakness.

Magic and Prayer

The SDA posit a functional equivalence between magic and prayer. This is apparent in the fact that prayer is conceived of as a substitute for magic; and prayer, like magic, loses its efficacy if it is publicly disclosed.

A former *Katolik* who, by his own account, had joined the SDA Church in order to put an end to his previously dissolute way of living, thus explained:

When I was outside [the SDA Church], I too used to perform magical spells when working in my garden or . . . that kind of thing. I did not invoke the Big Man, I did not call His name. I said magic over the garden or a ginger stalk . . . [laughs] . . . Then I planted sweet potatoes [laughs]. And the sweet potatoes grew very well by themselves . . . Then he[11] thought: 'Well, I performed the correct magic and my sweet potatoes are enormous, really enormous.' And he felt proud of it, he thought: 'It is I, I achieved this!' But after I joined the SDA, I said: 'Big Man, provide for everything', then I planted everything with the Big Man's power. I pray, I beg the Big Man to help me, then I plant my garden. It is the Big Man himself who makes everything grow. Later, I harvest and eat (Hermann Gunme, Vunabaur village).

Praying and performing magic are different means of achieving the same ends. The first utilizes the causal force of the relationship with God, while the second utilizes both the specific force of a given magic (some are stronger than others, some are 'correct' and others not) and the force of man's causal belief in his magic's powers. The same speaker thus observed:

If a man is very sick and I pray for him . . . the Big Man alone will hear my prayer, and can cure him. But if the Big Man wants to take him, He will take him back, He will take his breath back. It is exactly the same as magic! If a man tries with his magical spells, tries and is successful, then he will think: 'It's done, I have succeeded, I have succeeded with my magic.' And if he does not succeed, then he [the sick man] will die. It is exactly the same as prayer!

Magic and prayer do not have distinct fields of action. Just as, for instance, one can perform magic to kill a person, so can one pray to God to do so but it will ultimately be up to Him to satisfy, or not, this request. Though affected by human prayer, God will ultimately do whatever He desires, for '[the] Bible says that it rests with God alone to take revenge'. God's 'transcendence' thus operates as a structural etiology of failure. The non-accomplishment of the praying man's will is accounted for by the accomplishment of a will transcending it, the content, or intent, of which is unknown to man. Ineffective prayer does not denote human impotence but rather points to the power of the Almighty's will.

A forty-year-old Sulka, and full-time Adventist pastor, expressed it in the following way: 'In our custom [when performing magic], we dictate our law to God; we oblige Him to comply with our wishes. Whether God wants to or not, He must punish the man I want to punish. It is my wish, but not necessarily His. That is what's different now' (Petrus Karoyan, Ganai village).

However, Adventists are tempted to resort to magic when prayer proves to be ineffective. For, far from denying it, the Adventists acknowledge the power of magic when performed by those who believe in it – that is, the *Katolik*. As we have just seen, prayer and magic are functionally equivalent but magic is regarded as more effective than prayer as it short-circuits God's will, using Him as an instrument. Prayer, on the other hand, leaves less room for human wishes.[12] Some (fairly recent) converts to the Adventist Church avoid succumbing to this temptation by asking a *Katolik* to perform magic on their behalf . . .

SDA and Spirits

According to the SDA, the spirits (*kol*) dwelling in various parts of the Sulka physical environment can only be harmful to the people who believe in them and, for that reason, are afraid of them. A young SDA often went fishing in a river that other villagers carefully avoided, for it was known to be an abode for *kol* spirits. When asked about his foolhardiness, he replied: 'the spirits know I do not believe in them, so they can't harm me' (Pius Karingmae, Milim village).

This is the consensual view among the SDA. Incredulity is given instrumental value by using it as a protective strategy. Another informant thus said:

If you believe in the *kol* spirits they will kill you. If you believe in them . . . If you don't believe in them, then they can't do anything against you. When you go to a bad place, a place where spirits live, you must not be afraid of them. You must go. You must think only of the Big Man and you go. And you pray. You pray to God: 'God, I am going to this place. Stay with me and take care of me.' So you go fearlessly. Because if you start thinking: 'Oh, if I go there the spirits will kill me', then the spirits won't spare you. They know what you think, they know that you are afraid and they kill you. [Later, when] you come back home, you begin to feel ill: 'Oh! I went to this bad place and the spirits probably killed me . . .' If you are not afraid, nothing happens. If you are afraid, then your fear acts and something really does happen (Hermann Gunme, Vunabaur village).

As a protective device, the efficacy of disbelief is aimed not so much at the spirits as at one's own fears. This conception is not specifically Adventist but it is consistent with Sulka thought in general: the *kol* spirits' aggression is directed toward those who fear them. A common etiology for elephantiasis among the non-Adventists, for example, is walking through a swampy area where *kol* spirits dwell; but the spirits only punish those who fear walking there. To fear for one's life is to put it at risk. This principle does not apply to the relationship between humans and spirits alone. So long as one is fearless, it is said, there is no danger of being killed by a river crocodile or an ocean shark. Fear is here partially correlated to a sense of guilt as it is common knowledge that those who have committed some offence (theft or adultery, for instance) are more vulnerable to shark and crocodile attacks. It cannot be said, however, that this type of misfortune is bound solely to a punitive function. Others, those who are sick or whose 'image' (*nunu*) has been slain by a sorcerer, are also thought of as being particularly exposed to this form of aggression.[13]

The representation of the 'objective' relationship between humans and the various 'mystical' aggressors – *kol* spirits, sharks and crocodiles – must thus be understood in conjunction with a representation of the subjective economy of belief and fear (cf. Fredrikson 1991, 1994). The latter has, among other things, an explanatory power that the former alone cannot provide. In the context we have been examining, these 'meta-beliefs' (beliefs about believing) constitute what might be called an etiology of occurrence. The implicit question they seek to answer is: how to explain, given the formal principle of causality laid down by the custom, the perceived erratic incidence of misfortune? Just as disbelief can account for the failure of magic, so belief (or fear) can account for the specific occurrence of misfortune.

Disbelief, the refusal to succumb to fear or, alternatively, one's faith in one's own invulnerability, deprives the malevolent spirits of any hold over oneself, reducing them to impotence. In the same way, spirits are supposed to be harmless to white people. As they are unaware of the perils that surround them, or do not heed them, foreigners enjoy, so to speak, a natural – or more precisely, cultural – protection against them. Similarly, Whites are thought to be unable to benefit from good magic, and to be invulnerable to sorcerers' aggressions; their disbelief or unawareness places them beyond the reach of these powers. However, once they have been forewarned about them, and are afraid of them, foreigners become vulnerable too. In a word, and in the words of a *Katolik*: 'So long as you don't know that a place is dangerous, that place is safe' (Lulu Kak, Ploresel village).

Experiments in power

Faith alone kills, then. These views are shared by Sulka regardless of religious affiliation. The Adventists systematize them, working out a sceptical attitude which they utilize as an experimental strategy of power. They thus recoup the power they lost in renouncing magic, in relation to the *Katolik* who now appear more vulnerable than they. From this point of view, joining the SDA Church is a way of laying claim to extra-territorial status, so to speak, of adopting a posture of defensive disbelief. It is a means of separating one's self from fear and behaving in regard to the spirits as if one were unaware of their presence.

The SDA assign an experimental and demonstrative value to their attempt to overcome fear; they test the power of disbelief, just as they do to other aspects of their nonconformist behaviour. They play with the custom as with fire, but it is unquestionably a very reckless form of play. When considering the Adventists' experimental disbelief, one must realize the courage it demands. Let us ponder, for example, the case of this man, the only SDA of his village, alone with his doubts and his fear while defying the *kol* spirits that surround him:

> People talk a lot about spirits, but I don't believe in spirits. When I have to work in a spot which is said to be inhabited by spirits, I treat the spirits in an offhanded way.
> One day, I went with my child who was still small to make a new garden [in the bush]. Near the plot to be cleared was a big rock known as the abode of a female *kol*. I went to the garden to work and I began to chop down the branches of the trees. I threw the branches onto the rock while saying: 'If you really are a *kol*, you will kill me. If you are not a *kol*, you will not kill me and I will kill you.' That's what I said, without insulting it, I just spoke to it like that, but I didn't insult it. In the afternoon I came back home and I asked myself: 'This thing, will it kill my child or not?' Well no, it didn't kill him!
> In the evening . . . there was a terrible thunderstorm. The sky became completely dark, then there was lightning. My wife and some

villagers were very angry with me, and they blamed me: 'Look! You have provoked the *kol*'s anger, and it will avenge itself on us!' ... I didn't believe this.

The next morning, I found a [dead] snake hanging from the branch of a tree growing near my copra dryer. People said to me: 'Look, it's the *kol* you provoked that sent you this snake.' I answered them: 'If it had sent it to me, it would have put it on my house instead of in this tree' [laughs]. I think the lightning struck by itself and that this snake died by itself [that is without the *kol*'s intervention] because of ... I don't know. Maybe struck down by lightning or ... That's what I said to them. ... Nothing killed me. Neither me nor my son. Nothing. You know, if you believe too much in that, it kills you. If you don't believe, it can't't[14] (Oto Paranis, Guma village).

When SDA wish to publicize a meeting they are holding, they often do so by gathering in some spot known to house *kol*; when they set up camp in a coastal village, they go fishing near reefs said to be 'dangerous'. Every time they return safe and sound, they have won a cosmological victory over the powers that be, as well as over the *Katolik*. Through the stories of their individual and collective defiances, they demonstrate their control over the spirits and themselves, and their superiority over the *Katolik*.

The Sulka Adventists never actually deny the existence of the *kol*. On the contrary, it is by continuing to recognize their power that SDA can best demonstrate their unbelief and thus build up their reputation. They do however disapprove of the traditional (that is, *Katolik*) way of dealing with the spirits. In their eyes, the belief in *kol* spirits is, so to speak, a methodological, or strategic, error.

The *kol*, some Adventists say, were created by God; but the devil takes possession of these spirits as soon as one believes in them. If one does not believe in them, the devil cannot get a hold on them, and the *kol* themselves are therefore quite inoffensive. 'The devil takes advantage of people's belief', an Adventist argued. Denying belief within oneself, and thus controlling one's fear, would thus be a way of rendering the devil powerless.

This, however, is not an easy task. *Katolik* tell of Adventists whose acts of defiance resulted in illness (presumably because their disbelief was not strong enough to protect them from the spirits' malevolence). In the eyes of non-SDA Sulka, these misfortunes are experimental proof that custom reappropriates those who claim to have freed themselves from it. Every calamity suffered by an

Adventist is a victory won by the custom . . . The Adventists
counter, it will be recalled, by imputing their misfortunes to the
magic of the *Katolik*, whose efficacy is due to the fact they, the
Katolik, believe in its power to harm them.

Concluding Remarks: Christian Pagans and Pagan Christians

Earlier in the century, a missionary like Father Laufer was
surprised to find that these 'pagans' were in fact less pagan than
they could (or should) have been; they must therefore in some
sense be Christians, albeit unwittingly. At the present time, the
SDA Sulka are inclined on the contrary to regard the *Katolik* as
pagans who live under the delusion of being Christians – just
pagans with pagans' failings. The *Katolik*, they say, observe the
custom, that is, they worship idols and graven images (whether it
be a carved Christ in a church or a mask in the men's house),
perform traditional ceremonies, and believe (or do not deny
believing) in magic and evil spirits. Among other things, the
(Catholic) missionaries do not forbid the smoking of tobacco, the
chewing of betel nuts, the drinking of alcohol, tea or coffee; they
do not forbid the fashioning of masks, and allow the performance
of local traditional dances at the inauguration of churches. Are
they also not acting in a pagan way?

Describing a similar situation in the Southern Highlands of
Papua New Guinea, Holger Jebens makes observations that apply
equally well to the Sulka:

> Since the Adventists base their own identity largely on the observance
> of prescribed rules, an essential difference for them is that, as they
> put it, Catholics allow everything without prohibiting anything. From
> an Adventist perspective this means that Catholics do nothing more
> than continue the life they led before missionization. If the observance
> of prescribed rules is necessary for the transformation of adherents
> of traditional religion into genuine Christians, it follows that the
> absence of these rules means that such a transformation cannot take
> place. Thus, implicitly, the Adventists not only claim that the Catholics
> are not good Christians but, moreover, that they are not Christians at
> all . . .' (Jebens 1997: 39).[15]

Among the present-day Sulka, *Katolik* is thus a generic label used either to disqualify or to honour those who observe the custom. A derogatory term when used by the Adventists, it is a term of praise for the non-SDA who thus underscore their allegiance to the traditional Sulka way of living. Compared to the SDA, the *Katolik* are indeed traditionalists, those who, when sick, for example, have recourse to curing magic rather than 'believing in hospital', as the Adventists are said to do.

Another way of formulating this opposition would be to say that, for many Sulka today, Nut, the founding ancestor, was a *Katolik*, whereas God is an Adventist.

Acknowledgement

Many thanks to Charles Fredrikson (Centre d'Études Portugaises – École des Hautes Études en Sciences Sociales) for having made this paper readable in English. Although the analyses developed here are not binding on him, I wish also to say how stimulating his comments on this topic and other related matters, such as those presented in two of his papers (1991 and 1994) have been.

Notes

1. On the local reception of missionary activity, see for example the contributions in Barker (1990) and in Boutilier, Hugues and Tiffany (1978).
2. Since 1980, I've done fieldwork among the Sulka on four occasions (for a total of about 24 months); this ongoing research has been funded by the Centre National de la Recherche Scientifique (CNRS), Paris.
3. *E Nut vlou* (the 'great Nut') is the founding ancestor of Sulka society, and the 'father of the customs'. According to Sulka myths, *E Nut sie* (the 'lesser Nut'), his junior, is described either as his brother, a cousin or a mere homonym.
4. The notion of an ambivalent God, which Laufer found prevalent in the religions of many other New Britain societies (the Kilenge,

Bariai, Nakanai, Baining, among others), is viewed by him as a feature which strengthens the parallel with Christianized: '. . . that the same god, considered as the father and benefactor of mankind, might also have another aspect . . . that of some-body thirsty for revenge and often horrible reprisals . . . Is not this also, for many Christians today in the entire world, an unfathomable mystery?' (Laufer 1955: 60).

5. Though Laufer doesn't refer to it explicitly, there is a clear analogy here with the notion of *Urmonotheismus* developed by Father Wilhelm Schmidt in his monumental work, *Der Ursprung der Gottesidee: Eine historisch-kritische und positive Studie* (1912–55).

6. Sulka members of a movement disparagingly labelled 'cargo cult' by both Church and Administration also vehemently affirm that the Sulka are, or were, Christians in their own right, albeit unwittingly, and observed the Ten Commandments before the Sulka were evangelized (Jeudy-Ballini 1997).

7. Harris explains that for Father Wilhelm Schmidt, who strongly influenced missionaries like Carl Laufer, God's revelation, by which religion was given to men at the very outset of time, should be understood as 'a literal, personal appearance such as is described in Genesis' (1968: 391). In Schmidt's own words: 'It must have been a tremendous, mighty personality that presented itself to them . . . this personality cannot have been a merely internal image of the mind and imagination . . . Rather, it must have been really and truly a personality that presented itself to them from without, and that precisely by the power of its reality convinced and overwhelmed them' (Schmidt, quoted by Harris 1968: 391).

8. The Tok Pisin term *Katolik* has no equivalent – literal, peri-phrastic or metaphorical – in the vernacular. As for the Seventh-Day Adventists, they are designated solely by the initials SDA. I shall use these appellations unaltered through-out this chapter.

9. The Sulka do not have collective magic, nor do they have experts in magic. Every man or woman resorts to his or her own private magic, which is obtained through dreams or inherited.

10. For reasons of confidentiality, the names of my Sulka inform-ants have been changed.

11. Just as he laughs of his past actions and beliefs, thus distancing

himself from them, so the speaker at this point refers to his past self in the third person.

12. Commenting further about 'custom', the previously quoted informant affirmed that prayer was a traditional Sulka practice, an endogenous, not a specifically Christian, skill. 'In the days when we were not yet Christians, we prayed already, it was already prayer.' It was however misguided prayer: 'But', he went on, reverting to a more denunciatory attitude, 'our prayers were not addressed to God, but to the demon'. On other occasions, too, he defined magic as 'prayer to the demon'.

13. Even a sorcerer, it is said, is not invulnerable to these aggressions, and will take to avoid places infested with sharks and crocodiles, for his victim's *nunu* pursues him everywhere. This explains, among other things, why a sorcerer is not a successful hunter or fisherman.

14. *Kol* spirits are associated with snakes, and often assume their appearance; lightning is said to be an expression of their displeasure.

15. Sasha Josephides makes a similar observation about the Boroi people of New Guinea: '. . . there is even a possibility that Christianity is equated with Seventh-Day Adventism and Catholicism with traditional religion' (Josephides 1990: 60).

References

Aerts, T. (1978). The Old Testament through Melanesian Eyes. *Point* 2: 42–70.

Barker, J. (ed.) (1990). *Christianity in Oceania. Ethnographic Perspectives.* Lanham, New York, London: University Press of America.

Boutilier, J., Hugues, D. and Tiffany, S. (eds) (1978). *Mission, Church, and Sect in Oceania.* Lanham, New York, London. University Press of America.

Fredrikson, C. (1991). Certains l'aiment nature. *Sciences Sociales et Santé* 9(1): 21–37.

——— (1994). La duplicité de la femme: sorcières jouisseuses et disqualification féminine. In: Actes du Colloque *Ethnologie du Portugal: unité et diversité*, pp. 225–57. 1992. Paris: Centre Culturel Calouste Gulbenkian.

Harris, M. (1968). *The Rise of Anthropological Theory. A History of Theories of Culture.* New York: Harper & Row.

Janssen, H. (1975). Creative Deities and the Role of Religion in New Britain. An Evaluation of Carl Laufer's Anthropological Concern. In: H. Janssen, J. Sterly, and K. Wittkemper (eds), *Carl Laufer MSC, Missionar und Ethnologe auf Neu-Guinea. Eine Gedenkschrift für Pater Carl Laufer MSC gewidmet von seinen Freunden*, pp. 19–39. Freiburg, Basel, Wien: Herder.

Jebens, H. (1997). Catholics, Seventh-Day Adventists and the Impact of Tradition in Pairudu (Southern Highlands Province, Papua New Guinea). In: T. Otto and A. Borsboom (eds), *Cultural Dynamics of Religious Change in Oceania*, pp. 33–43. Leiden: KITLV Press.

Jeudy-Ballini, M. (1997). Culte du cargo ou culte du péché? Un rite mélanésien pour rendre Dieu meilleur. In: S. Tcherkézoff and F. Marsaudon (eds), *Le Pacifique-sud contemporain. Identités et transformations culturelles* pp. 111–34. Paris: CNRS Editions.

Josephides, S. (1990). Seventh-Day Adventism and the Boroi Image of the Past. In: N. Lutkehaus *et al.* (eds), *Sepik Heritage: Tradition and Change in Papua New Guinea*, pp. 58–66. Durham: Carolina Academic Press.

Laufer, C. (1946–9). Rigenmucha, das Höchste Wesen der Baining (Neubritannien). *Anthropos* 41–4: 497–560.

—— (1950a). Gott und das Aschenbrödel der Südsee. *Hiltruper Monatshefte*, pp. 184–7.

—— (1950b). Die Mission als geistiger Wiederaufbau der Menschheit. *Zeitschrift für Missionswissenschaft und Religionswissenschaft* 34: 261–78.

—— (1952a). Igal und Mana, eine religionwissenschaftliche Studie. *Zeitschrift für Missionswissenschaft und Religionswissenschaft* 36: 133–44.

—— (1952b). Notes on New Britain Religion. *Mankind* 4(9): 381–2.

—— (1955). Aus Geschichte und Religion der Sulka. *Anthropos* 50: 32–64.

Meier, J. (1945). Reminiscences. A Memoir. *Chronicle* special issue.

O'Neill, T. (1972). *And We the People. Ten Years with the Primitive Tribes of New Guinea.* Vunapope: Catholic Mission Press.

Schmidt, W. (1912–1955). *Der Ursprung der Gottesidee.* Münster: Ascherdorff.

Schneider, J. (1932). Sulka (und die weitere Südküste von Neubritannien). In: J. Hüskes (ed.), *Pioniere der Südsee. Werden und*

Wachsen der Herz-Jesu-Mission von Rabaul zum Goldenen Jubiläum 1882–1932, pp. 47–59. Hiltrup, Salzburg: [Missionshaus].

Turner, H.W. (1978). Old and New Religions in Melanesia. *Point* 2: 5–29.

Part V

Experiencing Outside Worlds

Chapter 9

Experiencing Outside Worlds: Tannese Labour Recruitment in the Second Half of the Nineteenth Century

Ronald Adams

'Traditional' Tannese Journeys

Before its boundaries were exploded by contact with traders from the 1840s on, the end of the known world for the Tannese was Mataso, a small island just to the north of Efate. For the great majority of Tannese most of their own island was beyond the range of immediate experience, with only a small proportion of men permitted to venture beyond their particular *niko* ('canoe') or territory, and even then only along traditionally-sanctioned pathways that led to precise destinations. These paths or roads (*rot* in the lingua franca, Bislama) linked the principal *yimwayim* (traditionally sanctioned meeting spaces) of the island and according to legend had been created by the *kapiel*, or magic stones. The *kapiel* had arrived on Tanna before the appearance of people and had brought with them a range of magical and cosmic powers that eventually were to reside with the men of Tanna. At some point in time the stones had fallen silent and affixed themselves along the tracks where they gave birth to the people and the clans, or tribes, of Tanna. Even today it is still believed that men, like the stones that gave rise to them, are implanted into the ground and bound to particular places that they are unable to leave without risking alienating the powers inherited from the *kapiel* – without risking losing their cultural identity: that 'existential aspect of those places where men live today as their ancestors did from time immemorial'. Being so fraught with risk, travel had to be strictly regulated – in theory by the dignitary known as the *yeremwanu* ('chief'), who controlled the flow of goods and the movement of people along every section of the paths passing through his *niko*. Only in exceptional circumstances could the *yeremwanu* himself move away from the place and the *kapiel* from which he drew his strength. Instead, another dignitary, the *yani niko* ('master of the canoe'), travelled in his name, proposing and organizing exchanges and meetings between different groups and, when necessary, directing the operations of war. This political control of space, this organizational expression of the essential relationship between man and place, left little room for innovation, and closely controlled the range of relationships available to local groups. Travel could not be for the Tannese (as it was for their European visitors) a neutral movement from one place to another. Rather, it was, as Bonnemaison has remarked, 'a journey in the cultural sense of the word – an experience imbued with meaning and ritual, inherent in the action of movement and sanctioned beyond the territory of identity, concluding with an encounter'. The man who risked a journey beyond the sanctioned limits, or along unfamiliar paths, was (to borrow Bonnemaison's metaphor) an explorer – facing many dangers but, if successful in creating a new connection, also winning great prestige.[1]

Post-European Contact Voyages

When regular European contact after 1842 increased the volume, frequency and especially the range of travel available to the coastal inhabitants of southern Vanuatu, an unprecedented number of Tannese men – and increasingly women – could contemplate their own voyage of exploration; and with the establishment of European plantations throughout the Pacific and in Queensland from the 1860s it became a virtual *rite de passage* for young Tanna men to undertake at least one journey of exploration abroad – to places as far afield as Australia, Fiji, New Caledonia, Samoa, Hawaii and the Carolines.

We will never know exactly how many Tannese undertook these journeys. Many of the engagements went unrecorded, and even when records were kept the island of origin was not always specified. Where it was, no distinction was made between 'old hands' and those recruiting for the first time until 1892, when the

Queensland government started compiling the statistics. There is anecdotal evidence that well before this time the Tannese were particularly well-travelled; and extrapolating from the available figures – though not discounting for re-engagements – it can be calculated that by the time the New Hebrides Condominium was proclaimed in 1906 as many as 1,200 Tannese had signed on for plantation work within the group (cf. Bonnemaison 1985: 67; Adams 1986). About the same number had engaged for Fiji (Adams 1984: 172; Siegel 1985). Possibly another one to two thousand were among the many thousands of ni-Vanuatu estimated to have worked in New Caledonia up to 1906.[2] Even larger numbers of Tannese were attracted to Queensland: by official reckoning, 4,241 between 1863 and 1904 (cf. Price and Baker 1976; Moore 1985: 25). Tannese also recruited in much smaller numbers for Samoa, Hawaii, Tahiti and even the western reaches of Micronesia.[3] In all, during the second half of the nineteenth century some thousands of Tannese were to be found spread throughout the Pacific and Australia – testimony to a deeply-felt urge, particularly but not exclusively among young men, to embark on lengthy journeys of exploration.

The prevailing missionary view, also at times the official British view, was that the recruits had all been kidnapped and then held in virtual slavery against their will. For missionaries the 'slave trade' was an 'unmitigated evil', with 'slavers' 'preying on the ignorance and credulity of the poor natives', 'deceiving, cajoling and exciting' the 'childish susceptibilities' of 'speechless savages' for 'musical attractions and offers of prizes', 'dragging down its helpless victims to a condition worse than that of beasts'.[4] Certainly in the early years of the traffic there were Tannese who, in the words of the missionary McNair, were 'seduced on board by false promises of tobacco, &c.', without 'understand[ing] anything about engagements'. Some were seized and dragged by the hair on board recruiting vessels, where they were detained at the point of a gun. Others were pressured into signing on after taking refuge on board during periods of inter-group fighting. Others were engaged while under the influence of alcohol.[5] Probably the most common abuse was the practice of pretending that the period of labour was only for a short duration. Another abuse was engaging labourers ostensibly for one place but then delivering them to another. Some Tannese signing on for Fiji and Queensland around 1884, for example, were delivered instead to New Caledonia or Samoa. In another reported abuse, ni-Vanuatu reluctant to work in New Caledonia's nickel mines signed on for other work in the French colony only to be despatched to the mines on reaching Noumea.[6] For every accusation of kidnapping and deception there is a corresponding report of eager Tannese volunteers. This is not the same as claiming that the recruits entered into freely negotiated contracts, or that they were not exploited by a system that valued people for their financial return: a system in which newly landed recruits were marched in gangs to the verandah of the owner's store where they were left for the inspection of intending purchasers and then sold off to the highest bidder; a system moreover in which fantastic profits were to be made. Perhaps Clive Moore's phrase 'cultural kidnapping' best sums up the essential imbalance resulting from the ability of European recruiters and employers to bring a 'more global outlook' to their dealings with the people of the south west Pacific. But as Moore notes, it is demeaning to the intelligence of Melanesians to presume that they continued to present themselves to be kidnapped from the same beaches on the same islands generation after generation (Moore 1985: 47; cf. Panoff 1979).

The individual motivations of islanders who did recruit would have been many and varied. According to Deputy Resident Commissioner Rason, some recruited to earn a good box with plenty of trade, some young men engaged to run away with another man's wife, or having had an affair with the woman were attempting to escape the husband's revenge. Others, he claimed, recruited because the marriage ceremony had ruined them and it was necessary to go away to earn money. Some sailed away to obtain arms. Others, according to Rason, simply wanted a change, and once on board the recruiting vessel would regret their action.[7] If Bonnemaison is correct, however, behind all these particular reasons, and imbuing the experience of recruiting with meaning and ritual, was the cultural dimension of the journey. It was a dimension beyond the imagination of Europeans like Rason, who proclaimed that what the 'natives' *really* wanted were habits of industry and moral uplifting, with a few trade goods thrown in for good measure – a rather convenient understanding when it came to remuneration. 'These people . . . get their food, and clothing, are housed and looked after and get some small wages besides', Richard Philp confided to his diary while visiting a Fiji plantation employing mainly Tannese labourers in 1872. 'I should

say it does them good to learn habits of regular, steady work.'
According to Acting Consul Thurston, the early ni-Vanuatu recruits
to Fiji were happy to a man: 'engaged by a respectable planter, all
clothed, housed, and fed well, and taught habits of cleanliness'.
They had even learned to cover their nakedness! Surgeon Comrie
of HMS *Dido* was particularly impressed with the general bearing
and discipline of the labourers who had been some time on the
plantations – an improvement that, in European eyes, reflected
great credit on their masters.[8] In New Caledonia even to work for
a less than reputable planter was considered to 'elevate' recruits
'a little above their savage state'. By this measure, the Tannese
working for the paternal Joubert in New Caledonia or the kindly
Graham in Fiji, with their weekend presents of tobacco, would
have experienced more than just a little elevation from savagery,
as reflected (so Europeans liked to suppose) in their working so
'well and willingly' for fourteen hours a day (Royal Commission
1869: 3, 45; cf. Palmer 1871: 15).

Changing Work Patterns

The work they performed was not confined to plantation labour.
In New Caledonia, for example, Tannese and other migrants
engaged in a diversity of occupations ranging from coffee
plantation hands and domestic servants, to labourers in stores and
on the wharves, to work in the mines. In Queensland, even after
the passage of the restrictive 1884 Act, time-expired labourers
continued to be employed as cooks, domestic servants, store
assistants, farm labourers and timbercutters. It is reasonable to
assume that there were also Tannese working in the proscribed
occupations of engineer, engine-driver, engine-fitter, blacksmith,
wheelwright, farrier, sugar boiler, carpenter, sawyer, splitter,
fencer, bullock-driver and mechanic; though the strengthening of
the trade union movement among European workers in the 1890s
eventually saw Melanesian workers confined to manual field
labour on sugar plantations. In Fiji the trend was the opposite,
with 'no immigrants . . . employed as field-labourers on sugar-
cane plantations' by 1906. There, besides cultivating coconuts,
indentured workers were to be found in sugar mills, stores,
butcheries and public utilities in Suva and Levuka. Even the
Tannese who recruited only within Vanuatu were exposed to a

radically new economic order, with cash crops ranging from bananas grown for export to introduced cotton, coffee, tobacco and maize, new production methods, a new sense of time-management and a view of human labour as a commodity with a price. As early as 1870 the Tannese engaged on Hebblewhite's Efate cotton plantation were learning to work with large, steam-driven gins; and even on the less-capitalized plantations they still had to be able to operate hand gins capable of turning out forty-five kilograms of cotton a day.[9]

In return for their labour, Tannese plantation workers in the 1870s were paid the equivalent of £2 or £3 per annum in Fiji and Vanuatu and as much as £10 (with an average of £6) in New Caledonia.[10] In the 1880s the minimum in Queensland was £6 per annum, with 'old hands' earning up to £12, much the same as in New Caledonia and within Vanuatu – though it is clear that a number of French planters on Efate systematically underpaid their labourers.[11] The view of human labour as a commodity to be bought and sold, with a precise monetary as opposed to social value, was further strengthened by the practice of augmenting wages with inducements to encourage speedy work. At Havannah Harbour, Hebblewhite gave a ticket to the value of about two pence (old currency) to every man who picked over fifteen kilograms of cotton a day, the accumulated prizes being paid weekly. In addition, a knife or similar article was awarded to the individual who picked the most cotton during one week. A similar system operated on some plantations in Fiji to encourage labourers to work on Sundays. Coming on top of the obligatory ten to fourteen hour working day Monday to Friday and half day on Saturday, it might be assumed that these piece-work arrangements would have reinforced an experience of 'work' as an alienated and alienating activity.[12] However, this presumes that 'work' remained divorced from other aspects of social life, and that labourers did not invest their life on the plantations with a meaning and a significance whose roots stretched back to their home islands.

Continuing Cultural Frameworks

As Clive Moore's and Patricia Mercer's studies of plantation life in Queensland have shown, the evidence suggests otherwise. Despite attempts to have them live in standard wooden barracks and houses, most labourers preferred to construct grass and leaf houses of traditional Melanesian design – though the longer they stayed in Australia the larger and more European their houses were likely to become, especially if they were married. But for the great majority of immigrants their dwellings provided a link with island-based spatial and cultural concepts, and a powerful buffer against alien worldviews. Even within the wooden barracks the separation of male and female quarters conformed to the familiar sexual demarcation, and with the large number of Tannese labourers on many plantations all-Tannese barracks would have been a feature on some of the larger estates (Mercer 1981: 24; Moore 1985: 211, 214). It was virtually impossible to strictly adhere to customary restrictions on sexual spacing within the confines of ships or plantation mills, or to exactly replicate traditional dwellings given the building materials available, but it was possible for recruits to maintain a sense of continuity and identification with their home islands.

Similarly, it was possible for recruits to sustain a sense of customary practices in the food they ate. Officially, after 1868 labourers in Queensland received European fare like beef or mutton, bread or flour, sugar or molasses and vegetables, though boiled meat and potatoes continued to constitute the mainstay of plantation rations, but, as Moore has shown, it was common for labourers to supplement their rations with what they obtained from hunting, fishing and bush foraging as well as what they grew in their own gardens. The cultivation of root crops and greens – including yams, taro and island greens specially imported by recruits – the hunting of kangaroos, possums and wild fowls, and the fishing for bream and flathead provided more than supplementary food. They also kept alive island-based horticultural, hunting and fishing magics and techniques and helped to maintain the political structure based on the possession of knowledge in these areas. Group-based expeditions and feasts also reinforced a sense of solidarity among Tannese co-labourers. At the same time, labourers were exposed to strange foods, to new magics and techniques, to tools and implements bereft of magical sign and to the realization that it was possible to successfully grow and collect food on land with which they did not have ancient connections and rights.[13]

A similar convergence of island-based and Western beliefs and practices occurred in the area of medical care, where customary magic and folklore and traditionally sanctioned use of herbs and plants for a wide range of ailments coexisted with the treatment provided by European doctors on the plantations and in the separate Kanaka wards and hospitals. Planters had been responsible for the medical treatment of their employees since 1868, and with the high incidence of respiratory, gastro-intestinal and infectious diseases among the Melanesian population of Queensland few Tannese would have escaped the need for some medical attention during their time in the colony. Given the Tannese view of the aetiology of disease, it is highly unlikely that the Tannese being treated by Western methods did not at the same time have recourse to more traditional remedies, or that they did not attribute their illness to some supernatural cause. Interviews with the descendants of Pacific islander labourers by Moore and Mercer revealed not only that tales of sorcery, angry spirits and ritual deaths were commonplace but that the practice of 'indigenous religion and magic' continued in Queensland as late as the Second World War (Mercer 1981: 50; Mercer and Moore 1976: 79–80; Moore 1985: 236–7, 272–3). Given that the Tannese, along with the Malaitans, had a reputation for clinging tenaciously to their 'custom ways', it was perhaps only to be expected that when several islanders died mysteriously on one Maryborough plantation, suspicion fell on a Tannese woman who was believed to have carried objects for sorcery in a cavity in her hair (cf. *Quarterly Jottings* No 95, January 1917: 2; Mercer 1981: 52–3). However, with his acknowledgment that certain areas of belief were 'held in abeyance or modified to fit their new circumstances', it is necessary to qualify Moore's conclusion that 'overall their traditional belief system continued to operate, allowing them to function culturally as Melanesians within European-controlled surroundings' (Moore 1985: 272–3). For the Tannese as much as for the Malaitan recruits to whom Moore is specifically referring, while beliefs and actions continued to have many points of contact with the 'systems' with which they had grown up, the holding in abeyance and the modification of 'certain areas of belief' constituted change to their 'belief systems', whether or not these are defined as 'traditional'. In terms of its impact on islands like Tanna, what is important is the extent to which labourers returned to their villages and attempted to apply the new means of dealing with sorcery, angry spirits and ritual deaths to which they had been exposed in the Kanaka wards.

In the same way, it is difficult to gauge the impact of the recruits' exposure to the cash economy and their awareness of the value of money. In the early years wages had been mainly, if not exclusively, paid in trade goods and it is not difficult to see how the prized 'trade box' could be readily integrated into existing exchange networks on Tanna. The trade box was never superseded, but with the passage of time there was a greater demand for payment in money, which could then be used back on Tanna to purchase guns and ammunition from resident traders and visiting vessels, to the extent that many recruits began to demand that the enlistment bonus, previously paid to their kin in goods, be paid directly to them in cash.[14] Time-expired labourers in the Maryborough district between 1884 and 1901 earned an average of £20/6/- per annum. Tannese like Jimmy Kalo, who recruited for Fiji aboard the *Clansman* in 1906, earned between £12 and £24 per annum with food (and up to £30 without food) under the Government-supervised terms of agreement.[15] In Queensland, Yarrowil, who had recruited from Tanna in 1880, had saved over £42 by 1903 in the Government Savings Bank; Konyea or Billy Tanna, who had arrived in 1881, over £35; Erranick, in Queensland since 1892, nearly £26. The 153 ni-Vanuatu, including ten Tannese, who were repatriated from Queensland on the *Sydney Belle* in 1906 had between them £265 in wages for the last three months and £741 withdrawn from the Savings Bank.[16] Savings accounts and cash in hand do not in themselves reflect a fundamental shift in values, which is more accurately gauged by how the money was ultimately spent rather than how much was accumulated over a period of time. Most islanders returning home appear to have continued to convert their cash into physical pleasure at pubs and brothels or into goods at plantation 'Kanaka stores' to take home in their large wooden trade boxes rather than hold on to their money. Nonetheless, the savings accounts are evidence of the Tannese being presented with new options, and of their ability to utilize the European economic order to their own ends (Mercer 1981: 62; Moore 1985: 188). Even for those Tannese who would appear to have been fulfilling 'traditional' ends when they willingly turned their backs on plantation life and returned home laden with goods, the new contexts in which they had acquired those goods inevitably invested them with a changed meaning and significance. In terms of subsequent developments on Tanna, more important than the amount of cash individuals like Yarrowil or Kalo were able to accumulate, was the knowledge of the operation of the colonial cash economy with which, along with their bulging boxes, nearly all recruits returned home.

New Layers of Consciousness

Ex-recruits also returned home with knowledge of the cultural and political dimensions of colonial society, combined at times with an unwillingness to accept the inferior position assigned to them by Europeans (cf. Mercer 1981: 54). In the case of Tannese recruits this unwillingness built upon a pre-existing ideology of rights based on the principle of reciprocity that underpinned all their social relations.[17] Some planters might have liked to suppose that their Tannese recruits were such good workers because they were both wonderfully strong and at the same time docile and affectionate (Eden 1872: 313, 326–7). The reason the Tannese worked so hard was not because they stood in affectionate awe of Europeans, however, but because they understood so well the nature of a contract. This cut both ways, and commentators who remarked upon the Tannese willingness to serve their masters faithfully also acknowledged their fierce determination to hold the employers to their side of the bargain. Thus the same Tannese recruits who would risk their lives one year defending their employers against alienated Fijians could rise up the next year and kill a planter because he was unable or unwilling to pay them off and return them home at the end of their term.[18] What the experience of colonial society did for the Tannese was to 'overlay', and in so doing transform, their understanding of human relationships based on the principle of reciprocity, with a new form of industrial–political consciousness which reflected their subordinate status both as 'workers' and as 'islanders' in European-dominated emerging capitalist societies. In New Caledonia the new consciousness was spawned by an indenture system in which police and government officials systematically conspired to cheat ni-Vanuatu workers (Shineberg 1991). Although labour regulations were more likely to be enforced in Queensland and Fiji, the operation of Masters and Servants Acts in the British colonies still served to institutionalize the subordinate position of ni-Vanuatu labourers. As Shineberg has commented, the planter 'mentality' was essentially the same in all the colonies, French or

British, 'where . . . the privileges of the white settlers appeared to them to be part of the natural order' (Shineberg 1991: 200). Evidence of islander resistance to this 'natural order' may be found in the Returns showing offences and convictions of so-called 'Polynesians' in Queensland in the 1880s and 1890s.[19] Only occasionally is it possible to identify Tannese offenders, such as:

Harry Tanna, sentenced to 12 months imprisonment for assault,
Tom Tanna, 2 months for damaging property,
Bob Tanna, 2 months for disorderly conduct,
Reg Tanna, 7 days for disorderly conduct,
Captain Tanna, 3 months for threatening language,
Jack Tanna, 2 months for assault,
Charlie Tanna, 6 months for aggravated assault,
Tom Tanna, 2 months for assault,
Joe Tanna, 1 month for larceny,
Yow Tanna, 3 months for aggravated assault,
Bob Tanna, imprisonment for possession of opium,
George Tanna, refusing to proceed to sea, 21 days,
Ned Tanna, drunk and disorderly, 24 hours,
Joe Tanna, 3 months for assault, and 1 month for attempting to escape from gaol,
Jack Tanna, 7 days for drunkenness,
Johnnie Tanna, 2 months for drunkenness,
Harry Tanna, 4 weeks for deserting ship,
Joe Tanna, 4 months for being drunk and obscene,
Tom Tanna, 7 days for drunkenness,
Dick Tanna, 3 weeks for being drunk and resisting police,
Jack Tanna, 2 months for assault.

In contrast to the Returns overall, where absconding from hired service, refusing duty and disobeying orders are the most common offences, a feature of the Tanna list is the absence of breaches of the Masters and Servants Act and related 'crimes', though it is possible that a significant number of Tannese are 'hidden' among the offenders identified only by a single European name. Regardless of the actual range of offences for which Tannese were convicted in Queensland, the important point in terms of subsequent developments on Tanna is that many Tannese would have returned home with alternative definitions of what constituted 'offences' against the person, property, morals and authority, and with knowledge and experience of a model of social organization similar to that which local Presbyterian missionaries – with the backing of naval force – were attempting to put into place on the island. While some Tannese returned implacably opposed to the new model, others saw in it an opportunity to forge novel alliances with missionaries, naval officers and other Tannese.

Emergence of New Identities

To varying degrees, Tannese returned from their journeys abroad with identities which transcended traditional descent lines – identities that found expression in the new European designations like Joe Tanna, Tom Tanna or Johnnie Tanna. The identification as 'Tannese' complemented their new roles as 'workers' *vis-à-vis* bosses, and as 'kanakas' *vis-à-vis* other workers. In Queensland time-expired and ticket-holding[20] recruits chose where and for whom they worked, negotiated with employers over wages, and took collective strike action – sometimes on the basis of descent group, language or island identity, at other times cutting across these lines. Parallel with their new industrial awareness went a knowledge of their legal rights as time-expired labourers took their complaints of maltreatment or conditions of service to the Inspectors of Pacific Islanders, brought assault charges against heavy-handed overseers and brought their employers to court under the Masters and Servants Act. Some, like Pacific Islands Association committee member Sandy Tanna, learned to use European meeting procedures to air their grievances and to organize politically across descent and ethnic lines to fight for their rights. Many attended Anglican and Presbyterian plantation missions not only to be baptized and confirmed as Christians but also to learn to read and write. Increasingly, they sent their children to mission and government schools.[21] It is impossible to know the extent to which all this 'changed' the Tannese. As Mercer has noted, it was common for groups to recruit together, often under the leadership of a man who had recruited before, and in the colony they maintained an informal network of communications, coming together at the end of their indenture or at any subsequent engagements to decide whether to stay or to return. In Fiji, it was policy under Thurston to keep recruits from the same village together during the period of indenture, even if they changed plantations.[22] Sunday was typically a time for visiting friends or relatives on neighbouring plantations, and through transfers or re-engagements kin could move closer together. More than many other groups, the Tannese continued to live in close proximity to each other, as at Herbert River where four Tannese families and one childless widower lived together in a settlement known locally as The Gardens. Even among those who planned to settle permanently in Queensland, a sense of Tannese identity was encouraged and nurtured, either self-consciously or through the efforts of other Tannese. Repatriated against his will and heading back to Tanna on the *Ivanhoe* in 1905, Harry Nogah (his wife having been detained in a Queensland leprosarium) found himself and his four young daughters surrounded and protected by the *Ivanhoe*'s five other Tannese, who marked out a separate 'Tanna space' in the men's quarters and declared it off limits to the other passengers. As the Immigration Officer commented: 'The Tannese would all camp together and . . . would jealously guard each other against any interference attempted by anyone but particularly a Solomon Islander.' Among the Tannese who stayed on in Queensland there was a similar *esprit de corps*, with a continuing preference for their children to marry partners also of Tannese descent. This identification as 'Tannese' was itself a new development generated by the recruiting experience, cutting across the customary descent lines defined by one's *niko*. As Mercer has documented, life in Queensland involved many such interactions with islanders who fell outside the circle of those who would 'traditionally' count as friends. Through their involvement with missions, their participation in political associations to improve conditions or oppose deportations, and even in their so-called inter-tribal fighting, with Tannese against Malaitan, or ni-Vanuatu against Solomon Islander, many Tannese labourers came to identify in varying degrees not just with fellow villagers, but with other Tannese, other ni-Vanuatu and other Melanesians (Mercer 1981: 59–60, 150–1, 168).

These new identifications did not necessarily contradict the traditionally sanctioned model of creating new connections with the outside world – at least not for Tannese men. For women to traverse such paths constituted a radical departure from the model, a deviation that threatened Tannese patriarchy. While the male guardians of the existing order might have dismissed and denigrated the women who recruited with their accusation that they were 'simply eloping', for the women themselves recruitment offered unprecedented scope for independence. Six months after leaving her village of Ibet in 1878 with four other women, Nuswoya (or 'Dinah') had moved from agricultural work on a Kirkcubbin plantation to (unspecified) duties at the Maryborough Visitors Club. Even after the 1884 restrictions in Queensland, female recruits were still frequently employed as cooks, domestic servants and children's nurses, having been taught new skills by mission teachers, female employers and other more experienced islander women. Although their rates of pay were consistently lower than men's, through the wages they earned women gained an unprecedented measure of economic freedom. There may well have been some Tannese among those women who enjoyed the independence of a savings bank account in their own name. Others might not have built up capital but returned home to Tanna celebrating Queensland for its 'Plenty MANO (dress) [and] plenty KI-KI (food)'. As well as experiencing material improvement, a number of women began to assume a larger role in public life than had been possible at home – like Numanipen, who remained an active Church member on her return from Queensland in 1899 despite her husband's 'heathenism'.[23] Some, like Yamei, would seem to have exercised an unprecedented degree of independence in choosing their own partner – though it is likely that a number of such liaisons were arranged by Tannese (or other) males on the same plantation.

Negotiating New Narratives of the Self

For the men and women who journeyed abroad, such innovation was always constrained by culture – though culture itself was constantly changing in the light of innovation. What Bonnemaison has described as the cultural voyages of those who recruited were simultaneously revolutionary experiences and affirmations of the need for all experience to serve 'traditional' ends. As Moore's and Mercer's research has shown, long after they left home recruits continued to eat similar food, sleep in a 'native' hut and practise their island magic, but the contexts were different. For recruits from Tanna, one of the new contexts was interaction and identification with other Tannese who did not belong to their immediate descent group – giving rise to what Speiser described as a strong sense of 'clannishness' among the Tannese – so that what they ate, where they slept and how they performed their magic came to be viewed as belonging to the whole of Tanna as well as a particular descent group such as the Kaserumene. Being so removed from the contexts on Tanna that had invested their actions and beliefs with meaning, however, meant that transplanted 'Tannese' food, huts and magic ran the risk of becoming fetishes, mere trappings of what it was to be 'Tannese'. For some Tannese, the voyage abroad so changed their sense of identity that Tanna no longer beckoned them as 'home'. For others, the journey so focussed and clarified their identification with 'home' that they were surely pierced to the soul as they pined for their own *niko*, their own *kapiel* and also, eventually, their own Tanna, thousands of miles away. Even for the latter, however, their canoe, their stones and their land could never, in the light of their journey, be the same again. Even if they viewed 'home' with a new-found commitment and reverence, it was located in a different, more global context, which invested 'traditional' food, huts and magic with new points of reference.

Working for money, being subject to different definitions of social and moral order, and (in the case of women) having additional scope for expressing independence from male control, added to the repertoire of the 'positions of enunciation' (to use Homi Bhabha's phrase) available to the people of islands like Tanna. Whatever term is chosen to describe the process (including 'hybrid', 'syncretic' or 'diasporic'), the critical factor in terms of understanding the meanings of Tannese cultural voyages is the recognition that the terms of cultural engagement, as Bhabha puts it, 'whether antagonistic or affiliative, are produced performatively', and should not be 'hastily read as the reflection of *pre-given* ethnic or cultural traits set in the fixed tablet of tradition' (Bhabha 1994: 2). From this perspective, it would be a mistake to view the Tannese cultural journeys described by Bonnemaison in terms of a static cultural model with which the Tannese identified. It would also be misleading to view them as giving rise to a fusion of 'traditional' and 'modern', in the sense of discrete identities coming together to constitute another self-contained (albeit composite) identity. Rather, they represent a dynamic process of negotiations between various cross-cutting identities – what Stuart Hall terms 'positionalities' – which constitute the sense of self according to the constantly changing contexts of 'tribe', 'clan', 'moiety', 'island', 'race', 'gender', 'class', 'tradition' etc. In the unfolding narrative of the self, particular positionalities will be enunciated, in the sense of being emphasized or privileged, *vis-à-vis* other possible positionalities. In the end, as Hall has observed in relation to more recent times and more familiar places, 'every identity is placed, positioned, in a culture, a language, a history. Every statement comes from somewhere, from somebody in particular. It insists on specificity, on conjuncture. But it is not necessarily armour-plated against other identities' (Hall 1986: 46; cf. Terry 1995).

Following Bonnemaison, we might conclude that the Tannese men and women who journeyed abroad in the second half of the nineteenth century experienced the 'outside world' in the light of 'Tannese culture', but we would also have to say that at the same time their experience and construction of 'Tannese culture' occurred in the context of their new engagements with the 'outside world'.

Notes

1. The analysis offered in this opening paragraph is based on Bonnemaison (1984 and 1985).
2. Personal conversation with Dorothy Shineberg; cf. Shineberg (1991: 187), where it is estimated that 12,550 ni-Vanuatu worked in the French colony up to 1925.
3. Bridges to High Commissioner, 9 August 1882, Western Pacific Archives (hereinafter WPA) (136/1882); Moses (1973); O'Connor (1968); Firth (1973); Acland, Remarks on Labour Traffic, 20 October 1884, Admiralty (hereinafter ADM) (1/6706); Goodenough to Admiralty, 15 November 1873, enclosed in Admiralty to Colonial Office, 18 February 1874, Great Britain. Parliamentary Papers (hereinafter PP) 1874; 'Statement of white men at Yap', 16 August 1883, 'Statement of New Hebridean natives at Yap', 17 August 1883, 'Statement of D.D. O'Keefe', 19 August 1883, WPA (159/1883).
4. 'Third Annual Dayspring Report', 1866, Reformed Presbyterian Magazine (hereinafter RPM) (1867:135); Paton to High Commissioner, 10 March 1882, WPA (50/1882); Quarterly Jottings (hereinafter QJ) (2: 9–10, 5: 14–5, 24: 1–3).

5. Palmer, 5 April 1869, PP 1871 (468) XLVIII; Royal Commission 1869: 4; Neilson to Kay, 11 December 1871, RPM (1872: 208); Paton to Kay, 1 July 1874, RPM (1875: 19).

6. Acland, 'A few remarks on the labour traffic', 20 October 1884, ADM 1/6706; Markham to Stirling, 10 February 1872; Layard to WPHC, 12 September 1887, 25 October 1887, WPA (238/ 1887, 282/1887).

7. Rason, 'Report of the Labour Traffic', 17 October 1902, printed in Australian No 178, Colonial Office (hereinafter CO) (888/ 11).

8. Sydney Morning Herald, citing a Brisbane newspaper, quoted in PP (1868–9, XLIII:29); Philp (1872); Thurston to Lambert, 4 September 1868, ADM (1/6054); Report of Surgeon Comrie, 21 May 1873, ADM (1/6261); Lt Harrington Martin to Chapman, 20 May 1873, ADM (1/6261).

9. James (1886: 151); Vict. 48 no 12, Cl. 12, cited in Moore (1985: 165–6); Moore (1985: 140–7, 161); Mercer (1981: 17–18); Fiji Legislative Council (1906); cf. Campbell (1872: 182–3, information from Hebblewhite).

10. Campbell (1872: 182–3); Report of Surgeon Comrie, 21 May 1873, ADM (1/6261); Royal Commission (1869: 3, 45, 50).

11. Cross to Commander-in-Chief, 21 March 1886, Australian Station Reports (hereinafter ASR) (1886); Moore (1985: 157, 170–1); James (1886: 150); Adams (1986: 50–7).

12. Campbell (1872: 182–3, information from Hebblewhite); Report of Surgeon Comrie, 21 May 1873, ADM (1/6261); Royal Commission (1869: 3, 45); Palmer (1871: 15); Moore (1985: 141).

13. Moore (1985: 226–7, 21 fn. 23); cf. Mercer (1981: 45–6); for Fiji cf. Report of Surgeon Comrie, 21 May 1873, ADM (1/6261).

14. Fiji Government Agent's Log for Marion Rennie; Cross to Commander-in-Chief, 16 May 1885, ADM (1/6815); Moore (1985: 157).

15. WPA (159/1883); Extract from Government Agent Popham's Log, September 1885, enclosed in Marx to Tryon, 28 October 1885, WPA (40/1886) Fiji Legislative Council, Polynesian Immigration Report for 1906; Nicholson to King, 2 November 1910, enclosed in King to WPHC, 7 December 1910; WPHC to King, 7 March 1911, WPA (30/1911); Moore (1985: 163).

16. Queensland Department of Immigration, Register of Savings Bank Accounts of Pacific Islanders c. 1870 – c. 1903; 489 Melanesians are listed in the register, with a total savings of

£3,370 in their accounts in 1903 – an average of £6/18/- per saver. The twenty-six identified Tannese had average savings of £9/6/-; Return for *Sydney Belle*, 3 May 1906, WPA (193/1906).

17. For what is still the most comprehensive account of Tannese social relations, cf. Guiart (1956).

18. Fijian Times, 2 April 1870, 29 March 1871, 5 April 1871.

19. Returns showing Offences and Convictions of Polynesians in the Colony of Queensland during the 10 years ending 31 December 1895; Returns of Polynesian Prisoners convicted from 1 January 1896 to 31 December 1899.

20. That is the 835 Melanesians resident in Queensland for over five years before 1 September 1884 who were not affected by the 1884 Act; cf. Moore (1985: 138).

21. Moore (1985: 168–9, 195, 314, 322, 327ff); Mercer (1981: 28–31, 98).

22. Thurston to Earl of Belmore, 30 March 1869, CO (881/2); Mercer (1981: 58–9).

23. Wawn to Immigration Agent Brisbane, 1 September 1882, WPA (151/1882); James (1886: 253); QJ (26: 11, 171); cf. Mercer (1981: 85–8).

References

Adams, R. (1984). *In the Land of Strangers: A Century of European Contact with Tanna, 1774–1874.* Canberra and New York: The Australian National University.

—— (1986). Indentured Labour and the Development of Plantations in Vanuatu, 1867–1922. *Journal de la Société des Océanistes* 42(82–83): 41–63.

Admirality (ADM) (Great Britain). Secretary's In-Letters, New General Series, London: Public Records Office; Microfilm, National Library of Australia.

Australian Station Reports (ASR). (1886–1907). Correspondence Respecting Outrages by Natives, Disturbances, &c., which have been the Subject of Inquiry . . . by Naval Officers in the New Hebrides. Royal Navy, Australian Station.

Bhabha, H. (1994). *The Location of Culture.* London: Routledge.

Bonnemaison, J. (1984). The Tree and the Canoe: Roots and Mobility in Vanuatu Societies. *Pacific Viewpoint* 25(2): 117–51.

—— (1985). Territorial Control and Mobility Within ni-Vanuatu Societies. In: M. Chapman and R. M. Prothero (eds), *Circulation in Population Movement: Substance and Concepts from the Melanesian Case*, pp. 57–79. London: Routledge & Kegan Paul.

Campbell, F.A. (1872). *A Year in the New Hebrides, Loyalty Islands, and New Caledonia.* Geelong and Melbourne: George Mercer & George Robertson.

Colonial Office (CO) (Great Britain). Confidential Prints.

Eden, C. H. (1872). *My Wife and I in Queensland.* London: Longmans.

Fijian Times (FT), Suva.

Firth, S.G. (1973). German Recruitment and Employment of Labourers in the Western Pacific before the First World War. PhD Thesis. Oxford: Oxford University.

Great Britain. (1871). Parliamentary Papers (PP). Correspondence Relating to the Importation of South Sea Islanders into Queensland, 1867–1868, XLVIII.

—— (1874). Correspondence Respecting Outrages Committed upon Natives of the South Sea Islands, XLV.

Guiart, J. (1956). *Un siècle et demi de contacts culturels à Tanna, Nouvelles-Hebrides.* Paris: Société des Océanistes.

Hall, S. (1986). Minimal Selves. In: L. Appignesi (ed.), *Identity: the Real Me*, pp. 44–6. London: Institute of Contemporary Arts.

James, S. (pseud. Julian Thomas, or the 'Vagabond'). (1886). *Cannibals and Convicts.* London: Cassel.

Mercer, P.M. (1981). The Survival of a Pacific Islander Population in North Queensland, 1900–1940. PhD Thesis. Canberra: Australian National University.

Mercer, P.M. and Moore, C.R (1976). Melanesians in North Queensland: The Retention of Indigenous Religious and Magical Practices. *Journal of Pacific History* 11(1): 66–88.

Moore, C.R. (1985). *Kanaka – A History of Melanesian Mackay.* Port Moresby: Institute of Papua New Guinea Studies and University of Papua New Guinea Press.

Moses, J.A. (1973). The Coolie Labour Question and German Colonial Policy in Samoa, 1900–1914. *Journal of Pacific History* 8: 101–24.

O'Connor, P.S. (1968). The Problem of Indentured Labour in Samoa under the Military Administration. *Political Science* 20(20): 10–27.

Palmer, G. (1871). *Kidnapping in the South Seas.* Edinburgh: Edmonston & Douglas.

Panoff, M. (1979). Travailleurs, recruteurs et planteurs dans l'Archipel Bismarck de 1885 à 1914. *Journal de la Société des Océanistes* 35(64): 159–73.

Philp, R. (1872). Diary, 19 August–13 December 1872, Fiji Museum 64.1, National Library of Australia Microfilm.

Price, C.A. and Baker, E. (1976). Origins of Pacific Island Labourers in Queensland, 1863–1904: A Research Note. *Journal of Pacific History* 11(2): 106–21.

Quarterly Jottings issued by the John G. Paton Mission Fund (QJ).

Queensland Department of Immigration. Register of Savings Bank Account of Pacific Islanders, c. 1870 – c. 1903. University of Queensland Microfilm.

Reformed Presbyterian Magazine (RPM), Edinburgh and Glasgow: Journal of the Reformed Presbyterian Church of Scotland.

Royal Commission, New South Wales. (1869). *Report of the Royal Commission Appointed to Inquire into Certain Alleged Cases of Kidnapping of Natives of the Loyalty Islands, &c.* Sydney: Thomas Richards, Government Printer.

Shineberg, D. (1991). 'Noumea No Good. Noumea No Pay': 'New Hebridean' Indentured Labour in New Caledonia, 1865–1925. *Journal of Pacific History* 26(2): 187–205.

Siegel, J. (1985). Origins of the Pacific Islands Labourers in Fiji. *Journal of Pacific History* 20(1): 42–54.

Terrry, L. (1995). Not a Post-Modern Nomad: An Interview with Stuart Hall on Race, Ethnicity and Identity. *Arena Magazine*, December.

Western Pacific Archives (WPA). Western Pacific High Commission Secretariat, Inwards Correspondence. National Library of Australia Microfilm.

Chapter 10

Intrusions into the Female Realm: The Medicalization of Human Procreation among the Kwanga in Papua New Guinea

Brigit Obrist van Eeuwijk

Introduction

This contribution inquires into some aspects of the relationship between traditional interpretations of fertility, gender and human procreation and those of modern health care. It is based on ethnographic studies conducted between 1980 and 1993 among the Kwanga of the Dreikikir area in the East Sepik Province. Among the Kwanga, traditional interpretations of fertility and human procreation were intimately tied to gender. To become a man, boys had to learn to control and steer the powers of their masculine bodies to achieve physical growth and procreative success in a cycle of initiations which took about 20 to 30 years to complete. Women had their own ritual to transform girls into future wives and mothers and to control their bodily capacity and potency at menstruation and childbirth.

Schindlbeck (1990) has documented how the men's cult began to crumble in the 1960s, shortly after intensified contact with the outside world and how, in the 1980s, Kwanga men struggled to evaluate and redefine their *kastom*. In this chapter I focus on the women's ritual. In the first part I offer a description and partial analysis of this ritual as I observed it in the early 1980s, when it still was a fixed and integral part of the Kwanga culture. I then explore reasons why, in 1993, women's initiations were no longer performed. My main argument is that the discarding of women's initiations signifies a fundamental transformation that can be partly explained as a local variation of the global process of 'medicalization'.

In Western societies, medicine has gradually assumed privileged knowledge and authority in solving the mystery of human procreation. The biological process of human fertilization was first understood and described in 1875 (Barnes 1973: 16; cf. Scheper-Hughes and Lock 1987: 19). In the subsequent decades the natural process of human reproduction came increasingly under the control of medicine. This process has been aided by the undoubted successes of technology and science. Pregnancy and birth – like menopause and menstruation – have increasingly been construed as medical conditions, and thus the proper subjects of medical diagnosis and treatment (Helman 1990: 145). The medicalization of human procreation is only one facet of a more general cultural transformation, namely the medicalization of life, which critical historians of Western societies (Illich 1976; Foucault 1980) have come to understand as a fairly permanent feature of industrialized societies. Few anthropologists have yet explored the medicalization of human procreation in Papua New Guinea, where it is occurring for the first time. With this contribution I hope to draw attention to this topic and to contribute to current work in this field.

Ethnographic Background

The Kwanga, about 13,000 people, settle in 25 villages that are perched on the southern foothills of the Torricelli Mountains. In many ways they still follow the *kastom bilong tumbuna*, the tradition of their ancestors. This tradition can be classified as a distinctive configuration of the yam culture complex that spreads along the coastal ranges. The Abelam and the Arapesh are probably the most famous representatives of this culture complex, which is characterized by ceremonial elaboration of yam cultivation, pig husbandry and large-scale food exchanges. Up to this date, the Kwanga primarily subsist on local food resources and their ability to use them. They practice an agroforestry system; gardening, forestry, animal husbandry, fishing, hunting, and collecting form integral parts of this system. Their political, economic and social life is founded, at least nominally, on patrilineages. A dual organization cuts across the descent system and forms the local cell of the men's cult network that spreads over the whole Dreikikir area.

In daily and ritual life, the Kwanga often refer to gendered domains representing two distinct bodies of knowledge, activities and objects: the *kastom bilong ol man* (masculine domain) and the *kastom bilong ol meri* (feminine domain). In their social separation of gendered domains the Kwanga draw on a well-known cultural theme in Papua New Guinea, namely opposition and complementarity of the sexes. Gender contrast is cast in physiological terms: masculine power and substance and feminine power and substance are symbolically portrayed as parallel as well as antithetical (see Keesing 1982). This theme finds its clearest and most dramatic expression in 'rituals of manhood' (Herdt 1982) and, where they exist as for instance among the Kwanga, in 'rituals of womanhood'.[1]

The Kwanga were first contacted by an Australian patrol in 1929 and repeatedly visited by labour recruiters in the 1930. The Second World War exposed them to a technology and military power hitherto unknown. In their 1944 offensive against the Japanese the Australians used numerous airstrikes and mistakenly dropped a bomb in a northern Kwanga village, killing at least five people (Allen 1976: 86, 91–6). The main thrust of the fierce fighting between the dogged Australians and desperate Japanese just missed the northern Kwanga villages; but news about the fighting reached the villages and caused confusion and anxiety.

After 1946, when a patrol-post was built in Dreikikir, Western influences multiplied and intensified. The area became part of a new subdistrict with headquarter in Maprik, 50 km to the east of Dreikikir. Permanent Catholic out-stations were established – for instance Bongos among the southern Kwanga in 1952 and Tau among the northern Kwanga in 1968. A striving for *bisnis* dominated the 1950s and 1960s and perhaps culminated in the 1970s in expectation of radical changes to be brought about by independence. In the northern Kwanga area, milestones in 'progress' were the construction of the Catholic missions, the opening of their community school, the building of a vehicle track, and their experiments with *bisnis* – for instance with cattle projects, passenger motor vehicles, trade stores and coffee production.

The fact that many of these experiments failed and most expectations were not fulfilled contributed to efforts to revive the

men's cult. However, in the 1980s, and even more pronouncedly
in 1993, the cult had many opponents among the Kwanga. On
several occasions, both informal and formal, Kwanga people
claimed that the cult members were liars and called the cult itself
a *rabis kastom* (rubbish or bad tradition).

The Kwanga Ritual of Womanhood

Women's lives and the feminine domain were, of course, also
affected by these changes introduced or imposed from outside.
Still, in the early 1980s, the devaluation of *kastom bilong ol man*
was much further advanced than that of women's *kastom*. In the
women's ritual small modifications had occurred, but Kwanga
women continued to perform their rites at every menarche,
menstruation and childbirth. The first, for obvious reasons, was
held only once in a woman's lifetime, but the second followed
women's biological cycle and the third was performed at every
birth. Anthropologists have often described one or the other or all
of these rites as if they were separate entities. I will attempt
to show that these women's rites among the Kwanga can be
understood as consecutive stages of a 'ritual of womanhood'.

The First Menstruation Ritual as Female Initiation

The first stage in many ways follows a classic initiation sequence,
as described, for instance, by Keesing (1982: 5–6). It is a significant
event, not only for the individual girl but for the social group of
adult women and the society as a whole. It is the largest public
event staged by and for women and it emphasizes women's visible
power to create and sustain life.

The first part of this ritual is characterized by submission,
liminality and a climate of secrecy. As soon as the girl spots blood
for the first time, she has to go into seclusion and follows a
prescribed regimen, both positive (washing only in ginger-water)
and negative (avoiding certain soups, scraped coconut and any
greens used in the preparation of soups). The girl's 'fat', so the
dogma has it, decreases *(sabi ragau)*, if she does not avoid these
foods, and increases *(sabi hau)*, if she washes with ginger-water.[2]

Bikpela meri, that is post-menopausal women, and other women of her kin group take care of her and pass their secret knowledge (*save bilong ol meri*) about menstruation and conception on to her. During women's rites, but also in daily life, women's knowledge is shrouded in secrecy. No man or child may overhear women's discussions of this topic. The period of seclusion is ended by ritual cleansing, which is also carried out in secrecy. In former times, the girl's skin on the breast, the shoulders and the upper arms was cut with scarification marks at this stage of the ritual; many older women still bear these marks. Younger women are said to be 'weak' because they refuse to be scarified. This is one of the minor modifications I observed in the early 1980s.

The rebirth of the girl into a new status and a new group can be illustrated by the following scenes of the ritual: Before the girl re-enters the community, other young women, particularly her *maagri* (mother's brother's children), dress and adorn her with women's heirlooms – shell necklaces (*kiasiki*) and shell wrist ornaments (*tamberugu*), with a new T-shirt and a new skirt, and with the most important Kwanga symbol of womanhood, a *sobo*-basket[3] full of banana, taro and firewood. The T-shirt and the new skirt represent, of course, also adjustments to modernity.

The mother's brother (*mango*) then leads the girl into her new life as an adult woman. He takes the girl by the hand and leads her to the centre of the open space, where not only the girl herself is on display but also several objects. These objects are: a piece of firewood, soup bowls, stewed yam, baked taro, coconuts, sugar cane, and greens for making soup. He hands one item after the other to the girl who has to perform certain ritual acts: she breaks the sugar cane across her head and knees, takes a bite of the stewed yams and the baked taro, holds the greens in her hand and points them to the right and left, and finally breaks the firewood by hitting it on the ground.

The women of the mother generation have painted their foreheads with lime and put on skirts made of banana leaves. They now step forward and dance around the group. Some of them hold a stick of wild sugar cane (*agri kombe*, new stick), others carry firewood on a headstring, and they all chant lamentations: 'Oh, oh, we can no longer ask her to scrape coconuts for us; oh, oh, we can no longer enter her house, that is over now; oh, oh, we can no longer eat her meals.' This last scene signifies that, from now on, the young woman has to observe the avoidance rules of a sexually mature woman.

That the girl is not only reborn into a new status but also into a group that is closed to others who do not or cannot belong is illustrated in the next scene. After this drama, everybody sits down to eat but women of reproductive age set themselves apart from the others by eating a special soup which was prepared by post-menopausal women. This soup is only cooked during women's rites and can neither be eaten by girls before menarche nor by men. The main ingredient is the pith of a banana (*klebi nglo*), which grows wild in the forest.

When night falls, the women get ready for the chanting of the *naina*-songs (*nainahugwa*). A group of women gather, turn their backs on the other participants, face the moon,[4] and begin to chant. The women take turns singing and resting until the day breaks. Their voices can be heard from far away. People in other hamlets, and even in neighbouring villages, comment: 'Can you hear it? Now they are singing the *nainahugwa* for so-and-so.'

In summary we can say that, by going through this ritual, the girl acquired the gender identity of Kwanga women. In the 1980s, all Kwanga women still passed through the same ritual. Each woman thus learned about her special responsibility as one who is endowed with a potential characteristic of her gender and dangerous to the other gender and the parent's generation.

In my opinion, the first menstruation ritual of the Kwanga can be interpreted as a female initiation. Allen (1967, in Keesing 1982: 5) draws a distinction between *initiation*, which inducts individuals into a defined social group, and *puberty* rites, which mark individuals' entry into a new status. Kwanga girls enter the new status of adult women and they are also inducted into the social group of (potential) female procreators. Female procreators are culturally marked as a social category by the ritual of womanhood, which clearly separates them from all the other social categories. Even in daily life a number of avoidance rules mark them as a separate category. At the communal eating of the *klebi* soup and the singing of the *nainahugwa* songs, they act as a social group.

Keesing (1982: 6) characterizes initiations as '*rites de passage* that introduce initiates collectively into a social group, or a series of them, through submission . . . and liminality, in a climate of secrecy: the initiates are reborn both into a new status and into a group closed to, and from, those who do not (or by virtue of their sex cannot) belong'. Apart from the fact that girls are not *collectively* introduced into the social group of women, the Kwanga first menstruation ritual fits this characterization of initiations. In other words, mirrored against the classic initiation sequence described for men's rituals, the Kwanga first menstruation ritual fulfils all but one criterion for an 'initiation', namely *collectivity*.

Marilyn Strathern (1993) inquired deeper into this issue and questions whether collectivity is, in fact, a distinctive mark. She argues that initiation practices gender the person, not as a 'complete' member – as incorporation through collective events might suggest – but as an incomplete being. She writes: 'Melanesian rituals make little sense as the social or cultural completing of a child; instead of making complete a person's incorporation into society, they prompt the simpler proposition that one kind of person is being transformed into another' (Strathern 1993: 45). The child is transformed, not just into an adult member of the society, but into a potential mother or father. According to Strathern, the child is regarded as composed of the acts of both its parents; in this sense, its gender is androgynous, a composite of male and female elements. Initiation, she continues, is conceptualized as a replacement of its andro-gynous body or image with one that is single sex: the child emerges as 'female' or 'male' to encounter its opposite male or female in the future.

If we interpret the Kwanga first menstruation ritual from this perspective, it certainly qualifies for the label 'initiation'. Kwanga women say that male and female blood becomes mixed during repeated intercourse; the child is thus composite of the mother's and father's blood substances. The replacement of the androgynous body of the child with that of a fertile woman is clearly elaborated in the ritual. Formerly, her new status was literally embodied, it was carved into her flesh (see Broch-Due, Rudie and Bleie 1993). It is still enacted in the coming-out ceremony when the initiate is adorned with women's objects, publicly performs women's tasks and finally eats women's soup. The new avoidance rules can also be understood against this background: a social separation from the parents and grandparents follows the transformation from girl to woman; the young woman has to move out of her parents' house, and her parents' and grandparents' generation can no longer eat what she has cooked.

Menstruation Rites

Menstruation is not marked with a public event. Still, in my opinion, the rites associated with it can be regarded as the second stage of the ritual of womanhood because they again emphasize women's visible reproductive power and provide a culturally defined mechanism to control it.[5]

When menstruation sets in, the woman quietly leaves the family home and goes to stay in the *mas aka*. While she is in seclusion, she may not enter men's living and sleeping quarters and gardens with growing yam in the ground and she may not peel, break and/or pound tubers, cut meat or scrape coconut for men. When she prepares food, she cuts up the greens and waits for a neighbour or the co-wife to peel and break the tubers. Using cane nippers, she then fills the food into the saucepan and puts it on fire. When the food is done, she takes it out of the saucepan and serves it to her family.

The proscriptions regarding food preparation and handling are very precise, not only in these rules for menstruating women but also in all other food avoidance rules construed by the Kwanga. An analysis (see Obrist van Eeuwijk 1992) has shown that the same food avoidance rules govern the relationships between members and non-members of the men's cult, between sexually mature children and their parents, and between women and men. All three proscribed ways of handling food reduce its firmness in a real and a figurative sense. The inside of the tubers and animals *(ome)*, like the vital organs of the human body, is protected by their skin. To peel or cut this skin means that the vulnerable part is exposed. The scraping of coconuts also means that a solid, hard substance is reduced to small pieces. Especially if a person who is thought to be loaded with reproductive power, be it a members of the men's cult, sexually active members of the children's generation or women during menstruation and in childbed, handles food this way, the food may become a carrier of this dangerous power. The person who then ingests this food also ingests the power and, if he or she belongs to the opposite social category, consequently falls ill.

These proscriptions point to the fact that the social body of Kwanga women – the representational uses of the female body in the Kwanga culture, encompasses much more than women's physical body. As Mary Douglas (1970), Scheper-Hughes and Lock

(1987) and others have shown, the female body, its natural fluid, menstrual blood, and its essences and powers are used to represent and to sustain particular views of social relations and of nature. These representations are embedded in beliefs about the radical psychological and physical difference between men and women mentioned earlier that also form the conceptual basis for the first menstruation ritual and for the men's cult. In fact, they are based on an even more comprehensive classification system of the Kwanga. This system is constructed of compound (hot-cold, wet-dry, strong-weak, hard-soft) qualities. The relations between such binary pairs are used to form analogies between the relations of men to women, certain plants to other plants, health to illness, ritual to secular, and so on.

After the flow of blood has stopped the woman performs a ritual cleansing of her body. She has now returned into a 'normal' state and can move back into the family house and resume her daily tasks.

Childbirth Rites

The childbirth rite is also a *rite de passage*. It constitutes the third stage of the ritual of womanhood. Like the menstruation rites, the childbirth rite is less spectacular than the female initiation yet it also follows a culturally defined pattern.

When it is time to give birth, the woman goes into seclusion. From this moment until the public feast, direct contact with her husband and all other men is cut off. If it is her first birth, or if she is scared, she asks the *bikpela meri* to help her. Most women, however, claimed that they managed on their own. When she is about to give birth, the woman squats over a 'bed' made of banana leaves or palm spathes. After delivering the baby and the placenta, she cuts the umbilical cord herself or calls a neighbour to do it. She carefully hides the placenta and the umbilical cord lest a sorcerer finds them. On the next day, female relatives prepare a special soup for the new mother, which is believed to increase her flow of milk. She is looked after by her neighbours, usually unmarried women of her kin. They bring water, firewood and do the cooking for her and her family until, about ten days after delivery, the woman performs a ritual cleansing rite and re-enters the family home. A few days later, the kindred gather at the house of the new mother to prepare and eat the special women's soup, as they did at her first menstruation ritual.

The sequence of seclusion, prescribed regimen and cleansing continues the cultural pattern established during the female initiation rite and perpetuated during the menstruation rite. In all three rites, the ultimate aim is to control women's bodily capacity and potency. This idea finds its clearest expression in the preparation and communal consumption of the *klebi*-soup which signifies conceptual links between the initiation rite and the childbirth rite. The Kwanga say: *klebi nambuhu, aha, ohmu aka kwambuhu, noomek igua* ('wild banana squeezed, eaten, her house hardened, garden to will go'). These beliefs draw on the class-ification system mentioned above: the eating of *klebi* is believed to make the uterus (house) *kwambu* (firm, hard, strong), the firmness of the uterus is considered as a prerequisite for resuming garden work. The implicit meaning is that women's bodily fluids and essences are dangerous for the growth of yam.

Nupela Rot: New Roads

During my fieldwork in the 1980s, the Kwanga performed these rites for all girls who reached menarche, all women during menstruation and all women who gave birth. In 1993, however, while discussing the stay of a girl in the coastal town Lae, her father recounted that she had her first menstruation there and remarked: 'We did not perform a *nainahugwa* for her; but that's alright, we have given them up anyway.' When I asked, why they had given it up, the mother replied: '*Em rabis kastom tasol, mipela bihainim nupela rot now.*' ('That's a "rubbish" custom, we now follow new roads.') By 1993, the Kwanga thus used the same derogatory term, namely *rabis kastom* ('rubbish' tradition), for the women's ritual as many of them already did ten years earlier for the men's cult. What are the new roads they want to follow?

Christian Faith and Public Health

With regard to fertility, gender and human procreation, the Kwanga first became aware of alternative understandings and practices through the missions. They learned about the Christian dogmas of creation and the moral order derived from them. The Christian faith as taught by different denominations offered new answers to the fundamental questions that formed the core of the Kwanga rituals. What are the cosmic forces that manifest themselves in the procreation and growth of humans, plants and animals, and how can man communicate with and possibly influence them?

As elsewhere in Papua New Guinea (Denoon 1989: 89) it was also the missions who first developed an interest in maternal and especially child health. In fact, the early administration health schemes were run by, and largely for, men; the care of women tended to fall to the missions (Frankel and Lewis 1989: 8). Nuns acted as nurses, and the mission organizations supported their maternal and child health activities. In the Dreikikir area a Catholic nurse set up an infant welfare hospital at the mission out-station Yassip in the early 1970s. She held mobile clinics at other mission out-stations, for instance in Bongos and Tau, travelling by aircraft or vehicle. Kwanga women with malnourished children were brought to Yassip, where they spent a week or two learning to prepare milk from dried milk and special meals for their children.

In the subsequent years, the infant welfare scheme of the Catholic Mission in the Dreikikir area became incorporated into the national Maternal and Child Health (MCH) services. This Division of the Public Health Department had been gradually built up after the Second World War (Denoon 1989: 87). It later adopted the global medical strategy coordinated by the World Health Organization. As in many other areas of the country, the mission organizations of the Dreikikir area, particularly the Catholic Mission, continued to be important in delivering MCH services of any kind. The national and provincial public health departments provided, at least in theory, a cash subsidy for staff and maintenance and organized the supply of drugs and basic medical equipment.

The Maternal and Child Health Clinics

As a result of the nationalization and internationalization, the MCH services became increasingly standardized (Gillett 1990: 130–1). The health centre is the key unit from which all health services to the rural people are organized. The officer-in-charge is responsible for all health activities in the area including the MCH activities. The MCH nurses and nurse aides have their base at the health centre and report there. They make visits, if possible monthly, to the villages, where they hold mobile clinics. All MCH clinics, in theory, have three essential antenatal functions: the identification of high-risk women for institutional delivery, prophylaxis for anemia, malaria and tetanus and the early recognition and treatment of diseases and problems of pregnancy. In addition, curative services are offered along with some family planning and health education. Another important function of the MCH clinics is the detection of nutritional disorders among the children under five years of age.

In 1984/85, an Australian Mercy Sister trained as a nurse, and a local nurse-aid, operated the MCH clinics in most villages of the area. Their base was the Catholic Mission and the Health Centre at Dreikikir. Travelling by vehicle or on foot they visited the villages and held mobile clinics about once a month in selected locations. These monthly clinics followed a ritualized pattern similar to that observed in other parts of the country (see Reid 1983). The children were weighed by the nurse-aid and examined by the Australian nursing sister who also plotted the weight on the weight-for-age graph in the children's health booklets, wrote comments in the clinic register and prescribed medications. The nurse-aid then treated and immunized them as soon as she had finished weighing. Antenatal examination and treatment were left until the end of the clinic. They were performed in the privacy of a house. If the nurse, based on her examinations, anticipated problems at childbirth, she advised the mother to come to the Rural Health Centre in Dreikikir when the date of delivery drew close. In 1984/85, this Rural Health Centre was staffed with a male Health Extension Officer, a male and a female nurse and six medical assistants.

On the fixed day, the Maternal and Child Health team arrived around 10 a.m., weighed, examined and treated the under-five-year-old children and the pregnant women, and left around 3 p.m. for the base in Dreikikir. There, the nurse and nurse-aid usually had a late lunch and then attended to additional clinical and administrative tasks (for example to unpack, clean, sterilize and refurbish the equipment, to keep various records and statistics). The next day, they returned to conduct the clinic for another Kwanga village, or they moved on to another division. In other words, within about five hours, the team unpacked the equipment, set it up, saw seventy to eighty children and a few pregnant women and packed up again to perform additional tasks in Dreikikir.

This brief description may suffice to illustrate that, at the MCH clinics, Kwanga women were confronted with a new ritual and a body of new and foreign knowledge, practices and objects. The clinic routine was rather hectic; individual consultations were rarely longer than five minutes. It stressed weighing, paper work and curative care. This is partly due to the fact that MCH patrols have been profoundly affected by the demand for statistical reporting and the meeting of numerical targets (Denoon 1989: 107). The nurse did not offer family planning advice and health education – at least not at the MCH clinics I observed. The mother–nurse interactions can best be described as a stylized, repetitive pattern of speech and behaviour. The nurse asked questions and gave advice in a straightforward, formula-like manner: 'When did you realize that you are pregnant? Why did you not come earlier? Is this your first pregnancy? Has the child been ill? What type of food does the child eat?'

Kwanga Women's Responses to the MCH Services

In the full swing of the 1970s, the infant welfare clinic was regarded as another step towards the new life style and – without giving up their old ways – women learned to acknowledge the expertise of the nurse in curing many diseases. In the early 1980s, attending the MCH clinics had become an integral part of the female domain. The Kwanga said that the *klinik* was 'something for the women'. It was very unusual for a man to go there, even if his wife was ill. Most women interrupted their daily routine only reluctantly, but they obliged, mainly because their husbands and the *bikpela meri* urged them to do so.[6]

Women were more critical now than in the 1970s, not only about the MCH clinics but also about their own *kastom*. Many of their expectations raised by the new services had been disappointed: small children continued to fall seriously ill, and many women still died from complications in childbirth. Women partly attributed this situation to disparities in urban and rural income and living conditions. Although their experience space was more limited than that of their husbands – only seven out of 106 interviewed women had ever seen the provincial capital Wewak – they were well aware of the fact that urban people and government employees working in rural areas (such as teachers, aid post orderlies, MCH nurses) had a different life style.

An examination of women' views on child feeding and growth (see Obrist van Eeuwijk 1992) has shown that Kwanga women mainly accepted the curative services of the MCH clinics, which resulted in a perceptible alleviation of suffering. They did not object to treatment and advice if they agreed that their child was ill but they also consulted a local healer, either simultaneously or consecutively. Kwanga women were convinced of the power of medication in the form of tablets but even more so in the form of injections because patients had frequently been cured of fever, pain and other easily recognizable symptoms after receiving this treatment. The weighing of children and the plotting of their weights on the weight-for-age graphs, however, was in their eyes *samting bilong ol nurse tasol* (something that is only of concern for the nurse); Kwanga women could not see what use weighing had in relation to the health of their children.

With regard to pregnancy and birth, some women followed the advice of the nurse to come to the antenatal clinic or to give birth at the Rural Health Centre in Dreikikir. Most women, however, did not consult the nurses until the last few months of pregnancy and preferred to give birth in the village. A few women said they felt ashamed to give birth in the presence of strangers, especially if they were men. Others said they had already given birth several times without any problems; why should they inconvenience themselves and their relatives by spending a lot of time in Dreikikir? If problems arose during a village birth, the woman was rushed to the Rural Health Centre, if necessary on a stretcher carried by her male relatives.

Kwanga women often complained about the way they were treated by the MCH staff at these monthly clinics. After one of the not-infrequent quarrels between the mothers and the nurse, a woman found precise words for a feeling shared by many in such situations: 'Why do they tell us how to care for our children? Have we not learned it from our mothers and grandmothers?'

Several women said that the MCH clinics did not offer any support where they most needed it, namely in the field of contraception. They had heard rumours about powerful contraceptive methods available through the health services but could not obtain any precise information from the Catholic nurse. A woman who already had six children, for instance, used a local contraceptive method. She consulted a *bikpela meri* who used a certain leaf to 'steam' women – a common part of local healing rituals. The Kwanga believed that one could thus catch the 'soul' (*masik ome*) and wrap it into the leaf. The *bikpela meri* folded the leaf, tied it up and told the woman to hide the bundle in her house. She instructed her that if she wanted to become pregnant again, she should fetch the bundle, open it and throw it into a river or water pool. The woman told me that she got pregnant without breaking the bundle. For several days, she loudly complained and had heated arguments with her husband. She then asked me for advice and called their own methods *giaman maresin* (quack medicine). Another woman chased her husband with a glowing piece of firewood because he had tried to have intercourse with her while she still breastfed her infant. This was a breach of the post-partem taboo that says that parents should not resume sexual intercourse until the last child is weaned; it is believed that the semen will mix with breast-milk and thus harm the child. In reality, parents often quarrelled and even fought about this issue. For the women, the post-partem taboo was a 'method' for natural child spacing but most of them would have preferred to have a safer method. Whether their husbands would have agreed is another issue.

In 1993, the MCH clinics were held by Papua New Guinean nurses who were Catholics but not nuns. Maybe the encounter with fellow Papua New Guineans who were trained to provide these services and to use the equipment led to changes in Kwanga women's attitudes to the new ritual of MCH clinics. It certainly looked as if they had come to accept the MCH services as a *nupela rot*, as a new road they wanted to follow.

Discussion and Conclusions

Medical pluralism, the coexistence of differing medical traditions, is now a common pattern in most parts of the world and also in Papua New Guinea, as the accounts collected by Frankel and Lewis (1989) illustrate. In their introduction Frankel and Lewis reflect on the concept of 'pluralism'. They point out (1989: 32) that in philosophy pluralism contrasts most obviously with monism, whereas discussions of medicine in Papua New Guinea are most often and obtrusively couched in a different form – that of dualism or pluralism. The contrast, and opposition, they continue, is presented as one between Western medicine and the local system. Although they admit that it is extremely easy to fall into this dualistic way of thinking, they claim that it is misleading. Their main argument is that we cannot think of dichotomies because local modes of treatment of the sick are not usually formulated as a unified system of theory, practice and medical institutions. The local forms are not matched against Western medicine as one system against another. They postulate substituting the concept of dualism with that of pluralism and refer to Chambers (1983, in Frankel and Lewis 1989: 32) who propagated pluralism as an ideology, a view that is based on an agnostic openness to evidence and argument. Such a view would involve a commitment to consider other points of view; it would acknowledge multiple causation, multiple objectives and multiple interventions and it would be critical of unicausal explanation, of single objectives, and one solution. Frankel and Lewis do not suggest that pluralism is consciously held as an ideology by many Papua New Guineans but they point out that the statement of agnostic openness to alternative approaches fits quite well with views that some Gnau people express to the effect that others may have different ways from them of explaining and dealing with problems of illness and they may also be right. They quote the Gnau, an ethnic group of the West Sepik Province in Papua New Guinea, saying that really it is better to have two or more possible ways of doing something than just one.

The Kwanga made similar statements as the Gnau, and, as the preceding section has shown, they experiment with different approaches to restore or maintain health. If their children are ill, Kwanga women seek treatment and advice at the MCH clinics or at the aidpost, and they consult a local healer, either simult-aneously or consecutively; they attend MCH clinics and turn to *bikpela meri* for contraceptive advice and measures. Many other examples could be cited to bear evidence of medical pluralism among the Kwanga.

At the same time, the Kwanga themselves, like many other Melanesian societies, use the notion of *kastom* to draw a distinction between what they define to be traditional knowledge, practice and object (*kastom*), and what they perceive as foreign or innovative (*nupela rot*). Examples from various Melanesian societies have shown that *kastom* experiences fluctuating moral evaluation over time and that the definition of its bounds and its moral evaluation are continuing political processes (see for example Lindstrom 1982; Jolly 1994). At present, we have seen, the Kwanga use the derogatory term *rabis kastom* for women's rituals and for the men's cult.

Both rituals related to fertility, gender and procreation and were among the most elaborate coherently organized parts of the Kwanga religion. At the risk of constructing a system that is my own invention rather than theirs, I argue that Kwanga interpretations of body physiology, namely their notion of opposition and complementarity of men's and women's bodily fluids, essences and powers, were tied in not only with gender but with the embodied world. The Kwanga understood their body as a microcosm of the universe. Their interest in menarche, menstruation and childbirth was part of their general concern about the procreation of life. They tried to make sense of the mystery of women's visible reproductive power, which continually manifests itself in menstruation and procreation, and its physical products – menstrual blood and children. This visible power was attributed to cosmic forces also observed in other manifestations, particularly in the growth of plants and animals.

The main conclusion of this contribution is that the dissemination of the Christian faith and its creation theory, the introduction of health services for women and children and the subsequent take-over of these services by national and international medical institutions made a decisive contribution to the devaluation of *kastom*, particularly to the devaluation of the ritual of womanhood. First the Church and then increasingly the medical institutions offered alternative understandings and practices relating to human procreation and gradually assumed authority backed by the power of the state. In the process the Kwanga, and especially Kwanga women, lost their control over their body and its reproductive capacity. What they had understood as a natural manifestation of cosmic forces, and tried to control in the ritual of womanhood, came increasingly under the control of medicine.

As a result, menarche and menstruation lost their cultural significance. The logic of scientific medicine evaluates physiological processes in terms of their health risks. Measured against this scale, menarche and menstruation are of negligible importance, whereas pregnancy, child birth and infancy rank very highly. Biomedicine focuses by definition on biological reproduction[7] and, as health *risk* is the main criterion, on the reproductive health of *women*. Without biomedical intervention, the health risk at childbirth is statistically very high. Papua New Guinea, where 60 per cent of the women deliver at home, is believed to have one of the highest maternal mortality rates in the world (Gillett 1990: 99). It has been estimated that two to three women die every day in Papua New Guinea as a direct result of being pregnant (Gillett 1990: 103). By shifting the focus to health aspects of pregnancy, birth and infancy, the conceptual chain linking menarche, menstruation and childbirth has been damaged.

Moreover, the Kwanga have heard rumours about contraceptive pills and injections. Even though they have not tested these special pills and injections themselves, they tend to believe in their effectiveness because they have become convinced of the power of medication in the form of tablets and injections, which are available to them. Many Kwanga do not doubt that the white man's medicine has solved the great mystery of how human beings can manipulate women's procreative powers.

I suggest, therefore, that the concept of medical pluralism offers only a partial understanding of what is happening among the Kwanga. The point I wish to make is that the Kwanga are able to reorder the social and cultural framework of their daily lives so as to shape their own experience of human procreation but this happens within a wider framework of powerful political and cultural forces. Scheper-Hughes and Lock (1987) use the term 'body politic' to refer to the regulation, surveillance, and control of bodies, for instance in procreation and sexuality. In pre-colonial time, Kwanga village societies had their own body politic, which exerted its control over individual bodies; with their integration into the colonial and later the national society, however, the state, or institutions backed by the state, namely the Churches and national medical service, gradually take over. For the Kwanga, Western medicine, and particularly the MCH services, were and still are, closely tied up with Christianity. For me as an outside observer, the Catholic Church certainly continues to exert control, particularly in the field of family planning, but in general I consider the medical services and their body politic to have a more profound impact on women's *kastom*. I therefore suggest that the concept of medicalization offers a new perspective for our understanding of the fundamental transformation currently taking place in the female realm among the Kwanga.

Notes

1. Other researchers (Lutkehaus and Roscoe 1995) use the term 'gender rituals' for female initiation in Melanesia and argue that female initiation rites express more than cultural notions of femininity, narrow definitions of reproduction, or coming of age rituals. Instead, they write, these gender rituals play an important role in other life cycle rituals and in the political and economic organization of society.
2. This prescribed regimen seems to be based on similar concepts of body physiology as Biersack (1982) describes for the Paiela, namely that physical growth affects the fatty underlayer of the skin, the 'inner' rather than the 'outer' skin. The Kwanga use the term *sabi* for the fatty 'inner' skin and *masambi* for the 'outer' skin. If my interpretation is correct, the Kwanga assume that the maturation of girls is a natural process that can be enhanced by a certain regimen.
3. Among the Kwanga and as in many other Papua New Guinean societies, certain activities and objects are gendered. One type of gendered object is the durable basket made of palm spathes. The men call their basket *antombongri*; it is rather small in size, oblong and carried on the shoulder. Women make much bigger baskets called *sobo* which they carry on their backs, suspended from a headsling. It is difficult to imagine a northern Kwanga woman without a *sobo*. When she returns from the gardens, the basket is filled with yams, taro, banana, several leaf bundles of green vegetables, perhaps topped with an orange pandanus and several pieces of firewood. When she goes down to the water-hole, she stows the dirty pots and dishes in it. When she goes to break firewood or to gather green leaves, she takes it along. Without *sobo*, there is not food, say the northern Kwanga women.
4. Like other societies in Papua New Guinea, for instance the Paiela (Biersack 1982), the Kwanga conceptualize the moon *(niaka)* as female, cold, and ultimately responsible for growth.

By singing towards the moon, Kwanga women express a symbolic link between the reproductive power of their own body and that of the moon.

5. Like many other Melanesian societies (Hauser-Schäublin 1977/78) the Kwanga have a set of rules that restrict women's movements and activities as well as their social relations but not their food choices.

6. Their clinic attendance is remarkably high: over a period of 24 months from 1983 to 1985 it ranged from 84 to 100 per cent according to clinic registers.

7. Beginning in the nineteenth century, medicine and other disciplines increasingly narrowed their focus on material and natural aspects of the human body. Life has become regarded as a 'matter' (Hauser-Schäublin 1991: 324). The underlying philosophy is in fundamental contrast to, for instance, Kwanga views and Christian views of procreation. Hauser-Schäublin (1991: 328) characterizes the contrast as follows: '*So haben Gedanken von "Seelen", "Geist" und "Lebenskraft", die eine transzendentale Dimension im Menschen anerkennen und dem Leben einen sinnhaften Platz im Kosmos geben, in der Betrachtungsweise von Gewebe und Zellen sowie im Umgang damit, der Manipulation dokumentiert, keinen Platz.*'

References

Allen, B.J. (1976). Information Flow and Innovation Diffusion in the East Sepik District, Papua New Guinea. PhD Thesis. Canberra: Australian National University.

Barnes, J.A. (1973). Genitrix:Genitor::Nature:Culture? In: J. Goody (ed.), *The Character of Kinship*, pp. 61–73. London: Cambridge University Press.

Biersack, A. (1982). Ginger Gardens for the Ginger Woman: Rites and Passages in a Melanesian Society. *Man* 17: 239–58.

Broch-Due, V., Rudie, I. and Bleie, T. (eds) (1993). *Carved Flesh/ Cast Selves: Gendered Symbols and Social Practices*. Oxford: Berg.

Denoon, D. (1989). *Public Health in Papua New Guinea: Medical Possibility and Social Constraint, 1884–1984*. Cambridge: Cambridge University Press.

Douglas, M. (1970). *Natural Symbols. Explorations in Cosmology*. Harmondsworth: Penguin.

Foucault, M. (1980). *The History of Sexuality. Vol. 1. An Introduction.* New York: Vintage.

Frankel, St. and Lewis, G. (1989). Patterns of Continuity and Change. In: St. Frankel and G. Lewis (eds), *A Continuing Trial of Treatment: Medical Pluralism in Papua New Guinea*, pp. 1–33. Dordrecht, Boston, London: Kluwer Academic Publishers.

Gillet, J.E. (1990). *The Health of Women in Papua New Guinea.* Goroka: Papua New Guinea Institute of Medical Research.

Hauser-Schäublin, B. (1977/1978). Vom Terror und Segen des Blutes, oder: Die Emanzipation des Mannes von der Frau. *Wiener Völkerkundliche Mitteilungen* 19/20: 93–116.

—— (1991). 'Verwandtschaft' und ihre 'Reproduktion'. Vaterschaft, die Entleiblichung der Frau und die Entseelung des Menschen. In: B. Hauser-Schäublin (ed.), *Ethnologische Frauenforschung*, pp. 307–31. Berlin: Dietrich Reimer.

Helman, C. (1990). *Culture, Health and Illness.* Oxford: Butterworth-Heinemann.

Herdt, G.H. (ed.) (1982). *Rituals of Manhood. Male Initiation in Papua New Guinea.* Berkeley, Los Angeles and London: University of California Press.

Illich, I. (1976). *Medical Nemesis.* New York: Pantheon.

Jolly, M. (1994). *Women of the Place: Kastam, Colonialism and Gender in Vanuatu.* Chur: Harwood Academic Publishers.

Keesing, R.M. (1982). Introduction. In: G.H. Herdt. (ed.), *Rituals of Manhood. Male Initiation in Papua New Guinea*, pp. 1–43. Berkeley, Los Angeles and London: University of California Press.

Lindstrom, L. (1982). Leftamapim Kastom: The Political History of Tradition on Tanna (Vanuatu). In: R.M. Keesing and B. Tonkinson (eds), *Reinventing Traditional Culture: The Politics of Kastom in Island Melanesia*, pp. 316–37. Mankind. Special issue 13(4).

Lutkehaus, N. and Roscoe, P.B. (eds) (1995). *Gender Rituals: Female Initiations in Melanesia.* New York and London: Routledge.

Obrist van Eeuwijk, B. (1992). *Small but Strong: Cultural Contexts of (Mal-) Nutrition among the Northern Kwanga (East Sepik Province, Papua New Guinea).* Basel: Wepf.

Reid, J. (1983). Educating Mothers: How Effective are MCH Clinics? *Papua New Guinea Medical Journal* 26: 25–8.

Scheper-Hughes, N. and Lock, M.M. (1987). The Mindful Body: A Prolegomenon to Future Work in Medical Anthropology. *Medical Anthropology Quarterly* 1(1): 6–41.

Schindlbeck, M. (1990). Tradition and Change in Kwanga Villages. In: N. Lutkehaus *et al.* (eds), *Sepik Heritage: Tradition and Change in Papua New Guinea*, pp. 233–40. Durham: Carolina Academic Press.

Strathern, M. (1993). Making Incomplete. In: V. Broch-Due, I. Rudie and T. Bleie (eds), *Carved Flesh/Cast Selves: Gendered Symbols and Social Practices*, pp. 41–51. Oxford: Berg.

Chapter 11

The Chuukese Women's Status: Traditional and Modern Elements[1]

Beatriz Moral

Chuukese women's status, because of its characteristics and complexity, is like a house of mirrors. The elements that are involved in it are numerous, varied and contradictory. I have classified these elements into two categories: traditional and modern. The present situation is the result of a volatile mixture that, at the moment, is unstable and very corrosive and in which the opposing elements are still reacting.

Traditional Elements

What was the women's situation in Chuukese traditional society? To reconstruct women's status in the most accurate way, as well as Chuukese society in general, it is fundamental to consider these elements: matriliny, identity, lineage, land, incest taboo and male superiority (Moral 1997).

First of all, it is necessary to point out that Chuukese society is matrilineal. The most important relationship is between the sister and the brother; this structures the pattern of the relationships between women and men in general. The matrilineal structure of kinship is the key to approaching Chuukese women's status, and the framework where the rest of the elements are going to find their place and meaning. The concepts we will consider here have to be analyzed within this framework.

Let us consider first the concept of 'individuality' and its characteristics. Or rather we should talk about the lack of that idea. Among the Chuukese, an individual can only be defined and identified by belonging to a lineage, by the relationship of kinship that links the individual to a group of people that has an identity. The individual is a nobody outside of this group. All activities are geared to strengthening and maintaining the well-being of the lineage, it being the provider and protector of all its members. The *eterekes* (lineage or matri-group) provide for the basic needs that allows the survival of its members, like food, space and care. Outside the *eterekes*, there is hunger, solitude and death.

In addition to providing the basic living and survival conditions, the *eterekes* is an organizing system in which each member has her/his own role and hierarchical place. It also defines the individual's identity through its characteristics as a group (such as its history, ancestry, lands, knowledge) as well as the position of the individual in the group (by its sex, age, kinship relationship with other members of the group and the position between the siblings of the same sex). The position in the group defines the rights, duties and privileges (or the lack of them) of the individual: identity, function, role, rights, duties, hierarchy and tasks of each member are defined by the group, inside the group as well as in the community. An individual, by himself or herself, is a helpless being who does not have any tools to survive and whose whole existence is menaced.

The *eterekes* includes not only the descendants of a common female ancestor, but also their lands.[2] Kawai[3] clearly explains the relevance of the relation between the land and the *eterekes*:

> The permanence of the *eterekes* and the permanency of the land exist in an *indivisible relationship*. Partition of the land is therefore thought as being equivalent to dissolution of the *eterekes*. Man and land comprise a unity, so to speak, and because of this men exist along with the land. Conversely, humans who hold land jointly are kinsmen . . . As one informant aptly put it, 'we are man because we hold land. If we have no land we are like birds with no branches to rest on'. Land provides men with food and is the foundation of life. It is the basis of all human activity (Kawai 1987: 121, my emphasis).

A recognition of the essential value of the land is shown in Chuukese culture through the idea of unity between the members of an *eterekes* and its land – what Kawai calls an 'indivisible relationship'. This relationship – which links land and people and makes them a unity - is not to be broken under any circumstances.

The fact that the dead people have to be buried in the land of their *eterekes* is one response to this necessity because this unity goes beyond life and it has to be maintained.

Giving or losing a piece of land has the same meaning as losing one of the members of the *eterekes*. The loss of one or the other is explained by the metaphor of a body that loses one of its parts. Losing one member or piece of land threatens the survival and the well being of the *eterekes*. Therefore, keeping this unity – the only entity that gives identity and protection – is absolutely fundamental.

As we have just seen, land has a determinant role in the composition and keeping of the *eterekes*. A woman is responsible for maintaining this unity between the land and the group, and because of it she has a key role. She is responsible for the land, and for averting any division and segregation of it within the *eterekes*, and she has to make sure that its transmission is done according to custom.[4] Women render possible, maintain and transmit that 'essential substance' that gives unity and identity to the individuals of an *eterekes* and to its land.

Women in Chuukese society are responsible for keeping this unity. With regard to the land, women are responsible for making sure that the transfer of lands inside the *eterekes* is not interrupted and that the unity is not broken. To the individuals who constitute the group, women are the ones who guarantee the survival of the clan by bringing in new members[5] (giving birth to children for the *eterekes*) and preserving the peace and harmony between its members as well as with other *eterekes*. Through the guarantee of the unity of the family group on the one hand, and the guarantee of the unity of the land, on the other hand, the unity between *eterekes* and lands is assured, thus fulfilling the primary goal.

The pillars of the Chuukese social structure are found in the basic triangle formed by women, land and *eterekes*. Land and *eterekes* constitute a vital, structural, functional and transcendental unity, and women make it possible, protect it and maintain it. Kawai describes this women's symbolical role: 'Women serve as the symbolical medium between men and the land ... In the thinking of the Trukese, not only are women the source of humans, but they are also the bearers of the land and the *eterekes* ... In symbolic terms, land is women and women is land and that is all there is to it' (Kawai 1987: 121).

Besides the importance of the symbolic value of the land, we also have to bear in mind its economic value, as well as its role in the distribution of political power. This link between women and land puts women in a position in which they can control one of the most important of the few sources of wealth, power and prestige.

Fertility is another powerful link between women and land. The woman's fertility and the land's fertility are both sources of survival, continuity, wealth and power. It is the union of both fertilities that makes the *eterekes* strong: women bring children and the land brings food. Kawai finds that the woman's fertility – her reproductive capacity – does not only concern human beings, but also concerns land: 'What is apparent . . . is that with the use of *owupwu*, "giving birth to", similar concepts of regeneration are expressed with regard to both the land and the human procreation of the *eterekes*, or matrilineal group' (Kawai 1989: 121).

The equivalence of both fertilities does not point to anything other than the relevance of her role, her responsibility in (pro)creation, sustenance and maintenance (continuity) of the family-group. Her alliance with the land happens to be so essential that woman and land finally become one: '. . . land is women and women is land and that is all there is to it' (Kawai 1989: 121).

The dark side of this position of women in Chuuk is the silence under which they have to live. This silence is the compulsory result of the combination of two fundamental elements of Chuukese culture: the incest taboo and the assumption of a male superiority.

First of all, let us consider the consequences of the incest taboo. In Chuuk this taboo concerns basically the relationship between sister and brother. Even if it also extends to other levels of kinship, the principal realm is between sister and brother, giving the pattern of reference for the rest of the relations. All the male members of a woman's clan are classified as her brothers; that is to say that there are very few occasions in which there are no brothers around. The fundamental rule of this taboo is: the brother has to be kept physically away; he should ignore his sister's sexuality and anything to do with it. Therefore the sister has to erase any kind of sexual connotation from her behaviour, body and presence.

For other reasons that we are not going to discuss here, the woman – because her genitals are the main symbol of sexuality (Gladwin and Sarason 1953: 254; Moral 1996, 1997) – is seen as a hypersexual being. So rules of modesty become very strong and an obsession because everything that comes from her has sexual connotation, even simply her presence. The ideal behaviour for a sister is to pretend that she is not there (that is the only way for all sexual connotations to disappear).

Another consequence of the incest taboo is the impossibility of women taking part in any public discussion. The reason for this is that there will always be brothers in the audience. Women's interventions have to be made in silence if they are not to transgress the rules that the taboo imposes; that is why verbal strategies and alternative paths have to be taken by women to take part in the decision-making processes.

The presumption of a male superiority only strengthens this situation. Males are considered as more capable, stronger and endowed with the gift of loquacity. Women are, by definition, weak, dependent on men and, of course, lacking the gift of the word.[6]

How could all this be articulated in the decision-making processes? In Chuuk, as well as in the rest of the world, women also use strategies through which they circumvent their exclusion from these processes. In Chuuk, women do that with more legitimacy than in other societies because of the exceptional structural place they hold. The sexual division of responsibilities and duties is divided in two ways, which have very few points of intersection. In this division of power men's responsibilities are always more prestigious than women's. However, there exists an instance that is outside of this parallel structure: the unity of the *eterekes*. Confronting any threat made to this unity would be a female's responsibility, which is above any male title and prestige.[7]

This responsibility gives women the last word, *but* has to be performed in silence. In the old days, the simple presence of a woman in a battlefield was enough for the conflict to end, without a single word said. Her drastic decisions would have been communicated through a male member who would have been considered a spokesman. This responsibility is exclusively limited to occasions when the unity and harmony of the *eterekes* is threaten and never outside these limits. This role as guardians of the unity is still performed (even though it has lost a lot of its former strength), as was shown during the temperance movements in 1976.[8]

The Modern Elements

The foreign influences in Chuuk have been numerous: Spanish, German, Japanese and North American. Lets also add Christianity. The strongest influences have been the Japanese, the North American and the Christian. Here we will only consider the last two, not only because they are the most recent but also because they are the ones which have brought more changes and had more repercussions.

The presence in the Chuuk lagoon of the first Protestant missionaries (New England Congregationalists) goes back to 1879 (Hezel 1972). They were the first foreigners who established a permanent residence in Chuuk. The Catholic missionaries (German Capuchins) appeared in the lagoon in 1912 (Hezel 1991).

Chuuk has been under the United States' political and economical control since the Second World War, although they had interests in this area before that time. From the Second World War until 1989, Chuuk was a Trust Territory of the United Nations under the United States' supervision. In 1986 the Federated States of Micronesia were established (of which Chuuk is one of the four states) under a democratic system and a constitution copied from the North American one. Today, the link with the United States is still in force because of a huge economical dependency and because of the Compact of Free Association.

There is a common point between the Christian and the North American influences: both of them share a strong male ideology. The consequences of this bias for Chuukese women's status have been fatal.

Let us first see the effect of Christianity. As we have seen before, the rules for modesty derived from the incest taboo could almost be compared to Victorian morality. The missionaries knew how to turn this to their benefit. They introduced in this frame the idea of sin and the idea of woman as the incarnation of evil and temptation. They kept the form but they changed the contents: they kept the highly integrated modesty rules but they substituted the idea of sex as a sinful activity for the incest taboo. It is necessary to point out that Chuukese do not consider sex as inherently bad; it is wrong only if the brother heard of it or if it is done with a taboo person.

The traditional contents were not removed. Nowadays both – incest taboo and sin – exist together, the pressure and the control women have to bear through their sexuality have become stronger. Another consequence of the Christianization has been the nuclearization[9] of the family through the model in which the father is considered as the head of the family. Not only is religion responsible for this but I think that it has been one of its most important promoters.

Given the relevance of the *eterekes* in structural and symbolical level, the nuclearization of the family implies a series of important changes. One of the results of it is the weakness of the *eterekes* as a structuring force and a weakness of the links between the members of the *eterekes*. Its traditional function is belittled because it lacks relevance to the new nuclear reality of the families. All the roles are redefined and in this transformation women lose the power that the role of responsibility for the survival and harmony of the most important structural unit of the society used to give them. The woman's role of guardian loses all its meaning; she loses the control over the land (because of the loss and change of meaning land used to have for the family group) and she also loses the capacity to participate in the decision-making processes, because the decisions now taken concern other and new values in which women have no say. In this redefinition of roles, men become the heads of the family unit; thus, male power is legitimized and strengthened.

The disintegration of the *eterekes* as the basic structural unit implies the disintegration of the Chuukese traditional society as such, the dissolution of female power and competence and the legitimization of male power.

Another effect of the disintegration of the extended family is the disappearance of the protection that women's families used to give them against the abuses of their husbands. Traditionally, women were protected by their families because they had the right and obligation to do so for all the members of the *eterekes*. Nowadays, this kind of intervention would be taken as an encroachment on the husband's authority. He is the only person who has power over his wife. As a result of this loss, 'domestic violence' is considered inherent to marriage.

The United States has introduced many changes in Chuuk and I believe that only a few of them have not left evident consequences. Here we will just talk about the ones I consider most important. On the one hand, the idea of women as hypersexual beings, weak and dependent on males, has been reinforced through the media. Even if TV has only arrived in Weno (the capital of Chuuk) in 1993, videotapes are common on the island, as they are in the other islands where TV has not arrived yet. The most viewed movies are the typical 'sex and violence' North American films in which women always play a role full of sexual connotations. On the other hand, the United States has closed almost all the ways women had to participate in the decision-making processes through 'modernization' and democratization of the government. Nowadays very little is left of the traditional governing structures, where women used to have ways of participating, their own domains of action and the respect that went with it. Chuukese have identified the functioning of the democratic system (or of any modern government) with the public domain, with men and honorary titles. Women do not have the right to be in the public arena, basically because it is the place of men.

The two main consequences of government forms that the United States has introduced are: first, that they have legitimized male power through democratization and because they have considered men as valid interlocutors as their power is the most apparent and institutionalized (which does not mean that it is the most effective); and second, that they have displaced female power from its traditional state of silence (which does not mean that it was not efficient) to a point where it is in danger of disappearing because of an attitude of totally ignoring it. Christianity, for its part, has also collaborated to reinforce this idea through the introduction of relevant male characters like the priest or the minister, not to mention God and Jesus Christ – and through its attitude of neglecting the value of the female role.

The introduction of primary and superior education has given a serious blow to traditional knowledge, especially because it has been understood as the only access to the new political and economical power. The new educational system (added to the disintegration of the traditional forms of government and of the *eterekes*) has come with the almost total disintegration of the mechanisms of transmission of traditional knowledge, which has degraded women's situation. Since the traditional role of women as guardians was practised in silence, the respect they enjoyed did not come from their public participation but from the fact that this role was a 'loud secret' that was transmitted in the intimacy of the family. It was something known by everyone, not because of its public and evident character but because its importance and function were transmitted from generation to generation. As a result of the breakdown of this chain, the female's basic function as guardian of the unity of the *eterekes* has almost been forgotten, and, if it has not, its relevance has.

Conclusions

The conclusions of all this are the following:

1. *The weakening of women's power.* The reasons for this are first, the *family nuclearization* – which implies the weakness of the *eterekes* as the basic structural unit, and therefore a loss of the importance of the functional role of women, and secondly, the *breakdown of the mechanisms of transmission of traditional knowledge* – which provokes a gap in the knowledge on women and lessens the recognition, prestige and respect their roles traditionally used to hold. Thirdly, the *introduction of modern or democratic government* – which blocks any possibility for women to take part in the decision-making processes, as the political arena is understood as a public domain, a place of prestige and titles, exclusively masculine.

2. *An increasing control on women's sexuality,* as well as on their behaviour and movements in general, because of, first, the *introduction of the idea of sin in the realm of sexuality* using the modesty rules that concur with Christian morality in their configuration (those rules increase and refine the control over female sexuality) and, secondly, the *reinforcement of the idea of woman as a hypersexual being,* no only because of Christian religions, but also because of a kind of image that comes to Chuuk through North American media, which strengthens the necessity of control over female sexuality.

3. *Diminution of the protection of women because of family nuclearization.* This nuclearization weakens the bonds within the *eterekes,* and the protection the group provides for women; the nuclearization *increases the husband's authority,* against which women have neither weapons nor protection.

4. The present situation is like a hybrid born from past and present. The traditional elements have not totally disappeared, but they still have enough weight and presence – more at an unconscious and symbolic level than as part of the official discourse.

Women's role as guardian of the transcendental unity of the *eterekes* still remains in its original form, as well as in other expressions. It is now adapted to the new circumstances, such as in women's associations, which are the current guardians of the well-being and harmony of the communities.

Notes

1. The two-years' fieldwork for this research has been made possible thanks to grants given by the Wenner-Gren Foundation for Anthropological Research, Euskal Herriko Emakumeari Buruzko Ikerketarako Mintegia / Seminario de Estudios de la Mujer de la Universidad del País Vasco, and Emakunde / Instituo Vasco de la Mujer del Gobierno Vasco. I would like to thank these institutions as well as my friend Maxine Becker and my friends in Guam and Chuuk, who helped me during my stay in Micronesia, my translator Anne Catherine Connolly and Mac Marshall for his comments on this chapter.
2. In the two most important ethnographies about property and land transmission in Chuuk (Goodenough 1951; Parker 1985), the relevance of matriliny concerning land has not had the full attention it deserves. The main way to transmit land is through the *eterekes*. There are however other practices. Goodenough and Parker seemed to me fascinated by the complexity of these practices and never to have fully accounted for the main way of transmission of the land, missing the opportunity of getting at the deeper meaning and role of women (especially from a symbolic point of view).
3. Kawai is one of the few anthropologists who has given the symbolism of land and women and their relationship in Chuuk the relevance they deserve. In other authors publications, this point is hinted at but never handled thoroughly. See also Thomas (1980) and for Yap Alkire (1989).
4. Nowadays, this feeling that women are the keepers of the land becomes evident in a tendency to justify the fact that the lands are registered under their names (even if these lands come from their parents, that is to say, outside the *eterekes*), arguing that

women don't want to sell them to obtain cash but that they take responsibility for keeping them and transmitting them to their offspring; doing the opposite of men, who seem to be more interested in having cash so as to spend it on ephemeral goods.

5. Chuukese also say that women bring land through the children they have with men from other *eterekes* because the children always receive land as a gift from the *eterekes* of their fathers, which enhances the mother's *eterekes*.

6. See J. Caughey (1977).

7. The division between female and male power is widely discussed by Weiner (1976): The female power would concern the 'cosmic sphere' while the male power would concern the 'social sphere'.

8. For more information about temperance movement in Chuuk see Marshall and Marshall (1990).

9. For more information about the consequences of the breakdown of the extended-family see Hezel (1987a, 1987b, 1989). He attributes an important part of the responsibility for this breakdown to economic changes.

References

Alkire, W. (1989). Land, Sea, Gender and Ghosts on Woleai-Lamotrek. In: M. Marshall and J. Caughey (eds), *Culture, Kin and Cognition: Essays in Honor of Ward H. Goodenough*, pp. 79–94. Washington DC: American Anthropological Association.

Caughey, J. (1977). *Fa'a'nakkar: Cultural Values in a Micronesian Society*. Philadelphia: Department of Anthropology, University of Pennsylvania.

Gladwin, T. and Sarason, S.B. (1953). *Truk: Man in Paradise*. New York: Wenner-Gren Foundation for Anthropological Research.

Goodenough, W. (1951). *Property, Kin, and Community on Truk*. New Haven: Department of Anthropology, Yale University.

Hezel, F. (1972). The Westernization of Truk: A Backward Glance. *Micronesian Reporter* 4: 25–31.

—— (1987a). Truk Suicide Epidemic and Social Change. *Human Organization* 46(4): 283–91.

—— (1987b). The Dilemmas of Development: The Effects of Modernization on Three Areas of Islands Life. In: S. Stratigos and P.J. Hughes (eds), *Ethics of Development: The Pacific In the*

21st Century, pp. 60–74. Port Moresby: University of Papua New Guinea Press.

—— (1989). Suicide and the Micronesian Family. *Contemporary Pacific* 1(1): 43–74.

—— (1991). *The Catholic Church in Micronesia: Historical Essays on the Catholic Church in the Caroline-Marshall Islands*. Chicago: Loyola University Press.

Kawai, T. (1987). Females Bear Men, Land and Eterekes: Paternal Nurture and Symbolic Female Roles in Truk. *Senry Ethnological Studies* 15: 107–25.

Marshall, M. and Marshall, L. (1990). *Silent Voices Speak: Women and Prohibition in Truk*. Belmont: Wardsworth Publishing Company.

Moral, B. (1996). Sobre la interesante concepción de los genitales en Chuuk (Micronesia). *Revista Española del Pacífico*, 6: 111–136.

—— (1997). Conceptualización de la mujer, el cuerpo y la sexualidad en chuuk (Micronesia). PhD Thesis. San Sebastián: Universidad del País Vasco.

Parker, P.L. (1985). Land Tenure in Trukese Society: 1850–1980. PhD Thesis. Philadelphia: University of Pennsylvania.

Thomas, J.B. (1980). The Namonuito Solution to the 'Matrilineal Puzzle'. *American Ethnologist* 7(1): 172–7.

Weiner, A. (1976). *Women of Value, Men of Renown: New Perspectives in Trobriand Exchange*. Austin: University of Texas Press.

Part VI

Appropriating New Forms of Knowledge

Chapter 12

Showing the Invisible: Violence and Politics among the Ankave-Anga (Gulf Province, Papua New Guinea)

Pierre Lemonnier

Like all other Angans, the Ankave are a great-man society. The prominent political figures are (were) the masters of initiations – and until recently the strongest warriors – although their authority over the rest of the community is restricted to times of active warfare or initiations. Male domination is the main social inequality. At the core of the mutual and crucial relationships that link warfare, male initiations and gender lies the notion that women's sexual physiology is generally harmful to men, dangerously debilitating for warriors and, therefore, a threat to the very survival of the tribe. Male initiations are a time when young boys are transformed into fierce and fearless adult men. Simultaneously, the domination of men over women is reaffirmed, and all the local groups in a given valley are brought together for a common undertaking. Also consistent with the great-man type of social organization described and analyzed by Godelier (1986) is the striking absence of intergroup ceremonial exchanges of wealth and of status or role based on the manipulation of wealth.

The Ankave socio-cultural life nevertheless shows some striking contrasts with that of northern Angans.[1] In particular: they have brideprice and place no emphasis on sister exchange in marriage; female blood and its substitutes, and not semen, is considered the key substance for fetal growth and the maturation of initiates; there is no ritualized homosexuality during male initiations; women enjoy relatively high status in everyday life; and cooperation is almost absent between people of the same sex (Bonnemère 1996). Also, unlike northern Angans, where up to four types of great men are found (Godelier 1986), the great warriors and the masters of the initiations were the only Ankave great men. Warfare and feuding ceased forty years ago and so there are no more great warriors among the Ankave, as young men no longer have the opportunity to demonstrate their fighting skills. However, male initiations still take place every five years or so and are the most important collective event.

What has been the Ankave's answer to the disappearance of half of their political offices? As we shall see, their power structure is still evolving, often in an experimental fashion. However, all avenues currently being explored by prospective Ankave leaders are based on the possession of particular imported knowledge, even if it is sometimes from just next door.

Despite the establishment in 1950 of an important government station and a mission at Menyamya, less than two days walk from the nearest Ankave village, and although first contact was in 1951, their territory was still considered unpacified in the mid-1960s (Weber 1965–6). The Ankave have remained relatively apart from the socio-economic transformations observed in more densely populated areas of Papua New Guinea and receive none of those services the modern world provides. For instance, there is no aidpost, no school, no road, no bush store, nor airstrip in the Suowi valley – where I have done most of my fieldwork since 1982 among the 250 people who live near Ikundi and in the surrounding hamlets. The health situation is disastrous by any standards and infant mortality rate (for children under twelve months) reaches 35 per cent. No official census was taken before 1990 and it was only in 1992 that a Lutheran evangelist started to teach children and adults to read and write.[2] It was not until 1993 that a patrol officer (from Menyamya) came into the area without official purpose, but just 'to see the place and listen to the people'.

There is neither cash-cropping nor mining nor forestry in the region, so that the small amount of money to be found in the villages has been earned by the three dozen men who worked on plantations in the 1960s and 1970s, and then by labourers on airfield sites. Today, most cash comes from the still-active sale of bark capes to neighbouring tribes. This money is used almost entirely for brideprice and compensations. People rarely buy food or tobacco in the bush stores located on the other side of the high mountains that bound the Ankave valleys to the east. Apart from clothes, steel axes, bush-knives and scarce aluminium saucepans are the only industrial goods to be found in each family. Since the end of the 1970s, only one or two men from Ikundi have gone to work on plantations. The most common foreign destination of the Ankave are the neighbouring Iqwaye valleys of Lagai and Jalerwalie, where they stay with kin or friends, and Menyamya, where they do not remain overnight because they feel unsafe. Recently the Lutheran evangelist took forty people (among whom ten were women) to the Markham Valley. In the absence of navigable rivers, the hinterland of the Gulf of Papua is never visited. The most frequent incomers are Iqwaye speakers from Lagai, because of ongoing intermarriage and friendly bonds established long ago, when many of them took refuge with the Ankave. Most diggers on the sporadic airstrip construction site are also Iqwaye. More irregular visitors are Lutheran nurses (once a year), police parties (once every three years or so) and anthropologists.

In short, several factors account for the relative isolation of the one thousand Ankave. First of all, they live in a remote and sparsely populated area (just over one person per square kilometre) at the intersection of three different provinces: Gulf, Morobe and Eastern Highlands. Far from roads and days away from the nearest patrol post in their district, they are virtually ignored by the administration. Secondly, as refugees regularly displaced by stronger groups, the Ankave still fear most of their neighbours. And last, their Iqwaye friends tell them tales of the fierce groups to the east in order to discourage them from visiting the Government station to get a better price for the few items they sometimes buy. The Ankave's own awareness of the violence of the police adds to their reluctance to see the wide world. Altogether, up to now, the Ankave have a very partial view of the state, of the Church and of the market. The last forty years have nevertheless been characterized by a tremendous amount of change and discovery.

'We Are not True Humans', and Other Weird News from the Outside World

As elsewhere in inland New Guinea, the most important item of information to enter the Ankave country was that white-skinned newcomers had powerful means to forbid fighting. Warfare and feuding declined rapidly, which allowed some men to travel to places they had hardly heard about until then. The Ankave also had to modify the use of the various means of violence they had at hand, but I shall come back to that later. Other 'knowledges' that filtered through were: 1) information on other cultures; 2) the discovery of entire sets of means of acting on the material world; 3) the revelation of Christianity.

It would be interesting to know what bits and pieces of information about the outside world have been put together in different places and times by various peoples and how this partial knowledge has been absorbed and possibly transformed to make sense. I will only point to the incredible variety of areas of which a group such as the Ankave has suddenly become aware. Such data range from statements on peoples located at an unthinkable distance ('Germany is in Europe') to information about distant neighbours ('there is gold near Wau and rascals in Lae'); and from revelations about their own recent past, for instance clues about the huge frightening insects that flew over the Ankave country (air combat during the Second World War), to confirmation of the ancestors' knowledge, for instance on the presence of expanses of water at the ends of their world. Everybody knows, too, since the new bank-notes (issued in 1975), that Papua New Guinea is an entity encompassing dozens of tribes and places, some of which have been visited by plantation workers.

Knowledge of techniques comprises both the observation or use of artefacts outside the Ankave territory proper and the acquisition of know-how regarding new devices and technical practices. Geographical or historical information is very often added to the Ankave's own store of knowledge without any sizeable influence on their way of life and world-view – but for the general feeling that white-skinned foreigners have immense power over the material world – but some imported technical knowledge is now included in the daily routine, mainly in the use of steel axes, machetes and files, which have had important (and well-known) consequences on the rhythm of labour. Other industrial artefacts are to be found either in small quantity (hinges, hammer, saw), or rapidly out of order (hurricane lamps, transistors) for lack of batteries, kerosene or mere interest. However, aside from steel tools, the most important technical innovation was the collective decision, taken around 1988, to put most pigs on one side of the river so that garden fences would no longer be needed, which has totally transformed the landscape.

Knowledge about Christian history, moral conceptions and practices deserves special mention. Today some Ankave are quite knowledgeable about biblical history and geography, and most believe that the events they are told about did happen, notably because they mistake the drawings shown to them for photographs. However, there is no form of syncretism between their own 'religious' beliefs and Christianity. Christian information simply confirms some of the ancestors sayings. For instance, a given founding couple is sometimes equated with Adam and Eve. Or both Ankave and Christian morality condemn adultery and theft. The main results of mission activity are literacy – which is too recent (1992) to be assessed in detail – and the restrictions that an irregular series of mission envoys has tried to lay down (without any lasting result).

Basically, these New-Guinean *pastor* or *misin* attempt to make the Ankave behave in a way that runs counter their habits. To meet for Sunday service or to build the evangelist's house, for instance, contradicts the remarkable absence of cooperation in Ankave social practices. Similarly, to settle in a particular hamlet opposes the Ankave's preference for dispersal. They have permanent houses in hamlets established between 800 and 1400 m altitude, but they often scatter into temporary forest camps in order to hunt, trap eels, or exploit semi-domesticated trees. Meetings, for them, are associated exclusively with war, initiations, or funerals. Some novelties introduced by the Church are generally appreciated: the school, Western clothes. Others are highly controversial. In particular, when the *misin* spoke of barring people wearing loincloths and bark capes from school, or tried to prevent the Ankave performing male initiations, many people were appalled.

These prohibitions are accompanied by an explicit and brutal condemnation of the normal Ankave way of life. In 1993, two sacred objects were broken and thrown in the (*misin's*) toilets for being 'satanic'. Also 'backward' were people daring to refer to their ancestors or wearing loincloths, not to speak of those helping the anthropologists! The bannings and contempt explain why the Church representatives are invariably driven out of the valley and why these restrictions last only as long the evangelist himself lasts.[3]

The way the Ankave are compelled to renounce their 'satanic' customs and to behave 'well' is shrouded in latent violence. For the most part, this violence is a moral one, for the person reputed to be acting in the name of God and who is associated with the introduction of health services or literacy clearly embodies an overwhelming influence, the kind a *misin* needs to convince people they are not real human beings until they are baptized![4] Furthermore, no effort is ever made to clarify the links between Church and state power. For instance, one *pastor,* who wanted to prohibit male initiations, spread the rumour that violators would be jailed by the police. Similarly, when a helicopter hired by the provincial government is planned to visit the area, people argue that the aircraft is in fact the evangelists'. Equally confusing is the way some Church-related people organize communal work (for example on the airstrip), with much horn blowing, calling roll and shouting, which reminds the Ankave of military parades seen here or there. Nor should one underestimate the persuasiveness and compelling force exerted by half-a-dozen tall, healthy young male members of some visiting Christian youth organization. Crowned with the prestige conferred by immaculate clothes, a pair of sport shoes, and a guitar, they lord it over everyone, at least until their love of card playing cuts them down to the level of ordinary sinners.

In turn, a portion of the mission workers authority is shared by those Ankave men (rarely women) who choose to become familiars of the *pastor* and his family. These are the one or two men who translate the pastor's speeches, live near his house and help him with food or work. In return, they receive clothes and, unlike other people, soap to do their washing. They are generally the first informed of the pastors plans and opinions. Usually one of these men is appointed 'Church committee' (*sios komiti* in Tok Pisin) to report on community life and is (wrongly) reputed to persuade villagers to respect the will of the Church when the pastor is not around.

Until now, and although more than half of the adult population has been baptized, Christianity has had almost no lasting effect on the Ankave's moral code or on their residential patterns. Thus, notwithstanding a ban on initiations, which raised some fuss, the Ankave initiated all the boys old enough as soon as the *pastor* left. The most radical and durable effect of the recent lengthening of the pastor's visits in the area was the 90 per cent conversion from bark capes and skirts to shorts, shirts and blouses between 1990 and 1992. Another tangible change has been that, whereas in 1988 the pastor's family made up the major part of the audience, today most of the people who happen to be in the village attend the Sunday service, provided it is led by a professional Church worker (otherwise no one takes the initiative for a Sunday meeting). As mentioned above, the incentive to gather in one village has poor results. Generally, a new *misin* does not settle in the hamlet where the previous church was, so that several families move their main residence to be near the newcomer, but, to the *misin*'s despair, the hamlet is deserted after a few weeks. When a *misin* leaves the valley, the people go back home and let the church fall into decay. Mission influence on the Ankave remains limited. Yet, Christian workers have shown an indisputable capacity to impinge on the Ankave way of life, even though for short periods of time only (rarely a full year). This is nevertheless all new to the Ankave who, as a rule, did not use to let anyone order them around, except their fight leaders or masters of initiations, on well-defined occasions. A *misin*'s power disappears as soon as he leaves the valley, and the incipient authority of his familiars immediately evaporates. However, the mere possibility that new political figures can have their say in the Ankave's life is certainly the biggest consequence of their discovery of Christianity. A similar situation can be observed as a result of the spreading of two other types of knowledge in the area, namely, the existence of the state and that of specialists able to identify cannibal flying spirits.

Mi bai i go long opis![5] How to Give Shape to an Unseen State

The majority of the Ankave's encounters with the (Australian, then Papua New Guinea) administration have been police parties rushing into the valley to investigate rumours of fights or murder. In 1953, one of the very first patrols to enter the valley enabled the Iqwaye refugees long established above Ikundi to return peacefully to their own land. Intratribal feuding went on for some time, but by around 1965 the Ankave themselves were asking the administration in Menyamya or Kaintiba to come to arrest serious trouble-makers. At that time, a *kiap* (patrol officer) from Menyamya appointed as first *luluai* a man chosen for his ability to speak Tok Pisin. Then a *tultul*[6] was selected by a government patrol. Later on, most 'leaders' were 'Church committee' designated by the

Lutheran mission of Kwaplalim, near Menyamya. Quite often, such a *sios komiti* 'puts his name' or 'takes a number' at the *kiap*'s 'office' as well. It also happens that a man decides to take on such a role and tells the administration about it after vague agreement by the villagers. Furthermore, a *gavman komiti* can be a *sios komiti* at a later time, and vice versa. In practice, it is often impossible to specify the institution (state or Church) to which a given *komiti* is supposed to refer. Both types of 'leaders' have the same functions: to arbitrate local courts (Tok Pisin *kot*), to translate officials' speeches, to act as spokesperson, and to inform the administration of major law-and-order or health problems. In all cases, it is only when people actually come to him to complain that an appointed or self-designated 'leader' is considered an acting *komiti*. In the Suowi valley, a dozen men have played such a role since the mid-1960s.

Kots are informal meetings during which alleged prejudices of all sorts are publicly exposed and arbitrated by one or two *komiti* working together. Marriage and adultery, pig damage, thefts, assault and battery, and insults are the most common complaints heard. Murders are also always dealt with locally, whether or not the administration is informed. With no exception, these are incidents that would invariably have led to more or less full-blown fights before 1960 (Bonnemère 1992).[7] On a given day, people gather near someone's house. The litigants put some money on the ground (one to three kina), to be taken by the *komiti* as a payment if the dispute is settled. Then they expose their case and answer the *komiti*'s questions. The *kot* usually goes on for hours. Quite often the disputants and the *komiti* come to an agreement, and one (or both) litigant(s) is (are) asked to give a certain amount of money to the other as a fine or reimbursement. Then everybody starts chewing betel nuts. It is often the case that the winner, too, is found to be at fault in some way and is asked to pay a fine, although smaller than what he himself receives. Frequently no agreement is reached, which leads the participants to meet again, and possible to choose another *komiti* as arbiter. Tricky cases are sometimes solved with the help of a visiting Iqwaye *komiti*. (Conversely, Ankave *komiti* participate in Iqwaye *kots*). As a last resort, if no accord is achieved, the complainant can threaten his opponent and the audience with 'going to the office', that is taking the case to the police in Menyamya. Such a threat is also what compels the defendant to come to the *kot*.

Asked by the anthropologist about the *kots*, informants refer to the fear of being imprisoned: 'When I want to kill my wife, I think about jail! I could no more see my kids! I do think about that!' 'Before, we would have killed the culprit on the spot! Now, there are *kots* and we do not respond.' Together with the dreaded coming of policemen, the prospect of spending years in a far-away prison is the prime mover behind the Ankave's intense participation in the local *kots*, which are held at least once a week on average. Also constant is the reference to the *kiaps' opis* as the ultimate recourse for solving conflicts peacefully *entre soi*. At the same time, such a reference is a reminder of the indisputable and unquestioned ban on fighting.

However, rather than trial and jail, what the Ankave have experienced from the very beginning of their encounter with the state is the brutality of the police forces. Many Ankave have been arrested in the last 35 years but most have escaped during the journey to Menyamya. Only one man has served a sentence of several months (for killing his wife) after giving himself up to the police.[8] Police parties visit the area very irregularly, something like every three years. They do not come in response to a particular crime, but because the Ankave from Angai have denounced some law-and-order problem (needless to say, the Ikundi reciprocate within a few years). In this case, appealing to the administration is clearly a means of getting an outsider to commit the intratribal violences that are now forbidden. In other words, the Ankave's encounters with the police have few links with reprehensible activity *per se*. On the other hand, they have learned that anybody can suffer from police brutality. It is only a matter of being in the wrong place at the wrong time.

In practice, the Ankave only report to the police when a murderer has been seen killing someone and has been captured on the spot. If there are only presumptions of murder, they will wait for a patrol to come around, a very unlikely event. If ever an administrator visits the area when such accusations are in the air, nobody says a word to the authorities. Everybody knows that to call for a police party can result in blows and losses for all – obviously a good reason to conceal doubtful cases from the administration. Rather than a real threat, 'to go to the office' is mainly a rhetorical reminder of the state's ultimate power, but as the coming of the police force to the valley is something to be avoided at all costs, the power in question is not so much that of treating the dozens of cases that are dealt with in the *kots* as that of enforcing the ban on fighting. In the absence of government services and presence, a *kot* gives shape to an unseen state, of which the Ankave know the only unchallenged ability to forbid warfare and feuding.[9]

The Rise and Fall of the *bos sanguma*

The Ankave's enthusiasm for *kots* and their masterminding of the police strikes in intervalley rivalry are only two of the consequences of Australian arrival. All informants agree that another direct result of the ban on fighting was the intensification of the evil-doings of two categories of invisible figures: *azia'o'* (sorcerers) and *ombi'*. The former are mere human beings who can induce fatal illness by pronouncing a spell (an *azia'o'*) while manipulating particular substances. Sorcery was particularly active in the 1960s and 1970s, a time when epidemics killing more than a dozen people at a time were attributed to specialists from other Ankave valleys hired by people from Ikundi.

Ombi' are cannibal spirits living inside a human host (male or female, adult or child) who directs them. They attack those against whom their master has some grievance. After entering various animals, notably fireflies, they come up to their victim and enter his/her body in order to cut open an organ (notably the liver) or the flesh, which leads to malaria-like symptoms. They can also block the blood flow with some object in order to create pain and illness; or steal and hide a victim's spirit. Recently, *ombi'* have destroyed important parts in planes and have been credited some air crashes. In all cases their ultimate goal is the victim's death because they collectively eat the decayed flesh of recent cadavers during secret meetings in the forest. Whereas sorcerers' acts are generally a punishment inflicted on people who have stolen something, *ombi'* chastize those who have failed in a sharing obligation (Lemonnier 1992, 1998). For the Ankave, the *ombi'* are the most feared of all evil spirits. Altogether, they are held responsible for the majority of fatal illnesses.

Shamans identify the causes of illness. They are helpless in the face of sorcery (for only the sorcerer can cancel what he has caused) but they can treat the body disorders resulting from the *ombi''*s action. With the help of their familiars, they remove from the victim's body the objects inserted by an *ombi'*, and they repair damaged organs. When standing guard around mortuary platforms, they are also able to see and indicate attacking *ombi'* to people around who drive them away with arrows. However, *ombi'* approaching a cadaver are not identified but only seen by shamans as wind or shade. In the past, the Ankave nevertheless suspected some persons of being *ombi'*, in particular when a dying person named her/his murderer. *Ombi'* (invariably women in this case) were then wounded or killed. In any case they were mutilated. When they died on the spot, they were thrown into the river. The mutilation and the throwing into water both recall *ombi'* life habits, for these beings come apart (here the trunk, there an arm, etc.) during the dances that accompany their cannibalistic feasts, and some of them are supposed to live under water, in pools.

In the lowland valley of Sinde, the toll of endemic malaria is such that the killing of suspected *ombi'* accounts for many deaths. Malaria and revenge killings (ten victims, year in, year out) would jeopardize the very survival of this small population if new arrivals from Angai did not regularly fill the demographic gap. The Ankave are fully aware of the consequences of a high rate of *ombi'*'s attacks and reprisals, and they advance this process to explain the extinction of several hamlets or clans in the past.

Assaults by *ombi'* have been increasing over the last decades. According to the Ankave, for fear of government sanction, people who were ready to wound or kill opponents with bows and arrows now launch more discrete invisible cannibalistic attacks. Whether these aggressors were already *ombi'* or became *ombi'* only recently is unknown. A few years ago, *ombi'* were such a constant threat and matter of concern for the Ankave that some were enthusiastic when they heard that specialists able to fight the *ombi'* were now to be found in a neighbouring southwestern Anga tribe, the Naotije (or Kamea). Called *bos sanguma* (in Tok Pisin a person who can fight evil spirits), these specialists have a new type of knowledge that allows them to identify and denounce people who harbour an *ombi'*. The Ankave of Angai were the first to obtain this knowledge, in 1981–2. One man got it from SDA friends in Komako (a one-day walk west, in Kamea country). Another was informed by people he met in Kerema, far away on the coast of Papua. Both of them then transmitted (free) their knowledge to a few persons they appointed as *bos sanguma* in hamlets other than their own. By 1986 there were a half dozen new seers around Angai.

In Ikundi, everything started in 1987 when two *komiti* decided
that it was vital to put an end to the *ombi'*'s activities and asked a
bos sanguma from Buu (near Angai) to intervene. A meeting was
organized and nearly a hundred people came (more than one third
of the valley's total population). The *bos sanguma* had come with a
very active leader from Buu. Both men first described Ikundi as a
backward place where people perpetually destroyed each other
through *ombi'* aggressions. The *misin* then insisted that only in such
a *ples bus*[10] were satanic habits like killing and cannibalism (*ombi'*
practices) to be found. Modernity was at the core of the speeches
that day. Several men from Ikundi stood up and declared that,
because they did not respect the government law and renounce
non-Christian behaviours, *ombi'* would exterminate the Ankave.
The usual argument 'you will then become true humans' (when
ombi' are removed from their hosts) was also advanced. Similarly,
the visiting *bos sanguma* explained that, after his struggle against
the *ombi'*, the group would be healthy and numerous again. *Ombi'*
were therefore portrayed as responsible for several of the
misfortunes the Ankave lament, namely: being a small group
pursued by stronger parties for centuries; having to grapple with
a high mortality rate and still being far from all government
services ('we are like pigs and dogs!'). Not surprisingly, the
audience accepted by acclamation that six men and three women
proposed by the seer from Buu' be appointed *bos sanguma* for the
Ikundi area. Although the first specialists in the other Ankave
valley were said to have received their knowledge from former
bos sanguma, I heard nothing about a teaching process in Ikundi.
Rather, all the active *bos sanguma* (only three in fact) told me that
they had themselves realized they had the power to spot and fight
the *ombi'* well before 1986. At any rate, the man from Buu showed
the new specialists how he himself proceeded. Above all, he was
the one who publicly detected and acknowledged the new *bos
sangumas'* powers.

Bos sanguma have two main types of activities. They detect *ombi'*
inside a person's body, or they recognize *ombi'* in their dreams,
and they protect the community from approaching *ombi'*. In
practice, a *bos sanguma* lines people up, designates those who
harbour such an evil spirit and asks them to give up their harmful
doings. If there is no specific accusation, suspects are not bothered.
Whether the *bos sanguma* then extracts the *ombi'* from his human
host is unclear to most informants. When questioned about a death,

the *bos sanguma* does not directly accuse a person of having secretly cannibalized the victim. He designates somebody as an *ombï'* and then tries to get him or usually her to confess to a particular crime during a *kot*. 'You have a bad skin!' 'I have seen you wandering around at night!' 'I have seen a woman in a dream, I want her to raise her hand!' 'How can you explain the firefly that came out of your body the other day?' are the kinds of question that are supposed to induce a confession. I have seen orphans or women without much support enjoined for hours to tell the truth. The *bos sanguma*'s other areas of action are less clear. The general feeling is that they are able to stop approaching *ombï'* and shout so that they run away, or put a mark on the ground that prevents them coming any closer. Whether they can destroy *ombï'* is not known. Last, some have curing abilities that resemble those of shamans. They receive a small sum of money (two to four kina) or a chicken in payment for their work.

The outcome of the *bos sanguma*'s activities in recent years has been different in Ikundi and in Angai. In Ikundi only half of the dozen people who have been publicly accused of having cannibalized a person having recently died have been brought to *kot*. Some are said to have confess their aggression, but in all cases I witnessed, no one ever admitted to being an *ombï'*. One accused man ran away. Another ridiculed the accusation and left the *kot*, without further consequence. Altogether, no serious sanction was ever taken against suspected *ombï'*, at most a few small compensation payments. Seers were active in 1990, but by 1993 there were no more *bos sanguma* around Ikundi. People waking up with a frog in their throat still surmise an *ombï'* attack during the night and wonder what sharing obligation they might have missed, but suspected *ombï'* are no longer questioned and *bos sanguma* are never mentioned. In Angai, on the other hand, the influence of the new specialists had more profound consequences, for two women were killed and mutilated in 1987 and 1990 after a *bos sanguma* accused them of being *ombï'*. The police came, but the murderers fled into the forest. These cases were settled locally by *kots*, which ordered compensations (about 200 kina) to be paid. However, the activity of *ombï'* hunters has now sharply decreased. First, the oldest *bos sanguma* in the valley was about to be killed because people thought he was himself an *ombï'*. Then, following a Sunday service, a young man explained to 150 people that the Church denied the existence of *ombï'* and that the consequences of the *bos sangumas'* actions were not only against the law of Papua New Guinea, but above all, sinful. Furthermore, he warned everybody that he would himself capture troublemakers and take them to the authorities. Later on a similar event took place in Buu. These speeches apparently corresponded to a general feeling, for in 1994 only one *bos sanguma* was said to be still active in a remote place on the southern border of the Ankave territory. However, only time will tell if the *bos sanguma* era has really come to an end among the Ankave.

Leaders at the Crossroads

Among the Ankave, the great warriors and the masters of the initiations are the only categories of great men. Shamans are not great men. They are not involved in warfare or initiations and they have no political power whatsoever. Skilled hunters, too, are seen as ordinary people. The ban on fighting has deeply transformed the political structure. To be sure, men's status as warriors, their bravery and their ability to protect the community remain central to the culture and social organization, and are regularly celebrated during male initiations; and from time to time men armed with bow and arrows can still be seen rushing at supposedly incoming enemies, but, while 27 Ankave were killed during fights with the neighbouring Iweto tribe between 1920 and the early 1960s, tensions with these long-standing enemies has led to mere shouting since then. Some men carry in their bodies their dead fathers' special fighting powers, but, for lack of opportunity to demonstrate them, none is considered to be a *kwi'ji'* or a *toexwi'*, that is a great warrior. In other words the great-man category of great warrior is now in a latent state. The only active great men are the masters of the initiations, who remain the sole organizers of the entire community's life for several weeks, a notable feat considering the acute reluctance of the Ankave to do anything in common or to obey other people.

In this context, *komiti* and *bos sanguma* appear as two incipient political figures. Both directly follow from the need to find new means of settling social conflicts since the *Pax Australiana*. Both deal with the uncovering of invisible realities. A *kot* gives some substance to the vague idea of an omnipotent state, the manifestations of which cannot otherwise be seen from the Ankave valleys.

Unlike the distant agents of the government (who are almost totally unaware of them)[11] *komiti* act in and for their own community, which they remind that solving conflicts peacefully is the best way to submit to the compulsory ban on fighting and to avoid encounters with the police.

Bos sanguma were a means to get rid of growing numbers of *ombɨ'* by revealing the latter's normally hidden face and identity. Their denunciations led to violence judged inopportune in the contemporary context. In the end they disappeared altogether because of the opposition of persons convinced that these new specialists infringed on both state and Church laws. But, above all, the *bos sangumas'* behaviour did not fit with particular aspects of the Ankave's socio-cultural organization.

Basically, *ombɨ'* have to remain unknown. On the one hand, so the Ankave say, the *ombɨ'*'s origins and 'lifestyle' are those of an anonymous gang (Lemonnier 1998), which is obviously incompatible with a process of naming *ombɨ'*. On the other hand, as shown by the 1987 and 1990 events in Angai, the disclosure of their identity leads to outbursts of violence that could turn into lasting feuds, so that the person able to identify *ombɨ'* would have the power to spark hostilities against particular families and, more generally, to threaten tribal unity. The Ankave's awareness and explanation of the demographic situation in Sinde allow them easily to imagine what would happen if *bos sanguma* had carte blanche.

This certainly explains several ambiguities surrounding these specialists' activities. First, in Ikundi at least, *bos sanguma* themselves were very careful not directly to accuse people of being *ombɨ'*: rather, suspected *ombɨ'* were asked to confess their hidden state. Similarly, the first *bos sanguma* in the valley repeatedly stated that he would exercise only if the entire gathering he was addressing asked him clearly to do so. I have also seen an audience order a man to keep quiet as he was pressing a *bos sanguma* to name the *ombɨ'* responsible for a given aggression.[12] The difference between merely arousing suspicion and a full accusation may be only one of degree when a *bos sanguma*'s indication still leads to a revenge killing, but it does indicates a will to restrain the seer's activity.

Even the status of the new specialists is blurred. Without exception, *bos sanguma* were regularly accused, in private, of being *ombɨ'*, too! I also heard numerous stories of *bos sanguma* accusing each other openly of being *ombi'* and then agreeing that they had abandoned their former speciality in order to become seers. Similarly, no one was surprised that the women killed as *ombi'* in 1987 had previously been appointed *bos sanguma*. As for shamans, they carefully distinguish their own ability to sense *ombi'* and to remove the objects inserted in their victims body from the *bos sanguma*'s power to see *ombi''*s faces and to remove human flesh from the victims. Finally, not only was the *bos sanguma* period of short duration, but these potentially highly influential figures were associated in part with the hated beings they were supposed to fight, which was a good way to undermine their incipient political power, if necessary.

None of the other figures born from the contact with the outside world are similarly controlled. Some of these 'new positions' (aid-post orderly, *misin*'s translator) do not need to be because they are rapidly abandoned, their holders soon tiring of their responsibilities. Others do not confer much power anyway. In particular, even the influence a few *komiti* have achieved remains incipient. It sometimes happens that a *komiti* manages to be both judge and judged and imposes an agreement favourable to his own interests, with the help of a fellow *komiti* to whom he will return the favour. However, most *komiti* have no way to impose their views, nor to rise above the rest of the population. In Ikundi, to date, only two *komiti* have made some money out of their position (a few hundred kina, at the most). They wear clean clothes and are among the richest men in the valley, but, except for a tendency to create a rise in the brideprices, their relative wealth has as yet had no political consequences, notably because the Ankave remain outside the market sphere.

What is important to note is that, like all other contemporary *a'mini'wa'* (important men) these two *komiti* would not have derived much from their position if they were not also involved in some other new activity. Apart from one of the *i'pa'ni'xano* ('initiate's fathers' – masters of the initiations) whose command is still total during male initiations, all of the three or four influential Ankave men are people who have held various offices in the past, or who now hold several simultaneously. For instance, the man presently being trained in Menyamya to become the first Ankave evangelist had previously opened the one-and-only store to have existed in the valley (for a few months in 1988). He also tried to make money by keeping an uncastrated pig to serve the villager's sows (a complete failure). Similarly, the *sios komiti* who was the most active opponent of male initiations in 1993 distinguished himself by his involvement in the 1994 ceremonies. Even the man presently in charge of the first- and second-stage initiations was acting as an orderly a few years ago and is now also a *komiti*.

The most powerful men in the valley are no exception to these attempts to accumulate bits of influence in order to seize some real political power. One is currently a *sios komiti*, but was the most active *bos sanguma* around (although often privately accused of being an *ombi'*). He was also *gavman komiti* for several years. To him, the rule is clearly to turn anything to good account. Together with a close male relative recently elected to the *komuniti gavman* in Kwaplalim, he has succeeded in monopolizing relations with the administration – that is the information flow. Their main achievement is probably to have built houses in the best places to profit from the opening to the outside world: next to the *pastor's* house, and right beside the future airstrip, although on another clan's land. When people work on the future airstrip, they are the ones who cook and distribute the rice provided by the government. They also distinguish themselves as the only ones to be paid, although they do not dig. Any visiting official stays at their house, and the first radio link with the District Services network was also installed in their house.

Until now, their accumulated prestige has not been transformed into direct authority over the rest of the population, but their habit of the Government station has already allowed them to convince the police to come and arrest (and beat) two men they wrongly accused of murder, although most people agreed that the 'victim' was in fact drowned in a river flood. The accused were soon released, but as both of them are the main representatives of the clan on whose land the future airstrip is being built, it is clear that having them jailed would have left the two 'leaders' with their hands freer to settle there. The behaviour of these two 'leaders' is contested in private, even by their fellow clan members, and yet the two men's current settling on 'foreign' land is consistent with their clans ongoing expansion. They are criticized notably for not acting as proper spokespersons for the whole community. They may therefore be replaced soon, but I would predict that they will not be far from the aidpost and the school when these come to Ikundi, in a few years.

In the absence of great warriors, the masters of the initiations, who hold the sacred objects and secret knowledge to meta-morphose boys into warriors, are presently the only Ankave great men. Because there were no ceremonial exchanges of wealth, there was no 'economic' base for power in this society. As the market economy remains out of reach, there still is none. *Bos sanguma* appeared as one answer to the displacement of violence toward hidden quarters, but their particular monopoly on the invisible world gave them a political power unheard of among the Ankave, who rapidly rid themselves of these ambiguous seers. None of the other new roles the Ankave have tested is prominent enough to allow its holder to compel others to obey his decisions. In this context, the incipient leaders are those whose knowledge of the changes in neighbouring tribes has enabled them to accumulate several roles. The most influential men are standing by, next to prospective centres of socio-economic transformations. No one knows how prestige, economic power and political influence will interact in the future, but control of the flow of information is clearly the best strategy for seizing power of any kind when it appears.

Notes

1. On Northern Angans see Herdt (1981, 1987) and Godelier (1986).
2. A one-day walk south of the Suowi, in the valley of the Ankave-Swanson river where the remaining 700 Ankave live, a missionary from the Summer Institute of Linguistics started a school in vernacular in the early 1980s at Angai. In 1987 an airstrip has been opened. Since the missionary has left the area (1992), the school is regularly ran by a handful of Ankave, men and women. The airstrip is hardly usable by fixed-wing aircraft. From here onward, the ethnography I present concerns the Suowi river valley, but for mention of Angai or of the third Ankave valley (Sinde, fifty inhabitants).
3. *Misin* has tried to settle around Ikundi since the end of the 1970s but real mission work started between 1982 and 1987, when

Lutheran evangelists were in the area half of the time. Two of them were chased by the Ankave because of adultery. For their part, these *misin* were successful in preventing their Seventh Day Adventists (SDA) colleagues to settle in the valley. Then there were no mission workers around for four years, until the arrival of a Church worker from the Markham, in 1992. There have never been two Church workers at the same time.

4. As some colleagues will know, to hear old and close friends come and explain that they have become men the month or year before is a very unpleasant experience.

5. Tok Pisin for 'I'll go and refer to the patrol officer's office'.

6. *Tultul* and *luluai* were the titles of the leaders appointed in German New Guinea. They were retained by the Australians. Two Ikundi men are still called by their former function.

7. Between 1930 and 1965, a dozen inhabitants of the Suowi valley were killed in feuds. Cauri shells have never been used in *kot*, which stresses the link of this institution with modern times. So does its Ankave name: *kotɨxɨ*. Unlike in big-men societies (Strathern 1972, 1985), there was no possibility of compensation to settle conflicts among the Ankave, except for peace ceremonies. On traditional and 'imported' village courts, see Berndt (1962), Epstein (1974), Reay (1974), Zorn and Bayne (1975).

8. Another man was jailed for ten years for his wife's murder, but the killing took place in Lae where he had been living for years.

9. Just for the sake of comparison, I must add that this fear of police and respect of ban on fighting is by no way shared by all Anga groups. Twelve years ago the entire population of another Anga valley took refuge in the surrounding forest for a few weeks while police parties armed with tear gas and incendiary grenades were in the villages. According to the villagers, due to the use of helicopters there were not much to do to but run away, but no one felt threatened and the men would challenge the police to follow them in the forest. As for the destruction of houses, it leads to no other comments than 'there are lots of trees in the forest to built new houses!'

10. A remote place. In the discourse of an active catechist, this expression indicates an area outside of government influence where the Church must impose 'civilized manners' (my terms) by all means.

11. For instance, for several years, the administration thought that the *komiti* for Ikundi was reporting on a place located in another tribe's and language group's territory.
12. On a similar reluctance to name invisible witches, and, more generally, on the changes in mediumism due to the irruption of the government and mission, see Schieffelin (1977).

References

Berndt, R.M. (1962). *Excess and Restraint.* Chicago: University of Chicago Press.

Bonnemère, P. (1992). Suicide et homicide: deux modalités vindicatoires en Nouvelle-Guinée. *Stanford French Review* 16(1): 19–43.

—— (1996). *Le pandanus rouge. Corps, différence des sexes et parenté chez les Ankave Anga (Papouasie Nouvelle Guinée).* Paris: CNRS Editions/Editions de la Maison des Sciences de l'Homme.

Epstein, A.L. (1974). Moots on Matupit. In: A.L. Epstein (ed.), *Contention and Dispute: Aspects of Law and Social Control in Melanesia,* pp. 93–112. Canberra: Australian National University.

Godelier, M. (1986). *The Making of Great Men. Male Domination and Power among the New Guinea Baruya.* Cambridge: Cambridge University Press.

Herdt, G. (1981). *Guardians of the Flutes. Idioms of Masculinity.* Chicago and London: University of Chicago Press.

—— (1987). *The Sambia. Ritual and Gender in New Guinea.* New York: Holt, Rinehart, Winston.

Lemonnier, P. (1992). Couper-coller. Attaques corporelles et cannibalisme chez les Anga de Nouvelle-Guinée. *Terrain* 18: 87–94.

—— (1998) Maladie, cannibalisme et sorcellerie chez les Anga de Papouasie Nouvelle-Guinée. In: M. Godelier and M. Panoff (eds), *Le corps humain. Supplicié, possédé, cannibalisé.* Paris: Editions des Archives Contemporaines.

Reay, M. (1974). Changing Conventions of Dispute in the Minj Area. In: A.L. Epstein (ed.), *Contention and Dispute. Aspects of Law and Social Control in Melanesia,* pp. 199–239. Canberra: Australian National University.

Schieffelin, E.L. (1977). The Unseen Influence: Tranced Mediums as Historical Innovators. *Journal de la Société des Océanistes* 33(56–7): 169–78.

Strathern, M. (1972). Official and Unofficial Courts. Legal Assumptions and Expectations in a Highland Community. Canberra: Australian National University. *New Guinea Research Bulletin 47*.

—— (1985). Discovering Social Control. *Journal of Law and Society* 12(2): 111–34.

Weber, R.E. (1965–6). Kaintiba Patrol Report No. 2, 1965–6. Waigani: National Archives.

Zorn, J. and Bayne, P. (eds). (1975). *Lo Bilong Ol Manmeri: Crime, Compensation, and Village Courts*. Port Moresby: University of Papua New Guinea Press.

Chapter 13

'Big Man' and 'Big Woman' in the Village – Elite in the Town. The Iatmul, Papua New Guinea

Milan Stanek and *Florence Weiss*

The authors analyze the adaptation strategy of the first and second generation of migrants from the Sepik River to Rabaul, New Britain, by means of a case study. Part one, 'the modernization project' (by M. Stanek) deals with the first successful entrepreneur coming from a village of the Iatmul. Part two, 'the women in the modernization project' (by F. Weiss) deals with the role of his wife and daughter in the entrepreneurial effort. Old and new cultural patterns are considered, as well as social conflicts and the inner integrative attempts of individuals. We also touch upon the methodological questions that seem inevitable when transgressing the confines of classical social or cultural anthropology.

The Modernization Project

The Active Man, a Successful Entrepreneur

The individual I put into the focus, is a man called Landu.[1] He was born at the beginning of our century in the village of Palimbei on the middle reaches of the Sepik River. In his childhood and adolescence (in the 1920s and 1930s) he experienced the establishment of the Australian colonial administration in the Sepik Region and plantation work in the centres of economic activity, located quite far from the Sepik.

As a young man (in the 1940s) he experienced the Japanese invasion and the retreat of the Australians. Then he took part in the war as a sergeant under Japanese command. What he came to know in terms of technology and levels of organization surpassed everything he knew before, in the context of his own Papuan culture or of the colonial context. After the war he was judged by a military tribunal for collaboration with the enemy and condemned to eight years of forced labour. So he experienced, at the end of the 1940s and in the 1950s, the discipline of the penitentiary (near Rabaul) and the corresponding forms of work organization. He advanced quickly to a leading position and commanded large work teams of prisoners numbering up to 200 men.

In the 1960s he received land from the colonial administration (in the Long Valley near Rabaul) and set up a plantation. This was his own agricultural firm producing – under his management – copra, and later cocoa for export. When I got to know him in 1972 (during his brief visit in his native village where I did my fieldwork at that time) he was at the peak of his entrepreneurial career. After the first ten years of effort his firm became profitable and Landu started to diversify – he established a transport firm running up to six lorries.

The profitability of both copra and cacao production sank in the 1980s as a consequence of the fall in international prices. Small firms especially – like Landu's – ceased to be profitable at all for a period of time. When I visited his plantation in the Long Valley in 1988, the yearly output was already at a very low level and of the transport firm no more then one vehicle remained. Landu waited for a rise in prices, not embittered so much as even minded. In accordance with his age – he was almost as old as the century – he had no motivation to start a new sort of entrepreneurial activity.

The Modernization

Throughout his life, Landu had experienced the influence of new – from the standpoint of his community – external powers, which were highly organized and in many practical concerns superior. These were able to influence profoundly the very conditions of his everyday life. First, it was the colonial officers, better armed and better organized, then the Japanese and the Allied armies, finally the world-wide networks of international trade.

He was born into a small community, one of the approximately 10,000 small political units existing on the island of New Guinea which, at the beginning of the century, did not know any centralized political power, neither within these units nor in a wider context on the regional level. What we call in Europe or in Asia the macro-social context, simply did not exist at that time in Melanesia. Landu has watched from the beginning the establishment of this macro-social context in his country and contributed in his own way to its stabilization.

We designate this process 'modernization'. In this we do not follow the sociology of development, which was out to change the world practically and believed in the progress of mankind. Rather, we follow the notions of the critical, if pessimistic sociology, which constituted itself on foundations laid down by Max Weber (1864–1920).[2] In his conception, the modern macro-social context is characterized – besides its centralized political power with its multifarious administrative bodies – by an economic system, operating on a large territory, with its highly rationalized organizational forms both within the single enterprise as well as among a larger number of them. On the one side we have the stable shell (*Gehäuse*, as Weber puts it) of the bureaucratic macro-structure of state and industry and on the other side we have the individual and his primary group. The latter, in the process of modernization, takes on either the role of an agent and representative of this process or the role of its victim. Evidently, the individual (and his primary group) can become an adversary of the modernization – but this does not constitute an alternative leading to another issue than the two formerly stated. Weber describes the modern world, on the grounds of his sociological analysis as well as on the grounds of the overpowering *Zeitgeist*, as a prison. He did not believe, that this organizational shell could be destroyed and removed, nor did he believe that there was any possibility of discovering an individual escape route out of this.[3]

An active individual in the macro-social context of the modernization is forced to take a series of corrective actions upon himself, be he an entrepreneur like Landu or his employees taking on different subordinate roles in a given institutional context like an agricultural firm or transport firm. These corrective actions concern, in the first line, time and money management, performance and proficiency attitudes, and the maximization of profit in a well-conceived financial structure. Lastly, what completes the

whole effort is corrective action across the generations securing
the family career beyond the grave of the founder.

The Original Cultural Background

The conditions of Iatmul village life – be it the economy with its
specific co-operation and exchange relationships or the kin system
as a means of communication and as an aspect of political
organization, or ritual and mythology – have been studied already
for some sixty years.[4] On the background of this knowledge we
are well able to isolate some so-called traditional elements in the
behaviour and in the reasoning of Landu and of other Palimbei
migrants in Rabaul.

For instance, the characteristic institution of the 'big man', the
whole pattern of mobilizing followers by a leader, can be perceived
when Landu employs his kinsmen at his plantation, when he
harnesses his women to this undertaking, and when he organizes
a never-ending redistribution of wealth in the form of gifts. The
attitude of the rest of the Palimbei migrants toward his achievement confirms this observation: not only that he is acknowledged
and designated as big man, *nsambindu* in Iatmul language, he also
has to stand up against the hostility of his countrymen when his
position seems to become more and more stable. The fact that the
son of Landu renounced the role of big man in building his own
career – without harnessing the support of kinsmen – in an exclusively international and multiethnic milieu, confirms once more how
far Landu himself relied upon the 'traditional' cultural concepts.

I consider this approach – looking for traditional patterns and
opposing them to the new ones – as narrow and deficient, although
not false. This approach allows us to see the composite character
of the observed social phenomenon – the individual does not
simply continue the 'old' pattern, nor does he simply acquire a
'new' one. Evidently social change is not possible without some
cultural continuity. Notwithstanding that Landu finds himself continually in conflict between the rationality of the big man role and
the rationality of the commercial undertaking, it is precisely this
difficult junction that creates – to the extent he is able to bear the
resulting tensions - the very condition of his success. The success
of Landu, in turn, opens new prospects for his son.

This approach remains unsatisfactory because it operates

merely on the level of cultural patterns. It does not open the way to the consideration of the drama of a struggling individual (and his primary group) who makes strategic decisions, makes headway or experiences his limits, changes himself and his immediate social context and, lastly, creates for his children and his grandchildren a set of conditions pushing his family into the significant changes of an unanticipated future. In the culturalist approach the description of a social phenomenon – in our case the first and for a time the only successful entrepreneur of Palimbei – breaks down in two static series of cultural patterns: the Iatmul big man and the modern manager. These two can be at best superimposed, somehow intertwined, or one can be dislodged by the other. In the latter case the result would be a person who remained a good big man and became a bad manager or the reverse. A sociological approach, although more dynamic, is often also unsatisfactory. For instance, in the framework of organization analysis it achieves seldom more than a brochure for the use of the apprentices of managerial art. It remains limited to the question of how a Papua becomes a successful businessman.

The Interdisciplinary Horizon

It became evident some time ago that a narrow culturalist approach does not meet its objectives and a genuine interdisciplinary approach is required. Many anthropologists make use of conceptions borrowed from economics, politology, sociology, psychology and biology, to name just some disciplines. The retreat of anthropologists into the realm of mere ideology, where they only consider patterns of thought, has met its end. Symbolic anthropology, with its philosophical or semiological approach, seems to me not to grasp anything more than its own pattern of thought. The reaching out of the anthropologists into the cultural world of modernization takes another path: we study the colonial situation and its heritage, urbanization, the international political and economical links, and arrive inevitably at the world system as an object of study in its own right. In this movement we realize that the small groups we were occupied with dissolve in this maelstrom. We have no more to do with this or that particular language or culture group, instead we are concerned with the managers, the officials, the workers, the unemployed and criminals.

In the effort to describe the social and cultural change in Papua New Guinea – represented here by the case of the big man and entrepreneur Landu – I proceed in two different interdisciplinary directions: the ethno-sociological and the ethno-psychological. Each represents a particular instance of analytical modelling.

The sociological approach, as developed by Max Weber and in the more recent Anglo-American conceptions, first puts the active individual into focus, and then ascertains the macro-social conditions pertaining to his situation, especially the regionally active intermediate conditions at the middle level of abstraction. Now it becomes possible to study the social conflicts arising among the actors as well as between the actor and the institutional context as dynamic elements of the general social structure. Now it becomes possible to study the social drama, the dilemmas of the actor, his strategies, the externally given motives of his actions, his errors and failures, the fruits as well as the burdens of success, or the marginalization and destitution.

The psychological approach, as developed by Sigmund Freud (1856–1939) and the more recent psychoanalytic conceptions,[5] furnishes a method to study the inner conflicts of the individual migrant who, in the course of his life, internalized successively two different cultural worlds. The integration of these two internal psychic realities is never possible without troublesome cognitive and emotional internal conflicts. A successful internal psychic integration or its reverse, the internal suppression of particular aspects of the one or the other cultural world, lead to diverse personality developments and personality disorders conditioning the social performance of the actor.

The Anthropological Fieldwork as Starting Point

At this point of our reasoning the question arises of why do we not simply say, 'well, our research is based entirely on the sociological approach'. Or, 'we apply the psychoanalytical method in Papua New Guinea'. Why do we insist on a particular anthropological approach, why do we speak about 'ethno-sociology', 'ethno-psychoanalysis' and so on? The reason is not so much the preference for this or that theoretical model or for any particular combination of these models; it is rather the consistency and compelling character of the anthropological fieldwork method.

I would not dismiss any theoretical conception coming from any discipline (sociology, psychology, anthropology, biology). The existence of conflicting models that are logically incompatible or not connected one with the other does not simply invalidate one of them. We know that different lines of interest or different purposes produce different theoretical models. To be sure, it is indeed our task to invalidate theories, nevertheless, it remains a poor exercise just to point out the logical inconsistency of a theoretical model or to adduce some new facts inconsistent with it. Our more important parallel task is devising new models that do not ignore the facts that have been highlighted by the other models. In this field of model-building anthropology has produced some very specific conceptions, but the need to integrate a particular anthropological approach into the interdisciplinary joint effort is not founded primarily on the importance of some typically anthropological model-building. In my opinion, it is the typically anthropological tradition of fieldwork that constitutes a challenge and an impulse for theoretical progress within both sociology and psychology.

Let us remind ourselves of the main features of the anthropological fieldwork method:

• We study a relatively small group numbering seldom more than one hundred persons connected among themselves by a rather dense co-operation and communication network.
• We allow ourselves quite a long period of time for this study – between six months and up to several years.
• The main settings in which we collect our information are longer series of open-end conversations with one person. These should be well documented so as to ascertain not only their content but also the development of the relationship between the informant and the researcher.

These three maxims describe the standard procedure most anthropologists employ. In spite of this, the anthropologists very often neglect to describe in their publications the relational context in which they received their information. They are also often reluctant to render the statements of their informants in full, and even more so in specifying their own contributions to the conversations with the informants. So we attach a fourth maxim to our catalogue:

- The setting of the conversations should be thoroughly described as an integral part of the publication of the results if the latter should be considered as of some use in model-building. The informants should be well visible in the final rendering as persons making statements within a more or less developed relationship with the researcher.

However, imprisoned in its own fieldwork strategy, anthropology would never in surpass the confines of a case study. When we strive to make general statements by means of more abstract models, it does not help at all to multiply the typical anthropological case studies. Even a larger number of such studies does not constitute, in my opinion, a sufficient base for generalization. For this reason it is necessary to widen the scope of observation. We need to consider a greater number of overlapping larger groups, embedded in a more comprehensive macro-social structure. Here the anthropological fieldwork method is no more practicable and we are induced to use the results of empirical social science, produced by the means of standardized questionnaires even if it does not allow the typically anthropological immersion in a case, deepening of knowledge or due consideration of individual informants. The anthropologist himself does not have to produce the results typical of empirical social science, nevertheless, he has to be able to extract them from the work of sociologists, economists, social statisticians and so forth and link them in a meaningful way with his own particular case study.

The anthropological case study of a small group appears against the background of sociology or economics as a restriction of the field of observation. In consequence, the knowledge of detail and analysis of individual behaviour can be developed further than by any other method. In comparison with the psychoanalytic approach the anthropological study appears as a widening of perspective; it furnishes material elucidating the social and cultural context of the dyadic relationship between the patient and the analyst. The insights into the psycho-dynamics of transference and counter-transference produced by the psychoanalytic method can thus be completed by the small-scale social context of the therapeutic dyadic relation – the inner conflicts as well as the inner integrative effort within the individual can be linked with the dynamics of social structure.

In the preceding paragraphs we circumscribed two basic

components of the methodological construction in ethnology (social and cultural anthropology): 1) the fieldwork and the resulting case study represent the starting point, 2) yet before we try systematic comparisons – in view to be able to make general statements – we have to build up interdisciplinary connections (in our demonstration in the sociological or psychological direction).

After this we are ready to try a meaningful comparison. We do compare at any point of time during the research activity, so to say from the scratch: in planning our trip, in devising the research strategy, during the fieldwork etc. but systematic comparison becomes possible only in an advanced phase of work, after having realized a meaningful, detailed description and analysis of the cases under consideration and after having embedded these in their corresponding macro-social context, eventually elucidating the inner psychic dynamics in connection with the social process.

If these two components of methodological construction are in fact basic, we have to accept an essential dependence of ethnology on several further disciplines, even before we start the systematic comparative effort. From this it does not follow that we would not value the results of the typical anthropological thinking, such as theories of culture or semiologic analyses. We simply observe how narrow its base is and how dependent it is. On the other hand we do not see any possibility to dispose of the anthropological fieldwork method – we cannot simply do sociology or do psycho-analysis and so on. When we retain the primary anthropological research strategy, we are forced to construct an ethno-sociology, ethno-psychoanalysis or another hyphenated anthropology.

The typical immersion in a case study – with a small number of informants, long fieldwork, an individual and his primary group – constitutes our genuine anthropological starting point as well as the point of arrival. The individuals who were our partners during the fieldwork appear twice in the whole process: first in the field, making statements in the context of the relationship with the researcher, then in the publications where this context has to be reconstructed and elucidated.

The Women in the Modernization Project

We start our reasoning with the following questions:

- What new social and economic circumstances are the women confronted with through the modernization process, and how do they cope?
- Under what conditions do they become an active agent of this process, if they do not try to side-step the new circumstances?
- In case they take part actively in the modernization process, in what concerns are they forced to change themselves and to adapt to the new situation?
- What contradictions and conflicts result out of accepting the change and what solutions remain open to the women?

From the remarks up to now it is clear that the initiator of new projects – in the case we are considering – is a man. Therein lies a general tendency evident in the entire world: men are in general more directly concerned with modernization than are women. They are quicker to become direct partners of the representatives of the colonial administration, they are the first to be integrated into the business connections of the colonial economy, and so on. Women are also concerned with modernization, although initially in an indirect way. This is the reason men, from the viewpoint of know-how, are sooner in a position to participate more actively in the modernization process. The women of Papua New Guinea had to overcome these disadvantages and it was only in the 1970s that they were successful at obtaining better positions and opening their own businesses.[6] We want to take a close look at exactly how these circumstances affected Landu's wife and his daughter.

The Group and the Localities

The group that we researched comprises three generations of a patrilineal kin-group: Landu, his daughter Langalagwi, his son Murendu and their children. Added to this are the marriage partners: Landu's wife Wanse, Langalagwi's husband Nselmbange and Murendu's wife. Connected with them is a circle of distantly related persons and unrelated persons.

m Landu	f Wanse, wife of Landu
m Murendu, Landu's son	f Langalagwi, Landu's daughter
(and his wife)	(and her husband Nselmbange)
children of Murendu	children of Langalagwi

Two localities stand in the foreground: on the one hand the agricultural firm 'Long Valley', and on the other the Palimbei settlement in the town of Rabaul, the northern quarter.[7] The plantation is situated about two hours from Rabaul by car. Landu, his wife Wanse and six employees, three women and three men, live there. The region is agricultural hinterland of Rabaul. The entire infrastructure of businesses, bank, post, and outlets for copra and cocoa are found in Rabaul. So Landu travelled to the town at least once each month.

The second important part of the family lives in the northern quarter. This settlement is a well-defined division within the larger town ring that runs around the town centre. It comprises over forty houses. Over 300 people lived here in 1988 (the proportion of females to males being about equal). Landu's daughter, Langalagwi, her husband Nselmbange and their children also live here. Their house is the only one that, like an Australian house, is built of prefabricated material. It stands out noticeably from the other houses of the settlement built from gathered boards. If Landu or his wife come to the town, they live here. Landu's son Murendu lived here until he took a job as manager of an automobile sales agency. At that time he moved into a house in a quarter of the town at the disposal of the firm for its higher employees. He visits his sister Langalagwi in the Palimbei settlement on a weekly basis.

The basic strategy of both family divisions, the agricultural firm 'Long Valley' and the northern quarter, became to fight for a tangible place in the new circumstances. The agricultural firm represented the self-supporting gainful work that, during the 1950s, meant an income and a connection to modern conditions. The people there worked the land that in the town is scarce. The family members in the town represented employment, access to education and close association with other groups of Palimbei migrants (potential employees for Landu's firm). Landu had recognized this from the beginning. He sat astride two horses: land and town, an agrarian firm in his possession, and on the other hand the regular employment of family members in the town.

The Wife Wanse: Modernization without Housewifeization[8]

Everyone, especially Landu was constantly aware that his project was only realizable with the participation of his wife Wanse. She is what the Iatmul call a strong woman. Like Landu, Wanse grew up in Palimbei. In contrast to him, she had neither gone through the school of co-operation with the Australians and Japanese, nor through forced labour. When Landu was convicted by the Australians for his collaboration with the Japanese and had to serve time in a prison in Rabaul, she went about her business undisturbed by the village neighbourhood's rejection, and she held firmly to her relationship with him. When Landu proposed that she move with him to Rabaul after his release, she was agreeable. She was the first woman to move to a colonial town. With the departure from the village she paid the price of separation from her relatives, loss of the women's group, and having to find her way among entirely new, to her unknown, circumstances. At the same time we can say that she was willing to take a active part in the project of her husband.

Wanse took responsibility for important functions in the agricultural firm. On the one hand she was a hard worker, she planted coconut palms and cocoa plants, she cut grass and helped with the harvest. On the other hand she grew garden produce for the family and for the employees. She sold part of her produce to the inhabitants of the northern quarter and tobacco, grown as a supplement, to a Chinese merchant. Her proceeds gave security for years by providing a regular income until the produce from the plantation could be sold. She could buy their first car from her revenue. In addition, Wanse did the housework: She cooked food for the contract workforce and she took care of their son Murendu.

It was important for relationships with the inhabitants of the northern quarter that Wanse sold part of her produce to them. Her trade took her regularly to her daughter's house. The women were happy to buy from her because it was cheaper than buying at the market.

As Wanse, together with Landu and her children, left the village and undertook the agricultural business, she came into contact in various ways with the new socio-economic circumstances. She took part in extensive projects designed by her husband. What came with this? She had to make her way in a small, isolated group. And she was confronted with a money economy: the produce for which she worked yielded part-wise subsistence, a larger share was sold for cash. All of these are especially violent changes for a woman who grew up in a village community. On the other side, her everyday work changed little. As in the village she was responsible for the organization of the household and for work outside the house on the plantation. From her background in the village, accustomed as she was to managing her independent business, Wanse could retain her independence in the new circumstances. Her sphere of activity required her to be self supporting and also equipped her to manage her own revenue. Landu as big man stands parallel to Wanse as big woman. The basis for this is a co-operation model that stems from the village. The economic tasks of the sexes in the traditional Iatmul society are pooled. Women are responsible for providing, preparing and apportioning the food (fishing and marketing) and they are responsible for the small children. The men are artisans (houses, canoes). This distribution, which changed only in exceptional circumstances, has the result that men and women are in large measure dependent on each other. Both genders position themselves reciprocally to acquire or provide, on the basis of the labour division, any product or talent at their disposal. So the strength of a family, and the clan, is dependent on how well the co-operation between the marriage partners functions. Wanse and Landu could put the traditional model to use under the new conditions.

The Daughter Langalagwi: The Social Role of the Housewife

In distinction to Wanse, Langalagwi lived in the town. There was no land or river to make use of, but work on the land or river would in no way be expected of her. In contrast to her mother who, besides the important housework, attended to agricultural production, Langalagwi took on exclusively the organization of the household.[9] While Langalagwi's husband Nselmbange had regular employment and brought home money for the support of the family, Langalagwi became primarily relegated to housework: cooking, washing, cleaning and care of the children. This stands in stark contrast to the village where the women, besides their house work, accomplish production of more than 80 per cent of the essential nutritional needs. The roles switched: the men in the village, artisans and dependent on their women for food, became the providers; the women in the town lost their autonomous position to the men. The men became dependent upon their employers, the women upon their men. This draws an all-too-familiar picture. The fact that Langalagwi could not earn money with outside work distinguished her from her mother. And, a substantial difference exists in the tasks that are considered housework. I would like to cite the importance of the responsibility women take for the children's school attendance. This meant a complete reorientation for Langalagwi, as for all Iatmul women. Not only must they cook at a certain time for the children and dress them appropriately for school – they have to shadow them. Most Iatmul children offer resistance and refuse regular school attendance. The demands of school stand in direct contrast to the autonomy and individual initiative that is so important to the Iatmul. In traditional Iatmul society children get fully reprimanded but are hardly ever forced to do something. One waits until they begin something out of their own initiative. Now Langalagwi, in full possession of independence and autonomy characteristic of all Iatmul women, must demand subordination and obedience. Langalagwi tells her children, with all the courage she can muster, against her own impulses, to attend school regularly. What comes into being under the new economic conditions is what we call the invention of childhood, a process that was put into effect in Europe in the eighteenth century. Children became beings who had to be educated, and mothers in this way came by an important function. What would have been carried by the group and the social structure of the village was taken over by the adults in the town – mainly the mother and teachers.[10]

The education of the new generation was a part of her father's project. In contact with the Japanese and Australians he came to learn how important professional training is, in view of obtaining a good position in the new social context. Langalagwi's father and mother, and even she herself, were restricted from the white's educational offerings. It was now Langalagwi's task to make access possible for her younger brother and later her own six children. She had to assume a new role and to accept a new value. In comparison with her mother, Langalagwi had to make many far-reaching adjustments in the new circumstances; we could even speak of a real values change. Year after year she had to take pains that her brother and her children complied with the demands of the school, an effort that only brought fruit in the distant future, if the children got a good job.

I would like to mention one aspect of the relationship that developed between Langalagwi and me while doing my research. Langalagwi became one of the most important partners during our Rabaul research. I visited her at her house for many months and we held regular conversations. Langalagwi was noticeably different from the usual Palimbei woman whom I came to know in the village or in the town. She was more controlled and quieter and distinguished herself in this way from the more typically extroverted and expansive Iatmul women. She did not have a negative attitude toward me, but she held herself back. During my visits to her house she watched me and listened attentively. When we talked about something she always wanted to know my opinion. She was in possession of various experiences within the modern context and this influenced her attitude and behaviour toward me. My estimation of Langalagwi changed in the course of time. At first I perceived mainly her adaptation: her restraint, the orderliness of her household. Only with time, through our conversations, did it become clear that Langalagwi had really adapted, but in no way had she given up her own objectives. To the contrary, one could say that it was her adaptation that enabled her to pursue them. It became apparent that she was proceeding from a certain rivalry with her brother and was attending to the wish for equality. She made it possible for both of their oldest daughters to go to the mission school and today they are among the best educated women of the Palimbei migrants in Rabaul. So we could say that not only did her father follow a plan, but she did too, however, in direct connection with the future chances of her daughters. So her ability to prevail was concealed behind her conformity.[11]

The Price of Success

The capability to make one's way in the new economic circumstances and to work one's way up the social hierarchy has its price. It means forgoing rewards that are important in the village culture. The realization of the agricultural project led to distance from the other migrants for whom the climb was not so successful. Envy, hate, and open rejection are effective methods to punish social climbers. Landu's family had to feel this rejection. The Palimbei's portrayed Landu's plan to build up an agricultural business as nonsense. In the beginning no one wanted to start to work for him and he was called 'the crazy man'. (In response to this, he officially baptized his transport firm 'The Crazy Man'.) His regular visits and the sale of agricultural produce by his wife also had a purpose: to create the best possible relations, to secure the urban Palimbei's good will and to minimize the aggression.

Langalagwi's example makes it clear how difficult all their accomplishments were. In a way, by living in the town settlement, she was more exposed to the rejection and scepticism of the urban Palimbei than her father and mother on the distant agricultural land, and, more than her brother Murendu who moved out of the settlement after he became a manager.

Langalagwi has had a strange illness for many years. When she leaves the house and the surrounding garden she gets dizzy. She loses consciousness and falls down. All attempts to heal her have failed. There is only one way for her to leave the settlement and that is by car. She doesn't get dizzy in an car. Her brother, father or a sister from the mission fetches her from time to time and takes her around by car on excursions around the town. It is easy to grasp that something of the problematic of the successful modernization and the social conflict that accompanies the stratification is concealed in Langalagwi's illness. The other urban Palimbei also interpret it this way. The Landu family has certainly become rich, but they pay a price for it. Langalagwi has an incurable illness. The illness protects her from aggression and the people in the settlement feel sorry for her, and with her, for the entire Landu family.

Closing Remarks

The fact that Landu as well as the women of his family have been successful in the course of modernization process makes them an elite. Their achievement allows them to survive at a higher level and brings them different sorts of satisfaction. On the other hand, it brings them also a certain type of stress so well known to us. The aspects of modernization accepted by the family of Landu are also an integral part of our own social conditions in Europe or North America.

Notes

1. All the personal names have been altered.
2. Cf. Weber (1973, 1990).
3. The metaphor of the world as prison appears already in Shakespeare, so often quoted by Weber (e.g. Hamlet II, 2, line 245); cf. Weber (1980: 333), (1920: 521).
4. G. Bateson (1965) and M. Mead (1949) in the 1930s, the linguists in the 1960s and 1970s (e.g. Laycock 1973), the Basel team in the 1970s (B. Hauser-Schäublin, M. Schindlbeck, J. Schmid, M. Schuster, M. Stanek, J. Wassmann, F. Weiss); also, not without some importance, the early German explorers in 1909 and 1913, e.g. Reche (1913) and Behrmann (1922).
5. Parin, Morgenthaler and Parin-Matthèy (1980); Boyer and Grolnick (1989). For the Iatmul cf. Morgenthaler, Weiss and Morgenthaler (1984), Weiss (1996).
6. Boserup (1970) contributed substantially to our understanding of the women's social role in the colonial and post-colonial development. King, Lee and Warakai (1985) and *Women in Development* (1985) deal with same subject in the Papua New Guinea and Pacific context.
7. Cf. Weiss (1982, 1991).
8. With this neologism we mean the imposition of the social role of the housewife. The term has been introduced in Bennholdt-Thomsen (1983); cf. also Jacobi and Niess (1980).
9. The reason women in PNG found hardly any work outside the house is connected with the lead the men had in the colonial system on one side, and the suppression of the informal sectors on the other.
10. Cf. Ariès (1973); cf. also Weiss (1981, 1993).
11. For more about her life cf. Weiss (in press).

References

Ariès, P. (1973). *L'enfant et la vie familiale sous l'Ancien Regime*. Paris: Seuil.
Bateson, G. (1936/1965). *Naven, a Survey of the Problems Suggested by a Composite Picture of the Culture of a New Guinea Tribe Drawn from Three Points of View*. Stanford: Stanford University Press.

Behrmann, W. (1922). *Im Stromgebiet des Sepik: eine deutsche Forschungsreise in Neuguinea.* Berlin: Scherl.

Bennholdt-Thomsen, V. (1983). *Auch in der Dritten Welt wird die Hausfrau geschaffen – warum?* Stuttgart: Klett-Cotta.

Boserup, E. (1970). *Women's Role in Economic Development.* New York: Routledge.

Boyer, B. and Grolnick, S.A. (eds) (1989). *The Psychoanalytic Study of Society. Essays in Honor of Paul Parin.* Hove and London: Analytic Press.

Jacobi, C. and Niess, T. (1980). *Hausfrauen, Bauern, Marginalisierte: Überlebensproduktion in 'Dritter' und 'Erster' Welt.* Saarbrücken: Breitenbach.

Keesing, R.M. (1989). Anthropology in Oceania: Problems and Prospects. *Oceania* 60: 55–9.

King, P., Lee, W. and Warakai, V. (eds) (1985). *From Rhetoric to Reality?* Port Moresby: University of Papua New Guinea Press.

Laycock, D.C. (1973). *Sepik Languages: Checklist and Preliminary Classification.* Canberra: Australian National University.

Mead, M. (1949). *Male and Female: A Study of the Sexes in a Changing World.* New York: Morrow.

Morgenthaler, F., Weiss, F. and Morgenthaler, M. (1984). *Gespräche am sterbenden Fluss. Ethnopsychoanalyse bei den Iatmul in Papua-Neuguinea.* Frankfurt: Fischer.

Parin, P., Morgenthaler, F. and Parin-Matthey, G. (1980). *Fear Thy Neighbor as Thyself. Psychoanalysis and Society among the Anyi of West Africa.* London and Chicago: University of Chicago Press.

Reche, O. (1913). *Der Kaiserin Augusta-Fluss.* Hamburg: Friederichsen. (Ergebnisse der Südsee-Expedition 1908-1910, ed. by G. Thilenius, Vol. II A 1).

Weber, M. (1920). *Gesammelte Aufsätze zur Religionssoziologie, Vol. I.* (Edited by Marianne Weber.) Tübingen: J.C.B. Mohr.

—— (1968/1973) *Soziologie. Universalgeschichtliche Analysen. Politik.* (Edited by Johannes Winckelmann.) Stuttgart: Kröner.

—— (1921/1980). *Gesammelte Politische Schriften.* (Edited by Johannes Winckelmann.) Tübingen: J.C.B. Mohr.

—— (1990). *Wirtschaft und Gesellschaft: Grundriss der verstehenden Soziologie.* (5. rev. edition by Johannes Winckelmann, 4th print.) Tübingen: J.C.B. Mohr.

Weiss, F. (1981). *Kinder schildern ihren Alltag. Die Stellung des Kindes im ökonomischen System einer Dorfgemeinschaft in Papua New Guinea (Palimbei, Iatmul, Mittelsepik).* Basel: Wepf.

—— (1982). Abwanderung in die Städte. Der widersprüchliche Umgang mit kolonialen Ausbeutungsstrategien: Die Iatmul in Papua Neuguinea. In: D. Centlivres (ed.), *Un nouveau regard sur la ville. Contributions à l'ethnologie urbaine*. pp. 149–66. Bern: Schweizerische Ethnologische Gesellschaft.

—— (1991). Frauen in der urbanethnologischen Forschung. In: B. Hauser-Schäublin (ed.), *Ethnologische Frauenforschung. Ansätze, Methoden, Resultate*, pp. 250–81. Berlin: Reimer.

—— (1993). Von der Schwierigkeit über Kinder zu forschen. Die Iatmul in Papua-Neuguinea. In: M.J. van de Loo und M. Reinhart (eds), *Kinder: ethnologische Forschungen in fünf Kontinenten*, pp. 96–153. München: Trickster.

—— (1996). *Die dreisten Frauen. Ethnopsychoanalytische Gespräche in Papua-Neuguinea*. Frankfurt: Fischer.

—— *(in press)*. Vor dem Vulkanausbruch. Eine ethnologische erzählung. Frankfurt: Fischer.

Women in Development in the South Pacific. Barriers and Opportunities. Papers Presented at a Conference held in Vanuatu from 11 to 14 August 1984. (1985). Canberra: Development Studies Centre, The Australian National University.

Chapter 14

Why Do the Tiwi Want a New Township?

Eric Venbrux

Introduction[1]

'We got development really going!' With these words the Council President of the Tiwi township on Melville Island where I had conducted fieldwork at the end of the 1980s greeted me on my return after a three-years absence. The developments included a nine-hole golf course, a brand new supermarket, a tennis court, a restaurant annex take-away, a new social club with snooker tables, and the man's own fishing company. He enthusiastically envisioned further developments in tourism, market gardening and other enterprises. The stock of housing would be rapidly increased and improved in quality, the roads sealed, and lawns supplemented with palm trees would make the place even more attractive.

Obviously, the Tiwi leader embraced an ideology of 'development'. A great many of the township's achievements in this direction came to his credit. There were other development-oriented Tiwi leaders too. By the end of 1991, Tiwi people discussed an ambitious plan to establish an entirely new township. The group of leaders who had developed the plan stressed they opted for a modern township, not an outstation. Tiwi people approved of the idea. Why would the Tiwi want a new township?

Tiwi society has undergone dramatic changes over the past 100 years, although in many areas the Tiwi have adapted and retained their own value system. The Tiwi are an Aboriginal people, consisting of about 1,900 persons. Their lands, Melville and Bathurst Islands, are located north of the Australian coast in the

Timor Sea. Directly south of the islands on the mainland is the town of Darwin, the capital of Northern Territory (hereinafter NT). The majority of the islands' population lives in three predominantly Aboriginal townships that have developed from previous mission and government settlements: Nguiu on Bathurst Island, and Milikapiti and Pularumpi on Melville Island. A fourth major township is in the process of being established. It is called Rangku (or Wurankuwu) and is located in the northern part of Bathurst Island. The new township has its origin in the aspirations of a section of the Tiwi leadership.

To understand this case of 'self-determination' we need to understand more about the nature of Tiwi politics. The Tiwi of course are no 'cultural isolate' and their incorporation in the Australian nation-state must not be downplayed. Howard (1978) argues the leadership assigned to certain Aboriginal people is at its best inaccurate and at its worst inappropriate. In his view those who pass off as 'leaders' in fact are 'clients of white patrons'; they are cultural brokers. By their very position they cannot speak on behalf of the Aboriginal community. The message is that 'whites' dominate the political scene and Aborigines are merely victims or dupes, as in the case of the so-called leaders. Gerritsen (1981, 1982) takes issue with the notion of what he calls 'the romantic "Gee wiz" school' that there is equality in Aboriginal societies. Gerritsen further resists the stereotyping of Aborigines as victims or dupes, ignoring an Aboriginal person can be 'exercising individual initiative or desiring decent housing' and 'a manipulating, self-interested individual' (1981: 6). Rowse in turn has criticized Gerritsen for failing to come to terms with '[d]istinctive Aboriginal understandings of "power"' (1992: 26). Rowse calls for a theory (which he thinks is not within reach), or a series of case histories, 'which shows *how the powers emanating from the Aboriginal domain articulate with those manifest in the manipulations of government subsidy*' (1992: 27, my emphasis). In this essay I offer such a case study of brokers cum leaders in a 'traditionally oriented' group of Aborigines in northern Australia.

Aboriginal Politics

Until about the mid-1970s it seems anthropologists did not bother much about Aboriginal politics. Aboriginal societies were supposed to be egalitarian. Formal political institutions, such as chieftainship, could be hardly recognized. Meggitt, for instance, stated that Aborigines 'had no formal apparatus of government' (1964: 178). A good example of the 'no-government-no-politics' view in Aboriginal studies at the time is Sharp's article 'People without politics' (1958).

If we take a less narrow view of politics, however, as people competing with each other, in the words of Boissevain, 'for valued resources, for prizes which form the important goals of their lives' (1974: 232), then Aboriginal people can be seen as engaged in politics. In the latter sense, there is no doubt that Aborigines did and do have politics (see Hiatt 1986). When the tide began to turn and researchers realized Aborigines had politics after all a number of case studies appeared, such as those by Gerritsen (1981, 1982), Myers (1982), Bern (1989), Sutton and Rigsby (1982) and in volumes edited by Howard (1978, 1982) and Tonkinson and Howard (1990), to mention only a few. Myers's comment that 'the importance of the individual in Aboriginal societies and the deeply political nature of social life are hallmarks of contemporary anthropological work' (1986: 139) underscores things have radically changed. A matter of definition, however, resulted in the topic being ignored for a long time (Hiatt 1986). Consequently, we generally lack studies of Aboriginal politics from the time before European influence and intrusion.

A notable exception is Hart's study of politics among Tiwi people who were still living in the bush on Bathurst Island in the late 1920s. Hart claims these people had not been subjected to alien influences yet. Tiwi politicking, according to Hart, centred around 'the struggle for influence and prestige' (Hart and Pilling 1960). The acquisition of many wives – 'an index of prestige' – for Tiwi males was an important avenue to obtain influence over others. Women were the main food producers and their female offspring served the male relatives through the means of marriage deals to recruit political clients enabling them to gain even more influence. There were other avenues in this ongoing political competition as well, including ritual, foraging activities and fighting, which provided interrelated arenas. Really influential men were those who succeeded in setting up large camps (dwellings) of their own. Some thirty or more people could be found in these camps. Around the larger camps smaller satellite camps existed, dependent in part on the food surplus produced by the main camp. More often than not influential brothers cooperated. Future sons-in-law also tended to become members of the main camps. Hart called these camps 'establishments' (ibid.). 'To the building of such large establishments', says Hart, 'a Tiwi man devoted his life' (1970: 299). The establishment of the township by influential Tiwi men seems to be congruent with this important political goal of olden times. It occurred in about the same area as where Hart conducted his fieldwork. The people involved are closely related to those described by Hart. Furthermore, in the township a resource centre for the neighbouring outstations has been established, creating a situation not unlike the one with the smaller satellite camps of Hart's days. In the late-1920s, Padimo happened to be the top client of the most influential man in the north of Bathurst Island. His son, the island's main ritual leader, now has his own outstation there, being the most prominent client of the man who dominates the new township.

Hart's study of the Tiwi polity provides the present case with a historical dimension, which is rather unique. A number of ethnographers, from the early 1950s until now, have confirmed that Tiwi politics have not changed very much in style and aims (Pilling 1958; Brandl 1971; Goodale 1971; Grau 1983; Hart, Pilling and Goodale 1988; Venbrux 1995). What is at stake has remained very much the same. The 'struggle for prestige and influence' continues. Hart used the metaphor of an on-going card game, he writes: 'The Tiwi influence and career patterns can be best compared to a non-stop bridge game wherein the scores were never totaled up nor a new game ever started on a clean slate.' In this endless game, 'every new player had to start in the middle and make the best of whatever assets he had by way of kinship, clanship, household membership, and help from other players.' Hart continues, 'The "game" was one of trying to win friends and increase prestige and influence over others. The "assets" . . . were mostly intangible ones such as friendship, "help", goodwill, respect of others, control over others, importance, and influence' (Hart and Pilling 1960: 51–2).

From Hart's writings it becomes clear that success in the game hinged on the players' personality, skills, shrewdness, networking, long-term planning and scheming, strategic choices of residence, using one's 'assets' to the fullest, and the inevitable bit of luck. Only players who had shown 'cleverness' from early adulthood onwards could hope 'to reap the benefits' in the final stages of

their lives (Hart 1930, 1954, 1970; Hart and Pilling 1960).
Competitiveness was and is an important feature of Tiwi
culture. In contemporary Tiwi society it can be observed in the
sports and the arts, in ritual, in foraging, in marital claims, and, as
Altman points out, 'in the rivalry between community leaders to
demonstrate their ability to attract venture capital and establish
new and profitable enterprises' (1988: 261). The present-day,
formal political institutions form another arena in which Tiwi
people compete. An aim of the key players within this political
field is to attract government funding as a matter of prestige
and with its expenditure to exert control and influence over
others.

During this century Tiwi people, no longer confined to their
islands, have made moves to expand their networks to members
of the wider society, including people in high positions. As Pilling
put it thirty years ago, 'Tiwi know what goes on in the local white
political scene - not only at the level of the formal and probably
unimportant, but also at the level of the informal and more
important, and they are in a position to influence decisions by
major white leaders' (1965: 314).[2] With the passing of the *Aboriginal
Land Rights (Northern Territory) Act* of *1976*, they obtained security
of the ownership of their lands. Tiwi people decided to create their
own land council, separate from the Northern Land Council, in
the firm belief their interests were better represented by themselves
(see also Hart, Pilling and Goodale 1988: 127–45).

The delegates to the Tiwi Land Council formed a Tiwi-owned
business holding in 1986. They wanted, as the chairman of the
land council and the board of directors phrases it, to ascertain 'a
Tiwi economic foundation which is vital for our future independence and security' (Pirntubula 1989: 3). The Tiwi businesses include
joint ventures such as Tiwi Barge Services, Tiwi Pearls, Melville
Island Forest Products and Tiwi Tours (Pirntubula 1989). Established to decrease Tiwi people's dependency on government
funding, these businesses have to compete with other ones in the
global market economy. When the enterprises prove to be viable
the Tiwi might become less dependent on government welfare and
assistance but dependencies of another kind will have been
created.

The Tiwi have produced a war hero, Australia's first Aboriginal
movie star, national stars in the popular Australian rules football,
and famous artists. Tiwi politicians have represented both the

Country Liberal Party and the Australian Labor Party – that is, the two main political parties in the Northern Territory. Four Tiwi people have been elected to the Legislative Assembly. The current member, a former football star, was re-elected with a largely increased vote. In September 1994, this Tiwi man addressed the annual national conference of the Labor Party, in Hobart, speaking on Aboriginal issues.

Many Tiwi are extremely self-confident, outgoing, and sophisticated in 'whitefella' ways; to mention some of the qualities that facilitate their smooth dealings with bureaucrats, politicians and business people. Tiwi people's achievements often get a great deal of media attention. In addition, the islands' geographical location close to Darwin safeguards numerous visits of government officials.

In 1990, the Aboriginal and Torres Strait Islander Commission (ATSIC) was brought into operation in order to decentralize decision-making power, previously held by Commonwealth bodies administering Aboriginal affairs (Department of Aboriginal Affairs, DAA, and the Aboriginal Development Commission, ADC), to regional indigenous councils. Eleven members were elected into the Tiwi Islands Regional Council for Melville and Bathurst Islands, and one Tiwi person was elected Commissioner. The ATSIC regional council 'has the task of formulating and revising a plan for improving the economic, social and cultural status of indigenous residents of the region and to assist with its implementation' (Tiwi Islands Regional Council 1991: 7). The Tiwi were happy with their own regional council but for administrative reasons the boundaries of the regional council were enbroadened to include the western part of Arnhem Land and the Daly River area, resulting in the formation of the ATSIC Jabiru Regional Council, in 1993. The ATSIC Tiwi Islands Regional Council played a significant role in the establishment of the Tiwi township on Bathurst Island.

Territorial Politics

Each Tiwi person belongs to a matriclan (*imunga*), which is tremendously important in the field of marriage politics. Matriclans make other decisions concerning their members on this level as well. The scope of this chapter does not permit to discuss its political ramifications here. Instead, I want to concentrate on territorial politics in which patrilineages come to the fore. The islands are divided into districts of variable size. Such a district is called a 'country' (*murukupupuni*) by the Tiwi. Its members form a land-holding group, they are the 'traditional owners'. Membership in principle comes through the (father's) father, although the actual situation is far more complicated than that. There existed a certain measure of flexibility as to where people took up residence. Some degree of freedom that Tiwi have, to opt for or change residence, has to do with factors that legitimate attachments to the land: having been born there, when one's father (actual or classificatory) has been born or resided there, being near the location of a burial place of patrilineal relatives, and having spiritual associations with the land as expressed in ritual. Women not residing in their country used to retain membership of their country of origin; men tended to change it. Tiwi social organization can be seen as flexible and shows considerable room for manoeuvre (see Hart 1970; Brandl 1971; Venbrux 1993).

The Tiwi have a long history of fission and fusion of land-holding groups (cf. Pilling 1958). In the nineteenth century, for instance, Portamini, the most influential man in the country Rangku, sent his younger brothers away to Melville Island, where they founded their own countries. In one of these, Wurangku, the present-day township of Milikapiti is located, named after its founder Milewuri. Hart (1970) found that in the late 1920s one man's sons were dominating all three countries on Bathurst Island. Those who had moved away from their country of origin had simply changed their group membership.

There are quite a number of cases in which a group of powerful brothers spread. The sons of Puruntatameri, also known as Munkara, from Tikelaru, for instance, founded new countries in various areas on the Tiwi Islands. On the one hand, this had to do with marriage politics as a son-in-law went to live at the place where he got his promised wives from, to ascertain their delivery. On the other hand, it was related to tensions between the brothers. They were supposed to cooperate in getting wives from other matriclans with which they had exchange relations but at the same time they were competitors for the same category of women (cf. Brandl 1971). Fraternal generosity and fraternal strife went hand in hand. Another reason given to me for this spreading was that they could support each other in fighting from different locations.

Hence, in conflict with others they would not as easily be wiped out. Really influential men were even able to change the alignment of the matriclans. They amalgamated clans or split off a part of clan (cf. Pilling 1958; Venbrux 1993). Therewith they, directly or indirectly, increased the number of wives they could marry. Part of the political process was that an amalgamation of two clans happened not to be necessarily acknowledged by all its members (cf. Brandl 1971).

Sutton and Rigsby (1982) speak of 'the politics in the management of land and people'. Challenging Sharp (1958), they entitled their article 'People with politicks'. To put it briefly, individuals have a choice as to their attachments to land. Succession to land does not automatically follow from rules of descent; they have to be appropriated by living actors. There appear to be limitations to group-sizes: When a group becomes too large conflicts will occur and a number of people split off to take possession of vacated or less densely populated land. At least in pre-contact times, so Sutton and Rigsby suggest, by land-centred politics Aboriginal people 'managed to maintain a stable relationship between their population and their lands' (1982: 169). Sutton and Rigsby thus introduce the carrying capacity of the land as an additional factor. In the Tiwi case, I believe, primary importance should be given to the internal dynamics of society.

Tiwi lived in a favourable environment and this seems to have enabled them to establish relatively large population centres in various locations on the islands. McKnight shows that the increase in violence and fighting in what he calls a supercamp on Mornington Island was due to the high population and 'high relational density'. Compared with the pre-settlement small camps of about 20 closely related people, the more heterogeneous settlement of about 600 people where one had to fulfil obligations to numerous actual and classificatory kin present caused disharmonious relationships (1986).

It is precisely for this reason, according to the Tiwi leadership, that conflicts are rife in the township of Nguiu. Nguiu has a population of over 1,200. Some people from elsewhere did not want to go there because there were 'too many relations'; with their numerous demands they would be making life rather stressful. Clan members also have to support each other in fights. In Tiwi perception Nguiu has too many clans. Most of these matriclans represent quite a number of people. At the social club in the township a few hundred drinkers join together day after day (except on Sundays). When trouble arises it easily snowballs. Tiwi say the township has become 'too big'. Let me now turn to the township project.

History of the Township Project

In 1991, members of the Tunkwaliti patrilineage within the Tiwi leadership began talking about splitting off with their people from the existing townships, and mainly from Nguiu where most of them live. They wanted to return to their vacant country Rangku.

For example, when I asked Peter Tunkwaliti why they wanted a new township he said that his people wanted to get away from Nguiu because there was 'too much violence and pressure'. He described the situation as follows: 'It is as if you are in room with a lot of people, and the door and windows are locked. You can't breathe. When the windows go open fresh air comes in [making the sign of a breeze]. People can breathe.'

Another Tiwi leader, who has his own outstation on Melville Island, said Nguiu was 'too big'. It was better 'to split up' to a size of a small township like Pularumpi. There were 'too many tribes [matriclans] there'. Like in Pularumpi people 'respect each other better, all [are] relations, *close* relations'. Other Tiwi leaders, including the delegates to the Tiwi Land Council, were of the same opinion and they all agreed to the idea. The leader of the Tunkwaliti patrilineage had compiled a list of some 350 people who were supposed to take up residence there. In November 1991, the Councils of the three existing townships decided to give their housing allocation for one year to the new township Rangku. But why should the township have to be in Rangku?

To cut a long story short, there are several reasons. For any Tiwi man who does not think of himself as a nobody the life-long ideal is to return to one's country. Nowhere can you find as plenty and lovely food as in your own country. The graves of relatives there are a focus of successful hunting, healing and luck in various aspects of life. In conversations it turns up time after time: Tiwi people want to be seen as 'important', they are 'not rubbish', but 'king' or 'queen'. Young Tiwi people say they are 'important' when they have a job in which they are not 'bossed around'. The goal thus is to reach a certain degree of autonomy or self-determination, if I may use these words. Territorial rights give the 'traditional owners' a decisive say in matters which happen on their land. In other words, only on one's own land one can have a real power base.

The Tunkwaliti family is very strong in number. Tunkwaliti, who lived in the last century, is said to have had some forty wives. This may be exaggerated a bit, but anyhow he had a numerous offspring. Several of the most prominent Tiwi leaders today are patrilineal descendants of Tunkwaliti.

Peter, for instance, has been chairman of the Tiwi Land Council for a decade. He accumulated many other important positions, including chairman of the board of directors of the Tiwi business holding Pirntubula and of Melville Forest Products (a multi-million dollar enterprise), and director of Tiwi Pearls. He was also Council President of Nguiu and licensee and manager of Nguiu Sports and Social Club, exerting influence over others in controlling the flow of beer. His brothers Trevor and Paul have also prominent positions in various formal political institutions and business enterprises. Paul is the Council President of Milikapiti. Malcolm is another leader of significance.

The prime mover of the township project, however, is John Tunkwaliti. John was the Commissioner of ATSIC's Regional North West Zone, while Malcolm, Peter and Trevor were councillors of the ATSIC Tiwi Islands Regional Council and Malcolm an executive member. It must be noted that there are various close ties between different Tiwi leaders (the chairman of the council mentioned, for instance, was a strong supporter of the project).[3] John, an extremely articulate person, is still a councillor of the enlarged ATSIC Jabiru Regional Council. Within this new arena he has proven to be able to capture any meeting with the Arnhem Landers, no matter that the latter provided the chairman (an Aboriginal liaison officer, personal communication). John is director of the Tiwi business holding and of Tiwi Tours, the tourist enterprise owned for 50% by the Tiwi.

John Tunkwaliti has the advantage of being senior to the other leaders of his patrilineage. He received his education from the Roman Catholic Mission on Bathurst Island and in Darwin. He played for a Darwin football club and worked as a forklift driver in Darwin harbour. Next, he staked out a career in public administration in relation to Aborigines (Horton 1994: 1074–5). His influence due to his positions, forceful personality and charm has enabled him to 'help' other Tiwi people in need or trouble. John does not excel in ritual performances, but the fact that he has nine children contributes to his social status of a senior Tiwi man. Although he stays with only one woman at a time, he claims to have five wives.

In the early 1980s, John was the Commissioner of the Aboriginal Development Commission (ADC) for the Northern Territory. He has been Council President of Bagot (an Aboriginal community in Darwin on the mainland) and of Milikapiti. He worked as an officer in the NT Department of Transport and Works, worked for the (Commonwealth) Department of Aboriginal Affairs (DAA) and visited Aboriginal communities all over the NT. 'I know a lot of people, and a lot of people know me', he said to me, 'That's really good, you know.' He appears to be very well aware of his role as an Aboriginal broker par excellence. Brokers, according to Boissevain, are 'highly expert network specialists' (1974: 148). One only needs to walk with him through the mall in Darwin at lunchtime to get a feel for his extended and numerous cordial relations with white bureaucrats. 'John always get what he wants', was how a (white) field officer put it, 'he is a good battler'.

Both as ADC Commissioner and as member of the Aboriginal Benefits Trust Account (ABTA) Advisory Committee, he secured the Tiwi got a disproportionate piece of the cake in government grants (public monies and mining royalties, cf. Altman 1985: 200, 1988: 257–61). Although not *de jure*, he was the *de facto* Tiwi 'Minister of White Affairs'. For five years John was employed by the DAA as Community Adviser in Milikapiti, where he later was licensee and manager of the Milikapiti Social and Sports Club. Thereafter, because John was so valuable for Milikapiti to attract funding, it was decided he would be employed as public relations officer for the council. John's prominent position in Milikapiti – and of Paul in his footsteps – was mainly due to the local infighting between the 'traditional owners' there. Peter owed his position in Nguiu to the same phenomenon. Peter is also a vocal person with charisma.

So, in short, what we have here is a group of prominent Tiwi leaders with extensive and significant networks, experience, skills and ambition. People who have the support of numerous Tiwi relatives. People who have direct access to white people in power. People who take it for granted they deal with the latter on the basis of equality. But the real coup has yet to come.

As I said, the locus of power for Tiwi people is in their 'own lands', necessary to obtain a larger measure of influence over others. Well, that was what the Tunkwaliti group was lacking. Without an 'establishment' in their own country they never could run their own affairs.

John says he had been thinking for years about an outstation in Rangku. A white former patrol officer and community adviser in the islands remembers it being repeatedly discussed by Peter and other up-and-coming men of the Tunkwaliti patrilineage in the 1970s (personal communication). When John was working for the DAA he had 'helped' in providing a water tank and a small generator for his relatives who stayed in Rangku, in a camp with tin sheds. His grandfather Tampu, putting up two spears crossed, had made the 'law' that it was their area, no one else was allowed to hunt or gather there. He chucked out all other people, told them 'to piss off'. John's father Alicio used to camp there as well – that is, later in his life when he had settled down. John was approaching the years in which he, in Tiwi terms, would have 'to reap the benefits of his career' (cf. Hart and Pilling 1960).

John found a strong supporter in Frank Johnson, Council President for more than a decade in the smallest Tiwi township, Pularumpi.[4] Frank is said by Tiwi locals to 'run the place'. Frank controls the local Progress Association. In his capacity as manager of the store he decides on bookings to be made at the store, and as manager and licensee of the Social Club on the selling of beer. The keys of the petrol pump are in his possession. Consequently, people are dependent on him if they want to obtain fuel. With regard to the better housing and the relatively well-paying jobs at the council, it is helpful to be on good terms with him. People have to turn to him for a great many other favours as well. Behind his back, Frank is frequently criticized by the islands' white staff and mission personnel for his use of power, partly as a result of their frustrating inability to make an impact on the local political scene. For a Tiwi leader like John, however, Frank is 'a good man', 'a mighty man'. Both men try to make the best of two worlds and maintain politically significant networks in the wider society. They are pro-development but at the same time their aspirations are guided by the Tiwi value system.[5]

Frank came up with the idea of John having a new township. In the struggle for prestige and influence this would have several advantages for Frank. In the first place, it would cut down the other townships in size, Nguiu in particular: another means of making himself bigger and more important. Secondly, it would take John as an influential man out of Milikapiti, leaving Frank room for manoeuvre to increase his influence over Melville Island affairs.[6] Frank has a keen interest in traditional Tiwi ways. He restructured his local council by having the matriclans nominate councillors from their midst. In addition, he started a campaign to reinforce the decision-making power of the islands' matriclans in matters of justice. Although his father was not a Tiwi, he has been accepted as a 'traditional owner' in the country of his mother (Hart, Pilling and Goodale 1988: 133). Frank managed to become the Land Trustee for the northwest of Melville Island. He nominates the other delegates to the Tiwi Land Council from his country, Munupi.

I would like to push this a bit further and place it in the context of developments in the early 1990s. Renison Goldfields came along. The mining company wanted to explore the islands' beaches for minerals. Talk had it that Tiwi people would get their share of the billions of dollars profit from sandmining when it could go ahead. The 'traditional owners' looked forward to receiving 15,000 dollars for exploration of the beaches in their country. The Land Council signed an agreement with the mining company. The expectations were high. The pro-development leaders stand to gain. There was an opposition to the mining led by Tiwi women, and supported by conservationists from the mainland, fearing serious environmental damage and increasing health risks for Tiwi people. They petitioned the federal minister of Indigenous Affairs, who replied he was not in a position to interfere in the decision-making process of the Tiwi, formally represented by the Land Council. The all-male Tiwi Land Council had its way.

Traditional owners within the Land Council sought to establish or re-establish their territorial claims more strongly. The number of countries agreed upon in previous years was renegotiated. This led to the foundation of an additional country (on a formal level) in its own right, with a land trustee and delegates to the Land Council. For the 'Tunkwaliti mob' (a loosely structured group) it became an urgent matter to establish themselves on that land. This was the best way to secure the monies or royalties that would come from the mining there.

In anticipation of the new developments the Land Council's financial dealings were restructured. Instead of one account for all Tiwi people, the then-existent arrangement, the Land Council decided that they would have so-called Family Trust Accounts. Income from enterprises in a particular country would go directly to the 'traditional owners' of that country.

The mining business gave the impetus to this decentralization. At the same time, it can be seen as part of a long term process of fission and fusion, to which I referred earlier. Public subsidies, however, increasingly tend to become a factor of significance in the political dynamics of Tiwi society. Grants for the means of transport and communication, dwellings with amenities on outstations, and infrastructure facilitate the process of decentralization. The CDEP (Community Development Employment Program) scheme or 'work on the dole' program now allows for maintenance work on outstations to be undertaken. In Arnhem Land this has set in motion a process of a tremendous fragmentation: in the outstation movement of the 1990s, so I am told, outstations with a population of only two people can be observed.

Well, let's stick with the Tiwi for the time being. The best thing that could happen for the 'Tunkwaliti mob' occurred. The ATSIC regional councils were established. The Tiwi Islands became one of the twelve ATSIC councils in the NT. John Tunkwaliti was elected Commissioner. John had some expertise as an ADC Commissioner in attracting funding for housing. This function of ADC had now gone to ATSIC. With his own people and friends in place in the Tiwi Islands Regional Council little could go wrong.

Establishment of the New Township

When the need for a new township had been established through the Tiwi Land Council and the support of the three local councils came off, the NT Department of Lands and Housing also became involved. A working party was formed in the department. Its members helped in formulating a brief for a feasibility study. It would examine *if and how* the township could be established. From the department a kind of commitment was made that it eventually was prepared to invest a considerable amount of money, out of its budget for Aboriginal housing, in Rangku.

In the meantime, however, John had acquired power as ATSIC commissioner. For him it was no longer a matter of 'if and how' but *when* Rangku would be established. 'John went straight to the ministers', so I am told from different sides. 'I pushed really hard', he told me. As a result, the ATSIC staff of the regional council came under tremendous pressure. These public servants experienced insecurity in their new role, facing the dilemma of having to assist the Commissioner *and* being accountable for the spending of public monies. When I asked the federal Minister of Indigenous Affairs about his eventual involvement, he said it had been 'not much, not very much'. On further questioning, he said, 'I have heard about it, that is about all.' He might have made queries, and if not, the mere suggestion of top-level contacts would not miss having an effect at the lower levels in the bureaucracy. Anyhow, John pushed the right buttons, so to speak. The senior officer agreed to Rangku being built. The (commonwealth) funding was made available.

The area of the former camp there and its surroundings were cleared. An airstrip was made, the roads upgraded, a water supply created, a resource centre – accommodating a meeting room, an office, a kitchen, a workshop, a chiller room, a store annex beer outlet – and seven fully-equipped suburban-style houses were constructed, a watertower erected, a barge landing made, and so on.

Northern Building Consultants, who would initially do the feasibility study, were granted a contract to write a so-called community planning report on Rangku for the ATSIC regional council. The NT Department of Lands and Housing happened no longer to be involved in this. It turned out that the airstrip was in the wrong direction according to the guidelines of the Civil Aviation Authority. Another problem was that it flooded in the rainy season. (Since then, some other technical shortcomings have come to light as well.)

The consultancy report stresses that Rangku had to be a 'special place': a dream the consultants probably shared with the NT town planners, who were eager to grab the unique opportunity to design an Aboriginal township that would be 'culturally appropriate' (white town planner of the NT government, personal communication).[7] The report further states little thought had been given to the management of the new township, apparently under the assumption that when an infrastructure is put in place 'the community will work' (Tiwi ATSIC Regional Council n.d.). At the time I was in Rangku, in September 1994, another three houses were under construction, and these had to be finished before the end of the year. After these ten houses, more houses will be built. The estimate is that Rangku will have cost 15 million dollar when there are twenty houses. The ATSIC Jabiru Regional Council has approved in principal to continue funding Rangku as part of Tiwi Island ward. An additional application for funding a health clinic has been made to the central office in Canberra (and given priority).

'The Territory government did not yet acknowledge it', John complained to me, but 'most of the funding came from the federal government.' Time had come to play off the bureaucrats of the commonwealth and the NT government against each other.

Dealing with the NT Government Bureaucracy

The NT so far had paid only 10,000 dollars to cover administrative costs. 'They promise the world', according to John, 'It's a strange set-up.' The Tiwi leader said that he had shown his 'commitment' by his efforts to put up the township, in obtaining the huge investments by the commonwealth, and by actually living there with his family and others. John did expect nothing else of the NT government than to come across with 'operational funding'.

The NT Minister of Aboriginal Development and of Lands, Housing and Local Government told me that it was impossible to go ahead like John's 'personal lobby'. It took more time. In fact, the NT bureaucrats had been outmanoeuvred by their colleagues of the Commonwealth. 'Nothing has been done any more on it since then', one of the former said.

Nevertheless, the establishment of the township was an accomplished fact. Whether they liked it or not, they would have to join in as a result of a recent, mutual agreement between the Commonwealth and the States and Territories (Council of Australian Governments 1992). Besides, as could be expected, when Rangku would get local government under the NT Local Government Act, the NT government would automatically be responsible for the delivery of services and the like.[8] At this time, Rangku is still an incorporated Aboriginal association (the Wurankuwu Association Inc.).

The NT Minister made clear that he was supportive of the new township. In a note to his departmental officers he acknowledged Rangku as 'an emerging community'. He requested to bring

together a special working group. The NT government had failed
to formulate a policy with regard to emerging communities and
outstations yet. The Tiwi township-project forced them to do so;
Rangku would be the first case. The ATSIC initiative has also tied
part of their limited resources for the delivery of services to
Aborigines in the NT.

The (NT) Office of Aboriginal Development, the administrative
unit for 'coordination, communication and policy development
within the Aboriginal affairs area' (Office of Aboriginal Development 1993) acknowledged Rangku as a new community, not to be
treated as an outstation. The Wurankuwu Coordination Working
Party was formed. On 14 October 1994, it had its first meeting
attended by key representatives of the various NT government
departments and units (Lands and Housing, Local Government,
Health and Community Services, Education, the Power and
Water Authority and the Office of Aboriginal Development), the
administration of the Wurankuwu Association (Ernst & Young),
the ATSIC regional manager, and John Tunkwaliti (and myself).
Discussed were the state of affairs, where the problems lay, and
how servicing agencies could be triggered out. John was asking
for operational funding, a hospital and a school. He said that his
children would not go to school if the government did not provide
one. John further argued he could not held to be responsible in
the case of an emergency: there were no telephones yet, and in the
rainy season that was setting in the roads would be inaccessible
and the airstrip flooded. Therefore, the delivery of health services
was an urgent matter. People would be stuck in Rangku (leaving
the barge the only possibility to bring goods and food in).

To obtain access to operational funding from the NT government the place had to have local government. First, two issues
had to be resolved. The Nguiu local government area included
the whole of Bathurst Island so an agreement to annex out a
proportion of the Nguiu area had to be reached with its council.
Equally important, Rangku had to have a population of at least
hundred people. John said it was 'no problem'; there were a
hundred people (and there were 'easily thirty to forty kids' as thirty
children were needed to get a school). An excision of the country
Rangku on Bathurst Island could be made because this was up to
the traditional owners.

Thus far, John had achieved a great deal. The NT government
stepped up its efforts in creating a platform for the future

development of the township, preventing it from being paralyzed by bureaucratic struggles.

The Tiwi Domain

John's main problem was the Aboriginal arena. Rangku might have had a hundred Tiwi people if all visitors were counted. The actual size of the resident population lagged behind this. The negotiations with the Nguiu Council happened to be much more troublesome than suggested. It must be noted that they were the ones who would lose people, funding, and power.

One thing is for sure: attracting all the funding has earned John Tunkwaliti a lot of prestige. He is nicknamed 'Bob Hawke II' by Tiwi people at 'grass-roots level'. Tiwi people turned to him for help in obtaining housing, government grants for cars, boats and so forth. Before the establishment of the ATSIC regional council, the Land Council played a significant role in the distribution of things such as motor vehicles, dinghies with outboard motors and outstation equipment. 'Tunkwaliti City', as an informant in the offices of the Land Council called the township, had changed all this.

John says that, in time, some 750 people will be living in Rangku. This sounds fairly optimistic and makes one wonder if the problems would not be re-created that people were running away from in the first place. In the words of a son, John is 'the big chief' in Rangku. However, it is true that all the houses were occupied, the resident population still had to increase.

According to John, there is 'jealousy' in Nguiu. As the Nguiu local government is directly funded by the Commonwealth for upgrading the roads, and the funds are limited, the road to Rangku has a low priority. Nguiu received ATSIC funds for a car for the doctor to visit Rangku, but the car will be stationed at Nguiu. In a number of ways the Nguiu Council is reluctant to assist Rangku because the council is afraid to loose its established funding. The promised houses are no longer heard of.

Some people say the township is not located in Rangku but in their country, Pupatu (Malau), adding that John might give them a house so they can live there. John's ambition to include land belonging to the countries Tikelaru and Malau, where the outstations are, in annexing out an additional proportion from the

Nguiu local government area, means that traditional owners want what they can get out of the deal. That is, housing for their outstations.

A Malau leader, heading the outstation Wangaru, borrowed 4,000 dollars from John for a revision of the motor of his car, to be paid back in instalments. In a card game at Nguiu, it was not John, who put in most of the money, but his prospective followers who took the winnings. His wife participated in the card games all day, a pay-day meaning big money, but she could not 'find the numbers' either. In many subtle and less subtle ways the leader has to satisfy the demands of a followership. This accountability in Tiwi terms might bring a manager in trouble. John told me that he experienced it as the most difficult thing in his position, that he had 'to be strict'.

A leader needs followers, and a lot has to be done to make them happy and to keep them happy: the hopes are for the future, that people will come. Several who were listed as future inhabitants do not intend to, when asked. When I was in Rangku, the leader's children did not return from a trip to Nguiu at night – even they preferred to stay at Nguiu at this stage.

Initially, Rangku would be a 'dry community'. The place had been used before as an alcohol rehabilitation camp. John himself is a non-drinker. The idea, however, was soon abandoned. Too many fatal car and boating accidents had occurred because people were forced to get their beer from elsewhere. In September 1994 the township was without power, and without power there is no refrigeration for the beer. The small generator ran down (due to the 'kids'). The township had to wait for a new generator. Time after time the story was told that is was on its way on the barge.

The big problem is how to get people to Rangku; the leader needs his followers badly. The future health clinic, to be built after the rainy season, will enable people on dialysis who are currently living in Darwin to stay in Rangku on the islands. (A great many Tiwi people are believed to be affected by renal disease during the course of their lives.) Other facilities and services, taken for granted by mainstream Australians, might attract people too. John has cleared an area for a graveyard; in the future graves can be seen as a means to increase people's identification with Rangku.

The rainy season will be the real test. The community will be isolated. Wangaru, a neighbouring outstation, had already been evacuated in October because of the early rains.

Tiwi outstations hitherto have failed to become permanent. Paru on Melville Island is a case in point. There are six houses as good as new (cf. Hart, Pilling and Goodale 1988: 139) but no living soul is there. This is due to problems with the water supply. The most prominent leader of this area wants a new township like Rangku, but a bit farther away.

The case of the Tiwi township shows Aboriginal leaders/ brokers are able to use their 'whitefella power' (Gerritsen 1981) to increase their prestige within the Aboriginal domain, but also that influence over others in this arena is never unconditional. The rhetoric of mainstream politicians and policy-makers are still scattered with notions of (an egalitarian and homogeneous) 'community', 'representative democracy' and 'development' which for them appear to have a quite distinct meaning than they do have in the reality of Aboriginal practice.

Notes

1. The title of this paper has been suggested to me by Jon Altman. An earlier version of the paper has been presented at the Centre for Aboriginal Economic Policy Research, The Australian National University, Canberra, on 20 October 1994, and to the Basel Conference of the European Society for Oceanists, Basel, on 13 December 1994. I am grateful for the helpful comments and suggestions I received on these occasions. Further, I am indebted to the Tiwi and non-Tiwi people who provided me with information, and the leader of the new township for his approval of my study. This paper is based on field research in Melville and Bathurst Islands and in Darwin, northern Australia, in October–November 1991 and August–October 1994. Thanks are due to the Netherlands Foundation for the Advancement of Tropical Research (WOTRO), The Hague and the University of Nijmegen for their financial support. The present in this paper is at the time of (re)writing, November 1994. I have substituted pseudonyms for real names of Tiwi leaders. This chapter reflects the situation of the new township in September–October 1994. Les Hiatt's book *Arguments About Aborigines* (1996) contains a chapter called 'people without politics'. Unfortunately, it could not be included in the

discussion here because the book appeared after I had finished the paper and it had been typeset.

2. Pilling also writes that Tiwi people 'believe they have the ear of the Judge of the Superior court of the Northern Territory, the Director of the Welfare Branch, that is, the Director of Aboriginal Affairs, the Bishop of the Roman Catholic diocese for the Northern Territory, the Administrator for the Northern Territory, the local Commander of the Royal Australian Air Force, and the local Army Commander. In fact, this is largely true' (1965: 314).

3. Note that his wife Susan is a stepdaughter of the late Walei, an influential man of the Tunkwaliti family. An early stage of Walei's career has been described extensively by Hart (Hart and Pilling 1960). Walei acquired at least nine wives. According to Pilling (1976) he used to dominate a bush camp of 150 people in the 1950s.

4. He has also been the founding chairman of the Tiwi Land Council, Member of the (Northern Territory's) Legislative Assembly, founding chairman of the NT Association of Local Community Government Councils, and the first chairman of the ATSIC Tiwi Islands Regional Council.

5. Frank's current pet projects are banana plantations, fishing safaris and an annual golf-tournament called the Melville Island Classic.

6. Frank happens to be a maternal half-brother of the principal 'traditional owner' of the Milikapiti area. As a matter of fact, he is the second in line in their matriclan. This enables him to exert some influence in this realm, perhaps even more so because the Milikapiti leader in question is chronically ill and has to stay in Darwin.

7. See also Crough and Pritchard (1991) and Sanders (1993).

8. See Wolfe (1989) for a study of these local governments in the NT.

References

Altman, J.C. (1985). *Report on the Review of the Aboriginals Benefit Trust Account (and Related Financial Matters) in the Northern Territory Land Rights Legislation.* Canberra: Australian Government Publishing Services.

—— (1988). *Aborigines, Tourism, and Development: The Northern Territory Experience.* Darwin: North Australia Research Unit (ANU).

Bern, J. (1989). The Politics of a Small Northern Territory Town: A History of Managing Dependency. In: P. Loveday and A. Webb (eds), *Small Towns in Northern Australia*, pp. 165–76. Darwin: North Australia Research Unit (ANU).

Boissevain, J. (1974). *Friends of Friends. Networks, Manipulators and Coalitions.* Oxford: Blackwell.

Brandl, M.M. (1971). Pukumani: The Social Context of Bereavement in a North Australian Aboriginal Tribe. PhD dissertation. Nedlands: University of Western Australia.

Council of Australian Governments. (1992). National Commitment to Improved Outcomes in the Delivery of Programs and Services for Aboriginal Peoples and Torres Strait Islanders. Endorsed by the Council of Australian Governments, Perth, Western Australia, 7 December 1992.

Crough, G. and Pritchard, B. (1991). *Infrastructure Provision in Remote Aboriginal Communities in the Northern Territory.* Report prepared for the Central Land Council. Revised edition. Alice Springs: Central Land Council.

Gerritsen, R. (1981). Thoughts on Camelot: from Herodians and Zealots to the Contemporary Politics of Remote Aboriginal Settlements in the Northern Territory. Paper presented to The Australasian Political Studies Association 23rd Annual Conference, 'Australian Politics', Canberra, The Australian National University, 28–30 August 1981.

—— (1982). Blackfellas and Whitefellas: The Politics of Service Delivery to Remote Aboriginal Communities in the Katherine Region. In: P. Loveday (ed.), *Service Delivery to Remote Communities*, pp. 16–31. Darwin: North Australia Research Unit (ANU).

Goodale, J.C. (1971). *Tiwi Wives. A Study of the Women of Melville Island, North Australia.* Seattle: Washington University Press.

Grau, A. (1983). Dreaming, Dancing, Kinship: The Study of Yoi, the Dance of the Tiwi of Melville and Bathurst Islands. PhD dissertation. Belfast: Queen's University.

Hart, C.W.M. (1930). The Tiwi of Melville and Bathurst Islands. *Oceania* 1: 167–80.

—— (1954). The Sons of Turimpi. *American Anthropologist* 56: 242–61.

—— (1970). Some Factors Affecting Residence among the Tiwi. *Oceania* 40: 296–303.

Hart, C.W.M. and Pilling, A.R. (1960). *The Tiwi of North Australia*. New York: Holt, Rinehart, Winston.

Hart, C.W.M., Pilling, A.R. and Goodale, J.C. (1988). *The Tiwi of North Australia*. Third edition. New York: Holt, Rinehart, Winston.

Hiatt, L.R. (1986). *Aboriginal Political Life*. Canberra: Australian Institute of Aboriginal Studies.

—— (1996). *Arguments about Aborigines. Australia and the Evolution of Social Anthropology*. Cambridge: Cambridge University Press.

Horton, D. (ed.) (1994). *The Encyclopedia of Aboriginal Australia*. vol. 2. Canberra: Aboriginal Studies Press.

Howard, M. (1978). Aboriginal 'Leadership' in the Southwest of Western Australia. In: M. Howard (ed.), *'Whitefella Business'. Aborigines in Australian Politics*, pp. 13–36. Philadelphia: Institute for the Study of Human Issues.

Howard, M. (ed.) (1982). *Aboriginal Power in Australian Society*. St. Lucia: Queensland University Press.

McKnight, D. (1986). Fighting in an Australian Aboriginal Supercamp. In: D. Riches (ed.), *The Anthropology of Violence*, pp. 136–63. Oxford: Blackwell.

Meggitt, M.J. (1964). Indigenous Forms of Government Among the Australian Aborigines. *Bijdragen tot de Taal-, Land- en Volkenkunde* 120: 163–78.

Myers, F.R. (1982). Ideology and Experience: The Cultural Basis of Politics in Pintubi Life. In: M. Howard (ed.), *Aboriginal Power in Australian Society*, pp. 79–114. St. Lucia: Queensland University Press.

—— (1986). The Politics of Representation: Anthropological Discourse and Australian Aborigines. *American Ethnologist* 13: 138–53.

Office of Aboriginal Development (Northern Territory Government). (1993). *Office of Aboriginal Development – Annual Report 1992/93*. Darwin: Northern Territory Government.

Pilling, A.R. (1958). Law and Feud in an Aboriginal Society of North Australia. PhD dissertation. Berkeley: University of California.

—— (1965). An Australian Aboriginal Minority: The Tiwi See Themselves as a Dominant Majority. *Phylon* 26: 305–14.

—— (1976). Tiwi Gerontocracy. Unpublished manuscript. (Held

by the Library of the Australian Institute of Aboriginal and Torres Strait Islander Studies, Canberra).

Pirntubula Ltd Pty. (1989). *Tiwi Business*. Darwin: Pirntubula Ltd Pty.

Rowse, T. (1992). *Remote Possibilities. The Aboriginal Domain and the Administrative Imagination*. Darwin: North Australia Research Unit (ANU).

Sanders, W. (1993). Aboriginal Housing. In: C. Parris (ed.), *Housing Australia*, pp. 212–27. Melbourne: Macmillan.

Sharp, R.L. (1958). People Without Politics: The Australian Yir-Yoront. In: V.F. Ray (ed.), *Systems of Political Control and Bureaucracy in Human Societies*, pp. 1–8. Seattle: University of Washington Press.

Sutton, P. and Rigsby, B. (1982). People With Politicks: Management of Land and Personnel on Australia's Cape York Peninsula. In: N.M. Williams and E.S. Hunn (eds), *Resource Managers: North American and Australian Hunter-Gatherers*, pp. 155–77. Canberra: Australian Institute of Aboriginal Studies.

Tiwi ATSIC Regional Council. (1993). Wurankuwu Community Planning Report. Darwin: Wurankuwu Association Inc. with Northern Building Consultants.

Tiwi Islands Regional Council. (1991). *Tiwi Islands Regional Council Annual Report 1990/91*. Darwin: Tiwi Islands Regional Council, Aboriginal and Torres Strait Islander Commission.

—— (1993). *Annual Report 1992-1993*. Darwin: Tiwi Islands Regional Council, Aboriginal and Torres Strait Islander Commission.

—— (n.d.). Tiwi Islands Regional Council; Regional Plan for the years 1993–1995. n.p.

Tonkinson, R. and Howard, M. (eds) (1990). *Going it Alone? Prospects for Aboriginal Autonomy*. Canberra: Aboriginal Studies Press.

Venbrux, E. (1993). Under the Mango Tree: A Case of Homicide in an Australian Aboriginal Society. PhD dissertation. Nijmegen: University of Nijmegen.

—— (1995). *A Death in the Tiwi Islands. Conflict, Ritual and Social Life in an Australian Aboriginal Community*. Cambridge: Cambridge University Press.

Wolfe, J. (1989). *'That Community Government Mob': Local Government in Small Northern Territory Communities*. Darwin: North Australia Research Unit (ANU).

Chapter 15

Staging a Political Challenge: The Story of *Tokelau te Ata*

Ingjerd Hoëm

A Search for Ways to Bridge Existential Discontinuities

Tokelau is a tiny atoll society that consists of three atolls with approximately 1,500 inhabitants, and about 5,000 in New Zealand, and it is situated in the South Pacific, north of Western Samoa.

Since the mid-sixties, many Tokelauans have migrated to New Zealand, and from that time the forces of modernity have increasingly been felt in the atolls, represented by, for instance, a monetary economy, bureaucracy, outboard motors, videos, imported food and so on. Lately, the 'New Zealand experience' has started to filter into the Tokelau society, as a result of people returning from overseas.

The difference between life in New Zealand and in Tokelau, at least as it was in the early 1960s, can hardly be stressed too much. In the following, I shall present an example of how a group of Tokelauans attempted to bridge these existential discontinuities through the introduction of a new genre to express their experiences, namely popular theatre, also called theatre for community development. They did this with the explicit goal of 'keeping the culture alive' as they called it, however they did not think it detrimental to their cause to borrow freely from the tradition of popular theatre in doing so.

Members of the theatre group wished to raise issues that they considered to be of importance to Tokelau cultural identity, such as, for example, the traditional gender-role pattern and authority structure, and more recent matters, such as abuse, street-kids and dependency. To bring up such matters *for serious consideration* within the context of public, festive situations is definitely not common (in Tokelau or in New Zealand) and to do so can be said to run counter to all canons of Tokelau etiquette.

The individual actors all had in common (although they conceptualized it in different ways) a wish to explore their cultural identity and a will to experiment, to go beyond what is communally accepted in the process of doing so. Their personal motivations for embarking on such a quest varied; however, a common denominator may be found in the deeply felt need to find ways of expressing and articulating the particular concerns arising from the enormous changes Tokelauans have experienced during the last thirty years. In the face of the common tendency to focus on the positive sides of the Tokelau way of life, to stress harmony and to downplay conflict, this group saw it as its task to mediate between the old and the young, by articulating common experiences that are normally not voiced. In short, they were searching for a more viable conception of self-hood that could help people to 'face up to the challenges of the here and now' as they put it.

In doing this the members of the theatre group were negotiating codes of behaviour in a manner that may be described as 'deep play' in the Geertzian sense of the term (Geertz 1973: 432). That is, in challenging commonly held notions about cultural identity, the actors were in a sense 'playing with fire'. By this I mean that it was more than an alternative vision that was at stake for the actors. The attempt to achieve general recognition for the issues they raised was also of such a nature that it had a potential to affect their respective statuses within the communities.

Tokelau – Recent Developments

Tokelau's present political status in terms of UN classification is that of a non-self-governing territory, and it has been administered by New Zealand since 1925 (previously Tokelau was part of the British colony of the Gilbert and Ellice Islands). The indigenous political leadership has traditionally consisted of elders, all male, and everyday life is largely dominated by subsistence activities and is communally oriented. During the last years, as a result of pressure from the UN (through the New Zealand administration) to decolonize, an inter-atoll assembly has been delegated governmental powers. The relationship among the three atolls of Tokelau has traditionally been one of distance and animosity. Currently they are in a situation that forces them to cooperate and develop a sense of a common identity that may allow them to handle their external political affairs as one nation. As mentioned above, in Tokelau there has been a relatively recent growth in the importance of a monetary economy, and significant socio-economic differences between families have occurred. The present thus has a new hierarchy to cope with – one that can be said in many respects to be on a clear collision course with anything considered as Tokelau values. Moreover, there have emerged new forms of leadership that are not as yet really formally recognized, a fact which makes it extremely difficult to talk about, and deal with in any direct way.

The brother–sister relationship, described by Judith Huntsman as complementary, still has a practical and symbolic dominance, as the values of kinship, communality and sharing override those related to the nuclear family, such as individualism and so on. The strictness with which the norms associated with this way of life are upheld has changed with the changes in the economic and technological basis of the society during the last thirty years, however.

Another structural principle is of importance to us here, namely what Huntsman refers to as 'similar' or 'symmetrical' relationships. This relationship exists between any number of individuals or any group that occupy a structurally similar position, such as that between the members of any particular age group, within a group of brothers, between two sports teams and so on. That this relationship is highly context sensitive should be obvious from the fact that, for example, in the case of a group of brothers, the factor of relative age can as easily enter into the situation and thus turn the situation into one where the hierarchical principle is dominant.

This symmetrical principle allows for relationships that are *competitive*. This is what really sets them apart from relationships defined by the principle of complementarity where, in contrast, sharing, cooperation and self-effacing behaviour is expected. The symmetrical principle is epitomized in the practice of 'making sides', *fai-itu*, which results in the division of each of the three villages in Tokelau into two, structurally similar, and thus competing 'sides' or *faitu*.[1] All these group-formations take place on the basis of, and simultaneously create relations of, symmetry and competition. Fora created by the meeting of such 'similar' groups provide the only legitimate arena for overt expression of self-aggrandizement and competitive behaviour. Otherwise, such behaviour is undercommunicated and sanctioned if it occurs.

These 'similar' groups may compete because their activities, that is, what they do (games, fishing competitions and so forth) are not classified as serious, in Tokelauan, *mea tauanoa*, literally 'things of no account'.[2] In other words, their activities are defined loosely as games, and are subsumed under the broader category of entertainment. They do not have any political significance nor is any formal power vested in them. This does not mean that such issues do not occur between such 'sides', nor that these relationships and institutions are without political significance, but, as entertainment, the activities of these groups have no institutional link with the formal political structure.

A Shift in Leadership Structure and the Issue of Legitimacy

The reason why I have included this description of 'complementary' and 'symmetrical' principles governing relationships, is that it is precisely in this area that an interesting development is taking place. As I have pointed out, new forms of leadership are slowly emerging and it will help us to gain a better understanding of what is at stake in these new developments if we look at them in terms of these previously established power structures.

Organizations within the Tokelau communities in New Zealand, which had their outspring and rationale in symmetrical relationships – 'cultural activities and games' organizations – seem to have undergone a transformation, as yet covert, not formally recognized, towards taking on a more political role. Positions within the organizations have changed accordingly. A structural precondition for this development is a lack of institutional recognition of the elders' political power within the New Zealand society. The group of people who in practice assume most of the leadership functions at present, still constitute a symmetrical element within the Tokelau organizations. A change of their role into a more formalized position would presently be perceived as constituting an open challenge to the older authority structure. This has not been seen as desirable so far. It has not been felt to be necessary, partly out of a recognition of the important function the elders fill as arbiters of dispute, and also out of deference to older people's authority in general. In Tokelau itself the picture is somewhat different. This is due to two factors. Firstly, the elders still hold the formal power, and secondly, the group of individuals who are comparable to the new leadership in New Zealand, and who often overlap with them, mainly work in the Tokelau Public Service, and are thus at one remove from the formal political structures of Tokelau. Nevertheless, the tendency for younger people with a greater familiarity with the outside world and international politics to take over positions of responsibility is also present in Tokelau.

Looking at the situation from the perspective of social organization then, it is apparent that new differences between people have emerged. Moreover, these differences also correlate with highly varied life-trajectories, to an extent that never existed among Tokelau people before the 1960s. Seen from Tokelau, a main divide is between those who have been outside Tokelau and those who have not. Another main difference, which coincides with having been outside, is between those who work in the Tokelau Public Service and those who do not.

There is no easily detectable correlation between these categories and attitudes to Tokelau values versus the values associated with the *pakeha* or *papalagi* life style (such as consumerism and individualism) however. In practice all sorts of combinations exist. You find the staunch traditionalist being an avid consumer of karate videos, and the cultural activist who leads a most 'un-Tokelauan life' in his or her free time.[3]

What is at Stake?

In the process of turning this emergent form of 'symmetrical' leadership into a viable model, legitimacy is drawn from various sources such as Tokelau egalitarianism and political theories of democracy mixed with notions of ethnicity and nationalism.

Empirically, the present situation may be described as a precarious balance, for example illustrated by how, at least in New Zealand, the role of the elders has moved towards an increasingly ritual function, and the role of the younger has taken on more substance in processes of decision making. There is, as I have pointed out, a change in the function of the so-called symmetrical relationships, and the status of the age-hierarchy and the complementary relationships are affected as well. To put it simply, the complementary relationships, that is, regulating rights and responsibilities associated with gender and kinship, have lost some of its previous functions. The age hierarchy in Tokelau has gained a legal backing, but at the same time, the increasing number of young persons in positions of leadership weakens the overall authority of the elders. The 'similar' groups, exemplified by the sides of the village, are as always for recreational purposes, but do carry a potential informal political aspect.[4] This means that the so-called expressive culture is a potentially important factor in the political life. This is not new, but what is new is the way this has been used during the last ten years with the explicit aim of bringing about a sense of Tokelau nationhood, encouraging cooperation between the three, traditionally warring atolls.

In the post-war period, things Tokelauans did not have a part either within the educational system or in anything 'official', that is in political dealings with the outside authorities (cf. Huntsman 1980). The use of Tokelauan was restricted to informal, everyday contexts, and everything having to do with the pre-Christian world-view was stigmatized as belonging to the period of 'darkness' or *pouliuli*, to the shameful heathen past.[5]

The older generation of Tokelauans seem in the main, as a response to this stigmatization, to have adopted a strategy of accommodation. By becoming good Christians, morally pure and 'civilized' in every way, they earned the right to (self-) respect. In the different political climate of New Zealand in the late 1960s and early 1970s, however, a shift from such meek attitudes towards more confrontational ones took place amongst members of the younger generation. This change can for example be observed in the establishment of relationships and groups on a basis different from what had been the case earlier. A shift began to take place in the forming of groups, which changed from being based on atoll affiliation to being based on place of residence in New Zealand, and also on the basis of common interest (see also Wessen et. al. 1992). This may seem a minor change, but in fact it constituted a major challenge to the existing authority structure and to the position of the elders.

Among the young and middle-aged people who presently find themselves in positions of leadership, it is possible to detect at least two markedly different attitudes and strategies. These individuals have in common an upward mobility, they are better educated than the main proportion of the other members of the communities. The main difference lies in their attitudes towards their common past. To simplify, where the one glorifies the past and wants to maintain what Hooper calls the 'neo-traditional order', as epitomized by the – in their view – unquestionable authority of the elders (and the Church) and the other wants to pick the best from both worlds and develop new models of Tokelau self-hood.

It is not possible to ignore the quasi-political role played by the 'symmetrical' organizations in New Zealand. Whether it is sports teams, song-groups, dance teams or theatre groups, women's organizations or pre-schools, they all have in common a focus around the 'Tokelau culture', or the 'Tokelau language' and so on. In Tokelau, as I have described elsewhere (Hoëm 1990/1995, 1992) the quasi-political potential of the sphere of 'entertainment' or expressive culture has always been there, as may be exemplified through the institution of clowning, which sometimes takes the form of rather explicit political criticism and commentary.

What is new, however, is the feedback into the Tokelau institutions of 'the New Zealand experience', as expressed in the introduction of Tokelauan language, history and culture into the national curriculum in Tokelau, the establishment of a forum for debate such as newsletters on all three atolls, the writing of poetry, songs and drama, some of which carry highly critical messages and analyses of Tokelau's predicament in present times.

The distance between the vision held by the 'activists' and 'the rest' is sometimes considerable. In other contexts however, there is a high degree of sharing of vision.

The emergence of new forms of social differentiation and new forms of cultural expression has, as described above, been followed by changes in attitudes towards 'tradition', 'knowledge' and 'the culture'. Differences in these attitudes actually constitute a major divide between people. This change within the Tokelau communities may profitably be described by reference to the different models of 'knowledge' that people hold. The 'traditionalists' hold that to grow older is to grow wiser, and that old age is synonymous with possessing knowledge. This view was one of the cornerstones of social organization in subsistence-oriented Tokelau, where knowledge of the seasons, the stars, navigation techniques and, perhaps most importantly of genealogies as giving legitimacy to land claims, was vital for survival.

This knowledge is treated as esoteric, but it is simultaneously being taught in the schools, and presented in the atolls local newsletters. Moreover, it has always been presented in song, in storytelling and in speechmaking. There is an ongoing negotiation about what should be shared and it is often the case that in spite of a part of 'the culture', being circulated in newsletters or in speeches or songs, those who are not supposed to have that kind of knowledge quite simply don't pick it up. A new context for the development of selfhood is being established through various culturally significant events over time. There are, however, equally strong forces that pull in other directions.

On a personal level, individuals who are in a structurally similar position, that is, in what I call a symmetrical relationship, tend to compete with each other to achieve potential authority (*pule* or *mana*). It is still the case that privilege, wisdom and command are commonly taken to be natural prerogatives of age, but these assets are not of great value if they are not exercised. In this context, ethnicity enters as a relatively new factor, providing an alternative frame of legitimacy that holds the potential to override the traditional principles for inclusion and exclusion such as family ties, atoll ties, gender and age. Ethnicity and nationalism, as a frame of reference, carries a potential for legitimacy for the new leadership, while, or perhaps precisely because, it allows people to avoid making a fundamental break with the Tokelau culture.

I would like to stress that this is a potential, a promise, a vision of a possible bridge over the extreme discontinuities that particularly the younger part of the Tokelau population has experienced, and that it is not a given solution with a guaranteed outcome. To gain an understanding of what is at stake here, of what may lie behind some of the tensions and conflicts between differing definitions of reality as implied by 'the Tokelau way', an obvious starting point is quite simply the immense discontinuity between the 'life-world' in Tokelau and the one encountered when going overseas.

Moving Between Worlds

To give a brief impression of what this may be like, a man, one of the members of the theatre group, described his first overseas experience the following way: 'I went to New Zealand as a scholarship student when I was twelve . . . I do not remember what happened the first two years, except for having talks with some fellow Tokelauans who had arrived there earlier. They helped me. It was too different. I did not understand the language. No, I cannot describe that time, I don't remember it.'

Such experiences are very common, and whereas some people fix in their descriptions of that first time abroad on some uncommon feature as metonymic for the whole experience, such as that of seeing cars for the first time: 'I thought it was a dog' (another non-existent species in Tokelau), on lettuce ('on the boat to Tonga, I noticed people eating these green leaves') . . . and so on, or quite simply, 'how cold it was in New Zealand', I would say that all have in common a very marked 'before and after' tone, after marking a change so great that after having been overseas Tokelau never seems quite the same. As in, 'when I came back I couldn't believe how small the place was'.

The experience of such discontinuities as for example the fundamental and quite unsettling difference between the flat, lagoon and ocean-dominated, palm-fringed atoll landscape and the mountainous landscape of Samoa or New Zealand, may in fact be very hard to express in words. The move from the familiar to the unknown may be accompanied by a physical shock, but even this transition can of course become a routine. When it is a first time, however, and the move is from a situation where every face is known, and moreover, where everybody's presence is explicitly recognized by greetings and other phatic talk exchanges every time one meets, and the space one moves around in is approximately the size of a couple of football fields, it is understandable that a certain immediate 'agoraphobia' sets in.

The tendency in Tokelau to stay within the atoll-affiliation-based communities is largely perpetuated in New Zealand. The majority of the older generation have a minimal interaction with the surrounding society, and whereas this seem to change within the second generation of Tokelauans there, the level of interaction with the Tokelau communities is still high (see Wessen *et al.* 1992).

The image of Tokelau is cherished among the New Zealand Tokelauans, and is among other things perpetuated in songs that are sung at every gathering, praising the beauty and virtues of the home atoll, or in the later years, also of Tokelau as a whole. This image, however, is in most cases an image of the place as it was twenty or thirty years ago. In particular it relates to what is considered proper social norms, with respect to family (*kaiga*), gender-roles, and the hierarchy of age. It also perpetuates a certain view on the relationship between the atolls, and it is ultimately centred around the position of authority attributed to the elders.

In this way the scene is set for a fundamental ambiguity in the relationship between 'Tokelau Tokelauans' and Tokelauans in New Zealand. On the one hand, I would say that there is a profound sense of loss and inferiority on both sides. The people living in New Zealand are all too aware of the loss of the survival skills they possessed in Tokelau, and with this, the familiarity with that environment as a whole. They say that the 'Tokelauan Tokelauans' 'have the culture' and that they are losing it. On the other hand, 'Tokelau Tokelauans' tend to perpetuate an image of New Zealand (or other overseas countries, as unemployment levels have risen in New Zealand) as the promised land, and they often express a sense of the inferiority of their lifestyle compared with how it is assumed to be possible to live elsewhere. This contrast is often expressed as a difference between an 'easy life' (in New Zealand) and a 'hard life' in Tokelau. However, this may also express a certain proudness of the physical agility of people in Tokelau as compared with those in New Zealand, and in this and similar fashions, the images and relationships are negotiated and modified.

In line with the general stress on harmony and avoidance of direct expression of conflict, there is one trait that is marked on both sides, however, and that is a tendency to stress the positive sides of the Tokelau way of life, and of downplaying the differences between these life-worlds. In marked contrast to this, some among the new leaders see it as their task to mediate what they perceive as discontinuities by articulating common experiences among the younger generation. In doing this, an explicit goal is to help people coming to terms with and facing up to the challenges of 'the here and now', as it is said.

Those who are concerned with preserving the status quo, meaning Tokelau as it was approximately thirty years ago, articulate their arguments with reference to *aganuku*, which is commonly translated as culture in the sense of the legitimized and thus legitimizing tradition. Others argue in terms of contemporary practice, *tu* or *mahaniga*, and stress that what people in fact already do is not likely to go away, and that to be able to handle the difficulties of the present situation, everyday practice must be taken into account in a positive way as well.

That such discussions take place at all is in itself proof of the great changes in practice, in that this implies a common reflection on some very fundamental values and principles, something that was definitely not the case in the Tokelau of thirty years ago. What is at stake is quite simply how life is going to be for Tokelauans in the future, ranging from being largely a matter of life quality to being a question of having a life at all. The scenarios people envisage varies from a scene where everybody has to leave (and eventually become assimilated into the mainstream New Zealand culture) because of the greenhouse effect, to one of abject dependency and apathy in Tokelau and in New Zealand with the help of aid or social welfare and alcohol, to one where 'everything is as it were thirty years ago', to various more-or-less felicitous combinations of what is unique to Tokelau and what derives from the increased interaction with the outside world.

Setting the Stage for a Political Challenge

Early in 1990 some individuals from the Tokelau community living in the Hutt Valley area outside Wellington, New Zealand, took advantage of the fact that a large proportion of all the Tokelau communities in New Zealand was gathered for what is called the Easter Tournaments, which mainly consist of competitive sports and dancing.[6] They used this occasion as an opportunity to interview their fellow countrymen about their opinions on such gatherings, asked whether they felt satisfied with the status quo, and if not, enquired about what they would like to see instead.

Many of the interviewees responded that they were tired of what these gatherings had to offer. However, they greatly valued the opportunity to socialize with the wider community and participated to stay in touch with the 'feelings of Tokelau' that these gatherings brought up, particularly so that their children would not loose touch with their larger networks of kin and with Tokelau ways altogether. Younger people and quite a large number of women said that they wanted something more than 'just the sports and the dancing' and added that they wished to learn more about other aspects of their culture. The youth also expressed the view that they wished to be given licence to explore other forms of cultural expression. They were eager to explore new media and did not necessarily want to confine themselves to doing things the usual Tokelau way.

Encouraged by this response, the interviewers then proceeded to create something new to fill this need, and the result of this was what some years later came to be named *Tokelau te Ata*. This name can be read as a play on the English word theatre, but it also carries a second, 'deeper' meaning (cf. Thomas 1986) true to the canons of Tokelau poetry, namely 'Tokelau, the image', or 'Tokelau, the dawn' or perhaps most poignantly, 'Tokelau, the reflection'.

The production of the first play, which was called *Tagi*, meaning 'cry' or 'lament', was largely carried out as a collective effort. The base line was a general agreement that the play should be about Tokelau history. This choice was motivated by various factors, of which I would say a very important one was the role of history in Tokelau society. The *tala anamua*, stories about the past, a large proportion of which is about what is called 'the days of war', concern the atolls and the relationships between them in pre-*papalagi*, pre-Western and pre-Christian times. Although set in the past, and reflecting historical events and relations, the contents of these *tala*, and songs and speeches that contain references to the same material, has a direct relevance for, and is highly politically charged even when used today. Another factor contributing to this choice of topic was the simultaneous launching of the book *Matagi Tokelau* or 'wind, news, memories, vigour, life' (from) Tokelau, a collection of various accounts of Tokelau history, moving from 'origin traditions . . . to descriptions of the contemporary scene'.[7] The material contained in this book was used by the group as a source to Tokelau history. And finally, another great motivating factor was the strong wish expressed by many of the interviewees to learn more about their cultural heritage.

The role of the *papalagi* instructor within the group, apart from being one of the actors, was to provide some guidelines on how to form the material so that it could easily convey a message to an audience. The material, in addition to what was drawn from *Matagi Tokelau*, was provided by the other cast members, and the language was to be Tokelauan. This was quite a challenge to some of the younger cast members, who were more familiar with English.

The production process went largely as follows; the group decided on a theme, such as 'village life in pre-*papalagi* times', 'the slave traders', 'leaving for New Zealand' and so on. Everybody was then asked to come forth with associations to the theme. These associations were then enacted, and put together to form a scene. As the main frame was Tokelau history, and as this increasingly took the form of 'what has happened to our way of life during the last centuries?' the linking together of scenes became largely chronological. Songs were composed, among them the first *haumate* or lament to be composed in this century, and a great deal of soul-searching, hard work and practice took place. The script of the play as a whole was never written down, but notes with suggestions for dialogue, translations and ideas were circulated during the meetings.

The final product consisted of three main parts; the pre-*papalagi* times, the coming of *papalagi* and finally, the migration experience. The scenes were as follows;

Part One:

(1) the telling of the individual actors' genealogies, linking them together and to atoll affiliation
(2) the individual actors' statements of their personal purpose with the play
(3) the origin myths
(4) the days of war
(5) village life.

Part Two:

(1) First visit of *papalagi*
(2) the coming of Christianity
(3) the arrival of slave traders.

Part Three:

(1) The political developments concerning Tokelau during the last decades, cast in the form of a genealogy
(2) individual accounts of journey to New Zealand
(3) a party scene in New Zealand
(4) the first-born Tokelau child in New Zealand
(5) school, ban on using the Tokelau language
(6) street kids
(7) welfare, drink, incest

(8) speeches and sayings about family (*kaiga*) particularly as it relates to the role of women.

The individual actors' personal opinions on the issues raised in the play were quite varied, as for example illustrated by their reactions to the scene of the arrival of Christianity. Some were rather uncomfortable with this scene, feeling that they didn't want to 'make fun of the Church', whereas others didn't think that what they did in this scene went too far at all. Anyhow, all the cast members unanimously agreed that it was a good thing to raise the issues, and that a time had come where it was necessary to bring out in the open the 'underside' or difficulties relating to certain aspects of their way of life in New Zealand. In their opinion such issues were usually just denied within the community at large. At least it was not considered fitting to bring up these things in public situations.

Negotiating Codes of Behaviour: From 'Message' to 'Gift'

As I mentioned above, regardless of how the members of the group personally felt about the issues they raised in the play, they were all in agreement when stressing the importance of making these issues public.

Furthermore they were aware of the fact that to explicitly bring up social conflicts and address problems such as incest is definitely not considered seemly from within the parameters of the *fakaTokelau*. When they decided to do it anyway, it arose out of a conviction that, as they said, for people to continue to deny that these things happen only serves to perpetuate the difficulties and might in some cases even serve to make things worse.

The presentation of the play *Tagi* to the larger Tokelau community in New Zealand took place as part of the 'cultural activities' of the subsequent Easter Tournament held in April 1992 in the Pahina Hall in Porirua.[8] The audience was entranced, laughed, cried and joined in the singing of the songs. In all respects it was a great success. Afterwards, however, the community was divided in how it responded to the event and the messages contained in the play. Some young women were prompted by the particular scene dealing with the topic of incest to contact members of the group, telling them how they had had similar experiences, feeling for the first time that it was acceptable to talk about it. Many did identify with the migration experience, and again many were happy to see 'the culture come alive' as it was presented in the first part of the play dealing with the pre-*papalagi* times. Again many enjoyed the event more as a pure spectacle.

There were however others who objected to the play on various grounds. One objection was quite simply that the group's activities had not been sanctioned by the elders. Another, which struck somewhat deeper, was the objection to the explicit mention of 'indecent' things in public. The objection that was most frequently voiced however, was directed at the very opening scene of the play, where the individual actors come forth as their genealogical connections are called out. The genealogies were said to be wrong, or partly wrong, and the fact that the group had chosen to 'link' (*hohoko*) themselves through one of the possible 'paths' (*auala*) that they have in common instead of through others, was a major source of contention. As one man put it to members of the Nukunonu contingent (to which the majority of the theatre group where considered to belong), 'don't worry about that lot. They are from Atafu' (one of the other atolls). In other words, this man, who can be said to belong to the 'traditionalist faction' among the new leadership, tried to use the group's tools against it, using its members way of affiliating themselves as a means of excluding them. His arguments drew legitimacy from the sphere of Tokelau tradition, and had the potential of setting a large part of the community against the group and undermining the individual statuses of its members. The group's members' way of linking themselves genealogically was however deliberately chosen to show the community that even deeply rooted emotional identifications such as the one with ones home atoll (which their adversary played on) can and indeed must be transcended if Tokelau is ever to develop a national identity.

These issues then, and similar themes, became the talk of the community for a while, and it often took the familiar form of 'who are they to present these issues', referring to the role of the elders as the custodians of tradition. While this talk went on in the community, the group, 'wanting to stay on top of things' as they put it, conceived the idea of making a tour to Tokelau. In applications for funding to support this tour, the project was called 'the indigenous people's return to the homeland'.

A Play About Freedom, Masks and Emotions

In preparation for the tour to Tokelau, a second play was begun, and this time it was to focus on the tension between individualism and the communal, extended-family orientation in Tokelau. Whereas the first play was produced with the New Zealand Tokelau audience in mind, to counter what they called 'the cultural erosion' they perceived to be taking place there, this second play was produced primarily for a 'Tokelau Tokelau' audience. This goal affected the production process in interesting ways as it led to confrontations and reflections over the differences between life in Tokelau and in New Zealand, and also between the images held of Tokelau by cast members and the reality of life in Tokelau of 1993/94. (Some of the members had not been back to Tokelau since the early seventies.)

The theme of the play shifted from being about the present political issues facing Tokelau, to one about the situation of women, particularly relating to her role within the extended family. A very rudimentary sketch of this play is as follows. The main character of the play, Tima, has been abroad to get an education, and she returns to Tokelau thinking that she is there for a holiday. Her family has other plans for her, however. They want her to get married and settle down in Tokelau to look after her elderly parents. She becomes desperate when she realizes this; she tries to talk it out with her parents, but they tell her to be respectful and do as she is told. She tries to get support from an aunt, who, while sympathetic to her pleas, advises her that Tokelau needs people with her experience. The aunt tries to talk Tima's case at a family meeting, but this doesn't help either. Tima meets an old acquaintance who works as a teacher in the village, and he nearly manages to convince her to stay and work there, when they are discovered talking by her father and the teacher is beaten up. Thoroughly disgusted by the situation by then, Tima wants to leave. She rejects her suitor, but at this point the village priest intervenes and orders her to do as her parents says. The play ends with her getting married to a suitor not of her own choice but picked by her parents.

The form of this theatre then, is such that, at what is called 'the situation of maximal oppression', the audience is invited to intervene and change whatever they think is wrong or should or could be different with the story. The scenes of the play are then enacted again, according to the wishes of the audience, and if the audience agrees, the final scene is rerun, but this time with a song depicting women as powerful and as individuals in their own right.

While working on this play, some of the female cast members, who all identify strongly with Tokelau culture, and who are active members of the community in New Zealand, even though they differ in the character of their personal attachments, experienced some very strong emotional reactions when experimenting with possible scenarios. The starting point this time was a strongly felt wish to, as it was put, 'tell the women of Tokelau to stop hiding'. During discussions, it came out that they perceived the negative side of the behaviour of Tokelau women in general (both in New Zealand and in Tokelau) as being hypocritical and dishonest. They described women as not showing their true emotions, as manipulating, as gossips and as conformists. Scenes were tried out, such as 'a group of women sitting in a cooking house in Tokelau. An outsider comes, tries to learn and help with their work, but is only discouraged and ridiculed.' 'Family scenes, where father rules and mother always self-effacingly obeys him, even though he might be in the wrong.' 'The same, but with religion entering into it.' 'People walking on the road, the public area in the village, and, being outsiders, not observing what is considered to be proper etiquette in Tokelau when it comes to ways of walking, talking and clothing', and so on.

At this stage it became apparent that, on the one hand, everybody had experienced such behaviour and felt victimized because of it. The fact that they all were going to Tokelau only served to strengthen this feeling of intense discomfort as they knew that they themselves would soon be exposed to this aspect of village life. On the other hand, they could also recognize themselves as occasionally being in the roles of oppressors and victimizers, and this naturally felt deeply unsettling.

Parallel to this, the cast members began to realize that it would probably not be a very good idea to come to Tokelau with only a negative image of their way of life, based largely on their newly won freedom in New Zealand society, and then tell the people there what the group, as outsiders, thought that the people living in Tokelau should do about it. There were some quite heated discussions, where solutions ranged from defence of Tokelau etiquette to total rejections of these codes of behaviour. These discussions, prompted by the experimental enacting of the scenes, were cast in terms of 'masks', in the sense of , for example, 'what is the mask of the woman who is in control', 'what is the religious mask', and even 'what are the masks of the three atolls'. An immediate reaction, true to the initial position of wanting to 'tell the women of Tokelau to be themselves', was that the message should be 'for everybody to take off their masks'. This led to the intriguing question 'what is behind the mask'.

At this point opinions started to differ. Whereas one woman said that she saw behind the masks 'a very gentle Tokelauan', others stated that the masks are necessary for social life, that they are not only negative, but that they also contain and protect what is positive about life in Tokelau. The hermit crab was used as a metaphor, as it cannot survive without its shell.

I would analyze this dilemma by drawing on the observation made by Nico Besnier and others, to the extent that 'in these societies, emotions are defined in behavioural terms' (Besnier 1989: 89.) Obviously such a subtle difference very easily turns into crude stereotyping when one attempts to operationalize it. Dichotomies such as 'shame' versus 'guilt' cultures, or 'context orientation' versus 'context independence' are but some examples of this. However, this particular orientation meant that, when the group started experimenting, enacting alternative ways of behaviour, it immediately came up against some very fundamental principles informing its sense of identity.

Whereas some group members were aware of what was happening, and had such a confrontation as their explicit goal, many obviously did not. As one woman put it: 'I entered the group because I wanted to be a mother, because I am proud of being a mother. I wanted the community to see me that way, and I asked for such a role, but I didn't know that it would be this deep.'

As mentioned above, following the Tokelau way, behaviour in most public situations is characterized by a restraint on sexual matters, avoidance of conflict, avoidance of expressions of self-interest, and by a stressing of a sharing, caring and compassionate behaviour (*alofa*). In contrast to this restraint, competitive and boisterous behaviour is occasionally encouraged, that is, in recreational contexts, where what is happening is said to be 'of no account', *mea tauanoa*. On such occasions a main ingredient is clowning and the presentation of skits, *faleaitu,* and within this context, a person who is either beyond the 'dangerous' age or holds a respected position in the community may explicitly joke about sexual matters, and put himself or herself forward without being censored. If the behaviour is perceived as being *fai mea malie*, making sweet or nice things, for the enjoyment of everybody, it is accepted graciously. In most cases, a direct, confrontational style is likely to cause discomfort and to alienate the speaker.

During the tour to Tokelau, it became even more apparent than it had been in New Zealand that the members of the theatre group were used to different forms of interaction and communication than what is currently encoded as 'the Tokelau Way'. Moreover, these codes of behaviour were exactly what they wanted to challenge through the plays. They were confronted with these differences on many levels during the tour, and again the reactions to the plays varied. One immediate response to the plays was that 'this is not the truth'. What people actually meant by saying that differed. Some referred to the fact that individual scenes were incorrect. For example one depicted an arranged marriage, which people said did not exist any more in Tokelau. Others seemed rather to say that the play does not depict truthfully a story of somebody that they knew (as many skits or *faleaitu* do) and they therefore did not quite know what to make of it.

Again others saw the play as a true story in the sense that they thought that the characters played by the cast members were expressions of their personal beliefs and lifestyles, and this was by far the most difficult experience for the members of the group. One illustration of this is the story of how one morning, after the play had been presented the evening before, one old woman walked up to a man who played what he himself considered to be a role representing everything he hated about his culture – a Bible 'loving' patriarch oppressing his family. She said: 'I was so happy to see that you have turned out to be such a good person. Your mother would have been proud of you.' He related this afterwards, saying that he didn't have the heart to tell her how he really felt about the role that he had played. Other members of the group experienced increasing difficulties with separating themselves from the role they were playing in the eyes of the community, so much that when for example the woman playing the main female character reached her home atoll, she found it necessary to make a public statement saying that she was not the character she represented in the play.

Again, the plays were generally graciously received; people enjoyed being entertained, and some people were deeply moved by seeing the history of Tokelau, 'come alive' as they put it. The controversies surrounding the 'genealogies' part was avoided this time. The oldest man of the group went, upon coming to each of the atolls, to an elder known for his proficiency in genealogies, and thus the first scene represented different 'paths' (_auala_), linking the cast members to Atafu, Nukunonu and Fakaofo on the respective atolls. This relativistic and detached attitude towards atoll affiliation is highly unusual and went unnoticed as far as I know among the very few who travelled among the three atolls during the time of the tour.

The group held workshops on each of the atolls, teaching the methods of 'popular theatre' to those who were interested, mainly teachers. During these workshops, and also as a result of presenting these plays to a 'Tokelau Tokelau' audience, some members of the group came to question what they were doing. More particularly some of them began to wonder whether the form of the plays, being a particular development 'for the Third World' of a branch of Western radical, action theatre, in fact wasn't antithetical to Tokelau forms of performance and styles of communication. What in New Zealand had seemed to be a culturally neutral tool for allowing the messages to get across to an audience suddenly did not seem neutral at all.

Vilsoni Hereniko (1994), in an article about clowning as political commentary in Polynesia, makes an explicit comparison between skits or _faleaitu_ and popular theatre. He describes how the popular theatre form is 'popular in many third-world countries and now has counterparts in Vanuatu and Solomon Islands', and indicates the potential use of the 'indigenous form to disseminate developmental and educational information' in Polynesia. There is, however, a significant difference between the indigenous genre of _faleaitu_ or skits and popular theatre, in that the Tokelau skits are not really dedicated to 'dissemination of information'; they always stay within the boundary of the humorous. Clowns or skit-makers may address touchy topics they could not address within their ordinary capacities under the protection of the set-apart nature of the performance, and this may have socio-political consequences if someone in the audience later on decides to modify his or her behaviour and instigate a certain course of action because of what he or she saw caricatured in the performance. However, the inversions of ordinary roles that are the main topic of skits in Tokelau are only acceptable because it is not for real, because the performance takes place within a joking context.[9]

The actors' doubts were linked to a realization that the seriousness of their performance could be interpreted as an attack on the traditionally humorous cast of such performances. Following Hereniko's discussion of the historical links between clowning and politics in the region it seems generally to be the case that it is precisely this characteristic, humour, which serves to safeguard the expression of subversive statements. In other words, some of the members of the group began to worry that they were perhaps applying too strong a medicine, undermining the arena that allowed them to present their alternative vision in the first place.

Deep Play *and* 'Things of no Account'?

To conclude, then, in Tokelau recreational activities are defined as entertainment, as fun, as 'things of no account', *mea tauanoa*. This situational definition allows for a certain amount of flexibility when it comes to what people may actually present during public events. The theatre performances fitted neatly into this category and this meant that those who had serious objections to the plays being performed, or to any of the messages in the plays did not have to confront the issue directly.

However it was in fact striking during the performances in Tokelau how many of the elders – the old men holding formal political power – were absent, or were seated in the dark outside the meeting house, so as to avoid giving the event an explicit blessing by their presence. That they did so may indicate that they realized that the popular theatre performance was a different kind of animal from the ordinary skits, and that they recognized the group as communicating something more serious than just a playful challenge to their authority. During the Tokelau sojourn, the members of the group on the other hand actually moved closer in their definitions of what they were doing to local notions of festivity and prestation exchanges. From a framework where their perception of what they were doing was defined as to 'take a message to an audience' – dissemination of information as Hereniko phrases it – they were led step-by-step in the direction of an altogether different definition of the situation. This new definition of what they were doing, clearly more fitting in the context of Tokelau, was expressed as 'we are coming to Tokelau with a gift, to celebrate'. This is how the group came to present their intentions to the Council of Elders, when they were invited to attend their meeting at the beginning of their stay to explain the purpose of their visit.

The difference between what is done in ordinary performances (skit making or clowning) and what the group attempted to do with the plays can be described as a difference between a temporary inversion of codes informing identity (as is the case with ordinary performances) and negotiating codes of behaviour with the explicit goal of transforming commonly held conceptions of identity (as was the case with the plays). To challenge people's conceptions of their way of life, and to do it in a serious and direct way is unusual in Tokelau, and the group clearly felt that to enter the meeting house at the centre of the village to present this anomaly in front of everybody was a grave undertaking. To enter into the ritual space of performance with the goal of redefining the parameters of the culture was 'deep play' indeed for some of the members of the group and for those amongst the audience who share their vision.

Notes

1. Cf. Borofsky (1987) for a description of an institution that shows some interestingly similar features to the Tokelau 'sides', the *akatawa*.
2. See also Hooper and Huntsman (1976).
3. For a more detailed analysis of the situation in Tokelau, with a focus on variation in attitudes towards knowledge, see Hoëm (1990/1995).
4. Much in the fashion described by Cohen (1974).
5. For a more thorough description, see also Sallen (1983).
6. See Wessen *et al.* (1992: 133–6, 138–9, 143), for a detailed historical description of the development of this institution.

7. This book was produced by elders in Tokelau who collected the oral material. The compilation of the book took place with the assistance of the anthropologists Hooper and Huntsman affiliated with the University of Auckland, New Zealand.
8. This is the meeting hall of the Fakaofo community. The name means literally 'white pearl shell lure', and this is one of the treasures in Tokelau, the gift or *kahoa* that is given to a bride by the grooms parents as part of the wedding ceremony.
9. For a further description of Tokelau skit-making, see Hooper and Huntsman (1975).

References

Besnier, N. (1989). Literacy and Feelings: the Encoding of Affects in Nukulaelae Letters. *Text* 9: 69–92.

Borofsky, R. (1987). *Making History. Pukapukan and Anthropological Constructions of Knowledge.* Cambridge: Cambridge University Press.

Cohen, A. (1974). *Two-Dimensional Man.* London: Routledge & Kegan Paul.

Geertz, C. (1973). *The Interpretation of Cultures.* New York: Basic Books.

Hereniko, V. (1994). Clowning as Political Commentary: Polynesia, Then and Now. *The Contemporary Pacific* 6 (Spring): 1–28.

Hoëm, I. (1990/1995). *A Way With Words.* Bangkok: White Orchid Press; Oslo: Institute of Comparative Research in Human Culture.

—— (ed.) (1992). *Kupu mai te Tutolu. Tokelau Oral Literature.* Oslo: Scandinavian University Press, The Institute for Comparative Research in Human Culture.

Hooper, A. and Huntsman, J. (1975). Male and Female in Tokelau Culture. *Journal of the Polynesian Society* 84: 415–30.

Huntsman, J. (1980). *Tokelau Tales told by Manuele Palehau.* Auckland: Department of Anthropology, University of Auckland.

Matagi Tokelau. (1990, 1991). (Compiled by A. Hooper and J. Huntsman). Apia: Office for Tokelau Affairs and Suva: Institute of Pacific Studies, University of the South Pacific.

Sallen, V.G. (1983). Tokelau Scholars in New Zealand: Experiences and Evaluations. (Unpublished MA thesis). Auckland: University of Auckland.

Thomas, A. (1986). The Fatele of Tokelau: Approaches to the Study of Dance in its Social Context. (Unpublished MA thesis). Wellington: Victoria University of Wellington.

Wessen, A.F., Hooper, A., Huntsman, J., Prior, I.A.M. and Salmond, C. (1992). *Migration and Health in a Small Society. The Case of Tokelau*. Oxford: Clarendon Press.

Part VII

Epilogue

Chapter 16

The New Modernities

Marilyn Strathern[1]

As two examples of the formation of identities in the twentieth century, Clifford (1988: 148) cites first Picasso's cubist response to an African mask and then Leach and Kildea's film *Trobriand Cricket*. 'The film takes us into a staged swirl of brightly painted, feathered bodies, balls, and bats. In the midst of all this on a chair sits the umpire . . . He is chewing betel nut, which he shares out from a stash held on his lap. It is a bright blue plastic Adidas bag. It is beautiful.' He then adds that perhaps one can see the Adidas bag as 'part of the same kind of inventive process' as the African-looking masks that suddenly appeared in Picasso's pictures. Built on the missionaries' game, something amazing, he says, has been concocted from elements of tradition. It renders ethnography surrealist. The surrealist moment, he argues, is one 'in which the possibility of comparison exists in unmediated tension with sheer incongruity' (1988: 146). Such 'elements of modern ethnography tend to go unacknowledged by a science that sees itself engaged in the reduction of incongruities . . . But is not every ethnographer . . . a *reinventor* and reshuffler of realities?' (1988: 147, my emphasis).

Comparison and incongruity: Latour (1993: 10–1) would see these enabled by two modernist knowledge practices. On the one hand there are practices of separation ('purification') that create distinct but comparable zones, his own prime example being the distinction between human and non-human worlds; on the other hand there are practices of mediation ('translation'), which mix types of being; above all 'hybrids of nature and culture'. Such mixes proliferate, unofficially as it were, as a byproduct of making those pure distinctions – indeed he argues that 'the more we forbid ourselves to conceive of hybrids, the more possible their inter-breeding becomes' (1993: 12). Latour argues that moderns tolerate both practices provided they too are kept distinct. But '[a]s soon as we direct our attention *simultaneously* to the work of purification *and* the work of hybridization, we stop being wholly modern' (1993: 11, my emphasis). And that is because we – 'we' appears to mean we moderns who are Euro-Americans – would see our relations with others differently.

In this context Latour extolls anthropology as the discipline that tackles everything at once: 'every ethnologist is capable of including within a single monograph . . . the distribution of powers among human beings, gods, and non-humans; the procedures for reaching agreements; the connections between religion and power; ancestors; cosmologies; property rights' (1993: 14). He is referring both to anthropologist's holistic approach to the description of social life and to the mixes offered by their subjects. Anthropology makes explicit, then, practices of modernism ordinarily suppressed in the purificatory and rational ('constitutional') effort to keep descriptions of (say) the natural and social worlds distinct. His point is that hybrids have always been present: there never has been a modernism of only that exclusively rationalist kind. We always were non-modern. His model for the non-modern includes parts from worlds he deliberately calls pre-modern, summoning among others peoples from Papua New Guinea. He could, for instance, have cited the Trobriand Islanders.

Now Latour does not wish to take on the pre-modern world wholesale; he only wants to borrow bits from it. After all, he argues, the explicitness that pre-moderns give to hybrids (mixing human and non-human elements) has as restrictive a role as does their dogmatic separation in the hands of moderns. Indeed by making hybrids a focus of cultural practice, pre-moderns cannot realize the potential for experimentation that moderns allow by officially ignoring them.[2] Pre-moderns and moderns alike are one-sided in their explicit orientations; Latour hopes moderns can redress the (several) balance(s). So what new roles are anthropologists' accounts of Papua New Guinea required to play in these demo-cratizing gestures? Euro-Americans are being invited to become aware of their continuities with others: 'As collectives, we are all brothers' (1993: 114). Pre-moderns show moderns a part of the picture, how to be explicit about hybrids.

Where Latour is interested in the separation and mix of nature and culture, Clifford performs the same intellectual operation on the separation and mix of cultures. So if scientific anthropology upheld the distinctiveness of cultures, he can also point to the power of the implicit, here the unofficial side of ethnography that was always juxtapositional, surrealist (1988: 147), in response to the hybrid character of culture itself. The two arrive at similar declarations of symmetry, both on account of the hybrid forms they detect: Latour's symmetry between modern and pre-modern societies resonates with the symmetry of mutual inventiveness Clifford finds in the way cultures borrow from one another. How could one possibly have any quarrel with such a programme?

A New Invention?

'Inventiveness' has all the resonances of the enabling role into which anthropologists place cultural consciousness. They are delighted when peoples turn to their own ends artefacts and ideas introduced from elsewhere – the endless possibilities for re-configuration (e.g. Wilk 1995) – especially when that elsewhere is the anthropologists' own culture. Culture appears, in Turner's words (1993: 423), 'as the *jouissance* of the late capitalist consumerist subject, playing with the heady opportunities for self-creation that the ever-growing world of commodities appears to provide'. My interest in Latour's account is because he not only tries to introduce a certain symmetry between social formations (modern and pre-modern), as Clifford does between cultures, but extends that symmetry to the kinds of mix of human and non-human entities that Papua New Guineans have made familiar to the anthropologist. The first kind of symmetry is an evolved form of cultural relativism. The second symmetry opens up a perspective on the substance of Melanesian (my examples come from Papua New Guinea) knowledge.

Latour argues that the separation of culture and society from nature has both given social scientists their distinctive field and corralled them within it. Thus he extolls anthropology only insofar as its mixed accounts include technology, religion, the natural world and social relations; he castigates it for privileging the social. The anthropologist is all too likely to suggest that the one entity that pre-modern peoples fail to see for themselves is society. Since such people cannot separate knowledge from society, he says (1993: 99), the anthropologist has to point out the social construction. Moreover, on home ground anthropology fails even in such an attempt. He accuses it of focussing on areas of life identifiably 'social' (arcane rituals or remote communities), ignoring natural science among other things. Here too anthropologists should look to the networks, to the mixes of artefact and idea and person that make up life. In Latour's terms, 'networks' become visible as effects of mediation ('translation'), that is, as links between whatever (non)moderns perceive as different orders of knowledge.[3]

To reveal the hybrid constitution of an artefact appears a democratizing move precisely because its configuration of meanings (its network) emerges as the creation (the network) of many actants. An African mask is at once the work of individuals, the presentation of planes and surfaces and an object under an artist's eye. Human and non-human combine in the painting Picasso creates. Picasso owns the painting but not everything that went into its composition nor indeed the image derived by others from it. He may sell it, in which case it acquires an alienability that becomes owned by another.

This is of a piece with the discovery that cultures were never pure. Clifford goes to great lengths to demonstrate the impurity of cultures and he links it, especially in the Mashpee Indian land case, to problems of identity when identity is held to depend on unique continuities of form (culture) and substance (people). Looked at one way, the Mashpee were Indian, another way they were not (1988: 289). (Cross examination of Mashpee as witness to Mashpee identity: 'You don't eat much Indian food, do you? Only sometimes. You use regular doctors, don't you? Yes, and herbs as well' (1988: 286).) Clifford's political intention is both to celebrate the hybrid as a form in its own right and to insist that through people's inventiveness all cultures are hybrids. So what is a difficulty for the Mashpee Indian is illuminating for the cultural commentator. A hybrid cannot be pinned down, for its character-istics do not reside in any one part but in the way parts work together. It is thus a perfect trope for culture as recreative combination, in the same way as Latour's 'network' is a trope for the journeying, nomadic, extensiveness of any enquiry that pursues connections. One sees linked in one continuous chain (Latour's phrase) entities as incommensurable as the chemistry, global strategy and personalities that go to make up (say) a report on atmospheric pollution. Insofar as a hybrid identity (of the report) is distributed between diverse components, and insofar as no-one can claim to have traversed a network identical to anyone else's, the journeying enquirer in turn has license for cultural creativity him or herself.

I wish to reflect on the way in which anthropological knowledge enters other people's networks, and contributes its bit to hybrids. It needs to retain a critical edge. For the language of hybridity may otherwise lull cultural observers into a false sense of freedom. There seems no end to human inventiveness: If everything is negotiated all we need pay attention to are the negotiations. We can describe the traffic to and fro, or the networks along which things, as they travel, change their shape and utility, the plastic bag that becomes a container for betelnut, betel itself going on its own travels (cf. Hirsch 1990). However, the symmetries may not be quite what they seem.

There is already a difference in the role Clifford and Latour accord *inventiveness*. Clifford sees culture as a source of creativity; one symmetry between cultures lies in their capacity to absorb and make hybrids out of one another. Latour sees inventiveness of a particularly powerful kind lying only in the suppressed hybrids of modernism: 'we do not wish to become premoderns all over again. The nonseparability of natures and societies had the disadvantage of making experimentation on a large scale impossible, since every transformation of nature had to be in harmony with a social transformation . . . [W]e seek to keep the moderns' major innovation: the separability of nature that no one has constructed . . . and the freedom of manoeuvre of a society that is of our own making' (1993: 140). Freedom as well as a superior inventiveness belong to the moderns.

Behind the democratizing concepts of impure cultures and hybrid networks lie other asymmetries. They turn on Euro-American assumptions about identity and ownership: where 'we' see ourselves and what 'we' claim for Euro-American culture. These asymmetries should be leading the anthropologist to new questions about old modernist issues, namely about property and proprietorship, but they would not have to endorse the 'purification' side of modernism. They would not be questions about the boundedness of cultures or about keeping separate the components of our narratives – anthropologists know now not to ask these. Rather, they would be questions about the length of networks. On the horizon are a whole new set of claims to proprietorship (new in the same way as becoming conscious of the modernist work of 'translation' is new). They arise *out of* the very perception of hybrids, out of mixes of techniques and persons, out of combinations of the human and non-human, out of the interdigitation of different cultural practices. Not socially innocent, not without their own likely effects, they presage new projects for modernity.

I am intrigued by the fresh significance Euro-Americans have found in their concept of intellectual property rights. These establish property in the creative process by which new forms come into being. What is newly hybrid about some current patenting procedures is their innovative mix of human and non-human parts. What should make anyone wary are the massive financial interests that give patent holders political power. Let me return to Papua New Guinea in order to consider why this might be of any interest for the way ethnographers think about their materials.

Impure Cultures and Hybrid Networks

Clifford's Adidas bag is a double take. Something amazing, he said, had been concocted from the missionaries' game of cricket, which had in the process been 'rubbished'.[4] The Adidas bag becomes rubbished too. The aesthetics are not symmetrical: Picasso bestows new value on the African mask, elevates it to high culture, but a plastic bag taken out of its classy sports milieu is detritus. One would have to spell out the fact that Trobriand Islanders appreciate shiny surfaces to things – as a preference for tin roofing over thatch was once explained to me – in order to deprive the epithet 'plastic' of its connotations of tawdriness.

There is a further asymmetry. Although Clifford indicates a state of mutual inventiveness between European artist and Pacific islanders, *both* examples illustrate the reach of Euro-American culture. African mask and Adidas bag landed up in their strange contexts through the *same* process of travel and diffusion. Euro-American culture seems to have the longer arm, to reach everywhere, so 'we' can simultaneously recognize ourselves both in what we appropriate from others and in what they appropriate from us. We are not only here, we are also there: traces of ourselves on the Pacific island. So invention may appear either in the inventiveness of seeing new uses for goods or in the invention of the goods that others use. Rendering the Adidas bag intrusive or incongruous in a Trobriand setting is Clifford's technique for undermining the concept of cultural purity; yet it is intrusive only insofar as it is overdetermined as Euro-American. Latour formalizes this phenomenon in terms of length of network. There is a crucial difference of scale between modern and pre-modern societies. 'Comparative anthropology has to measure . . . effects of size with precision' (1993: 114). By this he means that 'the relative size of collectives [actors who work together] will be profoundly affected by the enlistment of a particular type of non-humans' (1993: 109). His example is that of a technological invention – Archimedes' pulley which enabled the king of Syracuse to build a military force with a quite new dimension of power. Latour does not take size as self-evident. Large events may have small causes, as large enterprises are sustained by countless small projects – the very size of a totalitarian state is obtained only by a network of statistics, calculations, offices and enquiries. Nonetheless, it is the massiveness of machines, and the power of non-human devices, which, in his view, divides (non)moderns from pre-moderns.[5] As does, he says, 'the invention of longer networks' (1993: 133).

Now that moderns are no longer removed from the pre-moderns, he asks what best might we keep of each? 'What are we going to retain from the moderns? . . . The moderns' greatness stems from their proliferation of hybrids, their lengthening of a certain type of network, their acceleration of the production of traces . . . Their daring, their innovativeness, their tinkering, their youthful excess, the ever-increasing scale of action . . . are features we want to keep' (1993: 132–3). In short, the modern *as inventor*.

What qualifies for inclusion in a network? It can only be an agreement that things are connected by some continuous enterprise. The tenuousness of such agreements is described by Mol and Law (1994) through the arresting example of blood tests for anaemia that gather together different sets of 'natural facts' on the journey from labs to hospitals to clinics to tropical outstations. What makes us think that the betel container is an Adidas bag is *the length of the network* that we presume: artefacts both flow and remain recognizably Euro-American in origin (cf. Thomas 1994: 40). What renders them hybrid are the multiplicity of factors by which the anthropologist would construct cultural identity: a Euro-American artefact 'found' and turned to new use through indigenous cultural inventiveness. Like us, you see, these Melanesians, although their networks are shorter.

Latour's interest in scale implies a certain mathematics. He suggests that one concept worth saving from pre-moderns is that of there being a multiplication of non-humans, such as we may imagine the overpeopled of the Manambu universe (Harrison 1990), with its thousands of named entities, persons not necessarily human. But do these enumerations indicate a multiplication of beings? One could as well imagine a clan universe divided into numerous manifestations of itself (Mimica 1988). Melanesians, we might argue, live in an already globalized, already scaled-up, world (Wagner 1991). Its power is that it can be infinitely divided. This is certainly the logic of bodily generation, whether one is talking of a clan body (say), or a person's. Conversely, bodies are always capable of revealing their composition, their mixed character. Across Melanesia, people divide themselves by kinship, and borrow from one another sources of nurture and fertility, as a clan is formed and nurtured by affines. Such networks are routed through persons, carried by the human and non-human traffic of spouses, land and wealth, longer or shorter as the case may be. Indeed we may measure the length of some networks in the immediate or delayed return of conjugal partners (Damon 1983): the disposition of debts (compensation claims) indicates who inhabits the networks, or portions of them. Perhaps Melanesian networks are not so much 'shorter' as measurable.

Papua New Guinean Hybrids

Latour does not give much in the way of examples of pre-modern hybrids. I must therefore seek them. Can we find objects of knowledge where the mix partakes of both human and non-human elements? What about the way people relate things? Godelier (1978/1986a) offers an example in the 'combined system' of property rights that prevails in societies such as Siane of the Eastern Highlands of Papua New Guinea.

As Godelier redescribes Salisbury's (1962) original account, Siane rules regarding material and immaterial property comprise two kinds: men exercise inalienable rights over lineage land, sacred flutes and ritual knowledge and personal rights over clothes, pigs and planted trees. Yet if from an economic point of view the system appears mixed, daily practice works much more like a purification strategy separating sacred from profane. Protocols concerning people's claims with respect to these two types of property suggest that Siane have to ensure that these categories of things are kept apart. At the same time what is being kept apart, in the difference between what a Euro-American might call the human (mundane) and non-human (spirit) world, are different aspects of the person. On the one hand, the person is a clan or lineage member, tied to his (and it is his rather than her) ancestors and descendants alike; on the other hand, the person is individuated through his own actions and claims. We might say that out of this composition of distinct elements persons emerge as hybrids of the human and non-human. Conversely, if sacred goods '"belong" *simultaneously* to the dead ancestors, to the living and to descendants yet to be born' (1978/1986a: 79, Godelier's emphasis) these are all so to speak one person (the lineage) with an interest in property – the lineage being divided between, a composite of, the dead, living and those to be born.

Similar divisions are found in the domestic pig,[6] to Euro-Americans a non-human entity also the work of human beings, a piece of technology that has played diverse roles in the evolution of Highlands societies (Lemonnier 1993). Siane pigs are held as alienable personal property by men, although such rights of disposal are qualified by other interests, not least by those of women (e.g. Sexton 1986). We may recognize in this combination separate interests held simultaneously together. Godelier adds an important piece of knowledge apropos Baruya, on the borders of the Eastern Highlands. Men alone transmit their rights in their father's land to their own children, and possess the sacred objects used during initiation to reproduce the strength of male warriors. Women can do none of this. But, he says, women do transmit to their daughters the magical formulae that will enable them to raise pigs, along with pig names (1982/1986b: 81). Creativity is thus distributed between men and women. Certainly, in the attachment that Gimi women (also in the Eastern Highlands) show towards their pigs, procreative overtones are evident. 'Gimi women carry shoats like babies inside netbags to their gardens . . . When one of [a woman's] pigs is killed and set out for distribution at a feast, she sits weeping beside the pile of charred slabs, swatting away flies, wearing the pig's tail around her neck and chanting its name' (Gillison 1993: 43). As a non-human child, the pig has a divisible identity, for it belongs as much to men as to women, and those slabs of meat may be payments for her own child's 'head' that its

father must give her paternal, and its maternal, kin (cf. 1991: 187).
Like a human pig, the child is equally hybrid by gender and by
relationship, containing both male and female elements in its
makeup, recognized in just such separations of maternal from
paternal kin.

In these brief examples, we encounter networks with distinctive
features. If these mixes of beings dead and alive, human and
porcine, appear to create 'hybrid' persons, it is because persons
create relationships by dividing themselves off from other persons,
as they may divide Euro-Americans from Melanesians as brothers
elder and younger to each other.[7] Relations make a difference
between persons. The discrete interests of men and women
partition the child or the pig into an entity composed of different
entities. Thus Wassman (1994) describes for Yupno how the body's
very limbs may be calibrated for different effects – like a Massim
axe (Battaglia 1983) – one side of the body acting as a support for
the other's procreative energy. These are not quite the hybrids of
Latour's discourse.

We would not have expected such hybrids to parallel a division
between nature and culture, for that was a modern Euro-American
invention, but there is more at stake than the difference between
moderns who deal in abstractions such as nature and culture and
pre-moderns who personify everything. Because nature could not
be conceived separately, Latour argues, pre-moderns cannot
experiment on the modern scale.[8] Their technologies, their non-
human partners, are less powerful. This puts limits on the effects
of their inventiveness. So what kind of knowledge lies in those
powers of procreation and creativity attributed to men's rituals
and to women's intimate attachment to their pigs? It is knowledge
about (that inheres in) relationships, for they have one interesting
dimension: such powers are expressible in terms of claims between
persons and rights to payment in the form of compensation.
Persons are in this sense the composite property of others.

The combination of rights to which Godelier referred is repeated
over again in other Melanesian formulations. Living persons are
known as just such combinations, and combination is a corollary
of the fact that rights are divided or partitioned between persons.
The composite substance of persons becomes public knowledge
(is decomposed) through mortuary ceremonies, for instance, which
render discrete other people's interests – they can be disaggregated
through (compensatory) exchanges (Mosko 1983). It is the person

him or herself, 'owned' by multiple others, who brings these diverse interests and persons together. Each of these others owns a part, if we wish to pursue the language of ownership; none owns the hybrid. What intrigues me in certain Euro-American formulations is precisely the way the only possible object of ownership turns out be a hybrid.

But one cannot simply re-assert cultural difference, constructing Melanesian practices by contrast with Euro-American ones. It must be shown that such discriminations matter. I ground my wariness by touching briefly on some of the consequences that anthropological models have had, and on attempts to clean them up; such attempts may bring in items of knowledge already at work in other domains and thus far from innocent in their implications. This will lead us back to the same point about ownership, since it deals with that other part of Latour's modern hybrid, viz. culture, from Clifford's perspective of composite cultures.

The New Culturalism

In his first letter home to his supervisor, Reed writes of the kinds of relations warders and inmates in Bomana gaol, Port Moresby, appear to have – very different from what he had expected. A group of warders expatiated on the point, contrasting Bomana with gaols in 'the West'. They told the anthropology student that the difference was 'cultural'.[9]

The warders were pointing to practices they regarded as Melanesian – the celebrated *wantok* system through which shared language, region or kinship provide a basis for identity and appeals to solidarity. Warders invariably had *wantoks* among the inmates who would ensure their safety. In borrowing the concept of 'culture', people appear to be doing what is done everywhere, fastening on certain 'customs' as diagnostic of their way of life. Indeed in areas of Melanesia, notably Vanuatu, the concept of *kastom* has become an organizing trope for the way people present differences between themselves and Euro-Americans (Jolly 1992). If the anthropologist is tempted to read 'culture' into this concept, the reading is also played back to the anthropologist.[10] But whatever else it may refer to, it is also used to signify difference.

Now Melanesians have their own explicit practices of differentiation. By gender, group affiliation, territorial defence, not to speak of the partitioning of people's relationships between diverse kin, difference is invariably translated into differences between persons. People divide themselves off from one another by their connections, in terms, for instance, of the land whose food they eat or the ancestors who keep them in health, or in relation to those who talk in their own tongue. What difference would it make for us to imagine such differences as 'cultural'? None at all perhaps, except that cultural identity has become a sign of the new modernities. Resting, first, on a hybrid person/entity long established in Euro-American thought (in which social anthropology has much investment) it, second, places special emphasis on a form of creativity one might call inventiveness.

First, the human and non-human elements that render the Euro-American person hybrid combine radically distinctive elements from the realms of nature and culture. The idea that persons are duplex creatures, carrying around at once themselves and their social roles, evincing in their individual actions the collective culture of which they are a part, has been one of the contributions of social anthropology to modern conceptions of the world. It has been anthropology's strength to identify the cultural component of people's lives and to point to those differences between persons that are not innate or given but arise from their societies, from the language they speak and the styles of life they lead. Indeed, this particular apprehension of culture is one of anthropology's exports.[11] Where it is exported, there also the authors see themselves – or versions of themselves. Debates about custom in Vanuatu include debates about how far Euro-American anthropologists may recognize 'their' concept of culture in ni-Vanuatu *kastom*.

Promoting the modern idea of culture to explain differences once put down to identities of a racial kind (that is, locked into the bodily inheritance and disposition of people) has always been taken as an act of enlightenment. 'The demons of race and eugenics appeared to have been politically . . . exorcized . . . in defense of human equality in cultural diversity' (Stolcke 1995: 2). Her reference is to the work of UNESCO after the Second World War, which defended cultural identity and distinctiveness in the Boasian tradition. Since then, such ideas, which 'seemed to be a peculiar obsession only of anthropologists, have now come to occupy a central place in the way in which anti-immigration sentiments and policies are being rationalized' (1995: 2). On the surface appears a new symmetry. Cultural identity is something to which everyone can lay claim; but when cultures are given a homeland and become identified with particular territories or countries, then cultural difference may work to exclusionary or asymmetric effect.[12] Stolcke encapsulates the widespread and novel exaltation of cultural difference in recent years in what she calls 'cultural fundamentalism'.[13] What is at stake is a definition of culture for a Europe uncontaminated by foreignness. Yet the idea of a European culture is not just racism in new guise (and Werbner (1997: 6) notes the irony of that equation for the anthropologist). On the contrary there is a perceptible shift in the rhetorics of exclusion, as Stolcke calls them. In the language of the anti-immigration Right, emphasis is not on the different endowment of the human races as on profound differences in cultural heritage. This modern separation of culture from other forms of identity is joined with them again in the further idea that people are naturally xenophobic.[14] People, it is held, prefer to live among their own kind. 'Contemporary cultural fundamentalism is based, then, on two conflated assumptions: that different cultures are incommensurable and that, because humans are inherently ethnocentric, relations between cultures are by '"nature" hostile' (Stolcke 1995: 6). Stolcke points out that it is the particular combination of appeal to universal abstract principles (everyone seeks identity) and the demands of nationalism (citizenship), coupled with European ideas about human nature (innate dispositions), that leads to the twin concepts of 'cultural heritage' and 'cultural alien'.[15] These two concepts hold in place the modern hybrid as persons (aliens) carrying culture (heritage) on their backs. In this view, culture makes a difference between persons.

Second, invention abounds. In the anthropologist's eyes Europe is inventing a culture for itself, drawing among other things on the anthropological invention of that concept, which has become imbued with the capacity for inventiveness itself. Social anthropologists might nowadays rush to point out the modernist fallacy of reifying cultures as though they were bounded like territories and not the impure, hybrid creature they (anthropologists) know them to be. Yet anthropology did not only invent cultures as discrete entities. Recall Clifford's shadow surrealism: it celebrated diversity between cultures in the further idea that culture lay in the very inventiveness with which people played off their differences from one another (Boon 1982). But anthropology's 'culture' is now an embarrassment. If one can lay claim to an invention, can one also disown it?[16] Or should one be inventing something afresh?

Turner feels that the specification of the essential properties of culture is no longer an academic matter for it has become a political one. So what 'essential property' of culture might a latter-day anthropologist identify? Turner answers his own question with reference to the Euro-American movement for multiculturalism with its unpredecented claim that 'cultures' (as such) are worthy of equal support and protection from the state. There is in his view now only one ground on which to elevate culture as a 'new category of collective human rights . . . a legitimate goal of political struggle for equal representation in the public domain' (1993: 425). This lies in 'the empowerment of the basic human capacity for self-creation' (1993: 427). Culture *is*, in his words, the active sense of collective self-production; cultures *are* the way that people have made themselves. If culture generates a capacity for culture, its essential property would appear to be inventiveness.

This is not quite as free as it sounds. In seeming to clean up the act, this freshly minted view of culture turns out to be currency already in circulation, an invention borrowed from others. Turner more-or-less says so himself. New social conjunctures at work in the late capitalist world, he observes, favour the development and political recognition of cultural identities: 'a metacultural network of forces, institutions, values, and policies which fosters and reinforces the proliferation of cultural groups' (1993: 427). A new modernity then? I would add the new proliferation of claims which have as their very rationale the reduction of proliferation[17] through efforts to limit (competing) claims. Late capital has investments in the ownership of, among other things, inventiveness itself.

The New Proprietors

The English term 'hybrid' came initially from the Latin for a cross between a wild boar and tame sow. It emerged in the late eighteenth century with the fresh definition of a cross between species. At the same time it was pressed into metaphorical service for anything derived from heterogeneous or incongruous sources. In British parliamentary language, public bills that affect private rights may be referred to as hybrid. However, of all incongruous sources which create the hybrid character of networks, for Latour the conjoining of nature and culture is paradigmatic. An example drawn upon elsewhere would also be germane here (see Strathern 1996b). In 1987 a Californian corporation discovered the hepatitis C virus.[18] Two forms of Euro-American knowledge are involved here. The virus was a discovery, that is, the unearthing of fresh knowledge about the natural world. But the means of detecting the virus involved an invention in the development of a blood test for which the corporation was granted a patent. The idea of licensing is old, and at least since the eighteenth century, again, has been applied to inventions (but see Brush 1993). This test met all the modern criteria for a patent – novel, produced by human intervention and, in the interests of at once protecting and promoting competition, capable of industrial application. The patent has been a commercial success: the British National Health Service will be charged more than £2 for every hepatitis C test it administers, estimated to be at the rate of 3 million a year.[19]

What was new about this patent application was that the invention included the genetic sequence of the virus; the very identification of the relevant DNA was an integral part of the test. Gene sequences have 'applicability' on the argument that genes themselves are the technology for the medicine of the future. One outspoken critic[20] has observed that there is only one set of DNA sequences to be identified in the human genome, and no claims to identification could be countered by further inventions/discoveries; the patent is protecting the company from competition, not promoting competition. This particular corporation was in effect laying claim to 'ownership' of the virus and its genetic variants.

What makes such patenting even conceivable is the factor of human intervention in the production of a life form. Here is an American commentary on 'immortal' cell lines, that is, cells made reproducible in the laboratory. Similar arguments have been made at the European parliament (M. Strathern 1996a).

> Many human cells have already been granted patents in the US on the basis that *they would not exist but for the intervention of the 'inventor'*, who extracted and manipulated them to reproduce indefinitely. The US patent office has said it does not intend to allow patents on human beings, drawing on slavery amendments to US law that prohibits ownership of human beings. But the office has not made it clear how

it intends to distinguish between human cells and human beings . . . Individual scientists, universities and companies may eventually have the power to design the genetic makeup of a fetus. Should they then be able to patent the DNA that allows them to confer certain traits on the child? (*New Scientist*, 12 January 1991, my emphasis)

The anthropologist would observe that what makes these human cells ownable is their hybrid status, and hybrid in Latour's sense. The gene sequence as an identifiable part of DNA is simultaneously cultural and natural. Neither cell nor technique stand alone. The inventor has rights *only in the hybrid*, that is, in the DNA sequence that he or she has isolated. For 'invention' consists in the way in which culture has been *added* to nature.

Now modern institutions always took persons as having components available to the inventiveness of others, most notably labour, which could be bought and sold as a commodity. In the same way as the Euro-American person is an already-existing hybrid, at once a living biological organism and a bearer of culture and society, its energies may be distributed between the creativity that is the sign of its own human life and the creativity that is appropriatable in the marketplace. In using labour for ends of its own, capital realizes a use the original owner cannot realize for him or herself. Similarly, if the kind of knowledge which science gains from the natural world through its own inventiveness is recognized by patent, then this is because new contexts and uses are created that make the original item into something else. Patents are claims to inventions, that is, to embodiments of inventiveness that others technically could but are forbidden from utilising. Hence the person from whom the modified gene cells come cannot claim 'ownership' of DNA produced in the laboratory.

Now one objection to corporation pursuit of certain patents in genetic medicine is that any one invention/discovery is only made possible by the whole field of knowledge that defines the scientific community. There are long networks here, and patenting truncates them: 40 names to a scientific article and six names to a patent application.[21] It thus matters very much over which stretch of a network rights of ownership can be exercised. Hepatitis C had been under investigation for twelve years before the virus was isolated. The patent counsel for the company that developed the test was reported as saying: 'We don't claim we did all the research, but we did the research that solved the problem' (*The Independent*,

1 December 1994). The long network that was formerly such an aid to knowledge becomes hastily shortened.

Conclusion

There are numerous contexts of creativity in Papua New Guinean societies. The disposition of labour is one; the role of the intellect in invention is another (cf. A. Strathern 1994a). This chapter has touched on bodily creativity in the production of persons for its suggestiveness about network length.

If it is the interdigitation of nature and culture that makes moderns place such high value on inventiveness (culture), they are valuing themselves as nature with culture added. Persons embody the capacity for invention. Inventiveness is only limited by, so to speak, the technological capacity to realize it. The hybrid nature of the Melanesian person works to rather different social effect. Against Latour, we may observe that there is no limit to (Melanesian) people's capacity to invent, innovate and elaborate on what they think up for themselves or borrow from others. With him, we may agree that the length of networks is limiting, but we need to understand the nature of this limit.

Limitation is not so much quantitative, for any entity or artefact is infinitely divisible, as qualitative. Networks have a measure to them insofar, that is, as *social relationships* are measurable. Persons are the products of networks – hybrid mixes of debt, land and wealth – which demarcate the kind of claims they make on other persons. So it is less personal inventiveness that is subject to the control of others than the extent or scale of people's claims. This is true whether one thinks of obligations owed to ancestors or debts with affines or the rules that separate intermarrying moieties or the compulsion with which gifts demand gifts in return. Persons are subject to distributive relations that lead to claims based on the capacity to body forth the effects of creativity. (The creator's efforts, including creation through nurture, are realized in the bodies of those whom they create.) The extent of such claims are in principle known in advance through the protocols of compensation payments.

I have introduced the language of ownership for a reason.[22] Late twentieth-century cultural politics makes it impossible to separate issues of identity from claims to the ownership of resources. This is a field with which anthropologists have long been familiar in Oceania. In relation to land rights or below surface explorations or fishing reefs, anthropologists have been sensitive to the implications of ownership. This extends to the ownership of rights in the personages and identities of the names that kin groups claim as theirs or of otherwise clandestine knowledge that constitutes ritual prerogatives. By and large in Oceania, however, anthropologists have not had to deal with the ownership of persons, in terms say of child labour or forms of servitude that call for parallels with slavery, nor indeed with idioms of ownership as characterize certain African authority systems. On the contrary, debate over the exploitation of labour aside, 'ownership' of rights in persons tends to surface in the context of claims established through bridewealth and other life-related prestations. Creativity is already taken care of in the disposition of a person's acknowledged sources in diverse others. Those other persons both create the hybrid and are guarantee that the hybrid as such cannot be owned. The compensation networks that keep such interests alive, the relations that sustain the durability of such a view, may prove more important than we think. That, by contrast, the US patent office *has to spell out* the fact that human beings cannot be patented is chilling. One might prefer to be a in world where such claims on persons had already been settled, carry obligations even, as the anthropologist may indeed think of the life-related payments that characterize exchange systems in Papua New Guinea. *Wantok* do not just exemplify custom. They exemplify partitioned persons distributed among many and owned by none.

Here we should disaggregate hybrids and networks. Melanesian networks of relations are so to speak persons literally laid out to their fullest extent, measured by their numerous relations, each segment also with its own measure; the hybrid person is the figurative, condensed product of such relations, a composite ownable by no single segment of them. Now it is both the strength of the kinds of networks imagined by Latour and their weakness that there is no pre-existing measurement to them. Seemingly limitless, they can be imagined without anyone having to decide who owns what bits or indeed whether one can own parts of the network at all. If his modelling corresponds to the kinds of chains evident in the way Euro-Americans recognize their own artefacts regardless of whose lap holds them, or evident in the creation of the hepatitis C test, then they correspond to chains that are open, like nature, to appropriation. Hybrid products can be claimed at any juncture, so to speak, and it is when hybrids are claimed for ownership that segments of networks are chopped off to support the claim. No-one would these days want to claim ownership of an idea or artefact on grounds of unique identity, yet there is no refuge for the social anthropologist in the idea of hybrids, networks and invented cultures either. These do not, of themselves, indicate a symmetrical, sharing morality. They are not of themselves the resistant, transgressive stands they might seem; not the revitalized assembly or parliament of things Latour so freely imagines. For neither a mixed nature nor an impure character guarantees immunity from appropriation. On the contrary, the new modernities have invented new projects that forestall such imaginings. We can now all too easily imagine monopolies on hybrids, and claims of ownership over segments of network.

Notes

1. This was written as a companion piece to the article that appeared as 'Cutting the Network' (M. Strathern 1996b).
2. Anyone who wishes to locate within a wider intellectual/ cultural history the very particular versions of 'hybridity' discussed here should consult Werbner and Modood (1997). I note that social anthropologists always had their counterpart purifications, not only in themselves subscribing to nature and culture as ontologically distinct zones, whatever other peoples thought, but in effect treating societies and cultures as distinct zones in relation to one another. Assumptions about the naturalness of cultural distinctions, about internal congruity and external difference upheld the scientific side of anthropology to which Clifford refers (see below).
3. This 'network' is not to be confused with that of standard sociological usage. See Law's discussion of networks in actor-network theory, which he characterizes as a 'vision of many semiotic systems, many orderings, jostling together to generate the social' (1994: 18).

4. From a Trobriander's comment in the film.
5. From the moderns, as he lists them (1993: 135), one would want to retain the separation of free society from objective nature, while from the pre-moderns the non-separability of signs and things, and from the post-moderns denaturalization. But also to be saved from the moderns are 'long networks', 'scale' and 'experimentation', although it is 'limits on scale' that are to be discarded from the pre-moderns.
6. There is no such single entity as 'the domestic pig'; the role pigs play in the circulation of values varies enormously. Law's emendation of Latour's 'immutable mobiles', materials easily carried that retain their shape, is pertinent. Mobility and durability, Law argues, are themselves relational effects. A material 'is durable or otherwise as a function of its location in the networks of the social' (1994: 102).
7. After Burridge (1960); my thanks to Melissa Demian for reminding me of this division. Andrew Strathern's (1994b) recent comments on how local groups may treat a multi-national company or even 'the government' as a 'rival clan' could be understood the same way.
8. But scale, and limits, are also *defined* by the field of effect. Lemonnier (1993) demonstrates how different regimes of production and exchange in Papua New Guinea mobilize the domestic pig to different ends. Its apparently pivotal role in some societies is taken in others by human beings (women) or by life-substituting substances (salt); conversely the animal may take on the characteristics of persons or of inanimate materials. As a consequence the pig works as a pulley or lever on human relations with quite unpredictable results. There seems no single relationship between animal husbandry, horticulture and politico-economic system: with neither particular social values nor particular technological developments determinant, people's experimentations result in 'some unexpected technical choices' (1993: 146). We may ask how 'large' the fields of effects are here.
9. I am grateful to Adam Reed (1997) then undertaking a study of discipline and punishment with the cooperation of the Corrective Institutions Service for letting me quote from his letter. See Sahlins (1993: 3–4).
10. Lissant Bolton (1994) has articulated several reservations about the equation.

11. For example, M. Strathern (1995). Turner (1993) argues the opposite thesis. He suggests that anthropology's definitions of culture have been left behind in the new movement of multiculturalism. This has as its aims a democratization of cultural difference – challenging cultural hegemony 'by calling for equal recognition of the cultural expressions of non-hegemonic groups' (1993: 412).

12. Turner distinguishes between critical multiculturalism, which seeks (within education) to use cultural diversity as basis for relativizing both minority and majority assumptions, and difference multiculturalism where culture 'reduces to a tag for ethnic identity and a license for political and intellectual separatism' (1993: 414). He identifies the latter with neo-conservatism. But helpful as introducing such distinctions is, they also overlook 'translation'; different meanings bleed into one another. 'Critical' and 'difference' stands will only hold apart momentarily, as his own citation of a similar, constantly collapsible, distinction in feminist politics makes clear.

13. Compare Josephides' (1992: 159) critique of 'cultural function-alism' on the part of anthropologists.

14. Cultural fundamentalism builds its case on traits supposedly shared as a universal by all people everywhere (cultural identity, xenophobia), which either leads to the demand that immigrants assimilate culturally to the world around them or else works as an ideology of collective exclusion.

15. Margaret Thatcher (the then Prime Minister of Britain) stated in 1978 that 'people are really rather afraid that this country might be swamped by people of a different culture' (quoted by Fitzpatrick 1987). Stolcke notes differences between the British and French versions, among others.

16. Latour would disown segments of modernity in selecting from pre-modern, modern and post-modern regimes his hopeful amalgam for a non-modern world. Inventions are easiest to disown when they fall into the hands of aliens – when the creative act of appropriation implies they (the aliens) have 'their own' uses for it (see Thomas 1991).

17. Latour voiced a need to slow down and regulate modernity's proliferation of hybrids (1993: 12), but through bringing them into his new democracy, not through controlling them through new forms of possession!

18. From *The Independent*, 1 December 1994. The observations which follow rests on a couple of reports and a broadcast. For a British statement of some of the complexities of the concept of ownership in relation to human materials see Nuffield Council 1995.
19. The occasion of the newspaper report was a High Court ruling in November 1994 that the corporation could exercise a legal monopoly to the testing kits. Current HIV tests cost about 50p each.
20. The geneticist Martin Bobrow speaking on BBC Radio 4 (3 December 1994).
21. Apropos breast cancer (case cited on BBC Radio 4).
22. Quite apart from the fact that the naturalness of possession is being newly championed in interpretations of Melanesian ethnography; Battaglia's critique includes some pertinent comments on ownership (1994: 640). For an important elucidation of the way persons' sources in others must be acknowledged see Errington and Gewertz (1987).

References

Battaglia, D. (1983). Projecting Personhood in Melanesia: The Dialectics of Artefact Symbolism on Sabarl Island. *Man* 18: 289–304.
—— (1994). Retaining Reality: Some Practical Problems with Objects as Property. *Man* 29: 631–44.
Bolton, L. (1994). Dancing in Mats: Extending *Kastom* to Women in Vanuatu. Unpubl. PhD thesis, University of Manchester.
Boon, J. (1982). *Other Tribes, Other Scribes: Symbolic Anthropology in the Comparative Study of Cultures, Histories, Religions and Texts*. Cambridge: Cambridge University Press.
Brush, St. (1993). Indigenous Knowledge of Biological Resources and Intellectual Property Rights: The Role of Anthropology. *American Anthropologist* 95: 653–86.
Burridge, K. (1960). *Mambu: A Melanesian Millennium*. London: Methuen.
Clifford, J. (1988). *The Predicament of Culture: Twentieth-Century Ethnography, Literature, and Art*. Cambridge MA: Harvard University Press.
Damon, F. (1983). Muyuw Kinship and Metamorphosis of Gender

Labour. *Man* 18: 305–26.

Errington, F. and Gewertz, D. (1987). *Cultural Alternatives and a Feminist Anthropology: An Analysis of Culturally Constructed Gender Interests in Papua New Guinea.* Cambridge: Cambridge University Press.

Fitzpatrick, P. (1987). Racism and the Innocence of Law. In: P. Fitzpatrick and A. Hunt (eds), *Critical Legal Studies,* pp. 119–32. Oxford: Blackwell.

Gillison, G. (1991). The Flute Myth and the Law of Equivalence: Origins of a Principle of Exchange. In: M. Godelier and M. Strathern (eds), *Big Men and Great Men: Personifications of Power in Melanesia,* pp. 174–96. Cambridge: Cambridge University Press.

—— (1993). *Between Culture and Fantasy: A New Guinea Highlands Mythology.* Chicago: Chicago University Press.

Godelier, M. (1978/1986a). Territory and Property in some Pre-Capitalist Societies. In: M. Godelier, *The Mental and the Material: Thought, Economy and Society.* London: Verso.

—— (1982/1986b). *The Making of Great Men.* Cambridge: Cambridge University Press.

Harrison, S. (1990). *Stealing People's Names: History and Politics in a Sepik River Cosmology.* Cambridge: Cambridge University Press.

Hirsch, E. (1990). From Bones to Betelnuts: Processes of Ritual Transformation and the Development of a 'National Culture' in Papua New Guinea. *Man* 25: 18–34.

Jolly, M. (1992). Custom and the Way of the Land: Past and Present in Vanuatu and Fiji. *Oceania* 62: 330–54.

Josephides, L. (1992). Metaphors, Metathemes, and the Construction of Sociality: A Critique of the New Melanesian Ethnography. *Man* 26: 145–61.

Latour, B. (1993). *We Have Never Been Modern.* London: Harvester Wheatsheaf.

Law, J. (1994). *Organizing Modernity.* Oxford: Blackwell.

Lemonnier, P. (1993). Pigs as Ordinary Wealth: Technical Logic, Exchange and Leadership in New Guinea. In: P. Lemonnier (ed.), *Technological Choices: Transformation in Material Cultures Since the Neolithic,* pp. 126–56. London: Routledge.

Mimica, J. (1988). *Intimations of Infinity: The Cultural Meanings of the Iqwaye Counting System and Number.* Oxford: Berg.

Mol, A. and Law, J. (1994). Regions, Networks and Fluids: Anaemia and Social Topology. *Social Studies of Science* 24: 641–71.

Mosko, M. (1983). Conception, De-Conception and Social Structure in Bush Mekeo Culture. In: D. Jorgensen (ed.), *Concepts of Conception*, pp. 24–32. *Mankind* special issue 14 (1).

New Scientist, London, 12 January 1991.

Nuffield Council on Bioethics. (1995). *Human Tissue: Ethical and Legal Issues*. London: NCB.

Reed, A. (1997). Anticipating Individuals: Contemporary Sociality in Papua New Guinea in the Practice of Imprisonment. PhD thesis. Cambridge: University of Cambridge.

Sahlins, M. (1993). Goodbye to Tristes Tropes: Ethnography in the Context of Modern World History. *Journal of Modern History* 65: 1–25.

Salisbury, R. (1962). *From Stone to Steel: Economic Consequences of a Technological Change in New Guinea*. Melbourne: Melbourne University Press.

Stolcke, V. (1995). Talking Culture: New Boundaries, New Rhetorics of Exclusion in Europe. *Current Anthropology* 36: 1–24.

Sexton, L. (1986). *Mothers of Money, Daughters of Coffee*. Ann Arbor: Michigan University Press.

Strathern, A. (1994a). Keeping the Body in Mind. *Social Anthropology* 2: 43–53.

—— (1994b). Crime and Compensation: Two Disputed Themes in Papua New Guinea's Recent History. *Political and Legal Anthropology Review* 17: 55–65.

Strathern, M. (1995). The Nice Thing about Culture is That Everyone Has It. In: M. Strathern (ed.), *Shifting Contexts: Transformations in Anthropological Knowledge*, pp. 153–76. London: Routledge.

—— (1996a.). Potential Property: Intellectual Rights and Property in Persons. *Social Anthropology* 4: 17–32.

—— (1996b). Cutting the Network. *Journal of the Royal Anthropological Institute* (n.s.) 2: 517–35.

The Independent, 1 December 1994.

Thomas, N. (1991). *Entangled Objects: Exchange, Material Culture and Colonialism in the Pacific*. Cambridge MA: Harvard University Press.

—— (1994). *Colonialism's Culture: Anthropology, Travel and Government*. Princeton: Princeton University Press.

Turner, T. (1993). Anthropology and Multiculturalism: What is Anthropology that Multiculturalists Should Be Mindful of it? *Cultural Anthropology* 8: 411–29.

Wagner, R. (1991). The Fractal Person. In: M. Godelier and M. Strathern (eds), *Big Men and Great Men: Personifications of Power in Melanesia*, pp. 159–73. Cambridge: Cambridge University Press.

Wassmann, J. (1994). The Yupno as Post-Newtonian Scientists: The Question of What is 'Natural' in Spatial Description. *Man* 29: 645–66.

Werbner, P. (1997). Introduction: The Dialectics of Cultural Hybridity. In: P. Werbner and T. Modood (eds), *Debating Cultural Hybridity: Multi-Cultural Identities and the Politics of Anti-Racism*. London: Zed Books.

Werbner, P. and Modood, T. (eds) (1997). *Debating Cultural Hybridity: Multi-Cultural Identities and the Politics of Anti-Racism*. London: Zed Books.

Wilk, R. (1995). Learning to be Local in Belize: Global Systems of Common Difference. In: D. Miller (ed.), *World's Apart: Modernity Through the Prism of the Local*, pp. 110–33. London: Routledge.

Notes on Contributors

Ronald Adams (PhD La Trobe University, 1978), is Professor and Deputy Director of the Europe-Australia Institute at Victoria University, Australia. He carried out fieldwork in southern Vanuatu in the 1970s and 1980s and in Papua New Guinea and New Caledonia. Recently he has turned his attention to issues of cultural formation and transformation in the Mediterranean islands of Malta. His publications include *In the Land of Strangers: A Century of European Contact with Tanna, 1774–1874* (1984, Australian National University Press), he is co-author of '*To Learn More than I Have*' . . . *The Educational Aspirations and Experiences of the Maltese in Melbourne* (1993, Victoria University of Technology, with L. Terry and H. Borland), and he has co-edited *Culture Contact in the Pacific: Essays on Contact, Encounter and Response* (1993, Cambridge University Press, together with M. Quanchi) and *Maltese Inscriptions of the Australian Landscape* (1996, Victoria University, with J. Ronayne).

Sir *Raymond Firth* (PhD 1927, London School of Economics, various honorary degrees from other universities) has been, in his distinguished career and among many other professorships, Professor of Anthropology at the London School of Economics from 1944 until his retirement in 1968, and is now Emeritus Professor in Anthropology, University of London. Besides his research in New Guinea, Westafrica and London, he has conducted extensive fieldwork on Tikopia (1928–9, 1952, 1966, 1973) and in Malaysia (1939–40, 1963). Apart from numerous books his writings include a series of articles published in international journals and his more recent works *Tikopia–English Dictionary: Taranga Fakatikopia ma Taranga Fakainglisi* (1985, Auckland University Press), *Tikopia Songs: Poetic and Musical Art of a Polynesian People of the Solomon Islands* (1990, Cambridge University Press, together with M. McLean) and *Religion: A Humanist Interpretation* (1996, Routledge).

Andrée Grau first studied dance before devoting herself to social anthropology, where she obtained her PhD (The Queen's University of Belfast, 1983). Currently, she is a Senior Research Fellow at the Roehampton Institute, London. She has been doing extended fieldwork among the Tiwi on Melville Island, Australia, worked with a performance group in London and did research among the Venda in South Africa and in Central and South India. Her writings include numerous articles about dance and the anthropology of performance.

Ingjerd Hoëm received her academic training in anthropology and linguistics at the University of Oslo where she obtained her PhD in 1996. Currently, she is Research Fellow at the Faculty of Arts, University of Oslo. She has conducted two years' fieldwork in Tokelau, Samoa and New Zealand (all locations relating to the Tokelau population) and is editor of *Kupu mai te Tutolu* (1992, Oslo and Oxford University Press), and author of *A Way with Words* (1995, Bangkok, White Orchid Press); her book *A Sense of Place: the Politics of Identity and Representation* is forthcoming.

Monique Jeudy-Ballini (PhD University of Paris X Nanterre, 1984) is a member of the Laboratoire d'Anthropologie Sociale and Chargée de Recherche at the Centre National de la Recherche Scientifique, Paris. Between 1980 and 1994 she carried out fieldwork (two years in all) among the different groups of the Sulka, East New Britain, Papua New Guinea. As her various articles show, her theoretical interest lies in the representation of sexual identity, the notion of work, adoptive practices, ceremonial art and messianic movements.

Lisette Josephides (PhD University of London, 1984) has taught at the University of Papua New Guinea, the London School of Economics and Political Science, and the University of Minnesota. She is now teaching at the Queen's University of Belfast. She has conducted extensive fieldwork among the Kewa in the Southern Highlands (1979–81, 1985–6, 1993), in Port Moresby and the East Sepik Province, all in Papua New Guinea. Her writings include numerous articles in readers and international journals and *The Production of Inequality* (1985, Tavistock).

Verena Keck (PhD 1991, University of Basel) holds a position as Lecturer at the Institute of Ethnology, University of Basel. She has carried out fieldwork among the Yupno people in Papua New Guinea (since 1986, twenty-two months), on Bali, Indonesia, (since 1992, twelve months) and among the Chamorro people of Guam (1993, 1997, 1998). Her writings include articles in international journals and *Falsch gehandelt – schwer erkrankt. Kranksein bei den Yupno in Papua New Guinea aus ethnologischer und biomedizinischer Sicht* (1992, Basel) and *Historical Atlas of Ethnic and Linguistic Groups in Papua New Guinea, Vol. 1, part 3, Madang* (1995, Basel).

Pierre Lemonnier (PhD 1975, University of Paris V), is Directeur de Recherche at the Centre National de la Recherche Scientifique (CNRS) and member of the Centre de Recherche et de Documentation sur l'Océanie, CNRS-EHESS, Université de Provence, Marseille. Between 1972 and 1975, he carried out two years' fieldwork in South Britanny and since 1978 he has done forty months' fieldwork among the Anga people, Papua New Guinea. He is author of *Guerres et festins. Echanges, paix et compétition dans les hautes terres de Nouvelle-Guinée* (1990, Editions de la Maison des Sciences de L'Homme, Paris), and has edited *Elements for an Anthropology of Technology* (1992, Museum of Anthropology, Ann Arbor) and *Technological Choices. Transformations in Material Cultures since the Neolithic* (1993, Routledge).

Beatriz Moral received her anthropological training at the University of Basque Country, San Sebastián, where she obtained her PhD in 1997. Between 1992 and 1994, she has conducted a two years' fieldwork on Chuuk, Micronesia, where she focussed on women, sexuality and body.

Brigit Obrist van Eeuwijk (PhD 1990, University of Basel) holds a position as Lecturer at the Institute of Ethnology at the University of Basel. She has conducted extensive fieldwork among the Kwanga people in the East Sepik Province of Papua New Guinea (1980, 1984–6, 1993), and among the Minahasa in Indonesia, among Turkish and Kurdish people in Switzerland and in Dar es Salaam, Tanzania. Her writings include *Small but Strong: Cultural Contexts of (Mal-) Nutrition among the Northern Kwanga* (1992, Basel).

Anna Paini (PhD Australian National University, 1993) is a Postdoctoral Fellow at the Department of Social Sciences, University of Turin. Between 1989 and 1992, she conducted 21 months of fieldwork among the Kanak of Lifu (Loyalty Islands) as well as archival research at the Archivio dei Padri Maristi in Rome. Currently, she is working on a book based on her PhD thesis (*Boundaries of Difference: Geographical and Social Mobility by Lifuan Women*).

Milan Stanek (PhD 1979 University of Basel) currently holds a position as Lecturer at the Verbund für Psychoanalytische Sozialarbeit in Berlin. He has conducted extensive fieldwork in Papua New Guinea (mainly in the East Sepik and New Britain Provinces between 1972 and 1989), in New Caledonia (1996) and, since 1990, he is doing research in Eastern Europe (Czech and Slovak Republics, Hungary and in the Former German Democratic Republic). Apart from numerous articles, he has written *Sozialordnung und Mythik in Palimbei. Bausteine zur ganzheitlichen Beschreibung einer Dorfgemeinschaft der Iatmul, East Sepik Province, Papua New Guinea* (1983, Basel), and *Geschichten der Kopfjäger: Mythos und Kultur der Iatmul auf Papua-Neuguinea* (1982, Köln).

Andrew Strathern received his training in classics and social anthropology at Cambridge University (PhD 1966). He has carried out long-term fieldwork among the Melpa speakers of Mount Hagen, among the Wiru of Pangia and more recently the Duna speakers of Lake Kopiago, all in Papua New Guinea. His current fieldwork sites also include Lowland Scotland. He has held the Andrew W. Mellon Professorship in Anthropology at the University of Pittsburgh since 1987, and is Director of the Center for Pacific Studies at James Cook University, Townsville. Three of his recent publications are *Landmarks: Reflections on Anthropology* (1993, The Kent State University Press), *Voices of Conflict* (1993, Pittsburgh), and *Body Thoughts* (1996, The University of Michigan Press).

Marilyn Strathern (PhD 1968, Cambridge) is Professor of Social Anthropology and Head of Department of Social Anthropology, University of Cambridge. She has undertaken fieldwork in the Mount Hagen area (since 1964), among the Wiru in the Southern Highlands, and in Port Moresby (all Papua New Guinea). Her writings include numerous articles published in international journals; she is author and editor of many books. Her most recent publications are *Big Men and Great Men. Personifications of Power in*

Melanesia (1991, Cambridge, co-editor with Maurice Godelier), *After Nature. English Kinship in the Late Twentieth Century* (1992, Cambridge), *Reproducing the Future. Essays on Anthropology, Kinship and the New Reproductive Technologies* (1992, Manchester and Routledge); she is also editor of *Shifting Contexts. Transformations in Anthropological Knowledge* (1995, Routledge).

Borut Telban is Research Fellow at the Scientific Research Centre of the Slovene Academy of Sciences and Arts. He carried out more than three years of anthropological research in Papua New Guinea, first in the Highlands and later in the Sepik region (twenty months in Ambonwari village). In 1994, he completed his PhD at the Anthropology Department, Research School of Pacific and Asian Studies, Australian National University, Canberra. For the academic year 1995–6, he was appointed to the Leach/RAI Fellowship in Social Anthropology at the University of Manchester. He is author of *Dancing through Time: A Sepik Cosmology* (1998, Oxford University Press).

Christina Toren studied at the University College London where she gained a BSC (Hons) First Class in Psychology and then at the London School of Economics where she took her PhD in Social Anthropology in 1986. She is currently Senior Lecturer in Psychology and Social Anthropology at Brunel University. Her field area is Melanesia and the Pacific where she has carried out several periods of fieldwork in Fiji (the first from 1981–3, the most recent in 1993). Her writings include numerous essays and *Making Sense of Hierarchy. Cognition as Social Process in Fiji* (1990, Athlone).

Eric Venbrux studied anthropology at the University of Nijmegen where he obtained his PhD in 1993. He is a WOTRO (Netherlands Foundation for the Advancement of Tropical Research) Post-doctoral Fellow in the Department of Anthropology/Centre for Pacific Studies of the University of Nijmegen, and a Research Fellow in the Department of Ethnology at the P.J. Meertens Institute of the Royal Netherlands Academy of Arts and Sciences in Amsterdam. He conducted fieldwork in The Netherlands, Switzerland and Australia. He is author of *A Death in the Tiwi Islands. Conflict, Ritual and Social Life in an Australian Aboriginal Community* (1995, Cambridge).

Florence Weiss (PhD University of Basel, 1979) holds a position as Lecturer at the Institute of Ethnology, University of Basel. She has carried out repeated and extended fieldwork in Papua New Guinea (mainly East Sepik and New Britain Provinces) between 1972 and 1988, and has done research in Westafrica, India and Mexico, and, since 1990, in Eastern Europe. Her writings include *Kinder schildern ihren Alltag. Die Stellung des Kindes im ökonomischen System einer Dorfgemeinschaft in Papua New Guinea (Palimbei, Iatmul, Westsepik)* (1981, Basel) and *Die dreisten Frauen: Eine Begegnung in Papua New Guinea* (1996, Frankfurt am Main).

Index